3rd International Symposium on Biochemistry of Exercise

3e Symposium international sur la biochimie de l'effort

REGULATORY MECHANISMS IN METABOLISM DURING EXERCISE

LE MÉTABOLISME AU COURS DE L'EFFORT PHYSIQUE ET SES MÉCANISMES DE CONTRÔLE

A collection of the formal papers presented at the *International Congress of Physical Activity Sciences* held in Quebec City, July 11-16, 1976, under the auspices of the CISAP-1976-ICPAS Corporation.

Recueil des communications présentées dans le cadre du *Congrès international des sciences de l'activité physique* qui eut lieu à Québec, du 11 au 16 juillet 1976, sous les auspices de la Corporation du CISAP-1976-ICPAS.

Compiled and edited by

Recueilli et édité par

FERNAND LANDRY, Ph.D.
WILLIAM A. R. ORBAN, Ph.D.

Published by

Publié par

Symposia Specialists Inc.
Continuing Education in Sports Sciences

Éditeur officiel Québec

Released through
SYMPOSIA SPECIALISTS, INC. · 1460 N.E. 129th Street
Miami, Florida 33161, U.S.A.

JOINT PUBLICATION / COPRODUCTION

L'Editeur officiel du Québec

Le Haut-commissariat à la jeunesse,
aux loisirs et aux sports du Québec

Symposia Specialists Incorporated

Associate producers/Producteurs délégués
Michel Marquis
Miriam Hochberg

WORLDWIDE DISTRIBUTION / DISTRIBUTION MONDIALE

Symposia Specialists Incorporated
Miami, Florida 33161 U.S.A.

SOLE DISTRIBUTOR FOR QUEBEC
DISTRIBUTEUR UNIQUE AU QUÉBEC

◆ Éditeur officiel
Québec

Library of Congress Catalog
Card No. 78-054584
ISBN 0-88372-106-6

Table ⊠ Table
of Contents des matières

LECTURES AT THE INVITATION OF THE
SCIENTIFIC COMMISSION
CISAP – 1976 – ICPAS
Conférences présentées à l'invitation de la
Commission scientifique
du CISAP – 1976 – ICPAS

INDIVIDUAL SCIENTIFIC CONTRIBUTIONS
Communications scientifiques individuelles

A COMMISSION SCIENTIFIQUE
HE SCIENTIFIC COMMISSION

L'Exécutif — The Executive

ernand Landry — *Québec*
résident — President

'illiam A.R. Orban — *Ottawa*
ice-président — Vice-president

aul Godbout — *Québec*
ecrétaire — Secretary

Membres — Members

erald Kenyon — *Waterloo*
rthur Sheedy — *Montréal*
oy J. Shephard — *Toronto*
ves Bélanger — *Québec*
ouvernement du Québec
uebec Government

Paul S. Woodstock — *Ottawa*
Gouvernement du Canada
Government of Canada

Jean Loiselle — *Montréal*
COJO

Laurent Bélanger — *Montréal*
APAPQ

Gordon R. Cumming — *Winnipeg*
CASS — ACSS

Gregg McKelvey — *Ottawa*
CAHPER

Gilles Houde — *Ville de Laval*
Le Secrétaire exécutif et trésorier
The Executive Secretary and Treasurer

Gilbert Michaud — *Québec*

CONSEILLERS INTERNATIONAUX
NTERNATIONAL ADVISERS

'r Hon. — Rt. Hon.

hilip Noel-Baker — *Grande-Bretagne*
résident — President — *Great Britain*

IEPS — ICSPE

audol Ruiz Aguilera — *Cuba*
ean Borotra — *France*
ünter Erbach — *Rép. démocr. allemande*
German Democratic Republic

Julien Falize — *Belgique–Belgium*
Vladimir Roditchenko — *URSS–USSR*
Franz Lotz — *Rép. fédér. d'Allemagne*
Federal Republic of Germany
Tetsuo Meshizuka — *Japon–Japan*
Leona Holbrook — *EU–USA*
Nadir M. Souelem — *Egypte–Egypt*

Le Congrès international des sciences de l'activité physique, 1976
a été placé sous le distingué patronage de L'UNESCO, Organisation
des Nations Unies pour l'éducation, la science et la culture.

The International Congress of Physical Activity Sciences, 1976
has been placed under the distinguished sponsorship of UNESCO,
United Nations Educational, Scientific and Cultural Organization.

Acknowledgements

The *Scientific Commission* wishes to express its deepest appreciation to the Director General of UNESCO, Mr. AMADOU MAHTAR M'BOW. for having granted the official sponsorship of his organization to the *International Congress of Physical Activity Sciences — 1976*.

The *Scientific Commission* also wishes to express its sincere appreciation and thanks to the governments, as well as to the associations, committees and groups which have provided the financial, scientific and professional assistance necessary for the planning, organization and conduct of the *International Congress of Physical Activity Sciences — 1976*.

FINANCIAL AND ADMINISTRATIVE ASSISTANCE
— THE GOVERNMENT OF CANADA
  · Health and Welfare Canada
  Fitness and Amateur Sport Branch
  · Secretary of State
— THE QUEBEC GOVERNMENT
  · Haut-commissariat à la jeunesse, aux loisirs et aux sports
  · Le ministère des Affaires intergouvernementales
  · Le ministère des Affaires culturelles
  · Le ministère du Tourisme, de la chasse et de la pêche

— THE ORGANIZING COMMITTEE OF THE OLYMPIC GAMES OF MONTREAL

SCIENTIFIC AND PROFESSIONAL COOPERATION AND ASSISTANCE
— International Council for Sport and Physical Education
  · International Committee for Sociology of Sport
  · International Committee of History of Sport and Physical Education
  · International Work Group for the Construction of Sport and Leisure Facilities (IAKS)
  · Research Group on Biochemistry of Exercise
  · Working Group on Sport and Leisure
— International Council for Health, Physical Education and Recreation
— International Society for Sports Psychology
— International Society of Cardiology
— International Sports Press Association
— Association internationale des écoles supérieures d'éducation physique et de sport (AIESEP)
— International Society of Biomechanics
— American Alliance for Health, Physical Education and Recreation (AAHPER)
— American Academy of Physical Education
— American College of Sports Medicine
— National College Physical Education Association for Men (USA)
— Council for National Cooperation in Aquatics (USA)
— Canadian Association for Health, Physical Education and Recreation (CAHPER)

  · History of Sport and Physical Activity Committee
  · Sociology of Sport Committee
  · Philosophy Committee

Remerciements

La *Commission scientifique* exprime sa haute appréciation au Directeur général de l'UNESCO, M. AMADOU MAHTAR M'BOW, pour avoir bien voulu accorder le patronage de son organisme au *Congrès international des sciences de l'activité physique — 1976.*

La *Commission scientifique* tient aussi à exprimer ses remerciements les plus sincères aux institutions gouvernementales, ainsi qu'aux organismes, associations et comités qui lui ont procuré les appuis financiers, scientifiques et professionnels nécessaires à la planification et au déroulement du congrès.

L'ASSISTANCE ADMINISTRATIVE ET FINANCIERE

— LE GOUVERNEMENT DU CANADA
  · Santé et bien-être social Canada
    Direction générale de la santé et du sport amateur
  · Secrétariat d'Etat

— LE GOUVERNEMENT DU QUEBEC
  · Haut-commissariat à la jeunesse, aux loisirs et aux sports
  · Le ministère des Affaires intergouvernementales
  · Le ministère des Affaires culturelles
  · Le ministère du Tourisme, de la chasse et de la pêche

— LE COMITE ORGANISATEUR DES JEUX OLYMPIQUES DE MONTREAL

COLLABORATION SCIENTIFIQUE ET PROFESSIONNELLE

— Le Conseil international pour l'éducation physique et le sport (CIEPS)
  · Le Comité international pour la sociologie du sport
  · Le Comité international de l'histoire de l'éducation physique et du sport
  · Le Groupe international de travail pour les équipements de sport et de loisir (IAKS)
  · Le Groupe de recherche sur la biochimie de l'effort
  · Le Groupe de travail Sport et loisirs

— Le Conseil international sur l'hygiène, l'éducation physique et la récréation (ICHPER)
— La Société internationale de psychologie du sport (ISSP)
— La Société internationale de cardiologie
— L'Association internationale de la presse sportive
— L'Association internationale des écoles supérieures d'éducation physique et de sport
— La Société internationale de biomécanique
— American Alliance for Health, Physical Education and Recreation (AAHPER)
— American Academy of Physical Education
— American College of Sports Medicine
— National College Physical Education Association for Men (USA)
— Council for National Cooperation in Aquatics (USA)
— Canadian Association for Health, Physical Education and Recreation (CAHPER)

  · History of Sport and Physical Activity Committee
  · Sociology of Sport Committee
  · Philosophy Committee

ACKNOWLEDGEMENTS

- · Exercise Physiology Committee
- · Psycho-motor Learning and Sports Psychology Committee
- · Biomechanics Committee
- · Administrative Theory and Practice Committee

— Canadian Council for Cooperation in Aquatics
— Association des professionnels de l'activité physique du Québec (APAPQ)
— Canadian Association for Sports Sciences (CASS-ACSS)
— La Ville de Québec
— L'Université Laval

The Scientific Commission extends its deepest gratitude to all the individuals who, in the last three years, have worked behind the scenes in a most efficient and generous manner.

By formal resolution of the Scientific Commission at its meeting of April 28, 1977, Messrs. Fernand Landry and William A.R. Orban, respectively President and Vice-President of the Corporation were mandated to carry out the production of the official proceedings of the CISAP-1976-ICPAS (resolution CS 77-01-11).

NOTICE

By decision of the Scientific Commission, *French* and *English* were adopted as the two official languages of the International Congress of Physical Activity Sciences – 1976.

In these Proceedings, the communications appear *in the language in which they were presented* for French and English and *in English* as concerns the papers which were delivered in either German, Russian or Spanish. Abstracts in the two official languages accompany each paper included in Books 1 and 2 and the seminar presentations in the other books of the series.

REMERCIEMENTS

- · Exercise Physiology Committee
- · Psycho-motor Learning and Sports Psychology Committee
- · Biomechanics Committee
- · Administrative Theory and Practice Committee
- — Le Conseil canadien de coopération en activités aquatiques
- — L'Association des professionnels de l'activité physique du Québec
- — L'Association canadienne des sciences du sport (CASS-ACSS)
- — La Ville de Québec
- — L'Université Laval

La gratitude de la Commission scientifique s'étend à toutes les personnes qui, au cours des trois dernières années, et trop souvent dans l'ombre, ont apporté leur efficace et généreuse collaboration.

Par résolution de la Commission scientifique à sa réunion du 28 avril 1977, MM. Fernand Landry et William A.R. Orban, respectivement président et vice-président de la Corporation, ont été mandatés pour effectuer la production des actes du CISAP-1976-ICPAS (résolution CS 77-01-11).

AVERTISSEMENT

Les langues *anglaise* et *française* furent adoptées par la Commission scientifique commes langues officielles du Congrès international des sciences de l'activité physique – 1976. De ce fait, les communications apparaissent au présent rapport officiel *dans la langue où elles ont été présentées* pour ce qui est de l'anglais et du français, et dans la langue *anglaise* pour ce qui est des communications qui furent faites dans les langues allemande, russe et espagnole.

Des résumés dans chacune des deux langues officielles accompagnent chacune des communications qui paraissent aux Volumes 1 et 2 ainsi que les présentations faites par les conférenciers invités dans les autres volumes de la série.

Preface

The staging of international scientific sessions on the occasion of the Olympic Games has become a well-established tradition.

The themes of the congresses held at the times of the Games celebrating the last five olympiads illustrate that the movement has indeed become multidisciplinary and international.

In choosing *Physical activity and human well-being* as the central theme of the Québec Congress, the Scientific Commission endeavored to offer to the eventual delegates from the entire world, on the eve of the Olympic Games of Montreal, a large and democratic platform for the sharing of knowledge and the exchange of viewpoints on the problems now confronting sport internationally. For each one of the *subthemes* retained in the program, four speakers of different disciplines and of international reputation were invited by the Scientific Commission to give their viewpoint or that of their discipline on the proposed subjects. Additionally, the Scientific Commission offered a series of twenty (20) seminars of monodisciplinary character, in which at least three specialists of international reknown were invited to express themselves on selected topics. One hundred and twenty-seven (127) speakers from all corners of the world thus accepted the invitation of the Scientific Commission and were present at the Québec Congress.

Over and above the thematic and disciplinary seminars which constituted the heart of its program, the Scientific Commission also reserved a large portion of the time to the presentation of individual scientific contributions in sixteen (16) different disciplines and in six (6) special events.

The work sessions, numbering more than eighty (80), made it possible for more than three hundred (300) authors from all corners of the world to present the results on their research and scholarly work.

The central objective of the whole Congress was to bring frontier knowledge pertaining to sport and physical activity in general to the attention of the maximum number of persons. To that effect, the invited speakers were urged to present — the results of the latest research or scholarly work on the subjects proposed — the most convincing facts or ideas — the disciplinary practices, questions or issues which were in greater debate or contention — whenever

Préface

La tenue de sessions scientifiques internationales à l'occasion des Jeux olympiques est une tradition maintenant bien établie. Les thèmes des congrès qui ont effectivement eu lieu aux temps de célébration des cinq dernières olympiades confirment certes la multidisciplinarité et l'internationalisme du mouvement.

En choisissant pour thème du Congrès *L'activité physique et le bien-être de l'homme*, la Commission scientifique canadienne souhaitait donner aux délégués éventuels du monde entier, à l'occasion des Jeux olympiques de Montréal, une plate-forme large et démocratique permettant un libre échange des points de vue sur les problèmes qui confrontent le sport partout. Pour chaque *sous-thème* retenu, quatre conférenciers de disciplines différentes et de réputation internationale furent invités par la Commission scientifique canadienne à venir donner leur point de vue ou celui de leur discipline d'appartenance sur le sujet proposé. En plus, la Commission scientifique avait prévu la tenue de séminaires à caractère monodisciplinaire, donnant l'occasion à au moins trois spécialistes, dans chacune des vingt (20) disciplines impliquées, de faire état des connaissances sur des sujets choisis. Un total de cent vingt-sept (127) conférenciers de tous les coins du monde répondirent ainsi à l'invitation de la Commission scientifique canadienne et furent présents à Québec.

Au delà des séminaires thématiques et disciplinaires constituant le coeur du programme, la Commission scientifique a voulu réserver une place importante du programme à la présentation de communications scientifiques individuelles dans l'éventail des disciplines impliquées.

Les sessions de travail, au nombre de plus de quatre-vingt (80), permirent à plus de trois cents (300) auteurs de livrer à leurs pairs de tous les coins du monde les résultats de leurs réflexions et de leurs recherches.

Le rapport scientifique que constitue la présente série de publications se veut donc un bilan général de ce que dit la recherche et de ce que sont les réalités de la pensée et de la pratique courante, à travers le monde, sur des sujets précis touchant l'activité physique en général. Notre Commission scientifique canadienne avait à cet effet incité tous les auteurs à faire ressortir — l'état des connaissances, des

possible, the various implications relative to the education, health, or well-being of the people.

It was judged acceptable at the Québec Congress that speakers addressing themselves to the same topics present complementary, differing or even opposed viewpoints on the subjects, questions or issues at stake. It was in the discussion periods, which were made an essential and integral part of all work sessions, that the data and the viewpoints were exposed to questions, commentaries and criticisms from the audience, in the full respect of democratic principles and of the basic regards due to each person.

The reports which constitute the present series of publications are in reality the responsibility of their authors; consequently, they should not be interpreted as necessarily reflecting the opinion of the editors or those of the members of the Canadian Scientific Commission.

We believe that in actual fact, the body of knowledge relative to the potential contribution of physical activity to human well-being will have progressed significantly at the time and as a result of the Québec session.

The series of volumes constituting the present scientific report illustrates, in our opinion, the fact that the Canadian Scientific Commission has endeavored to build a program which was consistent with the highest contemporary international standards. To that effect, the Scientific Commission had chosen to function on a democratic basis which it believes unprecedented in this type of international effort; both the quality and the representativity of the professional and scientific organizations which were invited to contribute to the total endeavor do indeed illustrate this fact.

The members of the Canadian Scientific Commission believe that they were correct in assuring that there would be place, within the framework of the CISAP-1976-ICPAS program, for contributions stemming from all the branches and sectors of human knowledge which may be interested, from one angle or the other, in physical activity and sports as contemporary phenomena.

The success of the Québec Congress is owed outright to the efforts of the members of the Scientific Commission, the International Advisors, the members of the Executive, the Executive Secretary and Treasurer as well as to those of the numerous collaborators who have in fact consecrated so much energy to the pursuit of the objectives. At the critical stages of our collective endeavor, the professional and scientific contributions of a large

travaux de recherche et des réflexions de pointe sur le sujet, — les faits et/ou les idées les plus convaincants, — les pratiques ou les questions en discussion et en contention, — le cas échéant, les implications diverses qui touchent l'éducation, le bien-être, la santé ou la qualité de vie des citoyens.

Il était bien sûr accepté au Congrès de Québec que des conférenciers différents présentent, sur un même sujet, des vues personnelles, complémentaires, divergentes, ou même carrément opposées. Ce fut à ce sujet dans les périodes de discussions, parties intégrantes de toutes les sessions de travail, que les données et les points de vue ont été exposés aux questions, aux commentaires et aux critiques, dans le plus grand respect cependant des principes démocratiques et des égards dus à la personne.

Les travaux qui paraissent à la présente série n'engagent donc en fait que leurs auteurs; ils ne doivent pas être interprétés comme reflétant nécessairement les opinions des éditeurs ou celles des membres de la Commission scientifique.

Nous croyons cependant que l'ensemble des connaissances relatives à la contribution potentielle de l'activité physique au bien-être de l'homme aura progressé de façon significative, au moment, et comme résultant de notre session de Québec.

Les divers volumes du présent rapport scientifique illustrent bien, croyons-nous, le fait que la Commission scientifique canadienne s'est appliquée à édifier un programme qui soit conforme aux standards les plus élevés de l'heure et a de plus choisi de fonctionner sur des bases démocratiques sans précédent dans ce genre d'effort international. Les qualités et la représentativité des organismes scientifiques et professionnels qui ont été mis à contribution dans l'ensemble du projet témoignent, entre autres, de cet état de choses.

Nous croyons avoir eu raison d'avoir voulu et d'avoir fait qu'il y ait place, dans le cadre des débats du CISAP-1976-ICPAS, pour des apports en provenance de toutes les branches du savoir humain qui s'intéressent à l'activité physique sous l'une ou l'autre de ses formes.

Le succès remporté par le Congrès de Québec ne saurait cependant que revenir de plein droit aux membres de la Commission scientifique, aux Conseillers internationaux, aux membres de l'Exécutif, au Secrétaire exécutif et trésorier, ainsi qu'aux nombreux autres collaborateurs, bref à tous ceux et celles qui, effectivement, ont mis la main à la pâte. Aux moments les plus importants de notre cheminement critique, les apports professionnels et scientifiques en

number of persons, foreigners as well as Canadians, have indeed been generous, efficient and noteworthy.

The co-editors

William A.R. Orban, Ph.D.
Vice-president of the
Scientific Commission

Fernand Landry, Ph.D.
President of the
Scientific Commission

provenance d'un grand nombre de personnes, étrangers et canadiens, ont été en effet on ne peut plus généreux, efficaces et marquants.

Les co-éditeurs

William A.R. Orban, Ph.D.
Vice-président de la
Commission scientifique

Fernand Landry, Ph.D.
Président de la
Commission scientifique

Foreword

It has been a great pleasure for the Research Group on Biochemistry of Exercise, associated with the International Council of Sport and Physical Education (U.N.E.S.C.O.), to hold its 3rd Symposium in the pretty City of Quebec. The members of the Group express their thanks to the Corporation of the International Congress of Physical Activity Sciences for the initial proposal by its Scientific Commission and for having hosted our Symposium in the framework of its interdisciplinary program. We are also indebted to our Canadian colleagues C. Allard, G. Métivier and A. W. Taylor who acted as our representatives to the Scientific Commission and gave the best of their efforts to make the Symposium a success. The previous two symposia in Belgium and in Switzerland dealt with the changes occurring after acute and chronic effects of short-term and prolonged physical activities. The major topic at the present symposium was regulation of muscular exercise or, in other words, "why and how" humans react to physical activity practice. From our middle-aged scientific knowledge of ten years ago we are now beginning to understand the sequential utilization of fuels in muscle contraction. By the study of muscle fiber types we are now almost prepared to predict the type of activity or sport for which a youngster would have the best potential for future performance.

This symposium tried to understand partially the rules of Nature with special attention to athletes. However, one should remember what Francis Bacon wrote 357 years ago: "We cannot command Nature except by obeying her."

We had the privilege to hear Professor E. A. Newsholme of the University of Oxford (Great Britain) as one of our academic speakers. All biochemists know his famous book written with C. Start on *Regulation in Metabolism*. He gave us a highly qualified integrated account of the metabolic regulation during physical exercise.

We are beginning to understand how humans adapt themselves to strenuous physical stress. However, what we consider as a remarkable adaptation from untrained to trained subjects is in fact a common mechanism to the other animal families. We are even overjoyed by the biochemical adaptation to the environment or exceptional capacities of some birds for strenuous exercise. The Olympic winner of avian species should be the hummingbird which performs flight

Avant-propos

Le Groupe de recherche sur la biochimie de l'effort, associé au Conseil international pour l'éducation physique et le sport (O.n.g. — UNESCO) a éprouvé un vif intérêt à tenir son troisième symposium dans la belle ville de Québec. Les membres du Groupe remercient la Corporation canadienne du Congrès international des sciences de l'activité physique de l'offre faite par sa Commission scientifique et d'avoir été l'hôte de notre symposium dans le cadre de son programme interdisciplinaire. Nous sommes aussi redevables à nos collègues canadiens, MM. C. Allard, G. Métivier et A.W. Taylor, qui nous ont représentés auprès de la Commission scientifique et qui ont fait beaucoup pour que ce symposium soit un succès. Les deux symposiums antérieurs, tenus en Belgique et en Suisse, traitaient des changements survenant chez l'homme suite aux effets aigus et chroniques produits par des activités physiques brèves ou soutenues. Le thème principal du présent symposium était la régulation de l'effort musculaire ou, en d'autres mots, la façon dont les humains réagissent à la pratique d'exercices physiques. Ayant dépassé le savoir scientifique moyenâgeux que nous possédions il y a dix ans, nous commençons maintenant à comprendre l'utilisation successive du combustible dans la contraction musculaire. Grâce à l'étude des fibres musculaires, nous sommes sur le point de pouvoir prédire le genre d'activité ou de sport pour lequel un jeune sujet aurait un potentiel qui lui permettrait d'accomplir des exploits.

Au cours de ce symposium, nous avons essayé de comprendre une partie des règles de la Nature, en portant une attention spéciale aux athlètes. Il ne faut toutefois pas oublier ce qu'écrivait Francis Bacon il y a 357 ans: "On ne triomphe de la nature qu'en lui obéissant".

Nous avons eu le privilège d'entendre, entre autres, le professeur Newsholme de l'Université d'Oxford (Grande-Bretagne). Tous les biochimistes connaissent son livre *Regulation in Metabolism*, écrit en collaboration avec C. Start. Il nous a fait une description complète et savante de la régulation du métabolisme pendant l'effort physique.

Nous commençons à comprendre comment l'être humain s'adapte à l'effort physique intense. Toutefois, ce que nous considérons comme une adaptation remarquable, c'est-à-dire le fait de devenir bien entraîné, n'est qu'un mécanisme courant chez les autres familles d'animaux. Nous sommes même étonnés de l'adaptation

migrations across the Gulf of Mexico, a nonstop journey of over 1,000 km. Taken as it stands, this must be sufficient to depress for some years our top marathon runners.

Professor P. W. Hochachka of the University of British Columbia in Vancouver (Canada) is a famous leader in studying these strategies among mammal and nonmammal organisms. In 1973 he wrote a fascinating book on this subject and we were glad to have him as second speaker for the academic session.

There was a need for authoritative introductions of the different topics of this symposium. This task was assumed by several scientists known for their special interest in the interrelationship between exercise and particular aspects of metabolism, namely: D. L. Costill (Muncie), J. Gergely (Boston), P. D. Gollnick (Pullman), J. O. Holloszy (St. Louis), H. Howald (Macolin), E. Hultman (Stockholm), L. B. Oscai (Chicago) and J. R. Poortmans (Brussels).

These authors introduced a critical survey on the biochemical changes that occur in animals (including humans) as a result of physical activities and the possible mechanisms controlling such changes. The general strategy and tactics of the metabolic regulation were covered from the subcellular compartmentation toward cellular, tissue and whole organism.

It is the hope of the Research Group on Biochemistry of Exercise that these Proceedings will give a useful outline of present knowledge of the regulation of mammalian fuel and energy metabolism during exercise.

Jacques R. Poortmans
*President of the Research Group
on Biochemistry of Exercise*

biochimique ou par les capacités exceptionnelles de certains oiseaux à fournir un effort intense. Le champion olympique de l'espèce avienne serait le colibri dont la migration, au-dessus du Golfe du Mexique, représente un vol ininterrompu de plus de mille kilomètres. Voilà qui est suffisant pour déprimer nos meilleurs coureurs de marathon pendant des années!

Le professeur Hochachka de l'Université de la Colombie-Britannique, à Vancouver (Canada), est un chef de file renommé pour son étude de ces stratégies chez les mammifères et chez d'autres espèces. En 1973, il a écrit un livre fascinant sur le sujet et nous étions heureux qu'il soit notre deuxième conférencier.

Les différents sujets de ce symposium devaient être solidement posés. Plusieurs scientifiques, reconnus pour l'intérêt particulier qu'ils portent aux rapports entre l'effort et les aspects particuliers du métabolisme, y ont vu. Ce sont MM. D.L. Costill (Muncie), J. Gergely (Boston), P.D. Gollnick (Pullman), J.O. Holloszy (Saint-Louis), H. Howald (Macolin), E. Hultman (Stockholm), L.B. Oscai (Chicago) et J.R. Poortmans (Bruxelles).

Ces auteurs ont présenté une étude critique des changements biochimiques qui se produisent chez l'animal (ainsi que chez l'homme) comme conséquence de l'activité physique, et des mécanismes contrôlant ces changements. On y a englobé la stratégie et les tactiques générales de la régulation métabolique à partir de la compartimentation sous-cellulaire en allant vers la cellule, le tissu et l'organisme entier.

Le Groupe de recherche sur la biochimie de l'effort souhaite que ces travaux donnent un aperçu utile de la connaissance actuelle sur la régulation du combustible chez les mammifères et sur le métabolisme énergétique au cours de l'effort physique.

Jacques R. Poortmans
Président du Groupe de recherche
sur la biochimie de l'effort

**Lectures at the Invitation
of the Scientific Commission
CISAP - 1976 - ICPAS**

**Conférences présentées
à l'invitation de la
Commission scientifique
du CISAP - 1976 - ICPAS**

Control of Energy Provision and Utilization in Muscle in Relation to Sustained Exercise

Eric A. Newsholme

The author discusses the reasons currently proposed to explain the constancy of the ATP/ADP concentration ratio in muscle and suggests that only a kinetic explanation may be satisfactory. The mechanisms necessary to preserve the kinetic efficiency of the processes involved in energy transfer are then presented. The most important energy producing pathways in muscle are also reviewed, with particular reference to glycolysis, the β-oxidation system for fatty acids and the citric acid cycle. An explanation is given of the means by which sensitivity in metabolic control can be increased. Increases in the capacity of the substrate cycles and the control mechanisms for fatty acid mobilization are commented upon with reference to endurance performances.

Introduction

There are three important questions concerning the control of fuel and energy supply for muscle. First, how is the rate of fuel oxidation in muscle regulated *precisely* to the energy requirement of the contractile system? Second, how is the rate of mobilization of fuel from the body's store regulated *precisely* to the rates of fuel utilization by the muscle? Third, how is the utilization of fuels by exercising muscle integrated in relation to the fuel requirements of other tissues? The metabolic basis upon which these questions can be formulated is provided in this section and some possible answers to the questions are given in the following sections.

The Role of the ATP/ADP Couple in Energy Transfer in Muscle

During muscular work chemical energy is converted into mechanical energy. The site of this energy exchange is the crossbridges between the contractile proteins, actin and myosin, and the energy is

Eric A. Newsholme, Department of Biochemistry, University of Oxford, Oxford, England.

3

used during the breaking and re-attachment cycles of the cross-bridges. The energy is obtained from the utilization of ATP [23]. The terminal phosphate group and the ADP moiety of ATP are transferred to the participating systems in the reaction. Eventually, inorganic phosphate and ADP are released so that when the net reaction is completed, ATP has been hydrolyzed. The resynthesis of ATP from ADP and Pi occurs via the degradative pathways of the cell. Thus, some of the energy made available in the oxidative reactions is conserved in the formation of ATP. Consequently, the energy conserved during catabolism is transferred to the processes that utilize energy (e.g., muscular contraction) via the ATP/ADP coupled system. In other words, the ATP/ADP couple transfers energy from the producing to the utilizing reactions (Fig. 1).

It cannot be emphasized too strongly that ATP is not stored in the cell: its concentration in muscle is only 5 to 7 mM [4] which would be depleted in less than a second during contraction unless it is resynthesized at a rate equal to that of utilization [35 (pp. 138, 139)]. Consequently, it is important, as illustrated in Figure 1, that when mechanical activity increases, the rate of fuel oxidation increases, so that the rate of ATP formation equals that of utilization. This statement is supported by the fact that the ATP

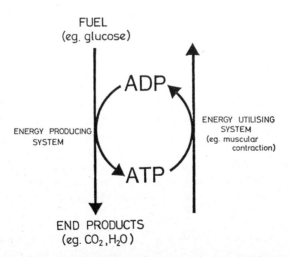

FUEL
(eg. glucose)

ADP

ENERGY PRODUCING
SYSTEM

ENERGY UTILISING
SYSTEM
(eg. muscular
contraction)

ATP

END PRODUCTS
(eg. CO_2, H_2O)

FIG. 1. The role of the ATP/ADP couple in energy transfer in muscle. The ATP/ADP concentration ratio remains remarkably constant under very different conditions of steady-state flux. There is no store of energy in this system, so that a change in rate of utilization of ATP must cause the same change in rate of production.

concentration remains remarkably constant when a muscle changes its mechanical activity, for example, the initiation of flight in the insect, which increases the rate of ATP turnover several hundredfold, produces a remarkably small change in the concentration of ATP or in the concentration ratio ATP/ADP (Table I). This observation strongly implies the existence of a regulatory mechanism that links the rate of ATP utilization with its formation, that this mechanism is exquisitely sensitive and that information is transferred very rapidly. This could be achieved through a feedback control mechanism (see section "Regulation of the Early Stages of Glycolysis").

That the ATP/ADP concentration ratio remains remarkably constant in muscle (and other tissues) is well established, but it is unclear why it should remain so constant, especially when it demands a complex metabolic control mechanism. A thermodynamic reason has been proposed [31]. For the purpose of energy transfer, a chemical reaction is most efficient at equilibrium (when the free energy change is zero) so that, for a given flux, the further a reaction is from equilibrium the larger will be the loss of energy as heat. Consequently, reactions involving the breakdown of ATP would be less efficient when the ATP/ADP concentration ratio was high and reactions forming ATP would be less efficient when the ratio was low. Hence the importance of constancy. Unfortunately, when the ATP/ADP concentration ratio is high, reactions in which ATP is synthesized become more efficient (and vice versa for the utilization processes). Since these factors should balance each other, arguments based on efficiency of energy transfer do not provide a satisfactory explanation for the observed constancy of the ratio. Furthermore, the actual change in free energy is small, despite large variations in the ATP/ADP concentration ratio [35 (p. 110)]. Another reason is that since ATP is involved in many reactions in the cell, a decrease in its concentration would reduce the activity of many cellular

Table I. Concentrations of Adenine Nucleotides and Pi in Locust Flight Muscle at Rest and After Flight

| Metabolites | Metabolite Concentration ($\mu mol/gm$ Fresh Wt.) | | |
	Resting Muscle	10 Seconds Flight	3 Minutes Flight
ATP	5.06 ± 0.20 (13)	4.58 ± 0.13 (19)	4.32 ± 0.10 (10)
ADP	0.43 ± 0.03 (7)	0.96 ± 0.05 (12)	1.10 ± 0.09 (10)
AMP	0.06 ± 0.01 (7)	0.12 ± 0.01 (10)	0.12 ± 0.02 (12)
Pi	9.30 ± 1.2 (9)	13.5 ± 1.2 (10)	11.9 ± 0.7 (9)
ATP/ADP	11.8	4.8	3.9

The data are taken from Rowan [42].

processes that require ATP. However, this explanation is unsatisfactory: for many enzymes the intracellular ATP concentration is considerably greater than the Km for ATP, so that reasonable variations in its concentration would make little or no difference to the catalytic activity.

The author considers that neither of the above explanations is acceptable but that a kinetic explanation may be satisfactory. Since ATP is chemically very similar to ADP, enzymes may have difficulty in distinguishing between these two compounds. This difficulty would manifest itself in competitive inhibition of the enzymes by either ATP or ADP, especially if the ATP/ADP concentration ratio changes significantly. Indeed, it is well established that enzymes with ADP as substrate are inhibited by ATP and vice versa [47] (Table II). If the intracellular ATP/ADP concentration ratio increased, the catalytic activity of some of the enzymes involved in ATP formation may be inhibited, whereas, if the ratio decreased, the catalytic activity of some of the enzymes involved in ATP utilization may be inhibited (Table II). It is unlikely that small changes in this concentration ratio would markedly inhibit activities of these enzymes, but any reduction in the activity of key enzymes could reduce the rate of ATP formation and/or the performance of work. In this way, what may be termed the *kinetic efficiency* of energy transfer (Fig. 1) may be reduced.

Although a reduction in kinetic efficiency in muscle may have little obvious effect in everyday life of a "normal" human subject enjoying the benefits of civilization, it could seriously interfere with

Table II. Inhibition of ATP-producing and ATP-utilizing Enzyme Activities by Adenine Nucleotides

Enzyme	Substrate	Inhibitor	Type of Inhibitor
Hexokinase	ATP	ADP	Competitive
3-Phosphoglycerate kinase	ADP	ATP	Competitive
Pyruvate kinase	ADP	ATP	Competitive
Creatine phosphokinase	ATP	ADP	Competitive
Phosphoenol pyruvate carboxylase	GTP	GDP	Mixed type
Fatty acyl-CoA synthetase	ATP	ADP	Competitive
Adenylate kinase	ATP	ADP	Competitive
Actomyosin ATPase	ATP	ADP	
Adenine nucleotide translocase	ADP	ATP	

The data are collated from Barman [3] except for actomyosin ATPase [30] and adenine nucleotide translocase. The inward transport of ADP by heart muscle mitochondrial translocase is not specific for ADP [5] so that an increase in the ATP concentration in the cytoplasm could reduce the activity of the translocase.

the performance of an athlete. It could also seriously interfere with the normal behavior of animals in the wild, in which maximal muscular capacity may be utilized in escape mechanisms, in predatory activities, in dispersal or migration and in the search for food. Thus, the development of sensitive and efficient mechanisms for the control of energy metabolism may be necessary to preserve the kinetic efficiency of the processes involved in energy transfer.

Fuel Stores in Human Subjects

The amounts of fuel stored in the different tissues in the average human subject are given in Table III. Glycogen appears to be a major store of fuel within muscle itself and it is utilized under both aerobic and anaerobic conditions [10, 35 (pp. 149-152)]. Glycogen is also stored in the liver and it is released as glucose into the blood during muscular activity [41]. Nonetheless, the amount of glucose stored in this form is small in comparison to other fuels.

Although triglyceride is present in skeletal muscle, the available evidence suggests that the energy required for contractile activity is obtained from blood-borne fat fuels. Triglyceride is stored primarily in adipose tissue in mammals and it is mobilized in the form of nonesterified fatty acids (NEFA) [16]. That NEFA can be used as a fuel by muscle is now well established for mammalian [12, 14] and avian muscles [6, 18]. However, the two other forms of fat fuel, triglyceride and ketone bodies, are quantitatively unimportant for energy provision during contractile activity [25, 39].

The extent to which amino acids can function as a fuel for muscle is uncertain. It has generally been accepted that amino acids are unimportant as fuels for muscle [10], but recent work on amino acid metabolism within muscle, the release of alanine by muscle and conversion of alanine to glucose in the liver has led to the theory that amino acid metabolism via gluconeogenesis may provide a quantitatively important source of energy for muscle in prolonged exercise [15]. This subject will not be discussed further in this review.

It is considered that of the blood-borne fuels, only glucose and fatty acids are significant in relation to energy provision for sustained severe muscular activity. Consequently, the control of fuel utilization must take into account differences in the quantity of these fuels in the body's stores (Table III) and the use of these fuels for tissues other than muscle. In particular, sustained severe exercise or sustained exercise under conditions of starvation must utilize fatty acids, since glucose reserves are totally inadequate to provide for

Table III. Fuel Reserves in the Average Human Subject

Fuel	Tissue	Fuel Reserves in Average Man kcal	gm
Triglyceride	Adipose tissue	100,000	15,000
Glycogen	Liver	200	70
	Muscle	400	120
Glucose	Body fluids	40	20
Protein	Muscle	25,000	6,000

The data are assumed to represent an average man weighing 70 kg (154 lb) and they are taken from Cahill and Owen [9].

sustained activity and they are reduced to insignificant levels by starvation. Nonetheless, the blood glucose remains remarkably constant during this activity. How does muscle utilize fatty acids and not glucose under these conditions and can it increase its rate of glucose utilization, if necessary? These questions are answered in the section "Interrelationship Between Fat and Carbohydrate Oxidation in Muscle."

The Flux-Generating Step in a Metabolic Pathway

Flux-Generating Steps and Control of Pathways

Metabolic pathways consist of a series of enzyme-catalyzed reactions which are linked by common reactants. The most important energy-producing pathways in muscle are glycolysis, the β-oxidation system for fatty acids and the citric acid cycle (together with the concomitant electron transport chain). Under conditions of rest or sustained muscular activity, it is likely that these pathways are in a steady state, that is, the flux through the pathway and the concentrations of metabolic intermediates are constant (although the flux will be considerably greater during activity than at rest). The importance of maintenance of a steady state in the ATP producing and utilizing systems has been emphasized in the "Introduction." In order to understand how a steady state can be established in a metabolic pathway, it is necessary to appreciate the significance of the flux-generating step.

In the following hypothetical metabolic system

$$S \xrightarrow{E_1} A \xrightarrow{E_2} B \xrightarrow{E_3} C \xrightarrow{E_4} P \xrightarrow{E_5}$$

substrate S is converted into end-product P, which is removed by a nonequilibrium reaction at the end of the system (E_5). The enzyme E_1, which catalyzes the first reaction in the system, must be saturated with substrate, so that variations in concentration of S, as the process proceeds, will not modify the activity of E_1. This enzyme catalyzes the flux-generating step, which is important in establishing the steady state. (If E_1 was not saturated with S, the rate of catalysis by E_1 would decrease continuously, so that a constant flux would be impossible.) The other reactions in the pathway must be regulated in such a way that they are able to accommodate the flux generated at E_1. In the simplest situation, these reactions will be regulated via changes in the concentrations of their pathway-substrate (i.e., A,B,C,P), which are termed internal effectors; an increase in the flux through E_1 will increase the concentrations of A,B,C and P, which will increase the activities of enzymes E_2, E_3, E_4 and E_5 (and vice versa for a decrease in flux). Since enzyme E_1 is saturated with substrate, its activity will be controlled by factors other than its substrate concentration, which are termed external effectors. Other enzymes in the pathway could be controlled by external as well as the internal effectors. However, it is important to emphasize that the external control of an intermediate step in the pathway (e.g., that catalyzed by E_3 above) must be coordinated to the control of E_1: an increase in the activity of enzyme E_3 alone would not change the flux through the pathway, but result solely in a decrease in the steady-state concentration of the intermediate B.

The biochemical details of the control of enzymes catalyzing flux-generating steps (and other reactions) that are relevant to the subject of this symposium will be described below. However, it is important at this stage to illustrate a general type of control mechanism that links the activity of the enzymes that catalyzes the flux-generating step with the external regulation of the activity of another enzyme in the pathway. If, in the hypothetical pathway given above, A is a feedback inhibitor of enzyme E_1 and X is an external regulator of E_2, as follows,

$$S \xrightarrow{\quad} A \xrightarrow{\quad} B \xrightarrow{\quad} C \xrightarrow{\quad} P \xrightarrow{\quad}$$

then control of the activity of E_2 by X will provide a feedback link to the flux-generating step, via the concentration of intermediate, A.

A major problem with such a control system is whether the concentration of A can change sufficiently to provide satisfactory control of E_1. For example, an increase in activity of E_2 (due to a decrease in concentration of X) will reduce the concentration of A, but if a reduction in concentration of A has to be large in order to increase the activity of E_1, this will reduce the activity of E_2 via internal regulation. Consequently, small changes in the concentration of A must produce large changes in the activity of E_1 (i.e., the control mechanism must be very sensitive). Means for increasing sensitivity in metabolic control are provided below.

Flux-Generating Step for Glucose Utilization in Muscle

A flux-generating step is identified by the following criteria: the reaction is nonequilibrium; the Km of the enzyme catalyzing the reaction is considerably lower than the substrate concentration in vivo and the flux through the pathway cannot be modified by changing the concentration of substrate of the putative flux-generating step. If these criteria are applied to the reactions of glycolysis in msucle (Table IV), it is obvious that glycolysis from glucose does not have a flux-generating step (whereas phosphorylase catalyzes such a step for glycolysis from glycogen) (Table IV). Consequently, the flux-generating step for glycolysis from glucose must be external to the muscle. It is suggested that hepatic phosphorylase, which catalyzes the degradation of liver glycogen to glucose I-phosphate, is flux generating for glycolysis in *muscle* (Table IV, Fig. 2). This is a metabolically important conclusion, since it emphasizes that a metabolic pathway* is not necessarily limited to

Table IV. Km Values for Nonequilibrium Reactions in Early Stages
of Glycolysis in Muscle and Substrate Concentrations
of These Reactions in Vivo

Reaction	Km for Enzyme or Process (mM)	Substrate Concentration (in Vivo) (mM)
Phosphorylase	1.0	20-30
Glucose transport	10.0	5.0
Hexokinase	0.1	<0.1*
Phosphofructokinase	c. 0.1†	0.1

*Intracellular glucose in muscle is difficult to measure precisely [35 (pp. 142-144)].

†The kinetics of the enzyme are such that if the enzyme is inhibited by ATP, the concentration of fructose 6-phosphate cannot be saturating [35 (pp. 106, 107)].

*A metabolic pathway is defined as those sequences of reactions that are initiated by a flux-generating step and terminate in a reaction preceding another flux-generating step or by loss of the end-product to the environment.

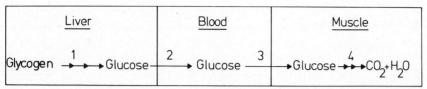

FIG. 2. The provision of glucose for oxidation in muscle by glycogenolysis in liver (1) represents the reactions catalyzed by phosphorylase, phosphoglucomutase and glucose 6-phosphatase; (2) represents the release of glucose by the liver; (3) represents the uptake of glucose by the muscle; and (4) represents the oxidation of glucose in muscle.

one tissue but can span several tissues. Thus, when the flux through glycolysis is increased during muscular activity, the rates of glycogen degradation and glucose release by liver must be increased to maintain a steady state in this pathway. (The bloodflow to the muscle is also increased by vasodilation which will increase the rate of transport of glucose to the muscle.) Furthermore, since hepatic phosphorylase is the flux-generating step for glucose utilization in muscle, the activity of this enzyme must be increased by a mechanism (i.e., via an external regulator) which is related to the rate of energy utilization by the muscle. Indeed, the more direct this relationship the better will be the maintenance of the steady state of the pathway.

The activity of hepatic phosphorylase is modified by the hormones adrenalin, glucagon and insulin; the changes in the concentrations of these hormones during sustained exercise are in the expected directions (i.e., the concentration of adrenalin increases, whereas that of insulin decreases) [46, 48]. However, a fundamental question is whether the changes in the concentrations of these hormones can regulate hepatic phosphorylase with sufficient precision to meet the energy demands of muscle during mechanical activity. The author considers that hormonal regulation alone cannot produce sufficient precision, so that an additional mechanism for the regulation of the flux-generating step is required. These mechanisms are discussed in the section "The Regulatory Link Between Muscle Glycolysis and Hepatic Glycogenolysis."

Flux-Generating Step for Fatty Acid Utilization in Muscle

Although the reactions of the fatty acid oxidation pathway are known, their properties are not as well established as those of glycolysis so that it is impossible to use properties of the enzymes to identify a flux-generating step. Nonetheless, the rate of fatty acid oxidation in muscle varies with the extracellular concentration of fatty acid [13, 17]. Thus, there is no flux-generating step for fatty acid oxidation in muscle, so that it is likely to be the lipolytic process in adipose tissue (Fig. 3) which is catalyzed by triglyceride lipase (together with di- and monoglyceride lipases). This provides another example of a metabolic pathway that spans more than one tissue, with the attendant problems of metabolic control. The activity of the lipase is regulated by a variety of hormones (e.g., glucagon, adrenalin, noradrenalin, insulin) whose concentrations change in the expected direction during sustained exercise (see above). However, in a similar manner to the mobilization of glucose from liver, it is unlikely that this type of control can provide sufficient precision in regulation of fatty acid release to satisfy the energy needs of muscle. Additional mechanisms of control are discussed below.

Flux-Generating Step for the Tricarboxylate Cycle

At the present time it is unknown which, if any, reactions of the tricarboxylate cycle are flux-generating. Candidates include the reactions catalyzed by pyruvate dehydrogenase (for entry into the cycle from glucose), citrate synthase and α-ketoglutarate dehydrogenase. The major difficulty in assessing this problem is the fact that the cycle is localized in the mitochondria, but methods are not yet available to measure metabolic intermediates in mitochondria of an intact muscle.

Control of Carbohydrate Utilization in Muscle

Short bursts of muscular activity probably rely on anaerobic degradation of glycogen to lactate for energy provision. The mechanism of control of degradation of glycogen in muscle has been

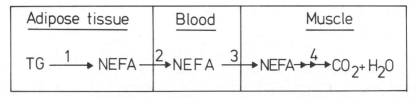

FIG. 3. The provision of fatty acid for oxidation in muscle by lipolysis in adipose tissue (1) represents the lipolytic reaction in adipose tissue; (2) represents the release of fatty acid by adipose tissue; (3) represents the uptake of fatty acid by muscle; and (4) represents the oxidation of fatty acids in muscle.

extensively reviewed so that it will not be discussed here [35 (pp. 153-185)].

In the early stages of sustained exercise (10 to 20 minutes) it is likely that glucose is the major fuel for the muscle. During this period, glycolytic flux (and the citric acid cycle plus electron transport chain) must be sufficient to provide enough energy for the demands of the contractile process. Consequently, the rate of glycolysis must be controlled in relation to the energy requirement of the muscle. However, since the total amount of glucose in the blood is very low (Table III), glucose must be released from the liver (from glycogen) at the same rate as it is used by the muscle in order to maintain the steady-state flux and the level of glucose in the blood (Table V and "Introduction"). Biochemical information on the properties of the enzymes which catalyze reactions in the early stages of glycolysis in muscle (and of phosphorylase and glycogen synthetase in liver) provides some insight into the mechanism of metabolic regulation of these processes.

Regulation of the Early Stages of Glycolysis

The three nonequilibrium reactions in the early stages of glycolysis that are regulated in relation to the energy requirements of the muscle are glucose transport, hexokinase and phosphofructokinase [35 (pp. 100-104)]. There is little information on the mechanism of the control of glucose transport. The activity of hexokinase is regulated by the changes in the concentration of glucose 6-phosphate, which in turn is regulated by the activity of phosphofructokinase. The mechanism of regulation of this latter enzyme by changes in the concentrations of AMP, Pi, fructose diphosphate and NH_4^+ has been discussed in detail elsewhere [35 (pp. 105-124), 44] (Fig. 4). However, the significance of the substrate-cycle between fructose 6-phosphate and fructose diphosphate, catalyzed by the simultaneous activities of phosphofructokinase and fructose diphosphatase, (Fig. 5) in the *precise* regulation of the rate of glycolysis in relation to energy utilization has not been extensively reviewed. This is discussed below.

The role of the fructose 6-phosphate — fructose diphosphate cycle in regulation of energy formation in muscle. A major problem in the regulation of glycolysis in muscle is sensitivity of the regulatory system to the changes in concentrations of metabolic regulators. Sensitivity in metabolic control of energy transference in muscles provides precision and improves kinetic efficiency of the ATP-producing and utilizing systems (see "Introduction"). The

Table V. Concentrations of Glucose, Long Chain Fatty Acids, Ketone Bodies, Glycerol, Insulin and Growth Hormone During Starvation and Exercise in Man and Rat

Concentrations in Serum (or Plasma) (mMol/L.)

Animal	Condition	Fuel or Hormone	Fed	*Days of Starvation*						
				1	*2*	*3*	*4*	*5*	*6*	*8*
Human	Normal, Resting	Glucose	5.5	4.7	4.1	3.8	3.6	3.6	3.5	3.5
		Long chain fatty acids	0.30	0.42	0.82	1.04	1.15	1.27	1.18	1.88
		Ketone bodies	c. 0.01	0.03	0.55	2.15	2.89	3.64	3.98	5.34
		Insulin†	c. 40	15.2	9.2	8.0	7.7	8.6	7.7	8.3
		Growth hormone	–	1.9	3.1	5.8	3.7	8.8	6.0	3.4

			Fed	*Days of Starvation*					
				3	*10*	*17*	*24*	*31*	*35–38*
	Obese, Resting	Glucose	4.8	3.6	3.8	3.8	3.8	3.8	3.7
		Long chain fatty acids	0.71	1.25	1.36	1.46	1.55	1.48	1.60
		Ketone bodies	0.1	1.62	5.30	6.22	7.05	7.21	7.19
		Glycerol	0.10	0.11	0.11	0.13	0.15	0.11	0.12
		Insulin†	>100	20	20	17	13	17	14
		Growth hormone	1.0	1.4	1.2	0.7	0.5	0.7	0.4

Concentrations in Blood (mMol/L.)

			Fed	*Days of Starvation*			
				1	*2*	*3*	*4*
Rat	Normal,	Glucose	6.34	–	4.76	4.36	4.28

	Resting	Time of Exercise (min)							
		0	10	20	30	40	60	80	90
Long chain fatty acids	0.66	–	1.31		–	–			
Ketone bodies	0.22	–	2.81		3.03	–			
Insulin*	28.7	–	4.2		–	3.35			
Rat 48 hr starved									
Glucose		3.92	3.64						
Long chain fatty acids		1.49	1.17						
Ketone bodies		3.39	1.92						
Human 3 hr after previous meal									
Glucose‡		5.0		4.7	–	5.0	5.0	4.7	–
Long chain fatty acids*		0.4		–	0.45	–	–	–	0.55
Ketone bodies		0.1		–	0.15	–	–	–	0.15
Glycerol		0.05		–	0.20	–	–	–	0.40

*plasma levels
†µU/ml
‡data taken from Hermansen et al [20].

The fed condition represents the absorptive state, and insulin levels are obtained from peak levels of an oral glucose tolerance test. The concentrations in starving normal man represent the average of six subjects, in starving obese man they represent the average of 11 subjects and in exercising man they represent the average of 9 subjects. The concentrations in rat represent the average of a large number of rats (>10). The data are taken from the following references: Cahill et al [9]; Hawkins et al [19]; Houghton [22]; Johnson et al [25].

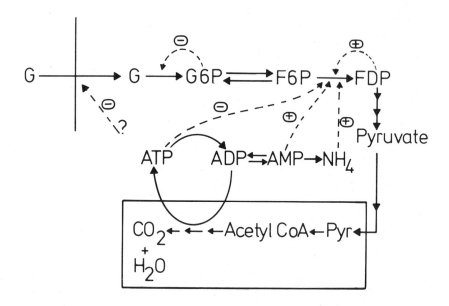

FIG. 4. Regulation of glycolysis in muscle at the glucose transport, hexokinase and phosphofructokinase reactions. The abbreviations G, G6P, F6P, FDP, Pyr represent glucose, glucose 6-phosphate, fructose 6-phosphate, fructose 1,6-diphosphate and pyruvate, respectively.

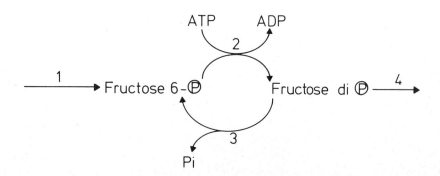

FIG. 5. The fructose 6-phosphate — fructose 1,6-diphosphate cycle. Reaction 1 represents the flux into fructose 6-phosphate from glycogenolysis or glucose utilization, or both. Reactions 2 and 3 represent phosphofructokinase and fructose 1,6-diphosphatase, respectively, and reaction 4 represents the flux into the remainder of the glycolytic pathway.

simplest mechanism to insure precision in the regulation of the rate of energy production is direct feedback control, i.e., the rate of ATP utilization directly controls the rate of glycolysis. This is provided by the phosphofructokinase-regulatory mechanism (see above). However, in muscle, the magnitude of the increase in rate of energy utilization from complete rest to maximal activity is large, so that the question arises whether the changes in concentrations of the metabolic regulators (AMP, fructose diphosphate, Pi and NH_4^+) are sufficient to produce the necessary increase in activity of phosphofructokinase.* Consequently, it has been suggested that a substrate cycle between fructose 6-phosphate and fructose diphosphate is present in some muscles so that the sensitivity of metabolic control at this enzymatic level is increased (Fig. 5).

The sensitivity in control provided by a substrate cycle is defined as follows:

$$\text{sensitivity} = 1 + \frac{\text{cycling rate}}{\text{flux}}$$

where sensitivity is defined as the relative change in flux/relative change in regulator concentration (see Newsholme and Crabtree [33] for derivation of equation). The ratio, cycling rate/flux, refers to the situation in the muscle under control (i.e., resting) conditions. Consequently, in order to provide an increased sensitivity over and above that provided by a noncycling system, the ratio, cycling rate/flux, must be high. However, it has been shown that a high rate of cycling produces a considerable amount of heat [33] and the maintenance of such rates for prolonged periods may result in hyperthermia. This problem is overcome if it is assumed that high rates of cycling (and therefore a large ratio cycling rate/flux) occur only when exercise is anticipated. Thus, it has been suggested that hormones, (e.g., adrenalin, noradrenalin) increase the rate of cycling between fructose 6-phosphate and fructose diphosphate in muscle during periods of anticipation or stress. This insures that if muscular activity follows the anticipation, so that ATP utilization is increased, metabolic control of fructose 6-phosphate phosphorylation will be very sensitive to changes in the concentrations of the metabolic regulators (i.e., AMP, Pi and NH_4^+). Consequently, the flux through

---

*The limits imposed on changes in concentration of metabolic regulators and the sensitivity of enzyme activities to these changes have been extensively discussed by Newsholme and Start [35 (pp. 69-76)]; Newsholme and Crabtree [32, 33]; and Crabtree and Newsholme [10].

glycolysis rapidly and precisely adjusts to provide sufficient energy for contraction.

In the absence of substrate cycling at this level, large changes in concentration of the feedback regulators may be required in order to regulate glycolytic flux. However, large changes in the concentrations of these regulators can only be obtained at the expense of large changes in the ATP/ADP concentration ratio, which could result in kinetic inefficiency of energy metabolism in muscle (see "Introduction"). The author suggests that athletic training, especially interval training, will increase the capacity of such substrate cycles, so that large changes in flux through the ATP-producing and utilizing processes will be obtained in muscle with minimum changes in concentrations of metabolic regulators. Consequently, kinetic efficiency will be maintained even at very high rates of ATP turnover.

The Regulatory Link Between Muscle Glycolysis and Hepatic Glycogenolysis

An increase in the rate of glycolysis in muscle demands a similar increase in the rate of hepatic glycogenolysis, if the overall pathway of glucose mobilization and utilization is to be maintained in the steady state.* How is this achieved? It is possible that mechanically active muscle releases an active regulatory compound(s) that stimulates hepatic glycogenolysis. This would provide a feedback link between the two processes that could produce precise regulation, especially if the rate of release of the regulator was proportional to the work performed by the muscle. At the present time, there is no evidence for such a regulator. Alternatively, small changes in the blood glucose level caused by changes in the rate of glucose utilization may regulate hepatic glycogenolysis. This would produce a direct feedback control mechanism. However, the problem of sensitivity of the regulatory mechanism arises, since the glycogenolytic system would need to respond to small changes in the blood glucose concentration. (See section "The Flux-Generating Step in a Metabolic Pathway.") Nonetheless, the elegant work of Hers and colleagues [21] has provided the basis for a sensitive regulatory mechanism in which the activities of both phosphorylase and glycogen synthetase can be controlled by small changes in blood

---

*If the rate of release of glucose is greater than that required by the muscle, the blood glucose level will rise and eventually it will be lost in the urine. On the other hand, if the rate of release is lower than required, the blood glucose level will fall: this would reduce the rate of glycolysis in muscle and hence limit mechanical activity.

glucose level. If this regulatory system is grafted onto a substrate cycle between glycogen and glucose 1-phosphate catalyzed by the simultaneous activities of these two enzymes, the system may be exquisitely sensitive to changes in the blood glucose level. The mechanism is described in more detail below.

Control of hepatic glycogenolysis by changes in the blood glucose level. The activity of the enzyme, glycogen synthetase, is inhibited by phosphorylase *a*. The proportion of the phosphorylase enzyme in the *a*-form is controlled, not only by the effects of hormones on the enzymes that interconvert phosphorylase *a* and *b*, but also by the hepatic glucose concentration. Thus, phosphorylase *a* binds glucose and, in this form, it is a better substrate for phosphorylase *a* phosphatase (i.e., the Km of the phosphatase for the complex, phosphorylase *a*-glucose, is lower than that for phosphorylase *a* alone [21]. Since an increase in the concentration of glucose in the blood will increase that in the liver, the proportion of phosphorylase in the *a* form will be reduced, when the blood glucose level increases. This will lower the activity of phosphorylase and hence the rate of glycogenolysis. Furthermore, the decrease in phosphorylase *a* concentration will result in the stimulation of the activity of glycogen synthetase. Thus, an increase in the blood glucose level will inhibit glycogenolysis and stimulate glycogen synthesis. If it is assumed that a substrate cycle between glycogen and glucose 1-phosphate exists in liver (Fig. 6), this will increase the sensitivity of the system to changes in glucose concentration. The author suggests that the combination of the complex regulatory interplay between phosphorylase and glycogen synthetase and a substrate cycle between glycogen and glucose 1-phosphate may provide an extremely sensitive control system so that it can respond to very small changes in blood glucose level. In this manner, changes in hormone concentrations in concert with changes in the blood glucose level may enable the rate of glycogen degradation to meet *precisely* the glucose needs of the muscle.

Control of Fatty Acid Mobilization by Adipose Tissue

Fatty acid oxidation provides a considerable proportion of the energy required for prolonged severe exercise (e.g., marathon running). Although the blood fatty acid level is one important factor controlling the rate of fatty acid oxidation, the energy demand of the muscle will undoubtedly play some part in the regulation of fatty acid uptake and oxidation. However, the biochemical mechanism of this latter control is unknown. Consequently, discussion in this

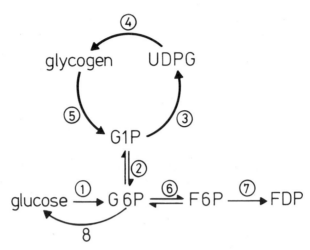

FIG. 6. Substrate cycle between hexose monophosphates and glycogen. The reactions are as follows: (1) hexokinase; (2) phosphoglucomutase; (3) UDP-glucose pyrophosphorylase; (4) UDP-glucose glucosyltransferase (glycogen synthetase); (5) phosphorylase; (6) phosphoglucoisomerase; (7) phospho-fructokinase. The abbreviations UDPG, G1P, G6P, F6P and FDP represent UDP-glucose, glucose 1-phosphate, glucose 6-phosphate, fructose 6-phosphate and fructose 1,6-diphosphate, respectively. The simultaneous activities of enzymes catalyzing reactions 3, 4 and 5 constitute the substrate cycle.

section will center upon the mechanisms by which the rate of fatty acid mobilization is regulated precisely according to the rate of utilization, so that a steady-state condition is achieved.

Hormonal Control of Lipolysis in Adipose Tissue

There are a large number of hormones that can increase the rate of lipolysis [43], but only insulin (and certain prostaglandins) inhibit lipolysis. During exercise, increases in the blood levels of the lipolytic hormones, adrenalin, glucagon and possibly noradrenalin, together with a decrease in the level of insulin may be responsible, at least in part, for the increase in the lipolytic rate (see above). However, the author considers that changes in levels of hormones (or nervous stimulation) cannot provide sufficiently precise control of rate of fatty acid mobilization to satisfy the energy requirements of the muscle: it seems highly unlikely that endocrine glands or even higher nervous centers can monitor accurately the work being done by muscular tissue at any instant of time. Nonetheless, the establishment of a steady state for the pathway of fatty acid utilization would appear to be fundamentally important for the metabolic well-being of the individual. Thus, if the rate of fatty acid mobilization exceeded that of utilization, the blood fatty acid level would increase continuously, such that it might reach levels that cause damage to various tissues.* On the other hand, if the rate of fatty acid mobilization was less than that of utilization, the fatty acid level in the blood would decrease, which would result in glucose utilization by the muscle (see section "Interrelationship Between Fat and Carbohydrate Oxidation in Muscle") and a fall in the blood glucose level. This could cause fatigue, which could be overcome only by a reduction in the energy expenditure by the musculature. Thus, hormonal control of lipolysis must be supplemented by a mechanism that provides a feedback link between the rate of energy utilization by the muscle and the process of lipolysis. Two such mechanisms, which are described below, may exist.

Ketone Body Control of Fatty Acid Mobilization

Ketone bodies (acetoacetate and 3-hydroxybutyrate) are produced in the liver by the partial oxidation of fatty acids to acetyl CoA, and conversion of the latter to acetoacetate via the hydroxymethyl glutaryl-CoA (HMG-CoA) cycle [35 (pp. 300-305)]. The blood level of fatty acids is one factor in the control of the rate of ketogenesis in the liver, so that if the concentration of fatty acids increases, the rate of ketogenesis increases and the concentration of ketone bodies in the blood is raised. It has been shown that in some animals including man [19, 24, 29] high levels of ketone bodies stimulate insulin secretion from the pancreas. Since insulin is a very potent antilipolytic hormone, this should reduce the rate of fatty acid mobilization. Furthermore, there is evidence that high ketone body levels can directly reduce lipolysis in adipose tissue [7, 19]. Thus, ketone bodies may reduce the rate of lipolysis by acting directly on the lipolytic system (although the mechanism of action is unknown) and indirectly, via insulin secretion. It is suggested that these effects provide a sensitive feedback control to relay information concerning the blood level of fatty acids to the lipolytic system (Fig. 7). If the rate of fatty acid mobilization exceeds that of utilization, the blood level of fatty acids will increase which will stimulate the rate of ketogenesis and increase the blood level of ketone bodies. This, in turn, will inhibit fatty acid mobilization. The

---

*High concentrations of fatty acids damage cell and mitochondrial membranes [1], uncouple oxidative phosphorylation [37], increase the rate of platelet aggregation [27], may result in fibrillation of the heart [36] and could be responsible for hypertriglyceridemia and eventual atherosclerosis [45].

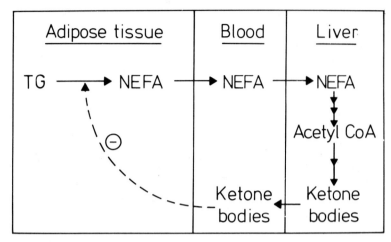

FIG. 7. The direct feedback control of lipolysis in adipose tissue by ketone bodies. TG represents triglyceride and NEFA represents nonesterified fatty acids.

opposite changes will occur if fatty acid utilization exceeds that of mobilization.

There are two pieces of indirect evidence to support this hypothesis. First, in starved rats, in which the levels of ketone bodies and fatty acids are raised, exercise lowers the blood ketone body level to a greater extent than that of fatty acids [22] (Table V). Second, the ketone body level is increased in human subjects after cessation of prolonged exercise [25] (Table VI). It is assumed that on cessation of exercise the rate of fatty acid mobilization will exceed that of utilization, at least transiently, since oxidation in

Table VI. Ketone Body Concentrations in Blood of Athletes
and Nonathletes During and After Exercise

| | Time (min) | Blood Ketone Body Concentrations (mM) | |
		Athletes	Nonathletes
Exercise	0	0.10	0.10
	30	0.15	0.15
	90	0.15	0.40
Postexercise	120	0.20	0.80
	150	0.25	1.10
	180	0.30	1.55

Blood samples were taken from the subjects prior to exercise during running, which lasted 90 minutes, and in the postexercise recovery period. The results are the means from 9 athletes and 18 nonathletes. Data are taken from Johnson et al [25].

muscle, but not mobilization from adipose tissue, will be reduced immediately. Thus, the blood fatty acid level will increase, which will stimulate ketogenesis and increase the level of ketone bodies in the blood, which should reduce the rate of lipolysis. Furthermore, the work of Johnson et al shows that the post-exercise ketosis is considerably greater in nonathletes than in athletes (even though the athletes did considerably more work than the nonathletes). This finding suggests that in athletes another feedback mechanism plays a more important role in regulation of fatty acid mobilization than the "ketone body" mechanism. The author suggests that this mechanism involves the triglyceride-fatty acid cycle in adipose tissue.

Feedback Control of Fatty Acid Mobilization
Via the Triglyceride-Fatty Acid Cycle

In adipose tissue, the process of lipolysis occurs simultaneously with that of esterification, so that triglyceride is broken down to fatty acids which are reactivated and re-esterified to form triglyceride (i.e., a substrate cycle) (Fig. 8). One advantage of a substrate cycle is the improvement in sensitivity of metabolic control mechanisms [33], and this may be particularly important for the effects of hormones and ketone bodies on lipolysis. Thus, small changes in the activity of the triglyceride lipase could produce large changes in the rate of fatty acid mobilization. However, the properties of the esterification and lipolytic processes permit the formulation of a theory of control of lipolysis by changes in the blood level of fatty

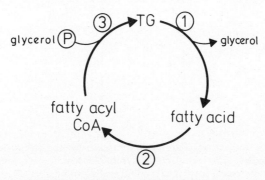

FIG. 8. The triglyceride-fatty acid substrate cycle. Reaction (1) is catalyzed by triglyceride lipase (plus di- and monoglyceride lipases; reaction (2) by fatty acyl CoA synthetase and reaction (3) represents the esterification process. TG represents triglyceride and glycerol (P) represents glycerol 1-phosphate. The simultaneous activities of enzymes catalyzing the three processes result in the substrate cycle.

acids. If the rate of fatty acid utilization by muscle increased (due to increased work), this would decrease the concentration of fatty acids in the blood and hence that in adipose tissue. Since the concentration of fatty acid in adipose tissue is not saturating for the esterification process [2, 26], a decrease in concentration would reduce the rate of esterification. Hence, the rate of fatty acid mobilization would increase. Furthermore, since fatty acids inhibit the activity of triglyceride lipase [8, 40], a decrease in the fatty acid concentration would increase the rate of lipolysis. Consequently, an increased rate of utilization of fatty acids in muscle, causing a decrease in fatty acid concentration in adipose tissue, will lead to increased mobilization of fatty acids from adipose tissue (Fig. 9). Of course, the opposite changes would result from a decreased rate of utilization of fatty acids in muscle.

Athletic training may stimulate the capacity of such cycles and increase the cycling/flux ratio so that an exquisitely sensitive control mechanism is produced. This could account for the minimal postexercise ketosis in athletic subjects (Table VI).

Interrelationship Between Fat and Carbohydrate Oxidation in Muscle

It is now generally accepted that fatty acid oxidation decreases glucose utilization by muscle.* This phenomenon may be of the

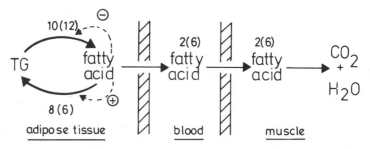

FIG. 9. Feedback control of fatty acid mobilization from adipose tissue via the triglyceride-fatty acid cycle. The numbers represent the (hypothetical) rates of the various processes. The numbers in parentheses indicate the changes in rates produced by an increased rate of fatty acid utilization by muscle.

---

*Experiments with isolated muscle preparations (perfused rat heart, isolated rat diaphragm and isolated soleus muscle [11, 34, 38]) demonstrated that fatty acid oxidation inhibits glucose utilization and oxidation by specific biochemical mechanisms; an increase in the blood fatty acid level, produced physiologically or artificially in animals or man, decreases the rate of glucose utilization [35].

utmost importance in long-distance running events. The energy expenditure during a marathon run is about 14 Kcal/min so that about 5 gm of glucose must be oxidized per minute to provide sufficient energy. Thus, under such conditions, the total extracellular glucose would be used within a few minutes and hepatic glycogen (at least, if the amount in the liver of the average man represents that in the marathon runner) within 20 to 30 minutes (Table III) (see section "The Regulatory Link Between Muscle Glycolysis and Hepatic Glycogenolysis"). Since the marathon lasts for well over two hours, another fuel must replace glucose. This fuel is long chain fatty acids, which are derived from the triglyceride stored in the adipose tissue. It is likely that after the first few minutes of exercise, fatty acids will be used to a progressively greater extent and that perhaps after 30 minutes they may be the major blood-borne fuel for muscle. Thus, in the early stages of the exercise, there will be a considerable increase, whereas in the latter part of the exercise, there will be a considerable decrease in glucose utilization. Nonetheless, the blood glucose concentration remains remarkably constant throughout this activity (Table V). The maintenance of the blood glucose level is important, since some tissues (e.g., brain, at least under these conditions, red and white blood cells and kidney medulla [9, 28]) utilize only glucose as a fuel. Consequently, the rate of glucose utilization (and mobilization) must be controlled so that it provides an important source of energy for the muscle in the early stages and an unimportant source in the later stages of exercise and yet the glucose level must remain constant throughout the exercise period. The author suggests that in the early stages, the control of hepatic glycogenolysis and, in the later stages, the inhibition of glycolysis by fatty acid oxidation are largely responsible for maintenance of the blood glucose level.

The regulation of glucose utilization by fatty acid oxidation is achieved, in part, by the inhibitory effect of citrate on the enzyme phosphofructokinase [35 (pp. 124-130)]. However, it is well established that an increase in the concentration of any (or all) of the de-inhibitors of phosphofructokinase (e.g., AMP, Pi, NH_4^+, fructose diphosphate) will reduce citrate inhibition of the enzyme and hence increase the rate of glycolysis and glucose utilization [34]. Consequently, if the rate of fatty acid provision to muscle provides just sufficient fatty acid oxidation for the energy requirements of the working muscle, an increase in work would reduce the ATP/ADP concentration ratio and increase glycolytic flux (see section "Regulation of the Early Stages of Glycolysis"). This would occur despite the inhibitory effects of fatty acid oxidation, since citrate inhibition of phosphofructokinase is relieved by AMP, etc. If the increased energy demand of the muscle could not be met by increased fat mobilization, the increased rate of glucose utilization would have to be maintained. This could result in a decrease in the local environmental concentration of glucose, which may result in fatigue. Consequently, the ability to mobilize fatty acids rapidly in response to increased workloads may be important in competitive distance running and this ability may be improved by athletic training (see section "Control of Fatty Acid Mobilization by Adipose Tissue").

References

1. Baker, P.F., Northcote, D.H. and Peters, R.: Nature 195:661-662, 1962.
2. Bally, P.R., Cahill, G.F. and Leboeuf: J. Biol. Chem. 235:333-336, 1960.
3. Barman, T.E.: Enzyme Handbook, vols I and II. Berlin, Heidelberg, New York:Springer-Verlag.
4. Beis, I. and Newsholme, E.A.: Biochem. J. 152:23-32, 1975.
5. Beis, I. and Newsholme, E.A.: J. Cell. Cardiology. (In press.)
6. Bilinski, E.: Can. J. Biochem. Physiol. 41:107-112, 1963.
7. Björntorp, F.: J. Lipid Res. 7:621-626, 1966.
8. Burns, T.W., Langley, P.E. and Robison, G.A.: Metabolism 24:265-276, 1975.
9. Cahill, G.F. and Owen, O.E.: *In* Dickens, F., Randle, P.J. and Whelan, W.J. (eds.): Carbohydrate Metabolism and its Disorders, Vol. I. London and New York:Academic Press, 1965, pp. 497-522.
10. Crabtree, B. and Newsholme, E.A.: *In* Usherwood, P.N.R. (ed.): Insect Muscle. London and New York:Academic Press, 1975, pp. 405-500.
11. Cuendet, G.S., Loten, E.G. and Denold, A.E.: European Association for Study of Diabetes Meeting: Munich 1975, Abstract no. 42, 1975.
12. Drummond, G.I.: Fortschr. Zool. 18:359-429, 1967.
13. Eaton, P. and Steinberg, D.: J. Lipid Res. 2:376-382, 1961.
14. Ekelund, L-G.: Ann. Rev. Physiol. 31:85-116, 1969.
15. Felig, P.: Ann. Rev. Biochem. 44:933-955, 1975.
16. Fredrickson, D.S. and Gordon, R.S.: Physiol. Rev. 38:588-630, 1957.
17. Fritz, I.B.: Physiol. Rev. 41:52-129, 1961.
18. George, J.C. and Vallyathan, N.V.: J. Appl. Physiol. 19:619-622, 1964.
19. Hawkins, R.A., Albert, K.G.M.M., Houghton, C.R.S. et al: Biochem. J. 125:541-544, 1961.
20. Hermansen, L., Hultman, E. and Saltin, B.: Acta Physiol. Scand. 71:129-139, 1967.
21. Hers, H.G.: Ann. Rev. Biochem. 45 (In press.)
22. Houghton, C.R.S.: D. Phil. Thesis. Oxford University, 1970.
23. Infante, A.A. and Davies, R.E.: Biochem. Biophys. Res. Commun. 9:410-415, 1962.
24. Jenkins, D.: Lancet 2:341-344, 1967.
25. Johnson, R.H., Walton, J.L., Krebs, H.A. and Williamson, D.H.: Lancet 2:452-455, 1969.

26. Kerpel, S., Shafrir, E. and Shapiro, B.: Biochim. Biophys. Acta 227:608-617, 1961.
27. Kerr, S., Pirrie, R., MacAulay, I. and Bronte-Stewart, B.: Lancet 1:1296-1299, 1965.
28. Krebs, H.A.: Essays Biochem. 8:1-34, 1972.
29. Madison, L.L., Mebane, D., Unger, R.H. and Lochner, A.: J. Clin. Invest. 43:408-415, 1964.
30. Maruyama, K. and Pringle, J.W.S.: Arch. Biochem. Biophys. 120:225-228, 1967.
31. Newsholme, E.A.: In Bartley, W., Kornberg, H.L. and Quayle, J.R. (eds.): Essays in Cell Metabolism. London:Wiley-Inter-Science, 1970, pp. 189-223.
32. Newsholme, E.A. and Crabtree, B.: Symp. Soc. Exp. Biol. 26:429-460, 1973.
33. Newsholme, E.A. and Crabtree, B.: Biochem. Soc. Symp. 41:61-110, 1976.
34. Newsholme, E.A. and Randle, P.J.: Biochem. J. 93:641-651, 1964.
35. Newsholme, E.A. and Start, C.: Regulation in Metabolism. London, Sydney and Toronto:Wiley & Sons, 1973.
36. Oliver, H.G. and Yates, P.A.: In Moret, P. and Fejfar, Z. (eds.): Metabolism of the Hypoxic and Ischaemic Heart. Basel:S. Karger, 1972, pp. 359-363.
37. Pressman, B.C. and Lardy, H.A.: Biochem. Biophys. Acta 21:458-466, 1958.
38. Randle, P.J., Newsholme, E.A. and Garland, P.B.: Biochem. J. 93:652-665, 1964.
39. Robinson, D.S.: Compr. Biochem. 18:51-116, 1970.
40. Rodbell, M.: Ann. N.Y. Acad. Sci. USA 131:302-314, 1965.
41. Rohr, P., Saint-Saens, M. and Monod, H.: J. Physiol. (Paris) 58:5-19, 1966.
42. Rowan, A.: D. Phil. Thesis. Oxford University, 1975.
43. Steinberg, D.: In Grant, J.H. (ed.): Control of Lipid Metabolism. London and New York:Academic Press, 1963, pp. 111-138.
44. Sugden, P.H. and Newsholme, E.A.: Biochem. J. 150:113-122, 1975.
45. Taggart, P. and Curruthers, M.: Lancet 1:363-366, 1971.
46. Vendsalu, A.: Acta Physiol. Sci. 49 Suppl. 173, 1960.
47. Watts, D.C.: In Schoffeniels, E. (ed.): Biochemical Evolution and the Origin of Life. North Holland, Amsterdam and London, 1971, pp. 150-173.
48. Wright, R.H. and Malaisse, W.J.: Am. J. Physiol. 214:1031-1034, 1968.

Le contrôle et l'utilisation des circuits producteurs d'énergie dans les muscles, par rapport à l'exercice physique soutenu

L'auteur traite des éléments couramment proposés pour expliquer la régularité du taux de concentration ATP/ADP dans les muscles et suggère qu'une explication ne peut venir que de la cinétique. Suit une présentation des mécanismes nécessaires au maintien de l'efficacité cinétique des processus compris dans le transfert d'énergie. L'auteur examine les plus importants circuits producteurs d'énergie, en s'arrêtant en particulier à la glycolyse, au système β-oxydatif des acides gras et au cycle de l'acide citrique. Ensuite vient l'explication des moyens permettant d'augmenter la sensibilité du contrôle métabolique. Commentaires sur la capacité accrue des cycles des substrats et sur les mécanismes de contrôle pour la mobilisation de l'acide gras, par rapport à des épreuves d'endurance.

When and How the Alpha-Glycerophosphate Cycle Works

P. W. Hochachka, C. French and M. Guppy

The α-glycerophosphate (α-GP) cycle, a mechanism for transferring reducing equivalents from the cytoplasm to the mitochondria, appears to take on prominent roles only in obligatorily aerobic muscles. From certain kinetic studies it appears that the α-GPDH catalysis is unidirectional and difficult to saturate; as a result, it supplies the muscle with an effectively unlimitable mechanism for sparking the α-GP cycle and thus respiration. The metabolic significance and other possible functions of the α-GP cycle are also discussed. It is concluded that all white muscle respiration probably is primed by the α-GP cycle whose operational limits are much more constrained than in obligate aerobic muscles.

Introduction

There is a requirement in the aerobic energy metabolism of all muscle cells for the presence of hydrogen shuttles — mechanisms by which reducing equivalents can be transferred from the cytoplasm to the mitochondria. Two such hydrogen shuttles are generally recognized as being the most important solutions to this requirement: the malate-aspartate shuttle and the α-glycerophosphate cycle. The malate-aspartate shuttle consists of the following components:

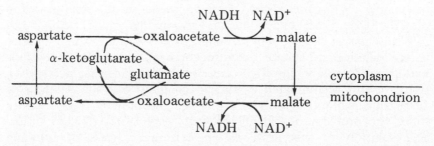

P. W. Hochachka, C. French and M. Guppy, National Marine Fisheries Service, Kewalo Basin, Honolulu, Hawaii, U.S.A. Permanent Address: Department of Zoology, University of British Columbia, Vancouver, B.C., Canada.

The functional properties of the malate-aspartate shuttle have been well described by others and no further discussion is necessary at this time. The properties of the α-glycerophosphate cycle (α-GP cycle), on the other hand, are not well known, which is perhaps surprising in that it is in a sense a simpler shuttle consisting of only one cytoplasmic arm:

$$\text{DHAP} \underset{}{\overset{\text{NADH} \quad \text{NAD}^+}{\longrightarrow}} \alpha\text{-GP}$$

and one mitochondrial reaction step:

$$\text{DHAP} \underset{\text{FADH}_2 \quad \text{FAD}}{\overset{}{\longleftarrow}} \alpha\text{-GP}$$

Because of the dearth of information in this area, we thought it useful for this conference to inquire into when and how the α-GP cycle takes on importance in muscle. From our analysis it appears that both its potential and its properties correlate with the O_2 dependence of muscle metabolism. At one end of the spectrum of O_2 dependence is to be found the obligatorily aerobic metabolism of insect flight muscle, and it is therefore convenient to begin our discussion with this system.

Highly O_2 Dependent Invertebrate Muscles

Insect flight muscle is one of the most metabolically active tissues known. It is usually loaded with mitochondria which are often precision packaged with respect to both the trachea (for efficient transfer of O_2) and the contractile elements (for efficient coupling between ATP formation and utilization). Of particular interest are those insect flight muscles that are powered exclusively or mainly by carbohydrate, such as those in the bee and the blowfly [16]. From our point of view in this paper, perhaps the most interesting "adjustment" of energy metabolism in these muscles is the deletion of lactate dehydrogenase (LDH). LDH activity is hardly measurable in the flight muscles of these insects; lactate, as a result, is not accumulated as an end product. But the deletion of LDH from mainline glycolysis in the bee and blowfly flight muscles raises the problem of balancing cytoplasmic $NAD^+/NADH$ ratios. The solution to this problem, an extremely active cytoplasmic α-GPDH, constitutes an important modification of the glycolytic system. It is relevant on two counts. In the first place, a highly active cytoplasmic α-glycerophosphate dehydrogenase forms the first arm of the α-GP cycle; in this process α-GP formed in the cytosol enters the mitochondria where it is re-oxidized to DHAP, sparking respiration in the process. DHAP in turn moves back into the cytosol to re-initiate the process. In anoxia, α-GP accumulates, but in steady-state flight, α-GP is neither accumulated nor depleted indicating that only priming quantities of DHAP are needed to drive the process. In the sense that DHAP initiates the process and is reformed by it, the process is cyclic; in the sense that no significant accumulation or depletion of either α-GP or DHAP occurs, the process is catalytic. The cycle thus constitutes an efficient mechanism for transferring reducing equivalents formed in glycolysis directly to the electron transfer system [16] and energetically it is distinctly advantageous. But the advantage is gained at the cost of the system's anaerobic capacities, and this brings us to the second and critical consequence of this modification in glycolysis. The presence of a high α-GPDH but no LDH reduces the *anaerobic* energy yield of this muscle to 1 mole ATP/mole G6P formed from glycogen or to *zero* mole ATP/mole G6P formed from glucose. More than any other single factor, it is this arrangement of α-GPDH and LDH that makes this metabolism so totally O_2 dependent. Not surprisingly, it is not widely found in nature. To our knowledge a similar metabolic organization is known for only one other group of organisms, the fast swimming predaceous squids [9]. Nevertheless, these few examples of dramatic aerobic metabolic potentials are instructive because they imply a fundamental reciprocal arrangement of α-GPDH and LDH (or its metabolic equivalent, octopine dehydrogenase in the cephalopods) that is apparently set in the genome through phylogenetic time. An identical relationship between these two enzymes occurs in ontogenetic time during flight muscle differentiation in insects [4]. The rule of thumb seems to be that α-GPDH is not utilized to any significant extent in redox regulation during anoxic stress (or in anoxia-tolerant organisms). The explanation as to why this should be the case comes from studies of the obligate aerobic systems: using α-GPDH under anoxic conditions leads to a serious drain of glycolytic carbon and to an effective drop in ATP yield per mole of starting G6P. That is why in anoxia, redox must be balanced by LDH or by metabolically equivalent reactions, such as, for example, octopine dehydrogenase, which takes on the function of LDH in many cephalopods [7]. In this context, we were understandably surprised when one of our colleagues (K.B. Storey) found α-GPDH and LDH and both at high activities in porpoise muscle [10]. Even in the diving turtle, *Psuedemys scripta*, the champion of all vertebrate anaerobes white muscle α-GPDH occurs at 30 to 50 units of activity, compared to about 300 units of LDH. Why should this be so? Interestingly, our major insights into this problem have come not from studies of diving animals where muscle metabolism [10] and muscle structure [21] are complex, but rather from studies of the tuna fish, where fiber organization is greatly simplified.

Tuna White Muscle Metabolism

The tuna fish is undoubtedly one of the most graceful and speedy of aquatic animals, as it would presumably have to be when faced with the dolphin as one of its potential predators. Of course it is also a predator feeding on a variety of pelagic prey organisms, including our fast swimming squid, *Symplectoteuthis oualaniensis* already alluded to above. More significantly, it offers an interesting experimental advantage in that the red and white muscles are ordered into discrete masses [5], unlike the setup in mammals where from an experimental point of view the fibers are rather hopelessly mixed. It was this characteristic coupled with the fact that tuna are "warm bodied" animals that first led us to choose them as an experimental system.

White muscle in tuna, as elsewhere, has substantially higher activities of glycolytic enzymes than occur in red muscle (Table I).

Table I. Activities of Glycolytic and Associated Enzymes
in Red and White Muscle of the Skipjack Tuna

Enzyme	Red Muscle	White Muscle
Phosphoglucomutase	48	154
Phosphoglucoisomerase	7	68
Glucose-6-P dehydrogenase	Undetectable	0.14
Aldolase	7	132
Triose-P isomerase	5	86
Phosphoglycerate kinase	32	318
Enolase	22	56
Pyruvate kinase	88	230
Lactate dehydrogenase	231	1858
α-glycero-P dehydrogenase	11	77
Aspartate aminotransferase	3	3
Alanine aminotransferase	1	0.1

Activities expressed as μmoles product formed/minute/gram wet weight of muscle at 25C under optimal conditions of pH and saturating concentrations of substrates and cofactors. Details of enzyme assays can be found in Hochachka et al [9] and in Storey and Hochachka [18].

As in dolphin muscle, both LDH and α-GPDH occur in high activities, over 1500 units of LDH and nearly 100 of α-GPDH. White muscle α-GPDH could have three potential roles: (1) it could serve an anaerobic function (i.e., NADH oxidation during anoxic stress); (2) it could play an aerobic role in priming the α-GP cycle; and (3) it could play a role in triglyceride formation or, indeed, mobilization [8]. In teleost white muscle, the first alternative is tentatively ruled out because α-GP is not accumulated to any significant extent during maximum swimming [6]. The third alternative is tentatively ruled out because triglyceride is neither accumulated nor significantly involved in energy metabolism of white muscle [12, 14]. The remaining possibility, then, a role in the α-GP cycle, seems the most likely. Several factors bear on this interpretation:

1. It is frequently observed that α-GPDH and mitochondrial α-GP oxidase occur in higher activities in white than in red muscle [1]. Whereas that alone tells us little regarding aerobic versus anaerobic α-GPDH function, the species distribution of the enzyme does. Thus, white muscle α-GPDH activities are highest in tuna, intermediate in the trout and lowest in the eel. That, too, is the order of the O_2 dependence of these species (the tuna being so O_2 dependent that they have to continuously swim to provide adequate gas exchange at the gills). Hence, it is reasonable to assume that α-GPDH is playing an aerobic function. Interestingly, white muscle preparations from fast swimming teleosts also display higher O_2 uptake than do preparations from slower swimming ones [14]. The correlations therefore are high α-GPDH activities, high O_2 consumption rates and high swimming velocities.

2. In fishes, white muscle fibers are recruited during steady-state swimming, a performance that is powered largely if not solely by an *aerobic* metabolism [3]. Again, this contribution may be greatest in the fastest swimmers such as the tuna. In accordance with this observation, tuna white muscle is known to contain unusually high concentrations of myoglobins and cytochromes [15]. That is why it is rather red in color and one reason why the Japanese prefer tuna sashimi to any other! These observations are also consistent with an aerobic function for α-GPDH in white muscle metabolism.

3. In at least two studies we are aware of, direct α-GP stimulation of respiration of white muscle preparations but not red muscle preparations is known [2, 20]. As we shall see, the magnitude of the observed stimulation is perhaps smaller than to be expected because of nonphysiological α-GP levels used in the studies. Nevertheless, the data encouraged us to look for direct evidence of

α-GP cycling in tuna white muscle. Working with low speed supernatant solutions of crude white muscle homogenates, we found that respiration showed a low sensitivity to malonate inhibition (unlike red muscle mitochondrial preparations) and a low sensitivity to the glycolytic poison, sodium fluoride. These observations were consistent with α-GP cycling. However, direct activating effects of α-GP could not be demonstrated in these preparations because of a high endogenous respiration (and, as we shall see, because the cycle is probably fully saturated with substrate). To demonstrate the activity of the α-GP cycle it was first necessary to introduce a block in the preparatory phases of the glycolytic path, somewhere *prior to the formation of DHAP.* Our way of blocking glycolysis in this region involved introducing the enzyme FDPase into crude homogenates of tuna white muscle. FDPase catalyzes the following reaction:

$$FDP \longrightarrow F6P \ + \ P_i$$

When present in the same compartment with PFK, catalyzing the following transphosphorylation

$$F6P \overset{}{\underset{ATP \qquad ADP}{\longrightarrow}} FDP$$

FDPase introduces a specific carbon and energy short-circuit into the pathway. Under these conditions, DHAP and other glycolytic intermediates in the terminal portion of the pathway are depleted and respiration rate drops dramatically. Now, most significantly, the addition of α-GP and NADH leads to a strong recovery of respiration; when the respiration rate is about 50% inhibited by the addition of FDPase, for example, α-GP and NADH at 2.5 and 1.0 mM levels, respectively, bring about a complete recovery of respiration. These experiments will be published in detail elsewhere. Suffice for the moment to emphasize that they, taken together with observations of relative enzyme levels (about 3 units of aspartate aminotransferase compared to about 80 units of α-GPDH), lead us to believe that *all* respiration in tuna white muscle is primed by the α-GP cycle, but its potential in red muscle is so low it cannot be demonstrated by comparable techniques. At this time, inhibition by NAD^+ coupled to competition for NADH constitutes the only known means by which the α-GP cycle in tuna white muscle seems to be regulated. Be that as it may, the currently available data lead us to conclude the aerobic glycolysis could certainly be coupled to the α-GP cycle in vertebrate white muscle, even if the potential would be low compared to that of, say, squid mantle, or bee flight muscle. This conclusion is further supported by kinetic studies of various α-GPDHs, since the enzyme in vertebrate white muscle is well suited for function in the α-GP cycle.

Properties of α-GPDH in Muscle With and Without LDH

To get at the question of how α-GPDH is regulated we compared the catalytic and regulatory properties of the enzymes from honey bee flight muscle and squid mantle with the homologous enzymes from tuna and turtle white muscle, and from skeletal muscle (mixed red and white) of the two diving animals, porpoise and seal. First let us consider the enzyme in muscles with an established functional α-GP cycle (Table II). In both the bee and the squid we found that α-GPDH has a low affinity for DHAP but an extremely high NADH affinity, being highest in the bee enzyme. The enzyme is thus poised to spark the α-GP cycle whenever DHAP becomes available. Since NADH pool size is obviously limited, the problem of NADH levels rising without limit does not arise even if the enzyme should become saturated with reduced coenzyme. By comparison, the DHAP pool size is less limited, and the high K_m for DHAP assures that high rates of cycling occur only when glycolytic rates (and hence DHAP levels) are high. Moreover, it prevents the enzyme from saturating with

Table II. Kinetic Properties of "Unidirectional" α-GPDHs from the Squid and Bee Compared to Those From Vertebrate White Muscles

| Species/Tissue | Kinetic Constant | Kinetic Constant (in mM) for | | | | Reference |
		DHAP	NADH	NAD	α-GP	
Bee flight muscle	K_m	0.24	0.005	1.6	2.0	[18, 19]
	K_i	0.005	0.001		10.0	[18, 19]
Squid mantle	K_m	0.15	0.015	0.14	1.0	[18, 19]
	K_i	0.012	0.114		over 15	[18, 19]
Seal muscle	K_m	0.14	0.015	0.6	0.5	*
	K_i	0.08	0.005	2.8	1.2	*
Turtle white muscle	K_m	0.09	0.015	0.25	0.3	*
	K_i	0.09	0.003	0.5	1.0	*
Tuna white muscle	K_m	0.072	0.014	0.4	0.25	†
	K_i	0.068	0.007	1.1	0.25	†

*Murphy, B. (unpublished data)

†Guppy, M. (unpublished data)

Enzymes purified by chromatography on G-100 Sephadex and on an agarose-hexane NAD affinity column were assayed in 50 mM imidazole buffer at 25C at pH 7.0 (except for turtle enzyme, at pH 7.4). Seal enzyme assayed at 37C.

DHAP and thus the more DHAP that is formed, the higher the α-GP cycling rates that can be achieved, a feature of obvious physiological advantage in extremely active tissues such as squid mantle and bee flight muscles.

Equally important, the product α-GP is a poor inhibitor of bee and squid α-GPDHs. That is why α-GP accumulates in muscle when these organisms are made anoxic. As we shall see, this cannot occur in tuna white muscle because of potent α-GP inhibition. Be that as it may, a far-reaching consequence of an α-GP *insensitive* α-GPDH is that during burst muscle work α-GP levels may be expected to reach a higher steady-state level allowing α-GP oxidase to work at closer to its maximum velocity, or alternatively, a sudden burst of cytosolic α-GPDH might lead to a pulse of α-GP production so as to spark α-GP oxidase. Either way, an α-GP insensitive α-GPDH seems advantageous to the bee and the squid.

A low affinity for α-GP contributes to another key element of the bee and squid enzymes: *unidirectional catalysis under in vivo conditions.* This element depends in part upon properties of the back reaction. Thus, when the back reaction is considered, both enzymes are remarkably sensitive to product inhibition, particularly with respect to NADH. In both cases, NADH is a strictly competitive inhibitor with respect to NAD, and the K_i values are 1.0 and 4.0 μM for the bee and squid enzymes, respectively. Similarly, DHAP is a competitive inhibitor with respect to α-GP and the K_i values for DHAP are likewise remarkably low, about an order of magnitude lower than the respective K_m values for the forward reaction (Table II). In functional terms what this means is that in both species, when the forward reaction is half-saturated with either DHAP or NADH, the back reaction is fully inhibited by either or both metabolites. On these grounds alone, then, one-way in vivo function, DHAP $\rightarrow$ α-GP, seems inevitable. This conclusion is bolstered by thermodynamic considerations (the reaction proceeding in this direction with a large, negative free energy change) and by the respective pH optima for the forward and backward reaction (the back reaction rates being reduced by two- to fourfold at physiological pH compared to optimal pH).

In tuna white muscle, α-GPDH purified by affinity column chromatography shows many of the same kinetic properties that we have already seen in the bee and squid enzymes. Thus, the activities are high (about 100 units, compared to values of 200 to 250 units in the bee and squid muscles), the forward reaction shows a sharp pH optimum at pH 7 while the reverse reaction shows an alkaline pH optimum, the K_m for DHAP (0.07 mM) is relatively high while the

K_m for NADH (0.014 mM) is low. Most of the features favoring unidirectional catalysis are also present at least partially preserved. Hence, on all these counts the tuna muscle α-GPDH seems similar to the homologues in bees and squids and thus seems fully capable of functioning with the α-GP cycle. When the effects of α-GP on the enzyme are considered, however, the similarities break down.

Turning "Off" Muscle α-GPDH

The constraints on the tuna system do not appear until we consider how α-GPDH is turned "off." In this connection, we searched diligently for potential regulatory metabolites [11] and for mechanisms by which α-GPDH activity can be blocked. In the bee and the squid ATP appears as the only possible candidate, K_i values being 2.0 and 0.6 mM for the bee and squid enzymes, respectively. Through this means it is clear α-GPDH activity could be integrated with the overall energy status of the cell. In this respect, the tuna enzyme is again similar, the K_i for ATP being about 1.5 (Guppy, unpublished data).

However, in tuna white muscle, ATP regulation by and of itself is clearly inadequate, since here *the specific kinetic and metabolic requirement is to turn α-GPDH "off" when LDH is "on"* (i.e., when the system is anaerobic, as during burst swimming). That requirement is absent in muscles with little or no anaerobic capacity. Most instructive in this context, then, are the following observations. First, when the temperature is increased, α-GPDH affinity for NADH falls, but LDH affinity for coenzyme rises (Guppy, unpublished data); thus, during burst swimming, when white muscle temperature is raised by about 10 C [17], emphasis is being placed on anaerobic glycolysis as α-GPDH capacity to compete for NADH is falling and LDH capacity to bind the same coenzyme is rising! That is one elegant way in which the flow of carbon and hydrogen to α-GP and lactate is controlled in tuna fish white muscle. The second and probably most significant way involves product inhibition of the enzyme, since tuna white muscle α-GPDH is extremely sensitive to α-GP. We attach particular importance to this observation, since a good (perhaps the best) metabolite signal for turning "off" α-GPDH when O_2 is limiting is α-GP accumulation. It is also instructive that α-GPDHs in all skeletal muscles thus far examined (tuna, porpoise, seal, turtle) display a relatively high sensitivity to α-GP (Tables II and III). That is why α-GP can serve as a signal to end its own further production *even if by comparison with lactate its accumulation during burst anaerobic glycolysis is modest.* In tuna, for example,

Table III. Kinetic Constants of "Reversible" α-GPDHs From Rabbit Liver
Compared to the Enzyme in Tuna Red Muscle and the Muscle From
the Dolphin, *Delphinus delphis*

Species/Tissue	Kinetic Constant	Kinetic Constant (in mM) for				Reference
		DHAP	NADH	NAD	α-GP	
Rabbit liver	K_m	0.02	0.004	0.2	0.68	[13]
	K_i	0.02	0.004	0.15	0.65	[13]
Tuna red muscle	K_m	0.05	0.007	0.15	0.2	*
	K_i	0.10	0.002	0.8	0.75	*
Dolphin muscle	K_m	0.02	0.005	0.17	0.15	†
	K_i	0.05	0.002	–	1.0	†

*Guppy, M. (unpublished data)
†Murphy, B. (unpublished data)
 Assay conditions as in Table II. Tuna enzyme assayed at 25C; dolphin enzyme assayed
 at 37C.

caught on line and hook and run to fatigue, white muscle lactate
levels increase from low values (4 mM or less) to nearly 100 mM,
while α-GP at the same time increases to only about 0.5 mM from
starting levels of about 0.05 mM (Guppy, unpublished data). Similar
though less dramatic differences have been observed by others [6].
In the presence of an active muscle LDH, such α-GP regulation of its
own production (and hence of α-GP cycling) seems both necessary
and sufficient *for insuring that the α-GP cycle respond to changing
NAD/NADH ratios only under aerobic conditions.* That perhaps is as
it should be, since hydrogen shuttling is unnecessary during
anaerobic glycolysis.

Metabolic Significance of the α-GP Cycle

For all of the above reasons, we tentatively conclude that white
muscle respiration in all vertebrates probably is primed by the α-GP
cycle, the more aerobic the muscle, the higher the potential activity
of the cycle. What advantages, if any, does it yield? What other roles
might it play? In other words, what is the overall metabolic
significance of the α-GP cycle in muscle? These questions can be
considered (1) in terms of substrate sources and the regulation of
glucose metabolism, (2) in terms of relative energy yields and (3) in
terms of recovery from bursts of anaerobic glycolysis. Thus, with
respect to substrate sources, it is worth emphasizing that the α-GP
cycle takes on a prominent role only in muscles that utilize glucose
as essentially the sole carbon and energy source (e.g., squid mantle,
bee flight muscle, tuna white muscle). We doubt that such a
correlation is without causal connections and propose that it allows a

tight integration of cytoplasmic and mitochondrial portions of energy metabolism *because both the carbon for oxidation and the protons and electrons for the hydrogen shuttle arise from a single substrate source.* However, more work is needed to bear out this idea and it is cast before you now only for heuristic reasons.

In terms of energy yield, for each spin of the α-GP cycle (or, per mole of G6P converted to pyruvate), 7 moles of ATP are netted, 4 moles through the α-GP mediated transfer of reducing equivalents to O_2, 3 moles through substrate phosphorylations in glycolysis. Compared to white muscles that convert G6P to lactate, this represents over a doubling of energy yield. However, in muscles using the α-GP cycle, the overall *aerobic* yield is 36 moles ATP/mole G6P, a value somewhat lower than the 38 moles obtained (by mammalian heart muscle, for example) when the malate-aspartate shuttle is used. Of these 36 moles of ATP, the formation of only 4 moles (i.e., only 1/9th the energy yield) is obligatorily linked to the α-GP cycle. In these terms, therefore, the α-GP cycle does not seem to represent an unusually advantageous system. But this minor energetic disadvantage can be readily outweighed if the muscle has available additional nonglycolytic sources of NADH for sparking the α-GP cycle. In the squid mantle, for example, free amino acid levels are high and reducing equivalents formed during the catabolism of amino acids could be utilized to drive the α-GP cycle [9]. In vertebrate white muscle, lactate is the most obvious candidate for this job.

As we have pointed out, during strenuous anaerobic work, lactate levels in white muscle of the tuna can reach startling (100 mM!) levels. Now, since the total NAD + NADH pool size is only about 1 mM, it will be evident that should even a modest fraction of this lactate be reconverted to pyruvate during recovery, the stage is set for a redox-based coupling between the LDH *back* reaction and the cytosolic α-GPDH *forward* reaction. This event in effect would "turn on" the α-GP cycle as shown below:

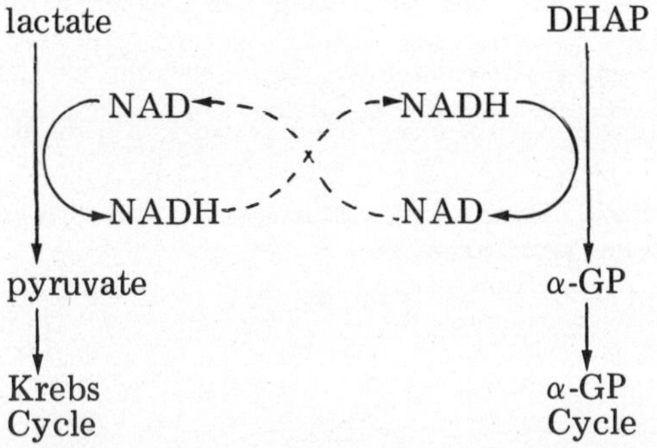

On the basis of this model, we would anticipate (1) that the activity ratio, LDH *back* reaction/α-GPDH *forward* reaction, should be approximately unity at least under physiological conditions of substrate, coenzyme and H$^+$ concentrations and (2) that lactate should stimulate white muscle respiration particularly in the presence of α-GP and NADH. Both predictions are in the process of being tested. If lactate is a good substrate for white muscle respiration, it is apparent that the energy yield that is linked to the α-GP cycle is similar to that obtained during aerobic glycolysis. Should all the 100 mM of lactate, for example, be fully oxidized in white muscle, a total of 1500 mM ATP would be netted by usual means while the formation of 200 mM ATP would be dependent upon hydrogen transfer via the α-GP cycle. That is, over 10% of the energy yield under conditions of lactate oxidation would be dependent upon the α-GP cycle, which in addition supplies muscle with a satisfactory mechanism for recovery from burst anaerobic work. Indeed, it may well have been this latter role in recovery from high lactate levels that most strongly favored the development of an aerobic α-GP cycle in muscle fibers whose characteristic work is undoubtedly anaerobic.

Acknowledgments

The National Research Council of Canada supported this work through an operating grant (to PWH). Special thanks are due Dr. Andrew Dizon for laboratory space and facilities and to the members of the *Buccaneer* and the *Anela* for capture of tuna.

References

1. Bass, A., Brdiczka, D., Eyer, P. et al: Europ. J. Biochem. 10:198, 1969.
2. Blanchaer, M.C.: Amer. J. Physiol. 206:1015, 1964.
3. Bone, Q.: *In* Hoar, W.S. and Randall, D.J. (eds.): Fish Physiology. New York:Academic Press. (In press.)
4. Bucher, Th.: Biochem. Soc. Symp. 25:15, 1965.
5. Carey, F.G., Teal, J.M., Kanwisher, J.W. and Lawson, K.D.: Am. Zoologist 11:137, 1971.
6. Driedzic, W.R. and Hochachka, P.W.: Am. J. Physiol. 230:579, 1976.
7. Fields, J.H.A., Baldwin, J. and Hochachka, P.W.: Can. J. Zool. 1976.
8. Harding, J., Pyeritz, E., Copeland, E. and White, H.: Fed. Proc. 33:2097, 1974.
9. Hochachka, P.W., Moon, T.W., Mustafa, T. and Storey, K.B.: Comp. Biochem. Physiol. 52B:151, 1975.
10. Hochachka, P.W. and Storey, K.B.: Science 187:613, 1975.
11. Hochachka, P.W. and Guppy, M.: *In* Jobsis, F. (ed.): "O$_2$ in the Organism" Proc. of a Fed. Proc. Colloquium, Professional Informational Service, Dallas. (In press.)

12. Holloszy, J.O. and Booth, F.W.: Ann. Rev. Physiol. 38:273, 1976.
13. Lee, Y.P. and Craine, J.E.: J. Biol. Chem. 246:7616, 1971.
14. Lin, Y., Dobbs, G.H. and DeVries, A.L.: J. Exp. Zool. 189:379, 1974.
15. Mastuura, F. and Hashimoto, K.: Bull. Jap. Soc. Sci. Fisheries 24:809, 1959.
16. Sacktor, B.: Biochem. Soc. Symposia, vol. 41. (In press.)
17. Stevens, E.D., Lam, H.M. and Kendall, J.: J. Exp. Biol. 61:145, 1974.
18. Storey, K.B. and Hochachka, P.W.: Comp. Biochem. Physiol. 52B:169, 1975.
19. Storey, K.B. and Hochachka, P.W.: Comp. Biochem. Physiol. 52B:175, 1975.
20. Thakar, J.H. and Ashmore, C.R.: Fed. Proc. 35:524, 1976.
21. Tulsi, R.S.: J. Anat. 119:39, 1975.

Modalité de fonctionnement du cycle des glycérophosphates

Le cycle des α-glycérophosphates (α-GP), l'un des mécanismes de transfert des équivalents réducteurs du cytoplasme à la motochondrie, ne semble jouer un rôle important que dans les muscles à caractère aérobie obligatoire. Certaines études cinétiques font croire que l'action catalytique des α-GPDH est unidirectionnelle et difficile à saturer; il en résulte qu'elle fournit au muscle un mécanisme efficace et illimité pour faire démarrer le cycle des α-GP et de ce fait la respiration. La portée métabolique et les autres fonctions possibles du cycle des α-GP y sont aussi discutées. On y conclut que toute respiration d'un muscle blanc est mise en branle par le cycle des α-GP dont les limites sont plus réduites que dans les muscles à caractère aérobie obligatoire.

Some Molecular Aspects of
Muscle Contraction and Relaxation

J. Gergely

Contractile proteins including those that are immediately involved in contraction as well as those that regulate it are reviewed. The interaction of myosin, a multi-subunit molecule, with actin in an organized subcellular system, the ATPase activity, the role of Ca^{2+} activation in troponin and tropomyosin complex are described relating biochemical to mechanical changes. Differences among muscle types cannot be classified on the basis of a simple criterion since genotype, expression of individual genes, and neural impulses and activity patterns effect changes of fiber type.

Introduction

A brief review of what are perhaps erroneously, as we shall see, termed contractile proteins seems most appropriate at this Symposium on the Biochemistry of Exercise. These are the proteins — and we shall include those that are not immediately involved in contraction but in regulating it — localized in the myofibrils. They are to be contrasted with the proteins freely dissolved in the cytoplasm or tied to structural entities in the mitochondria and involved in energy production or transformations of chemical energy culminating in the synthesis of ATP. They are also to be distinguished from those proteins that are characteristic of membranes — the plasma membrane, surrounding the fiber and continuing as the sarcotubular system into the interior, and the sarcoplasm, i.e., reticulum proper, constituting a closed membrane system within the cell. These membrane proteins are involved in various transport

J. Gergely, Department of Muscle Research, Boston Biomedical Research Institute; Department of Neurology, Massachusetts General Hospital; and Department of Biological Chemistry, Harvard Medical School, Boston, Mass., U.S.A.

The preparation of this manuscript was supported by grants from the National Institutes of Health (HL-5949), the National Science Foundation and the Muscular Dystrophy Associations of America, Inc.

processes, notably that of Na^+ in the plasma membrane and Ca^{2+} in the sarcoplasmic reticulum.

As mentioned above, the contractile proteins do not in reality contract. This idea grew out of the discovery that the chief constituents of the muscle fiber are organized into two distinct sites of filaments and that muscle contraction is not the result of shortening of some microscopic elements but rather of the sliding past each other of the two sets of filaments [32-34]. As the contraction proceeds and the sarcomere shortens, the filaments essentially maintain their length but change the extent to which they overlap (sliding filament theory). Therefore, the molecular basis of contraction is not to be sought in the overall length change of the constituent molecules, but rather in the repeated cyclic interaction between the constituents of the two sets of filaments — specifically, myosin in the so-called thick filaments and actin in the thin filaments. The latter, being anchored to the Z bands, are also the location of tropomyosin and troponin, the key regulatory proteins [15, 23, 31, 78]. The properties of these molecules determine structure — the filaments into which they are organized as well as the dynamic processes that provide the driving force for contraction.

Myosin Structure and Function

The architecture of the thick filaments and the crossbridges that emanate from their surface and interact with actin furnish an excellent example for relating molecular properties to structure and function in an organized subcellular system. Myosin is now recognized as a multi-subunit molecule (Fig. 1). There are two so-called heavy chains whose length is about 160 nm. These two heavy chains are over a long stretch intertwined in an α-helical coiled coil rod-structure while the two N-terminal ends form two distinct globules or, as they are often referred to, heads. The core of the thick filaments is made up of the rod portions [41]. Each head region contains a site for combination with actin and one for combination with ATP; each head is associated with two smaller subunits, the light chains [19, 64, 79, 81]. These light chains differ according to the type of muscle. We shall return to this point later. The lead regions, together with a portion of the rod, constitute the crossbridges that protrude on the surface of the thick filaments.

Mild proteolytic digestion of myosin with various enzymes (trypsin, chymotrypsin, papain) produces fragments that correspond to various functionally distinct proteins of the molecule [41]. Thus,

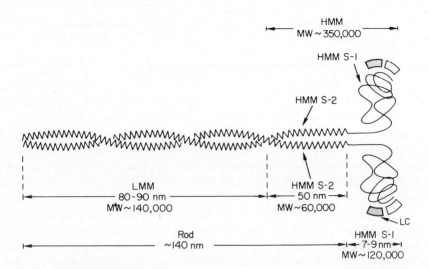

FIG. 1. Schematic representation of the structure of the myosin molecule based chiefly on Lowey et al [41]. The rod portion of the molecule has a coiled-coil α-helical structure. Hinge-regions postulated in the mechanism of contraction are at the junction of HMM S-1 and HMM S-2 and of HMM S-2 and LMM. It should be noted that HMM S-1 has one chief polypeptide chain while the other fragments have two. LC: light chain associated with the S-1 region. (Reproduced from Gergely [22].)

the interaction with actin can be investigated by using isolated single heads (subfragment 1) or a two-headed fragment (heavy mero-myosin) (HMM) that also contains part of the rod (subfragment 2). HMM is thought to correspond to a crossbridge in the intact system.

It has been suggested that myosin contains hinged regions [32]. Specifically, one would be at the junction of subfragment 2 and the head. Another hinge would exist at the junction of what is called light meromyosin obtainable by tryptic or chymotryptic digestion and subfragment 2. The physiological significance of these hinges is that they permit movement of the head with respect to the connecting link and of the connecting link itself with respect to the thick filament. These movements then play an important role in current schemes of myosin-actin interaction in vivo (see below).

According to recent experimental work, myosin actually pos-sesses the dynamic properties postulated for it. This work, in the laboratory of M. Morales and in ours, making use of fluorescence polarization [43] and saturation transfer electron spin resonance spectroscopy [72-74], respectively, has shown that the myosin heads are capable of independent motion with respect to the rest of the myosin molecule and are greatly slowed down on attachment to actin.

Actin-Myosin Interaction

While the fact that myosin has ATPase activity has been known since the classic discovery of Engelhardt and Ljubimova [17], recent work has uncovered some new and unexpected details [71, 75] of the mechanism of the crucial enzymatic reaction in the mechano-chemical transduction process in muscle. The classic, perhaps not explicitly stated, view has been that ATP combines in myosin and that the ATP myosin complex waits, as it were, for the hydrolysis to occur to be rapidly followed by the release of the product, viz., ADP and P_i. It had also tacitly been assumed before 1970 or so that the activation of ATPase by actin occurred by an accelerated hydrolysis of ATP bound to an actin-myosin complex. According to the current views the actual hydrolysis of ATP occurs rapidly whether myosin is or is not attached to actin, and the rate-limiting step is the removal of the products. The latter is a complex process, and currently several intermediate stages are postulated between the hydrolytic step and the removal of the products (Fig. 2). On the newer view, the

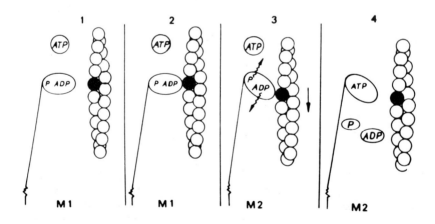

FIG. 2. Schematic representation of the crossbridge cycle coupled to the hydrolysis of ATP. M1 and M2 denote two possible orientations of the myosin head region (showing only one head) resulting from rotation between the S-1 and S-2 portions of HMM. The other point at which a hinge has been postulated is the junction of the connecting lines and the body of the thick filament, indicated by the break at the bottom left of each panel. (Reproduced from Mannherz et al [42].)

effect of actin would be the acceleration of the removal of the products from myosin. This changed view raises new questions concerning our understanding of the parallel relationship between ATPase activity and shortening velocity as originally reported by Barany [2]. This is an important problem if one tries to relate contraction velocity to metabolism in different types of muscle, a topic of considerable interest at this Symposium. Since, according to current views, the hydrolytic step occurs prior to interaction with actin and a given crossbridge spends only a fraction of the cycle time attached to actin, a simple explanation of this correlation is somewhat difficult. It cannot be simply assumed that the reason for the parallelism between shortening velocity and ATPase activity is that the slower the rate of ATPase reaction the longer the attachment of a crossbridge to actin, and thus the rate of contraction would be limited. In light of these considerations, the connection between biochemical and mechanical phenomena has to be probed at a deeper kinetic level.

A possible scheme to relate biochemical to mechanical changes is shown in Figure 3 in which two states $(AM.Pr)_1$ and $(AM.Pr)_2$ are

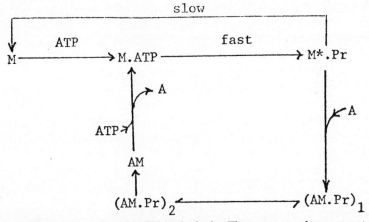

FIG. 3. Simplified scheme of ATP hydrolysis. The upper cycle represents the "idling" ATPase of detached myosin. The lower cycle represents actin-activated ATPase. The asterisk indicates a change in myosin conformation occurring on formation of the tightly bound products (ADP, P_i). $(AM.Pr)_1$ and $(AM.Pr)_2$ represent actin-myosin complexes differing in, say, the orientation of the myosin head (crossbridge) with respect to the actin filament. This change in orientation plays a crucial role in driving the two filaments past each other [35] and depends upon the internal flexibility of the myosin molecule. Contraction velocity would be limited by the average time a crossbridge spends in the AM states and not by the overall cycling time. M: myosin; A: actin. (Reproduced from Gergely [24].)

shown representing attached crossbridges with the products of ATP hydrolysis still on the myosin head. These two states correspond to attached states that differ in the angle the myosin head makes with the actin filament. Current molecular schemes of muscle contraction assume that the myosin head attaches to the actin filament making a roughly 90° angle with it and is eventually detached in a roughly 45° angled state. The two states are in rapid equilibrium as deduced by Huxley and Simmons [35] from experiments in living muscle involving rapid release and stretch. The existence of different attitudes of the myosin head with respect to the actin filaments in rigor and in contraction has been derived from x-ray and electron microscopic observations [27, 45, 54, 56] and, more recently, from changes in polarization fluorescence emission of extrinsic or intrinsic fluorophores in the myosin heads [4, 11, 12, 46].

The actin filaments not only contain the actin subunits that serve as sites of attachment for myosin but also carry the regulatory proteins, tropomyosin and troponin. We shall now turn to their consideration. The work of Weber and Ebashi and their colleagues [15, 78] led to the realization that unless highly purified actin and myosin are used, minute amounts of calcium ions (Ca^{2+}) are required for their interaction. This Ca^{2+} sensitivity was then tracked down to tropomyosin and troponin by Ebashi's group. It should be mentioned that in lower organisms Ca^{2+} control is exerted directly on myosin, although in some species both thick and thin filament control, as they have become known, exist [39].

Tropomyosin is localized in the thin filaments; and by virtue of its length, about 40 nm, one tropomyosin molecule spans the length of about seven actin monomers [15, 78]. Troponin, as established by Marion Greaser in our laboratory, consists of three subunits which are now generally referred to as TnC, TnT and TnI [25]. They denote in turn a calcium binding subunit, a tropomyosin binding subunit, and a so-called inhibitory subunit, the latter name having been given to it because it inhibits actomyosin ATPase whether or not calcium is present (Fig. 4). The complex consisting of three subunits plus tropomyosin inhibits the actin myosin interaction only if calcium is absent.

Let me discuss in some detail the TnC subunit where the primary event in the interaction with Ca^{2+} occurs. TnC exhibits strong homologies in its amino acid sequence with the calcium binding protein paravalbumin, found in various muscles. The function of the latter is unknown. It occurs in the sarcoplasm and is not attached to structural elements. Since the structure of paravalbumin has been

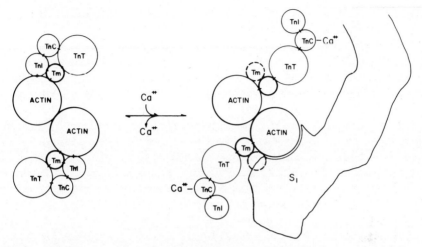

FIG. 4. Scheme of regulation of muscle contraction by troponin and Ca^{2+}. The relative positions of actin, tropomyosin and the head of the myosin molecule (S-1) in the model are essentially as shown. Key: A, actin; TM, tropomyosin; T, TnT; I, TnI; C, TnC. Left: relaxation in the absence of Ca^{2+}. Right: activation, $[Ca^{2+}]$ 1 μM. Suggested interactions between proteins are indicated by short connecting lines.

determined on the basis of x-ray diffraction data [36], it was possible for John Collins in our department [7], having established the amino acid sequence of troponin C, to find those regions that are likely to be involved in calcium binding. There are four such regions, in agreement with the direct calcium binding experiments [55], showing four calcium binding sites in troponin C. These four calcium binding sites can be divided into two classes differing in their affinity for calcium. The two high affinity sites also bind magnesium, while the two sites of somewhat lower affinity appear specific for calcium. Evidence obtained from these studies on myofibrillar ATPase suggests that binding of Ca^{2+} to these latter two sites is crucial in the interaction of actin and myosin.

Current work carried out in our laboratory, in collaboration with Drabikowski and his group, utilizing various fragments of troponin C, is aimed at establishing the location of different types within the primary structure [38]. Advances are being made with respect to the other troponin subunits as well. Thus, Smillie and his colleagues have sequenced TnT [47], while work in Perry's group has led to the determination of the sequence of TnI [83] and has made a start in identifying those regions in TnI and TnT that are likely to be in protein-protein interactions among troponin subunits and with tropomyosin and actin [50].

If we push our inquiry a step further we may then ask what molecular changes take place in the troponin complex, in tropomyosin and perhaps even in myosin and actin as Ca^{2+} activation occurs. The most immediate changes must and do occur in the calcium binding subunit of troponin. Here one has to distinguish between changes that are very impressive in vitro but may play a less important role in the regulatory event in vivo. Thus, binding of Ca^{2+} to sites of one class — the so-called high affinity sites — is accompanied by various conspicuous changes in the indicators of protein conformation — circular dichroism, ultraviolet fluorescence and electron spin resonance spectra, reactivity of the single -SH group, etc. (see Potter et al [55] for recent work and earlier references); but if, as some evidence suggests, these sites are always occupied in vivo either by Ca^{2+} or Mg^{2+}, one would not expect these changes to underlie the regulatory process. It is more likely that binding to the two remaining Ca^{2+} binding sites of lower affinity is strongly coupled to the activation process, but the conformational changes accompanying this process are not conspicuous. Indirect evidence for such changes in TnC can be deduced from changes in TnI attached to TnC. Therefore, the intensity of fluorescence of a dansyl label attached to TnI increases as calcium is bound to troponin C, as shown by Paul Leavis in our laboratory. This change occurs in the same calcium concentration range in which the ATPase activity of actomyosin is activated by Ca^{2+} rather than in the lower range that produces the large structural changes in TnC. Binding to the sites of lower affinity produces a change in TnI which is presumably involved in the regulatory process, and this change occurs through the binding of calcium to sites distinct from those that stabilize the structure of TnC.

The next question is this: How does the change produced in TnC, and indirectly in TnI and, perhaps, also in TnT influence actin-myosin interaction? The current view is that tropomyosin changes its position within the thin filament depending upon whether the muscle is active or relaxed [30, 32-34]. In relaxed muscle tropomyosin occupies a position in the thin filaments such that it blocks the interaction with myosin heads. There is evidence that the attachment of troponin to the thin filaments involves two sites: one involves troponin T and tropomyosin, the other troponin I and both actin and tropomyosin [30, 55]. In this view the calcium-induced change in TnC propagates to TnI, whereupon the linkage between

TnI and the thin filament is broken, and tropomyosin carrying the troponin complex attached to it by the troponin T subunit is allowed to move and activation ensues.

No doubt this picture is somewhat simplified and there are still many points that require a more thorough understanding. Thus, the possibility of changes induced in actin by the Ca-troponin interaction cannot be ruled out. Also, the significance in vivo of certain cooperative phenomena among myosin heads in the domain of the same tropomyosin molecule, emphasized by Weber and her colleagues, as well as the possible interaction among myosin molecules involving the domains of different tropomyosin molecules, has to be explored further. Actin, which usually has been regarded as playing a passive role in the interaction with myosin, may have dynamic properties, as revealed by recent studies utilizing quasi-elastic light scattering [21] and electron spin resonance [40, 72, 73] that deserve greater consideration in our thinking about contraction and regulatory mechanisms.

Finally, mention should be made of the regulatory processes that may be involved in the fine tuning of the response to Ca^{2+}. These are probably manifested in the inotropic effect of drugs and neuro-humoral agents (e.g. epinephrine) and in the influence of hormones on the contractile apparatus. This kind of control may depend on the phosphorylation of proteins [49, 50], in particular of a myosin light chain and of TnI. The increase in the phosphorylation of TnI [18] and decrease in the phosphorylation of the myosin light chain [20] accompanying the positive inotropic effect of epinephrine in cardiac muscle point in this direction.

Differences Among Muscle Types

There is no need to emphasize at this particular symposium the fact that muscle fibers of differing physiological (fast and slow) and biochemical (oxidative, glycolytic) fibers exist. Nor do I have to point out that the properties of these fiber types in a given muscle and individual affect performance in various types of activities. What should perhaps be emphasized is that the fibers cannot be classified on the basis of a simple criterion [16, 62]. This is indeed not surprising since the character of a muscle must be determined by many genes, and thus the genotype as well as the expression of individual genes within the genome can be a source of considerable diversity.

Myosin may serve as an example. The existence of differences among myosins with respect to ATPase activity and stability at higher pH has been known for many years [69]. The electrophoretic pattern of light chains on SDS gels has been used extensively to characterize myosins [64, 79] (Fig. 5). The three light chains in fast muscle myosin have been referred to as LC1, LC2 and LC3 in increasing order of mobility. LC2 can be removed with the thiol reagent 5,5'-dithiobis (2-nitrobenzoate) (DTNB, or Nbs$_2$ according to the more recent nomenclature) and has been known as the DTNB light chain. The remaining two are removed by alkali treatment and are known as alkali light chains, specifically A1 (LC1) and A2 (LC3). In fast muscle myosin each head contains a pair of Nbs$_2$ light chains and either a pair of A1 or a pair of A2. The fact that A1 and A2 do not occur in a 1:1 molar ratio makes it unlikely that each myosin molecule contains an A1 and an A2 light chain. In slow muscle myosin only two light chains are found migrating at electrophoretic velocities roughly corresponding to those of fast muscle LC1 and LC2. However, they can be clearly distinguished from their counter-

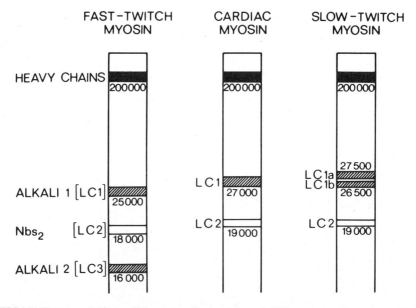

FIG. 5. Representation of the subunit structure of different vertebrate myosins. The patterns of light chains obtained by gel electrophoresis in the presence of sodium dodecyl sulfate are shown for fast-twitch, slow-twitch and cardiac myosins. Diagonal shading shows light chains containing thiol sequence. The values given for molecular weights are those apparent from gel electrophoresis. The Nbs$_2$ light chain is commonly called the DTNB light chain. (Reproduced from Weeds [79].)

parts in fast muscle myosin. In slow muscle myosin light chains occur in equal amounts so that each myosin can be thought of as containing one pair of LC1 and one pair of LC2. Recent work has shown that LC2 (both in fast and slow muscle) can be phosphorylated [49, 50], and there is considerable interest in the possible physiological significance of this process. A detailed discussion of cardiac myosin would be outside the scope of this paper, but it is worth mentioning that its subunit pattern is similar to, but distinct from, that of slow muscle myosin [64, 80].

Thus, the character of a given myosin molecule is determined by at least three genes coding for the heavy chain and the two types of light chain. If one takes into account the existence of isozymes and differences between the two heavy chains [10, 28] or between pairs of corresponding light chains occurring in the same molecule, as many as six genes may be involved. In addition, there are the genes determining the modification of residues [29, 37] in the primary sequence (methylation, phosphorylation). Thus, on the basis of myosin alone, a large number of fiber types may exist and the type I-type II histochemical classification based on ATPase activity is an oversimplification. A priori, there is no need to assume that a certain type of ATPase is uniquely coupled to a predominantly oxidative, say, or glycolytic metabolic pattern; recent fiber classifications indeed include more than the classic fast-glycolytic and slow-oxidative types. While it seems now clear that the light chains do not determine the ATPase activity of myosin itself, the interaction with actin and the actin-activated ATPase activity does not seem to be affected by the light chain present [77]. In whole muscle the velocity of muscle contraction appears to be correlated with the character of myosin, while the rate of tension development and relaxation is governed by the properties of the sarcoplasmic reticulum and by the components of the tropomyosin-troponin system, which also differ according to the type of muscle from which they have been obtained [48]. The functional significance of the chemical and structural differences in tropomyosin and troponin is not yet clear. Tropomyosin preparations contain two kinds of chains, α and β; the α chain is found in predominantly fast skeletal muscles, whereas the β chain is more abundant in slow skeletal muscles [8, 9]. While cardiac muscle myosin seems to resemble its slow skeletal muscle counterpart, cardiac tropomyosin contains only the α chain and is, therefore, similar to the fast skeletal muscle protein. Two of the troponin components, TnI and TnT, can be distinguished by their different electrophoretic mobility in cardiac muscle and in slow skeletal muscle [13, 70, 76].

The Effect of Changes in Neural Impulses
and Activity Pattern on Fiber Type

The existence of biochemical differences among muscles of differing functional characteristics has been useful in analyzing the role of neural factors and of the activity pattern itself imposed on a muscle and in determining its properties. The pioneering studies of Buller et al [5] and those that followed [65, 67] have shown that by connecting the cut nerves of a slow muscle to a fast one and vice versa, the physiological characteristics of the muscle change according to the new innervation. It has subsequently been shown that the changes in physiological parameters, viz., of contraction velocity and the time required for maximum tension development and relaxation, are accompanied by or result from changes in biochemical properties. Thus, in the transformation of a fast to a slow muscle there is a shift from glycolytic enzymes to oxidative enzymes [14, 26, 44, 58]; the myosin ATPase activity is reduced [3, 5, 6] and becomes alkali labile — characteristics normally found in slow muscles [67]. Quite strikingly, the myosin light chain pattern changes so that the light chains found in normal slow muscle appear in cross reinnervated fast muscle and vice versa [63, 67, 82]. Cross reinnervation also makes changes in troponin I [1]. The slower relaxation detected by physiological techniques in cross reinnervated fast muscle may have its biochemical correlate in the reduced calcium uptake rate of the sarcoplasmic reticulum [44, 65].

What is perhaps even more interesting, particularly from the point of view of exercise physiology, is that stimulation of a fast muscle with steady low frequency (10 Hz) mimicking the normal input in a slow muscle leads to a slowing down of the muscle producing essentially the same result as that obtained after connecting the nerve innervating the slow muscle to a fast muscle [61]. Subsequent studies revealed that these changes in physiological parameters are accompanied by marked biochemical changes, again indicating the transformation of the fast muscle into the slow one [53, 57, 65-68]. Glycolytic enzymes are replaced by oxidative enzymes and myosin in terms of ATPase activity, subunit pattern and methylation of a histidine residue, showing replacement of the protein found in slow muscle. The sarcoplasmic reticulum changes its activity in a similar way. It appears that changes in impulse activity produce the same results as a change in innervation, and the transformation of the muscle need not be attributed to the production of specific trophic substances by the motor neuron determining the properties of the muscle. More complex experiments [60] were able to show that the effects of cross innervation could be counteracted by applying a stimulation pattern corresponding to the original character, in this case, of a slow muscle.

In all these experiments it appears that stimulation of the muscle at a certain characteristic frequency, whether it comes from the nerve connected to the appropriate motor neurones or from an external stimulus applied to the intact nerve, leads to the activation of genes normally not expressed in that muscle. The question arises whether the change in the muscle characteristics is due to the replacement of fibers of one type, e.g., fast fibers by slow fibers, or whether individual fibers undergo a transformation by regression of the activity of one set of genes and activation of another. Our recent experiments provide direct evidence that the latter is the case [59]. We have studied the binding of specific antibodies against slow or fast myosin to sections of muscle fibers obtained after stimulation for various periods. Whereas the control fast muscle used in these experiments reacted only with fluorescent antibodies against fast myosin, stimulation led to the appearance of fibers showing staining with both anti-fast and anti-slow antibodies and eventually there was a complete reversal of the antibody staining pattern in that the originally fast fibers now stained with antibody against slow myosin. Pette [51] has obtained evidence from gel electrophoresis experiments on single fibers showing the presence of both types of light chain in the same fiber. The view that the transformation of stimulated muscle is the result of the transformation of individual muscle fibers was indirectly deduced by simultaneously following the transformation pattern of various components of the fibers. The fact that the shift from glycolytic enzymes to oxidative enzymes occurs before one sees substantial changes in the myosin light chain pattern is consistent with this view [57]. Pette et al [52] have recently also emphasized, on the basis of the disparity between the percentage of fibers transformed as judged on the basis of histochemical enzyme reactions, that one would require an internal rebuilding, as it were, of fibers rather than replacement of fibers of one type to those of another. These results may have an important bearing on the effect of various types of exercise on a specific muscle, but it should be borne in mind that in the intact organism the problem is rendered more complex. These phenomena may be a start on the long road toward a better understanding of the factors and mechanism that determine the expression of some genes and not those of others in a given muscle and may shed light on the problem of differentiation in general.

References

1. Amphlett, G.W., Perry, S.V., Syska, H. et al: Nature 257:602, 1975.
2. Barany, M.: J. Gen. Physiol. (suppl.) 50:197, 1967.
3. Barany, M. and Close, R.I.: J. Physiol. (Lond.) 213:455, 1971.
4. Botts, J., Cooke, R., DosRemedios, C. et al: Cold Spring Harbor Symp. Quant. Biol. 37:195, 1972.
5. Buller, A.J., Eccles, J.C. and Eccles, R.M.: J. Physiol. (Lond.) 150:417, 1960.
6. Buller, A.J., Mommaerts, W.F.H.M. and Seraydarian, K.: J. Physiol. (Lond.) 205:581, 1966.
7. Collins, J.H.: In Duncan, C.J. (ed.): Calcium in Biological Systems. Vol. 30. Symp. Soc. Exp. Biol., Cambridge Univ. Press, 1976, p. 303.
8. Cummins, P. and Perry, S.V.: Biochem. J. 133:765, 1973.
9. Cummins, P. and Perry, S.V.: Biochem. J. 141:43, 1974.
10. d'Albis, A. and Gratzer, W.B.: FEBS Lett. 29:292, 1973.
11. DosRemedios, C.G., Millikan, R.G.C. and Morales, M.F.: J. Gen. Physiol. 59:103, 1972.
12. DosRemedios, C.G., Yount, R.G. and Morales, M.F.: Proc. Natl. Acad. Sci. USA 69:2542, 1972.
13. Drabikowski, W., Dabrowska, R. and Barylko, B.: In Fleckenstein, A. and Dhalla, N.S. (eds.): Basic Functions of Cations in Myocardial Activity. Recent Advances in Studies on Cardiac Structure and Metabolism. Baltimore:University Park Press, 1975, p. 245.
14. Dubowitz, V.: J. Physiol. (Lond.) 193:481, 1967.
15. Ebashi, S.: In Campbell, P.N. and Dickens, F. (eds.): Essays in Biochemistry. Vol. 10. London:Academic Press, 1974, p. 1.
16. Eisenberg, B.R.: In Milhorat, A.T. (ed.): Exploratory Concepts in Muscular Dystrophy II. Control Mechanisms in Development and Function of Muscle and Their Relationship to Muscular Dystrophy and Related Neuromuscular Diseases. Amsterdam:Excerpta Medica, 1974, p. 258.
17. Engelhardt, W.A. and Ljubimova, M.N.: Nature 144:668, 1939.
18. England, P.J.: FEBS Lett. 50:57, 1975.
19. Frank, G. and Weeds, A.: Eur. J. Biochem. 44:317, 1974.
20. Frearson, N., Solaro, R.J. and Perry, S.V.: Nature 264:801, 1976.
21. Fujime, S. and Ishiwata, S.: J. Molec. Biol. 62:251, 1971.
22. Gergely, J.: In Walton, J.N. (ed.): Disorders of Voluntary Muscle, ed. 3. 1974, p. 102.
23. Gergely, J.: In Sanadi, D.R. (ed.): Chemical Mechanisms in Bioenergetics. American Chemical Society, 1976, p. 221.
24. Gergely, J.: In Jacob, R. (ed.): Proceedings of Symposium on Biophysical, Biochemical and Morphological Aspects of Hypertrophy. D. Steinkopff Verlag. (In press.)
25. Greaser, M.L., Yamaguchi, M., Brekke, C. et al: Cold Spring Harbor Symp. Quant. Biol. 37:235, 1972.
26. Guth, L., Watson, P.K. and Brown, W.C.: Exp. Neurol. 20:52, 1968.
27. Haselgrove, J.C. and Huxley, H.E.: J. Molec. Biol. 77:549, 1973.
28. Hoh, J.F.Y.: Biochemistry 14:742, 1975.
29. Huszar, G. and Elzinga, M.: J. Biol. Chem. 247:745, 1972.
30. Huxley, H.E.: In Heilmeyer, L.M.G., Ruegg, J.C. and Wieland, Th. (eds.): Molecular Basis of Contractility. Berlin:Springer-Verlag, Springer, 1976, p. 9.

31. Huxley, H.E.: *In* Bourne, G.H. (ed.): The Structure and Function of Muscle, Vol. I. New York:Academic Press, 1972, p. 302.
32. Huxley, H.E.: Science 164:1356, 1969.
33. Huxley, H.E. and Hanson, J.: Nature 173:973, 1954.
34. Huxley, A.F. and Niedergerke, R.: Nature 173:971, 1954.
35. Huxley, A.F. and Simmons, R.: Cold Spring Harbor Symp. Quant. Biol. 37:669, 1972.
36. Kretsinger, R.H.: Ann. Rev. Biochem. 45:239, 1976.
37. Kuehl, W.M. and Adelstein, R.: Biochem. Biophys. Res. Commun. 39:956, 1970.
38. Leavis, P., Drabikowski, W., Rosenfeld, S. et al: Fed. Proc. 36:831, 1977.
39. Lehman, W. and Szent-Györgyi, A.G.: J. Gen. Physiol. 66:1, 1975.
40. Loscalzo, J., Reed, G.H. and Weber, A.: Proc. Natl. Acad. Sci. USA 72:3412, 1975.
41. Lowey, S., Slayter, H.S., Weeds, A.G. and Baker, H.: J. Molec. Biol. 42:1, 1969.
42. Mannherz, H.G., Barrington-Leigh, J., Holmes, K.C. and Rosenbaum, G.N.: Nature (New Biology) 241:226, 1973.
43. Mendelson, R.A., Morales, M.F. and Botts, J.: Biochemistry 12:2250, 1973.
44. Mommaerts, W.F.H.M., Buller, A.J. and Seraydarian, K.: Proc. Natl. Acad. Sci. USA 64:128, 1969.
45. Moore, P.B., Huxley, H.E. and DeRosier: J. Molec. Biol. 50:279, 1970.
46. Nihei, T., Mendelson, R.A. and Botts, J.: Proc. Natl. Acad. Sci. USA 71:234, 1974.
47. Pearlstone, J.R., Carpenter, M.R., Johnson, P. and Smilley, L.B.: Proc. Natl. Acad. Sci. USA 73:1902, 1976.
48. Perry, S.V.: *In* Milhorat, A.T. (ed.): Exploratory Concepts in Muscular Dystrophy II. Control Mechanisms in Development and Function of Muscle and Their Relationship to Muscular Dystrophy and Related Neuromuscular Diseases. Amsterdam:Excerpta Medica, 1974, p. 319.
49. Perry, S.V., Amphlett, G.A., Grand, R.J.A. et al: *In* Carafoli, E., Clementi, F., Drabikowski, W. and Margreth, A. (eds.): Calcium Transport in Contraction and Secretion. Amsterdam:Holland Publishing Co. 1975, p. 431.
50. Perry, S.V., Cole, H.A., Morgan, M. et al: *In* Biro, E.N.A. (ed.): Proc. IX FEBS Meeting Vol. 31 Proteins of Contractile Systems. Budapest:Akad. Kiado, 1975, p. 163.
51. Pette, D.: *In* Jacob, R. (ed.): Proceedings of Symposium on Biophysical, Biochemical and Morphological Aspects of Hypertrophy. D. Steinkopff Verlag. (In press.)
52. Pette, D., Müller, W., Leisner, W. and Vrbova, G.: Pflügers Arch. 364:103, 1976.
53. Pette, D., Smith, M.E., Staudte, H.W. and Vrbova, G.: Pflügers Arch. 364, 1973.
54. Podolsky, R., St. Onge, R., Uu, L. and Lyman, R.W.: Proc. Natl. Acad. Sci. USA 73:813, 1976.
55. Potter, J., Leavis, P., Seidel, J. et al: *In* Carafoli, E., Clementi, F., Drabikowski, W. and Margreth, A. (eds.): Calcium Transport in Contraction and Secretion. Amsterdam:North Holland Publishing Co., 1975, p. 515.
56. Reedy, M.K., Holmes, K.C. and Tregear, R.T.: Nature 207:1276, 1965.
57. Romanul, F.C.A., Sreter, F.A., Salmons, S. and Gergely, J.: *In* Milhorat, A.T. (ed.): Exploratory Concepts in Muscular Dystrophy II. Control

Mechanisms in Development and Function of Muscle and Their Relationship to Muscular Dystrophy and Related Neuromuscular Diseases. Amsterdam: Excerpta Medica, 1974, p. 344.

58. Romanul, F.C.A. and Van der Meullen, J.P.: Arch. Neurol. 17:387, 1967.
59. Rubinstein, N., Sreter, F.A., Mabuchi, K. et al: Fed. Proc. 36:584, 1977.
60. Salmons, S. and Sreter, F.A.: Nature 263:5572, 1976.
61. Salmons, S. and Vrbova, G.: J. Physiol. 201:535, 1969.
62. Samaha, F.J. and Gergely, J.: In Siegel, G.J., Albers, R.W., Katzman, R. and Agranoff, B.W. (eds.): Basic Neurochemistry. Boston:Little Brown, Inc., 1976, p. 471.
63. Samaha, F.J., Guth, L. and Albers, R.W.: Exp. Neurol. 27:276, 1970.
64. Sarkar, S., Sreter, F.A. and Gergely, J.: Proc. Natl. Acad. Sci. USA 68:946, 1971.
65. Sreter, F.A., Elzinga, M., Salmons, S. et al: FEBS Lett. 57:107, 1975.
66. Sreter, F.A., Gergely, J., Salmons, S. and Romanul, F.C.A.: Nature (New Biol.) 241:17, 1973.
67. Sreter, F.A., Luff, A.R. and Gergely, J.: J. Gen. Physiol. 66:811, 1975.
68. Sreter, F.A., Romanul, F.C.A., Salmons, S. and Gergely, J.: In Milhorat, A.T. (ed.): Exploratory Concepts in Muscular Dystrophy II. Control Mechanisms in Development and Function of Muscle and Their Relationship to Muscular Dystrophy and Related Neuromuscular Diseases. Amsterdam: Excerpta Medica, 1974, p. 338.
69. Sreter, F.A., Seidel, J.C. and Gergely, J.: J. Biol. Chem. 241:5772, 1966.
70. Syska, H., Perry, S.V. and Trayer, L.P.: FEBS Lett. 40:253, 1974.
71. Taylor, E.W.: In Current Topics in Bioenergetics. 5:201, 1973.
72. Thomas, D.D., Seidel, J.C. and Gergely, J.: In Perry, S.V., Margreth, A. and Adelstein, R.S. (eds.): Contractile Systems in Non-muscle Tissue. Amsterdam:North Holland Press, 1976, p. 13.
73. Thomas, D.D., Seidel, J.C. and Gergely, J.: Fed. Proc. 35:1746, 1976.
74. Thomas, D.D., Seidel, J.C., Hyde, J.S. and Gergely, J.: Proc. Natl. Acad. Sci. USA 72:1729, 1975.
75. Trentham, D.R., Eccleston, J.F. and Bagshaw, C.R.: Quart. Rev. Biophys. 9:218, 1976.
76. Tsuki, R. and Ebashi, S.: J. Biochem. 73:1119, 1973.
77. Wagner, P.D. and Weeds, A.G.: J. Molec. Biol. 109:455, 1977.
78. Weber, A. and Murray, J.M.: Physiol. Rev. 53:612, 1973.
79. Weeds, A.G.: Eur. J. Biochem. 66:157, 1976.
80. Weeds, A.G. and Frank, G.: Cold Spring Harbor Symp. Quart. Biol. 37:9, 1972.
81. Weeds, A.G. and Lowey, S.: J. Molec. Biol. 61:701, 1971.
82. Weeds, A.G., Trentham, D.R., Kean, C.J.C. and Buller, A.J.: Nature (Lond.) 247:135, 1974.
83. Wilkinson, J.M. and Grand, R.J.A.: Biochem. J. 149:493, 1975.

Certains aspects moléculaires de la contraction et de la relaxation musculaires

Examen des protéines contractiles, autant celles qui sont directement impliquées dans la contraction que celles qui la règlent. L'interaction de la myosine, molécule à plusieurs sous-unités, et de l'actine dans un système sous-cellulaire organisé, l'activité ATPase, le rôle de l'activation du CA^{2+} dans la troponine et la tropomyosine s'y trouvent décrits en rapprochant les changements biochimiques et mécaniques. Les différences entre les types de muscles ne peuvent être classées en se fondant sur un simple critère puisque le génotype, qui est l'expression des divers gènes, les impulsions neurales et les types d'activités opèrent des changements de types de fibres.

Energy Production During Exercise

John O. Holloszy, William W. Winder, Robert H. Fitts,
Michael J. Rennie, Robert C. Hickson
and Robert K. Conlee

The pathway to energy production depends upon the work
rate and the type of skeletal muscle involved in the work. The
capacity for energy production is related to the biochemical
adaptation to exercise-training; the mechanisms for gearing
ATP production to ATP utilization; and the substrates
involved during exercise. The importance of fatty acids and
carbohydrates as substrates and the factors determining the
relative amounts of energy from their metabolism during
prolonged exercise is discussed.

Introduction

Muscle cells are unique in that they can perform mechanical
work and, in the process, increase their rates of energy production as
much as 300-fold. The metabolic rate of resting skeletal muscle is
low. It reflects the rate of ATP utilization required to maintain
cellular integrity (sodium pump, protein synthesis, etc.) and accounts
for only about 15% to 30% of a resting individual's O_2 consumption.
The rate of ATP production during work is closely geared to the rate
of ATP utilization which, in turn, is determined primarily by the
work rate. At the molecular level, the major factor determining the
rate of ATP hydrolysis is the number of crossbridges between myosin
and actin that are formed and broken per unit of time as the
myofilaments slide past each other. A portion of the increase in
energy utilization during work also occurs between contractions,
when ATP is required for recovery processes such as the uptake of
calcium by the sarcoplasmic reticulum.

John O. Holloszy, William W. Winder, Robert H. Fitts, Michael J. Rennie,
Robert C. Hickson and Robert K. Conlee, Department of Preventive Medicine,
Washington University School of Medicine, St. Louis, Missouri, U.S.A.

The research in the authors' laboratory is supported by NIH Grants
AG00425 and AM05341, and by a Muscular Dystrophy Associations of America
Neuromuscular Disease Research Center Grant.

Pathways for Energy Production
in the Different Types of Muscle

Skeletal muscle can regenerate the ATP required for work by means of both glycolytic and aerobic phosphorylation of ADP. The relative contributions of these two pathways to energy production depends upon the work rate relative to VO_2max and on the type of skeletal muscle involved in the work.

Work Rate

In an individual performing work of an intensity that he can maintain for only one or two minutes before becoming exhausted, as much as 30% to 50% of the required energy may be derived from conversion of glycogen to lactate [1-3]. In contrast, if an individual runs or bicycles at a pace he can maintain for an hour before becoming exhausted, "anaerobic glycolysis" probably provides only about 1% or 2% of the total energy [1]. Actually, during prolonged exercise, "anaerobic glycolysis" appears to be of importance only during the first few minutes before O_2 consumption has increased sufficiently to keep pace with the rate of energy expenditure. This is evidenced by the finding that muscle lactate concentration increases during the first few minutes of exercise, plateaus and then decreases during prolonged exercise [4].

Before discussing the second factor that determines which pathway of energy production is used, namely the type of skeletal muscle involved, a description of the different types of muscle fibers is necessary.

Types of Skeletal Muscle

Skeletal muscles have generally been classified on the basis of either their color or their contractile properties. Thus, muscles have been classified either as red or white, or as fast or slow. Considerable confusion arose when some authors began to equate fast with white and slow with red. The confusion was further compounded when investigators working with one species began to draw general conclusions regarding skeletal muscles of other species on the basis of their findings. It is now evident from available data that red muscle fibers can be either fast or slow contracting, and that major species differences exist. In most of the mammalian species that have been studied, the skeletal muscles are a mixture of three fiber types. In rodents, which have been most extensively studied, there are the fast-twitch white fibers which have a low respiratory capacity, a high glycogenolytic capacity, a low myoglobin content and high myosin

ATPase activity; the fast-twitch red fibers which have a high respiratory capacity, a high glycolytic capacity, a high myoglobin content and high myosin ATPase activity; and the slow-twitch red fibers which have a moderately high respiratory capacity, a low glycogenolytic capacity, a high myoglobin content and have low myosin ATPase activity [5, 6]. In many other mammalian species, including man, in contrast to rodents, it is the slow-twitch rather than the fast-twitch red fibers which have the highest respiratory capacity [7, 8].

Since white muscle fibers contain few mitochondria and have a low respiratory capacity, conversion of glycogen to lactate is the major pathway for regenerating high energy phosphate bonds during strenuous contractile activity. As has been shown by Cori [9], the rates of glycogen breakdown and lactate formation can be accelerated as much as a 1000-fold when a previously resting muscle is given a brief tetanic stimulus. However, although large amounts of ATP can be generated rapidly, this mechanism for regenerating ATP is self-limiting. There appears to be an upper limit to the amount of lactate that can accumulate before an individual is forced to stop exercising [2, 3]. Anaerobic glycolysis can probably serve as the primary source of energy for only 30 to 60 seconds of strenuous exercise. A possible explanation for this limitation is that the intracellular pH drops as lactate accumulates in muscle, and this results in inhibition of the rate-limiting enzyme phosphofructokinase [10].

Studies comparing the responses of the different types of muscle fibers to repeated electrical stimulation through the nerve have shown that the white fibers decrease their glycogen content and fatigue very quickly compared to the red fibers [11]. White muscle appears to be recruited infrequently during exercise that can be maintained for a prolonged period (i.e., endurance exercise) [12-14]. Red muscle fibers have small motor neurons that require less excitatory input for discharge than the larger motor neurons innervating white fibers; therefore, the red fibers are preferentially recruited during work of light and moderate intensity [15]. White fibers are recruited either when the excitatory input into the motor neurons increases to high levels during very strenuous work or when the red fibers become fatigued.

Thus, the white muscle fibers are specialized for short bursts of very intense work separated by prolonged periods of recovery. The slow red fibers have the potential for prolonged work of moderate intensity, with the rate of ATP utilization being matched by the rate of oxidative phosphorylation. The fast-red fibers combine some of the capabilities of the other two fiber types, since they have high capacities for both aerobic and anaerobic generation of ATP. When O_2 and substrate supplies are not limiting, the work rate that can be maintained for prolonged periods by a muscle is determined by its respiratory capacity.

Effects of Exercise-Training on the Capacity of Skeletal Muscle for Energy Production

The biochemical adaptations that occur in response to exercise have been reviewed in detail recently [6], so only those adaptations that affect the capacity for energy production will be mentioned briefly here. Prolonged endurance exercise-training results in increases in the capacities of muscle to oxidize fat, carbohydrate and ketones [6]. The mitochondria from trained animals' skeletal muscles exhibit normal respiratory control and tightly coupled oxidative phosphorylation providing evidence that the increases in the capacities to oxidize fat and carbohydrate are accompanied by a parallel rise in the capacity to generate ATP via oxidative phosphorylation.

Underlying the exercise-induced increase in the capacity of muscle to generate ATP from the oxidation of substrates are increases in the levels of the enzymes involved in the activation, transport and β-oxidation of long chain fatty acids, the enzymes involved in ketone oxidation, the enzymes of the citrate cycle, the components of the mitochondrial respiratory chain involved in the oxidation of NADH and succinate and of coupling factor 1. These increases in the levels of activity of a wide range of mitochondrial enzymes appear to result from increases in enzyme protein concentration. This is evidenced by increases in the concentrations of the cytochromes and in the protein content of the mitochondrial fraction of skeletal muscle. Electron-microscopic studies on human and on rat skeletal muscles have provided evidence that increases in both the size and number of mitochondria are responsible for the increase in total mitochondrial protein [6]. There are also changes in mitochondrial composition.

The exercise-induced adaptive responses of a number of mito-chondrial enzymes have been studied in all three types of skeletal muscle fibers in the rat. All three fiber types undergo adaptive increases in mitochondrial enzymes. However, the increase in mitochondrial enzymes in white muscle is small in absolute terms when compared to the responses of the red fiber types when the training program consists of prolonged continuous running at a moderate speed. The relatively small response of white muscle to this type of exercise is probably a consequence of minimal involvement of white muscle [12]. It seems likely that greater adaptive changes could be induced in white muscle by interval training with short bouts of work sufficiently intense to result in recruitment of the white motor units. Endurance training appears to have little effect on the capacity of skeletal muscle to generate ATP via anaerobic glycolysis.

Mechanisms for Gearing ATP Production to ATP Utilization

The rate at which working muscle cells consume oxygen is determined by the rate of ATP hydrolysis, which, in turn, is determined by the work rate. Oxidative phosphorylation is tightly coupled to electron transport; this means that O_2 cannot be utilized unless ADP and Pi are available. This coupling provides the mechanism by which the rate of substrate oxidation is geared to the rate of energy utilization. When muscle contracts ATP is split, and the levels of ADP and Pi rise. Of these two compounds ADP has the lower concentration in tissue and appears to be the rate-limiting factor. It appears that the ratio of ATP/ADP rather than the concentration of ADP per se determines the rate of O_2 consumption [16]. The increase in ADP with muscle contraction is damped by the creatine kinase reaction, which catalyzes the resynthesis of ATP by transferring the high energy phosphate from creatine phosphate (CP) to ADP. As a result CP concentration falls and creatine concentration rises.

If work is submaximal (i.e., requiring less than the muscle cell's maximum O_2 uptake capacity to balance the rate of energy utilization) ADP concentration will rise until respiration is turned on sufficiently to balance the rate of ATP splitting. The decrease in high energy phosphate concentration, the increase in Pi and the other concomitant changes simultaneously result in an acceleration of glycolysis as a result of an increase in phosphofructokinase (PFK) activity [17-20]. Much of the pyruvate thus formed will, of course, be oxidized in the mitochondria. However, some will also be converted to lactate, even though the cell is well oxygenated, because muscle contains a large amount of lactate dehydrogenase and has no mechanism for channelling pyruvate and NADH exclusively into the mitochondria [21].

If work is so intense that the rate of ATP utilization exceeds the muscle cell's capacity to regenerate ATP via oxidative phosphorylation, a much greater stimulation of glycolysis will occur. The concentrations of ADP and Pi will continue to rise (above the level needed to activate mitochondrial respiration maximally), and CP and ATP concentrations will fall either until (a) "anaerobic glycolysis" is activated sufficiently so that it, together with respiration, generates enough ATP to balance ATP utilization or (b) muscle contractile function is impaired and work output decreases.

In the above context, it is not surprising that muscles that have adapted to exercise training with an increase in respiratory capacity produce less lactate at any given submaximal work rate than untrained muscles that are otherwise comparable except for a lower mitochondrial content [22, 23]. It also follows that a higher work rate is needed to attain the same rate of lactate production in the trained as compared to the untrained state.

Substrates for Energy Production During Exercise

ATP hydrolysis at the crossbridges between myosin and actin provides the energy for muscle contraction [24]. Via the creatine kinase reaction, muscle stores of CP can function to rephosphorylate the ADP formed during muscle contraction. There is enough ATP and CP in skeletal muscle to support a few seconds of vigorous contractile activity. It is interesting that in the rat the "fast-twitch" types of muscle, which have the capability of performing short bursts of very intense work, have significantly higher concentrations of ATP and CP than "slow-twitch" muscle (Table I).

The major substrates that provide the energy for the resynthesis of ATP in muscle during sustained exercise are carbohydrate and fat. Catabolism of carbohydrate, in the form of glucose or glycogen, can regenerate ATP both via glycolytic and aerobic phosphorylations of ADP. Glycogen is a more efficient fuel for muscular work than glucose, because it results in the net generation of three ATPs for

Table I. Concentrations of ATP and Creatine Phosphate
in the Different Types of Skeletal Muscle in the Rat

Type of Muscle	Source	ATP	CP
		μmoles/gm Wet Weight	
Fast-twitch white	Superficial portion of vastus lateralis	8.10 ± 0.24	20.1 ± 0.9
Fast-twitch red	Deep portion of vastus lateralis	7.99 ± 0.13	19.6 ± 1.1
Slow-twitch red	Soleus	4.63 ± 0.14	13.8 ± 0.3

Values are means ± SE for six animals.

each glucose unit converted to pyruvate or lactate compared to two ATPs per glucose molecule transported into muscle from the blood. Complete oxidation of one glycogen-derived glucose molecule results in the formation of either 37 or 39 molecules of ATP, depending upon whether electrons from the NADH generated during glycolysis are transported into the mitochondria via the α-glycerophosphate shuttle or the malate-aspartate shuttle. The reason for this difference is that electrons that enter the mitochondrial electron transport chain via the α-glycerophosphate shuttle bypass the first site at which phosphorylation of ADP to ATP is coupled to electron transport.

The yield of ATP from oxidation of fatty acids varies with chain length and degree of saturation. The net ATP yield from the oxidation of two common fatty acids, palmitate and oleate, is 129 molecules of ATP/molecule of palmitate and 144 molecules of ATP/molecule of oleate. When energy yield is expressed in terms of substrate weight fat is a much more efficient fuel for muscular work than carbohydrate. The ATP yield is approximately 510 moles/kg of fat oxidized, compared to a yield of 228 moles of ATP from oxidation of 1 kg of muscle glycogen. This difference in energy yield per kilogram of substrate is further magnified when one considers that glycogen binds a considerable amount of water. Clearly, glycogen is a very heavy fuel which would limit mobility if stored in large amounts. Therefore, most of the body's energy reserves are stored as triglycerides in the adipose tissue. Glycogen stores are relatively small in mammals and can, at the most, provide the energy for only two to three hours of strenuous exercise.

Although fat is clearly the most efficient fuel in terms of portability, glycogen is a more efficient substrate in terms of energy yield per molecule of O_2 utilized during exercise. While fat oxidation yields only 5.6 moles of ATP/mole of O_2 consumed, muscle glycogen provides between 6.17 and 6.5 moles of ATP/mole of O_2 (depending upon whether reducing equivalents from cytoplasmic NADH enter the mitochondria via the α-glycerophosphate or the malate-aspartate shuttles). This is a most important point, which may help to explain why muscle glycogen appears to be indispensable for heavy aerobic exercise.

The Relative Importance of Fatty Acids (FFA) and Carbohydrate as Substrates for Energy Production in Skeletal Muscle During Prolonged Aerobic Exercise

The following section will deal only with metabolism in red skeletal muscle, because white muscle is minimally involved during prolonged exercise.

Generally, 65% or more of the O_2 consumption during heavy aerobic exercise is accounted for by oxidation of carbohydrate, as evidenced by R.Q.s of 0.90 or greater [4, 25-28]. During heavy aerobic exercise generally only about 10% to 20% of the oxidized carbohydrate is derived from blood glucose (i.e., liver glycogen) [4, 29-31].

Studies in which serial biopsies of the quadriceps muscle were obtained on men performing heavy aerobic work on a bicycle ergometer have provided evidence that the point of exhaustion at which the predetermined workload can no longer be maintained coincides with the depletion of muscle glycogen stores [4, 25-27, 32]. Furthermore, the duration for which heavy aerobic work at a given work rate can be maintained appears to be determined by the concentration of glycogen in the muscles at the beginning of exercise; muscle glycogen can be varied over a wide range of exhausting exercise and dietary manipulations. For example, Bergstrom et al [27] did a study in which young men who had been eating a normal mixed diet exercised to exhaustion at a workload requiring 75% of $\dot{V}O_2$ max; at the point of exhaustion muscle glycogen was depleted. They were then fed a diet of very high carbohydrate content for three days; this resulted in an increase in muscle glycogen concentration to twice normal levels. The subjects then again exercised to exhaustion at the same workload; duration of exercise was greatly increased. Muscle glycogen stores were again found to be depleted at the point of exhaustion. They were then fed a high-fat, high-protein, low carbohydrate diet for three days. Muscle glycogen levels were subnormal and the duration of exercise to the point of exhaustion was decreased. There was an excellent correlation between duration of exercise to exhaustion and muscle glycogen concentration at the beginning of exercise. Similar results, showing that muscle glycogen stores determine how long heavy aerobic exercise can be performed, were obtained in other studies [4, 25-27, 32]. Thus it appears that muscle glycogen is indispensable for the performance of heavy aerobic exercise.

Although heavy aerobic exercise cannot be continued after muscle glycogen stores are exhausted, an individual can exercise for a long time at moderate aerobic levels (i.e., 60% of $\dot{V}O_2$max or less) after his muscle glycogen is depleted [33, 34]. Thus, oxidation of fat can provide essentially all of the energy required by the working muscles during light to moderate aerobic exercise.

It is not clear at present why a supply of muscle glycogen is indispensable for heavy aerobic work but not for light work. One possible explanation relates to the greater efficiency of glycogen in terms of energy yield, with generation of 6.2 or more moles of ATP per mole of O_2 consumed, compared to 5.6 ATPs/O_2 for FFA. Theoretically, the same workload would require a higher O_2 consumption (i.e., would require a higher percentage of $\dot{V}O_2max$) when fat is oxidized than when muscle glycogen is utilized.

A second possibility is that substrate supply may become limiting when glycogen stores are depleted. Under normal physiological conditions, the rates of FFA and glucose uptake by muscle, plus the rate of intramuscular triglyceride hydrolysis, may be unable to keep pace with the muscles' energy demands during heavy aerobic exercise. This would make the rapid provision of pyruvate via glycogenolysis essential. Under normal physiological conditions plasma FFA concentration limits the rate of FFA oxidation [29, 35], while the rate of glucose transport into the muscle cell limits the rate of glucose oxidation during exercise. These limitations may well represent built-in protective mechanisms that guard against (a) very rapid glucose uptake resulting in hypoglycemia and symptoms of central nervous system starvation and (b) the development of high intracellular FFA levels which can result in inhibition of many enzymes and partial uncoupling of mitochondrial oxidative phosphorylation.

Factors Determining the Relative Amounts of Energy Derived From Fat and From Carbohydrate Metabolism During Prolonged Exercise

At a given metabolic rate, the rate of fatty acid oxidiation by a tissue appears to be determined by two factors. These are the concentration of fatty acids (i.e., substrate availability) and the capacity of the tissue to oxidize fat. When the metabolic rate is constant, at rest or during steady-state exercise, the rate of fat oxidation increases linearly with fatty acid concentration; saturating concentrations of free fatty acids do not appear to have been attained in studies in vivo [29, 35]. Thus, the availability of fatty acids to the mitochondria appears to be the rate-limiting factor for fatty acid oxidation at any given respiratory rate in vivo. However, at any concentration of fatty acids, the rate of fatty acid oxidation will be the highest in the tissues which have the greatest capacity to oxidize fat. For example, at the same FFA concentration the heart will oxidize fatty acids more rapidly than will skeletal muscle, and red muscle will oxidize fat more rapidly than white. Since the rate at which a substrate is utilized is a function of the level of enzyme activity, regardless of whether substrate concentration is at a saturating level, the muscles of trained individuals, with their greater capacity for fat oxidation, could be expected to oxidize more fat at the same fatty acid concentration than those of untrained individuals. In keeping with this line of reasoning, it seems well established that trained individuals derive more energy from fat oxidation and less from carbohydrate at the same submaximal level of work and $\dot{V}O_2$ than do untrained individuals [4, 25, 36]. It has been shown, using serial biopsies of the quadriceps muscle during a standardized bout of submaximal exercise, that men deplete their muscle glycogen stores less rapidly when they are trained than when they are untrained [4, 22, 25]. Exercise-trained rats deplete both muscle and liver glycogen less rapidly than untrained animals during standardized exercise tests [37, 38]. In a recent study [38], the total amount of glycogen utilized during a standardized bout of exercise was inversely related to the respiratory capacity of the rats' muscles. There was also a significant correlation between how long the animals could run before they became exhausted and the respiratory capacity of their muscles [38]. Since the animals had similar body weights and performed the same exercise, they must have had similar energy expenditures. Therefore, the more highly trained animals, which used less carbohydrate, must have oxidized proportionally more fat. Since plasma FFA levels tend to be lower in the trained than in the untrained state during submaximal exercise [39-42], the greater rate of fat oxidation in the trained state appears to be entirely due to the increase in the capacity of the muscles to oxidize FFA.

As mentioned earlier, muscle glycogen appears to be indispensable for performance of heavy aerobic work (defined here as requiring 70% or more of $\dot{V}O_2$max), and depletion of glycogen stores results in an inability to continue to perform heavy work. However, although glycogen is indispensable and provides the greatest portion of the energy during heavy aerobic work, FFA can provide a sizable share of the total energy. The contribution of FFA to the total energy supply during heavy aerobic work is quite variable and depends upon the plasma FFA level and the individual's level of training; values in the range of 10% to 45% of total energy derived from FFA oxidation have been reported [4, 25-28]. Clearly, the greater the percentage of energy derived from FFA, the longer it will be before glycogen stores are exhausted and the individual has to stop exercising. As discussed earlier, the trained individual derives a greater percentage of his energy from fat oxidation than the untrained during submaximal exercise. Thus, the increase in the capacity of the skeletal muscles to oxidize FFA induced by training could contribute importantly to the increased endurance of the trained individual by postponing the exhaustion of glycogen stores.

Since endurance exercise induces comparable increases in the capacities to oxidize fat and carbohydrate in skeletal muscle [43-45], one might ask why the trained individual oxidizes proportionally more fat than the untrained. The answer lies in the inhibitory effect that oxidation of FFA has on carbohydrate utilization. It has been well documented that glucose uptake, glycolysis and glycogenolysis are inhibited by oxidation of fatty acids in the heart [46]. It has recently been shown that increased oxidation of FFA also inhibits glycogenolysis and glucose uptake in the red types of muscle of exercising rats [47]. The mechanisms by which this inhibition of carbohydrate utilization is mediated are not fully understood. However, one important factor that has been well documented is the accumulation of citrate [48-50] which inhibits phosphofructokinase [18, 48] and results in the accumulation of fructose 6-phosphate and glucose 6-phosphate [48, 51].

References

1. Åstrand, P.-O. and Rodahl, K.: Text Book of Work Physiology. New York:McGraw-Hill, 1970, pp. 303-305.
2. Karlsson, J.: Lactate and phosphagen concentrations in working muscle of man. Acta Physiol. Scand. Suppl. 358:1-72, 1970.
3. Karlsson, J. and Saltin, B.: Lactate, ATP, and CP in working muscle during exhaustive exercise in man. J. Appl. Physiol. 29:598-602, 1970.
4. Saltin, B. and Karlsson, J.: Muscle glycogen utilization during work of different intensities. In Pernow, B. and Saltin, B. (eds.): Muscle Metabolism During Exercise. New York:Plenum, 1971, pp. 289-299.
5. Peter, J.B., Barnard, R.J., Edgerton, V.R. et al: Metabolic profiles of three fiber types of skeletal muscle in guinea pigs and rabbits. Biochemistry 11:2627-2633, 1972.
6. Holloszy, J.O. and Booth, F.W.: Biochemical adaptations to endurance exercise in muscle. Ann. Rev. Physiol. 38:273-291, 1976.
7. Burke, R.E., Levine, D.N., Zajac, F.E. et al: Mammalian motor units: Physiological histochemical correlation in three types in cat gastrocnemius. Science 174:709-712, 1971.
8. Dubowitz, W. and Brook, M.H.: Muscle Biopsy: A Modern Approach. London:Saunders, 1973, pp. 50-60.
9. Cori, C.F.: Regulation of enzyme activity in muscle during work. In Gaebler, O.H. (ed.): Enzymes: Units of Biological Structure and Function. New York:Academic Press, 1956, pp. 573-583.
10. Trivedi, B. and Danforth, W.H.: Effect of pH on the kinetics of frog muscle phosphofructokinase. J. Biol. Chem. 241:4110-4112, 1966.

11. Edstrom, L. and Kugelberg, E.: Histochemical composition, distribution and fatiguability of single motor units: Anterior tibial muscle of the rat. J. Neurol. Neurosurg. Psychiat. 31:424-432, 1968.
12. Baldwin, K.M., Reitman, J.S., Terjung, R.L. et al: Substrate depletion in different types of muscle and in liver during prolonged running. Am. J. Physiol. 225:1045-1050, 1973.
13. Gollnick, P.D., Piehl, K., Saubert, C.W. et al: Diet, exercise and glycogen changes in human muscle fibers. J. Appl. Physiol. 33:421-425, 1972.
14. Gollnick, P.D., Armstrong, R.B., Saubert, C.W. et al: Glycogen depletion patterns in human skeletal muscle fibers during prolonged work. Pflügers Arch. 344:1-12, 1973.
15. Henneman, E.: Organization of the spinal cord. In Mountcastle, V.B. (ed.): Medical Physiology, ed. 13. St. Louis:C. V. Mosby, 1974, pp. 636-650.
16. Davis, E.J. and Lumeng, L.: Relationships between the phosphorylation potentials generated by liver mitochondria and respiratory state under conditions of adenosine diphosphate control. J. Biol. Chem. 250:2275-2282, 1975.
17. Uyeda, K. and Racker, E.: Regulatory mechanisms in carbohydrate metabolism. VII. Hexokinase and phosphofructokinase. J. Biol. Chem. 240:4682-4688, 1965.
18. Passonneau, J.V. and Lowry, O.H.: P-fructokinase and control of the citric acid cycle. Biochem. Biophys. Res. Commun. 13:372-379, 1963.
19. Krzanowski, J. and Matschinsky, F.M.: Regulation of phosphofructokinase by phosphocreatine and phosphorylated glycolytic intermediates. Biochem. Biophys. Res. Commun. 34:816-823, 1969.
20. Lowenstein, J.M.: Ammonia production in muscle and other tissues: The purine nucleotide cycle. Physiol. Rev. 52:382-414, 1972.
21. Jobsis, F.F. and Stainsby, W.N.: Oxidation of NADH during contractions of circulated mammalian skeletal muscle. Resp. Physiol. 4:292-300, 1968.
22. Saltin, B. and Karlsson, J.: Muscle ATP, CP and lactate during exercise after physical conditioning. In Pernow, B. and Saltin, B. (eds.): Muscle Metabolism During Exercise. New York:Plenum, 1971, pp. 395-399.
23. Karlsson, J., Nordesjö, L.-O., Jorfeldt, L. and Saltin, B.: Muscle lactate, ATP, and CP levels during exercise after physical training in man. J. Appl. Physiol. 33:199-203, 1972.
24. Katz, A.M.: Contractile proteins of the heart. Physiol. Rev. 50:63-158, 1970.
25. Hermansen, L., Hultman, E. and Saltin, B.: Muscle glycogen during prolonged severe exercise. Acta Physiol. Scand. 71:129-139, 1967.
26. Hultman, E. and Bergström, J.: Local energy-supplying substrates as limiting factors in different types of leg muscle work in normal man. In Keul, J. (ed.): Limiting Factors of Physical Performance. Stuttgart:Georg Thieme, 1973, pp. 113-125.
27. Bergström, J., Hermansen, L., Hultman, E. and Saltin, B.: Diet, muscle glycogen and physical performance. Acta Physiol. Scand. 71:140-150, 1967.
28. Costill, D.L., Sparks, K., Gregor, R. and Turner, C.: Muscle glycogen utilization during exhaustive running. J. Appl. Physiol. 31:353-356, 1971.
29. Paul, P.: FFA metabolism of normal dogs during steady-state exercise at different work loads. J. Appl. Physiol. 28:127-132, 1970.

30. Rowell, L.B.: The liver as an energy source in man during exercise. *In* Pernow, B. and Saltin, B. (eds.): Muscle Metabolism During Exercise. New York:Plenum, 1971, pp. 127-141.

31. Paul, P.: Uptake and oxidation of substrates in the intact animal during exercise. *In* Pernow, B. and Saltin, B. (eds.): Muscle Metabolism During Exercise. New York:Plenum, 1971, pp. 227-247.

32. Ahlborg, B., Bergström, J., Ekelund, L.-G. and Hultman, E.: Muscle glycogen and muscle electrolytes during prolonged physical exercise. Acta Physiol. Scand. 70:129-142, 1967.

33. Christensen, E.H. and Hansen, O.: Arbeitsfahigkeit und Ernährung. Skand. Arch. Physiol. 81:160-171, 1939.

34. Pernow, B. and Saltin, B.: Availability of substrates and capacity for prolonged heavy exercise in man. J. Appl. Physiol. 31:416-422, 1971.

35. Paul, P. and Issekutz, B.: Role of extramuscular energy sources in the metabolism of the exercising dog. J. Appl. Physiol. 22:615-622, 1967.

36. Christensen, E.H. and Hansen, O.: Respiratorischen Quotient und O_2 — Aufnahme. Skand. Arch. Physiol. 81:180-189, 1939.

37. Baldwin, K.M., Fitts, R.H., Booth, F.W. et al: Depletion of muscle and liver glycogen during exercise: Protective effect of training. Pflügers Arch. 354:203-212, 1975.

38. Fitts, R.H., Booth, F.W., Winder, W.W. and Holloszy, J.O.: Skeletal muscle respiratory capacity, endurance and glycogen utilization. Am. J. Physiol. 228:1029-1033, 1975.

39. Johnson, R.H., Walton, J.L., Krebs, H.A. and Williamson, D.H.: Metabolic fuels during and after severe exercise in athletes and non-athletes. Lancet 2:452-455, 1969.

40. Johnson, R.H. and Walton, J.L.: The effect of exercise upon acetoacetate metabolism in athletes and non-athletes. Q. J. Exp. Physiol. 57:73-79, 1972.

41. Rennie, M.J., Jennet, S. and Johnson, R.H.: The metabolic effects of strenuous exercise: A comparison between untrained subjects and racing cyclists. Q. J. Exp. Physiol. 59:201-212, 1974.

42. Winder, W.W., Baldwin, K.M. and Holloszy, J.O.: Exercise-induced increase in the capacity of rat skeletal muscle to oxidize ketones. Can. J. Physiol. Pharmacol. 53:86-91, 1975.

43. Holloszy, J.O.: Biochemical adaptations in muscle. Effects of exercise on mitochondrial oxygen uptake and respiratory enzyme activity in skeletal muscle. J. Biol. Chem. 242:2278-2282, 1967.

44. Molé, P.A., Oscai, L.B. and Holloszy, J.O.: Adaptation of muscle to exercise. Increase in levels of palmityl CoA synthetase, carnitine palmityl-transferase, and palmityl CoA dehydrogenase and in the capacity to oxidize fatty acids. J. Clin. Invest. 50:2323-2330, 1971.

45. Baldwin, K.M., Klinkerfuss, G.H., Terjung, R.L. et al:: Respiratory capacity of white, red and intermediate muscle: Adaptive response to exercise. Am. J. Physiol. 222:373-378, 1972.

46. Neely, J.R. and Morgan, H.E.: Relationship between carbohydrate and lipid metabolism and the energy balance of heart muscle. Ann. Rev. Physiol. 36:413-459, 1974.

47. Rennie, M.J., Winder, W.W. and Holloszy, J.O.: A sparing effect of increased plasma fatty acids on muscle and liver glycogen content in the exercising rat. Biochem. J. 156:647-655, 1976.

48. Garland, P.D., Randle, P.J. and Newsholme, E.A.: Citrate as an intermediary in the inhibition of phosphofructokinase in rat heart muscle by fatty acids, ketone bodies, pyruvate, diabetes and starvation. Nature (London) 200:169-170, 1963.
49. Parmeggiana, A. and Bowman, R.H.: Regulation of phosphofructokinase activity by citrate in normal and diabetic muscle. Biochem. Biophys. Res. Commun. 12:268-273, 1963.
50. Garland, P.B. and Randle, P.J.: Effects of alloxan-diabetes, starvation, hypophysectomy and adrenalectomy, and of fatty acids, ketone bodies and pyruvate, on the glycerol output and concentrations of free fatty acids, long-chain fatty acyl-coenzyme A, glycerol phosphate and citrate-cycle intermediates in rat heart and diaphragm muscles. Biochem. J. 93:678-687, 1964.
51. Newsholme, E.A. and Randle, P.J.: Regulation of glucose uptake by muscle. 7. Effects of fatty acids, ketone bodies and pyruvate, and of alloxan diabetes, hypophysectomy, and adrenalectomy, on the concentrations of hexose phosphates, nucleotides and inorganic phosphate in the perfused rat heart. Biochem. J. 93:641-651, 1964.

Production d'énergie en cours d'effort physique

Les moyens de production d'énergie dépendent du taux d'effort et des muscles squelettiques impliqués dans le travail. La capacité de production d'énergie dépend de l'adaptation biochimique à l'entraînement, des mécanismes reliant la production ATP et l'utilisation ATP et des substrats exigés par l'effort. On discute de l'importance des acides gras et des hydrates de carbone en tant que substrats et des facteurs qui déterminent la somme relative d'énergie issue de leur métabolisme au cours d'un effort physique prolongé.

Energy Stores and Substrates Utilization in Muscle During Exercise

H. Howald, G. von Glutz and R. Billeter

Energy stores, sequence of fuel utilization and the comparative power output at the molecular level in the skeletal muscle cell are discussed. Utilization of different fuels in muscle metabolism clearly depends upon the intensity and duration of work: ATP and CrP can be depleted to about 70%-80% and 20%-30% of resting values, respectively, in heavy exercise leading to exhaustion; glycogen stores in the muscle cell can be completely depleted in long-lasting physical exercise, the pattern differing according to muscle fibers; and intramuscular triglycerides in aerobically trained muscle are utilized sparing glycogen stores and to prevent hypoglycemia and increase endurance capacity.

Introduction

The main energy supplying substrates in skeletal muscle are the energy-rich phosphates, glycogen and triglycerides [34]. Amino acids have been shown to produce only a minimum quantity of energy in normal muscle during work [25]. Some of the substrates needed for energy production are stored within the muscle cell itself or may be mobilized in extramuscular organs and be transported to the working muscle by the blood. This paper will deal with the cellular substrate stores and their utilization, whereas the problems of substrate mobilization, transport and uptake will be presented in the papers of Drs. Gollnick, Hultman and Oscai. Since there exists a number of excellent reviews in the field of muscle metabolism during exercise [21, 25, 26, 41, 44, 45], emphasis will be given especially to the development of new techniques for metabolic research in the muscle cell.

Historical Survey

For a long time, scientific studies on the use of fuels for muscular work depended mainly upon the analysis of respiratory gas exchange.

H. Howald, G. von Glutz and R. Billeter, Research Institute, Swiss School for Physical Education and Sports, Magglingen, Switzerland.

In 1896 Chauveau found a respiratory quotient of 0.95 during work and concluded that carbohydrates are the only energy source in these conditions [5]. In 1905 Zuntz et al were the first to show that the respiratory quotient depends upon the dietary fat intake in resting conditions as well as during exercise [49]. Bock et al in 1928 demonstrated an interrelationship of work intensity and the respiratory quotient [3] and Christensen et al in 1939 finally concluded that both carbohydrates and fat are utilized during rest and work [6, 7]. The same authors showed that the relative importance of these substrates to the energy supply depends upon the intensity and duration of work as well as on the type of diet prior to exercise. Margaria et al made valuable contributions in another field, namely, the anaerobic energy-supplying processes by distinguishing a so-called alactic part from the lactic acid production at very high work intensities [31].

The analysis of arteriovenous differences of substrates or metabolites in blood and the utilization of radioactive isotopes markedly extended our knowledge about muscle metabolism during exercise. Most authors agree that carbohydrates supply the major part of energy at onset of work and during high work intensities, whereas fat oxidation largely produces the energy needed during prolonged physical exercise at relatively low intensities [25, 27, 39, 42, 47].

The introduction of the biopsy technique by Bergström in 1962 [2] finally made it possible to obtain muscle samples in human subjects and to study exercise-induced metabolic changes at the tissue level. Mainly Scandinavian authors contributed to a large extent the most valuable information about the utilization of cellular substrates and the production of metabolites during different types of physical activity [22, 23, 45]. In the last few years, much interest was focused on the histochemically determined substrate depletion pattern of the different human muscle fiber types [8, 15, 16]. Most recently, methods were developed which enable us to assay metabolic processes in single muscle cells [10, 30].

Energy Stores and Sequence in Fuel Utilization

The cellular energy stores in human skeletal muscle are shown in Table I. The energy-rich phosphates ATP and creatine phosphate (CrP) constitute only a minor reserve, whereas glycogen and especially triglycerides provide for ample amounts of available energy on the local level [22]. The quantity of stored fuels evidently limits the total work that can be done. On the other hand, the maximum

Table I. Cellular Energy Stores in Human Skeletal Muscle

mMoles/Kg Dry Weight		Available Energy (mMoles ~ P/Kg Dry Weight)	
ATP	24.6	9.8	
Creatine phosphate (CrP)	76.8	61.4	
Glycogen (glycosyl units)	365	1'060	(Anaerobic)
		14'200	(Aerobic)
Triglycerides	48.6	24'520	

From E. Hultman and J. Bergström [22].

energy output depends upon the activity of the enzymes involved in the different metabolic pathways. Estimations of maximum power in human muscle are given in Table II. Splitting down of the energy-rich phosphates generates at least twice as much energy per unit of time as the anaerobic glycolysis does. The oxidation of free fatty acids produces only one half of the energy supplied by the oxidation of carbohydrates and the maximum flux of high-energy phosphates available from the oxidative utilization of fuels is also only about 50% of the one generated by the anaerobic glycolysis [34].

These estimations of maximum power output at the molecular level are well paralleled by maximum work outputs of top athletes. The energy stored in the form of ATP and creatine phosphate enables the human organism to work at very high intensities for a short period of time (weightlifting, 100 to 200 meter dash). The breakdown of muscle glycogen in the anaerobic Embden-Meyerhof pathway produces the high amount of energy needed in middle-distance running and other sports activities lasting up to two to three minutes of time; but at the same time, lactate production is creating a severe local and general acidosis with muscle and blood pH values as low as 6.3 and 6.8, respectively [18, 28]. The energy demand in

Table II. Estimated Maximum Flux of Energy-Rich
Phosphate from the Utilization of Different Fuels

Fuel Utilization		Maximum Power (mMoles ~ P/Kg · Sec)
ATP, CrP	→ ADP, Cr	1.6 – 3.0
Glycogen	→ Lactate	1.0
Glycogen	→ CO_2, H_2O	0.5
FFA	→ CO_2, H_2O	0.24

From McGilvery [34].

physical activities lasting more than two to three minutes is predominantly supplied by oxidative processes. While carbohydrates serve as the most important substrate in workloads of relatively high intensity and relatively short duration (rowing, etc.), the contribution of fat oxidation to energy production increases with the duration and decreases with the intensity of exercise (long-distance running, cross-country skiing, etc.). So the utilization of the different fuels in muscle metabolism clearly depends upon intensity and duration of work (Fig. 1).

Depletion of Energy-Rich Phosphates

ATP is depleted to about 70%-80% and creatine phosphate to 20%-30% of resting values in heavy physical exercise leading to exhaustion within 2, 6 or 16 minutes [23]. Special attention should be given to the fact that the tissue concentrations of ATP and creatine phosphate already fall to their final values during the first 2 minutes or work regardless of whether the load leads to exhaustion within this time or whether the exercise may be continued for 4 or even 14 additional minutes. Whereas the decrease of ATP concentration seems to be independent of work intensity [29], the depletion of creatine phosphate in muscle tissue seems to be linearly related to the workload at least in the range of 50% to 100% of maximum oxygen uptake [24]. The declines in ATP and creatine phosphate concentration seem to have little effect on the absolute ADP and AMP concentrations until near exhaustion [34]. However, when the concentration scale is magnified, a 60% decrease in total energy-rich phosphate content of muscle tissue would result in a more than 20-fold change in ADP and a nearly 700-fold change in AMP concentrations at constant pH, while the ATP concentration decreases only to 70% of its resting value [34]. These marked changes in ADP and AMP concentrations are responsible for the control of energy-supplying metabolic processes in the cytoplasm as well as in the mitochondria. Depletion of 40% of the total energy-rich phosphates or 60% of the resting creatine phosphate concentration causes an ADP-induced acceleration of anaerobic glycolysis at the level of phosphoglycerate kinase and pyruvate kinase and an acceleration of ADP transport into muscle mitochondria. The increased ADP concentration in the mitochondrial matrix then activates the oxidative phosphorylation or aerobic ATP production [34]. The changes in AMP concentrations enhance the anaerobic glycolysis at the level of phosphofructokinase.

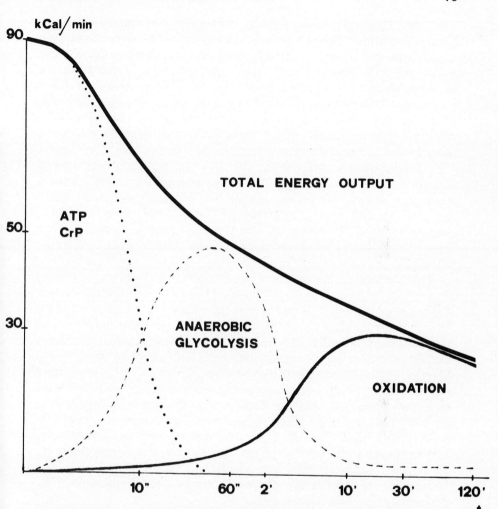

FIG. 1. Sequence and quantitative relationships of energy-supplying biochemical processes in human skeletal muscle. The duration of exercise is given on a logarithmic scale and the energy outputs are calculated on the basis of results performed by top athletes in the different activities concerned.

Glycogen Depletion

Glycogen is probably the substrate that has been studied in the largest number of investigations dealing with human skeletal muscle during the last ten years. The glycogen stores of the muscle cell can be completely depleted in long-lasting physical exercise and this can be demonstrated by electron microscopy as well as by biochemical methods using tissue homogenates. At a given submaximal workload demanding about 60% to 90% of an individual's maximum oxygen uptake, the glycogen content of muscle tissue is more or less linearly decreasing with the duration of exercise and is considered to be the limiting factor for muscular work [17, 22]. There is also a direct relationship between workload and the muscular glycogen decrease, which cannot be prevented by continuous glucose infusion [22]. Only at very low and highest work intensities does fatigue occur independently from the remaining glycogen concentration in muscle. Diet is considerably influencing the muscular glycogen content and thus an athlete's ability to sustain a higher speed for a longer time in endurance events. The best results are obviously obtained when eating a fat- and protein-rich diet for three consecutive days after exercise-induced depletion of the glycogen stores, followed by a three-day period with high carbohydrate intake prior to competition [1].

Histochemistry allows for a separation of at least two different fiber types in human skeletal muscle [13, 14]. Slow-twitch muscle fibers are bright and the fast-twitch ones are dark when staining for ATPase after alkaline preincubation [38]. Intracellular glycogen can be demonstrated by the PAS-stain [40]. In resting conditions there is usually no noticeable difference in histochemically determined glycogen content of the different fiber types [8, 15]. Prolonged bicycle exercise at an intensity demanding 60% of an individual's maximum oxygen uptake produces a selective glycogen depletion in the slow-twitch fibers, while "supramaximal" bouts of exercise at about 120% to 150% of $\dot{V}O_2$ max have been demonstrated to predominantly empty the glycogen stores of the fast-twitch fibers [8, 16]. This different glycogen depletion pattern has also been discussed to be a reflection of specific motor unit recruitment in the different types of physical exercise.

Although the validity of the subjective ratings of PAS-staining intensity has been demonstrated to be quite high in comparison to simultaneous determinations in muscle homogenates [8], the glycogen content and depletion in single muscle fibers should be investigated with more advanced techniques. In 1974 Essen et al [9] were the first to apply Lowry's technique [30] for dissection of freeze-dried human muscle samples. Parts of a muscle biopsy specimen are lyophilized at −30 C and placed under a binocular microscope. With fine instruments individual muscle fibers 2 to 3 mm long can then be dissected out. Small parts of the fiber ends are cut away and stained for ATPase with either alkaline (pH 10.3) or acid (pH 4.1)

preincubation in order to identify the fast- or slow-twitch characteristics of the isolated fibers [38]. Dark stain after alkaline preincubation is typical for the fast-twitch fibers, whereas the slow-
twitch ones stain darkly after acid preincubation. After fiber-type
identification, the remaining portion of the individual fiber is
weighed on a quartz fiber fishpole balance [30]. The weights of the
muscle fibers usually vary from 0.5 to 5.0 μg [9, 10]. The individual
fiber can then be placed in a capillary tube and glucose residues can
be analyzed fluorometrically according to the Lowry method after
hydrolysis [23, 30].

In a recent experiment, we measured the glycogen depletion in
isolated slow-twitch and fast-twitch muscle fibers in m. vastus
lateralis of a trained long-distance runner after different types of
exercise. Our subject had a $\dot{V}O_2$ max of 60.4 ml/min/kg and 65%
slow-twitch fibers. Biopsies were taken before and immediately after
a one-hour work period at 60% of $\dot{V}O_2$ max (220 w) and again
before and after six one-minute bouts at 150% of $\dot{V}O_2$ max (550 w).
We analyzed 186 individual muscle fibers with an average weight of
3.5 μg (Fig. 2). The resting glycogen content was equal in both fiber
types, but slightly higher before starting the intermittent exercise
experiment. Continuous exercise at 60% of $\dot{V}O_2$ max produced a
25% decrease in glycogen content of the slow-twitch fibers
($p < 0.001$), but only an 8% glycogen utilization in the fast-twitch
fibers ($p > 0.05$). The very intense intermittent exercise routine
predominantly depleted the fast-twitch fibers 50% ($p < 0.005$), but
the 32% decrease in glycogen content of the slow-twitch fibers was
also statistically significant ($p < 0.001$). Thus, we could not completely confirm earlier reports on histochemically determined glycogen depletion pattern in single human skeletal muscle fibers [8, 16]
with our direct quantitative method. However, the trend seems to be
the same and more laboratory work with more than just one subject
will be needed to further investigate this problem.

Depletion of Intracellular Triglycerides

The intracellular content of triglycerides in human skeletal
muscle is subject to large variations according to different authors
using chemical determination methods [22, 36]. Our own morpho-
metrical investigations have also shown a wide range of intracellular
lipid volume density, obviously depending upon age, sex and
endurance capacity of an individual [20, 37]. For a long time,
skeletal muscle lipids were considered to be of minor importance for
energy production during exercise [11, 12, 33]. Carlson et al in 1971

H. HOWALD ET AL

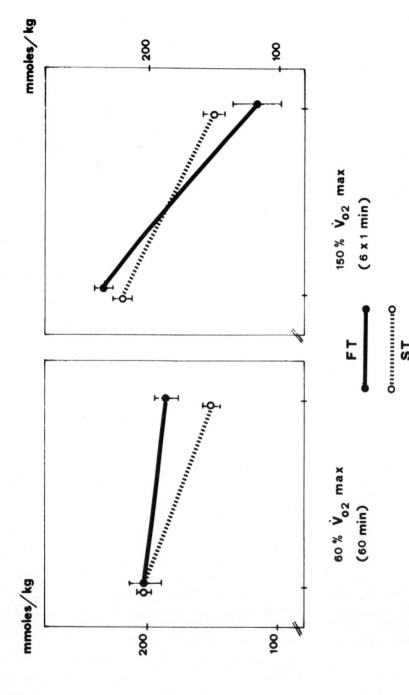

FIG. 2. Glycogen depletion in fast-twitch (FT) and slow-twitch (ST) individual human muscle fibers during moderate continuous and very intense intermittent bicycle exercise.

then clearly demonstrated that during long-lasting physical activity at 70% of the subject's maximal oxygen uptake, 75% of the energy supplied by fatty acid oxidation came from intramuscular triglycerides and only 25% from free fatty acids in blood [4]. Paul calculated that during the first 30 minutes of long-lasting physical exercise, intramuscular fat contributes 48% of the total caloric expenditure and that the plasma free fatty acids participation in energy production is rising only if exercise continues [39].

Distance runners specialized to very long distances up to 100 km show a much higher intracellular lipid content than untrained people and well-trained orienteers [20, 37]. In a morphometric study on seven runners covering the distance of 100 km in a mean time of eight hours and 49 minutes [37], we found an average decrease in intracellular lipid content of 74.7% (p <0.01) and a similar decrease in the number of interfibrillar glycogen granules (p <0.005). We calculated that out of the 7100 calories consumed during the 100 km run, 50% were supplied by fat oxidation and that the intracellular lipids contributed 25% of this substrate, the remaining 75% of oxidized free fatty acids coming out of the stores in adipose tissue.

Intracellular lipid droplets are predominantly located in the slow-twitch muscle fibers [46]. Saltin's group in Denmark measured a triglyceride concentration of 50.5 mmoles/kg dry weight for slow-twitch and of 18.1 mmoles/kg for fast-twitch fibers (personal communication). It is evident that a marked decrease in tissue triglyceride content after exercise points to an important recruitment of the slow-twitch fibers. Reitman et al found a 70% decrease of triglycerides in red and no change in white muscles of rats performing exhaustive exercise [43].

A higher intramuscular triglyceride content and higher activities of enzymes involved in the oxidation of free fatty acids [19, 35] enable the muscle trained aerobically to utilize more of this energy-supplying substrate and to spare its precious glycogen, thus preventing hypoglycemia and increasing endurance capacity.

References

1. Åstrand, P.-O.: Nutrition and physical performance. In Rechcigl, M. (ed.): Food, Nutrition and Health. Basel:Karger, 1973, vol. 16, pp. 59-79.
2. Bergström, J.: Muscle electrolytes in man. Scand. J. Clin. Lab. Invest. 14 Suppl. 68, 1962.
3. Bock, A.V., Vancaulaert, C., Dill, D.B. et al: J. Physiol. 66:162, 1928.
4. Carlson, L.A., Ekelund, L. and Fröberg, S.O.: Concentration of triglyceride, phospholipids and glycogen in skeletal muscle and of free fatty acids and beta-hydroxybutyric acid in blood in man in response to exercise. Eur. J. Clin. Invest. 1:248-254, 1971.

84   H. HOWALD ET AL

5. Chauveau, A.: C.R. de l'Acad. Sci. 122:1163, 1896.
6. Christensen, E.H. und Hansen, O.: Untersuchungen über die Verbrennungsvorgänge bei langdauernder schwerer Muskelarbeit. Skand. Arch. Physiol. 81:152-159, 1939.
7. Christensen, E.H.: Arbeitsfähigkeit und Ernährung. Skand. Arch. Physiol. 81:160-171, 1939.
8. Edgerton, V.R., Essén, B., Saltin, B. and Simpson, D.R.: Glycogen depletion in specific types of human skeletal muscle fibers in intermittent and continuous exercise. In Howald, H. and Poortmans, J. (eds.): Metabolic Adaptation to Prolonged Physical Exercise. Basel:Birkhäuser Verlag, 1975, pp. 402-415.
9. Essén, B. and Henriksson, J.: Glycogen content of individual muscle fibres in man. Acta Physiol. Scand. 90:645-647, 1974.
10. Essén, B., Jansson, E., Henriksson, J. et al: Metabolic characteristics of fibre types in human skeletal muscle. Acta Physiol. Scand. 95:153-165, 1975.
11. Fröberg, S.O.: Metabolism of lipids in blood and tissues during exercise. In Poortmans, J. R. (ed.): Biochemistry of Exercise. Med. and Sport 3, Basel:Karger, 1969, pp. 100-113.
12. Gollnick, P.D., Januzzo, C.D., Williams, C. and Hill, T.R.: Effect of prolonged, severe exercise on the ultrastructure of human skeletal muscle. Int. Z. Angew. Physiol. 27:257-265, 1969.
13. Gollnick, P.D., Armstrong, R.B., Saubert, C.W. et al: Enzyme activity and fiber composition in skeletal muscle of untrained and trained men. J. Appl. Physiol. 33:312-319, 1972.
14. Gollnick, P.D., Piehl, K., Saubert, C.W. et al: Diet, exercise, and glycogen changes in human muscle fibers. J. Appl. Physiol. 33:421-425, 1972.
15. Gollnick, P.D., Armstrong, R.B., Sembrowich, W.L. et al: Glycogen depletion pattern in human skeletal muscle fibers after heavy exercise. J. Appl. Physiol. 34:615-618, 1973.
16. Gollnick, P.D., Piehl, K., Karlsson, J. and Saltin, B.: Glycogen depletion patterns in human skeletal muscle fibers after varying types and intensities of exercise. In Howald, H. and Poortmans, J.R. (eds.): Metabolic Adaptation to Prolonged Physical Exercise. Basel:Birkhäuser Verlag, 1975, pp. 416-421.
17. Hermansen, L., Hultman, E. and Saltin, B.: Muscle glycogen during prolonged severe exercise. Acta Physiol. Scand. 71:129-139, 1967.
18. Hermansen, L. and Osnes, J.B.: Blood and muscle pH after maximal exercise in man. J. Appl. Physiol. 32:304-308, 1972.
19. Holloszy, J.O.: Biochemical adaptations to exercise: Aerobic metabolism. In Wilmore, J.H. (ed.): Exercise and Sport Sciences Reviews, Vol. 1. New York and London:Academic Press, 1973, pp. 45-71.
20. Hoppeler, H., Lüthi, P., Claassen, H. et al: The ultrastructure of the normal human skeletal muscle. A morphometric analysis on untrained men, women and well-trained orienteers. Pflügers Arch. 344:217-232, 1973.
21. Howald, H. and Poortmans, J.R. (eds.): Metabolic Adaptation to Prolonged Physical Exercise. Proceedings of the Second International Symposium on Biochemistry of Exercise, Magglingen, 1973. Basel:Birkhäuser Verlag 1975.
22. Hultman, E. and Bergström, J.: Local energy-supplying substrates as limiting factors in different types of leg muscle work in normal man. In Keul, J. (ed.): Limiting Factors of Physical Performance. Stuttgart:Georg Thieme Publishers, 1973, pp. 113-125.

23. Karlsson, J. and Saltin, B.: Lactate, ATP, and CP in working muscles during exhaustive exercise in man. J. Appl. Physiol. 29:598-602, 1970.
24. Karlsson, J., Nordesjö, L.O., Jorfeldt, L. and Saltin, B.: Muscle lactate, ATP, and CP levels during exercise after physical training in man. J. Appl. Physiol. 33:199-203, 1972.
25. Keul, J., Doll, E. and Keppler, D.: Energy metabolism of human muscle. Med. and Sport, Vol. 7. Basel:Karger 1972.
26. Keul, J. (ed.): Limiting Factors of Physical Performance. International Symposium at Gravenbruch 1971. Stuttgart:Georg Thieme Publishers, 1973.
27. Keul, J., Haralambie, G., Arnold, T. and Schumann, W.: Heart rate and energy-yielding substrates in blood during long-lasting running. Eur. J. Appl. Physiol. 32:279-289, 1974.
28. Keul, J.: Kohlenhydrate zur Leistungsbeeinflussung in der Sportmedizin. Nutr. Metab. 18 (Suppl. 1):157-170, 1975.
29. Knuttgen, H.G. and Saltin, B.: Muscle metabolites and oxygen uptake in short-term submaximal exercise in man. J. Appl. Physiol. 32:690-694, 1972.
30. Lowry, O.H. and Passonneau, J.V.: A flexible system of enzymatic analysis. New York and London:Academic Press, 1972.
31. Margaria, R., Edwards, H.T. and Dill, D.B.: The possible mechanism of contracting and paying the oxygen debt and the role of lactic acid in muscular contraction. Am. J. Physiol. 106:689-715, 1933.
32. Margaria, R., Aghemo, P. and Sassi, G.: Lactic acid production in supramaximal exercise. Pflügers Arch. 326:152-161, 1971.
33. Masoro, E.J., Rowell, L.B., McDonald, R.M. and Steinert, B.: Skeletal muscle lipids. Nonutilisation of intracellular lipid esters as an energy source for contractile activity. J. Biol. Chem. 241:2626-2634, 1966.
34. McGilvery, R.W.: The use of fuels for muscular work. In Howald, H. and Poortmans, J.R. (eds.): Metabolic Adaptation to Prolonged Physical Exercise. Basel:Birkhäuser Verlag, 1975, pp. 12-30.
35. Moesch, H. and Howald, H.: Hexokinase (HK), glyceraldehyde-3P-dehydrogenase (GAPDH), succinate-dehydrogenase (SDH), and 3-hydroxyacyl-CoA-dehydrogenase (HAD) in skeletal muscle of trained and untrained men. In Howald, H. and Poortmans, J.R. (eds.): Metabolic Adaptation to Prolonged Physical Exercise. Basel:Birkhäuser Verlag, 1975, pp. 463-465.
36. Morgan, T.E., Short, F.A. and Cobb, L.A.: Alterations in human skeletal muscle lipid composition and metabolism induced by physical conditioning. In Poortmans, J.R. (ed.): Biochemistry of Exercise. Med. and Sport 3. Basel:Karger, 1969, pp. 116-121.
37. Oberholzer, F., Claassen, H., Moesch, H. und Howald, H.: Ultrastrukturelle, biochemische und energetische Analyse einer extremen Dauerleistung (100 km-Lauf). Schweiz. Z. Sportmed. 24:71-98, 1976.
38. Padykula, H.A. and Herman, E.: The specificity of the histochemical method of adenosine triphosphatase. J. Histochem. Cytochem. 3:170-195, 1955.
39. Paul, P.: Effects of long lasting physical exercise and training on lipid metabolism. In Howald, H. and Poortmans, J.R. (eds.): Metabolic Adaptation to Prolonged Physical Exercise. Basel:Birkhäuser Verlag, 1975, pp. 156-193.

40. Pearse, A.G.E.: Histochemistry — Theoretical and Applied. Boston:Little, Brown and Co., 1961, pp. 832, 854, 899.
41. Pernow, B. and Saltin, B. (eds.): Muscle Metabolism During Exercise. Proceedings of a Karolinska Institutet Symposium held in Stockholm, Sweden, September 6-9, 1970. New York and London:Plenum Press, 1971.
42. Pruett, E.D.R.: Fat and carbohydrate metabolism in exercise and recovery and its dependence upon work load severity. Oslo:Institute of Work Physiol., 1971.
43. Reitman, J., Baldwin, K.M. and Holloszy, J.O.: Intramuscular triglyceride utilization by red, white and intermediate skeletal muscle and heart during exhausting exercise. Proc. Soc. Exp. Biol. Med. 142:628-631, 1973.
44. Rosell, S. and Saltin, B.: Energy need, delivery and utilization in muscular exercise. *In* Bourne (ed.): Structure and Function of Muscle, ed. 2. New York:Academic Press, 1973, vol. 3.
45. Saltin, B.: Metabolic fundamentals in exercise. Med. Sci. Sports 5:137-146, 1973.
46. Schmalbruch, H.: Die quergestreiften Muskelfasern des Menschen. Ergebnisse der Anatomie und Entwicklungsgeschichte. Band 43, Heft I. Berlin: Springer Verlag, 1970.
47. Wahren, J., Felig, Ph., Hagenfeldt, L. et al: Splanchnic and leg metabolism of glucose, free fatty acids and amino acids during prolonged exercise in man. *In* Howald, H. and Poortmans, J.R. (eds.): Metabolic Adaptation to Prolonged Physical Exercise. Basel:Birkhäuser Verlag, 1975, pp. 144-153.
48. Wilmore, J.H. (ed.): Exercise and Sport Sciences Reviews. New York and London:Academic Press, 1973, vol. 1.
49. Zuntz, N., Loewy, A., Müller, F. and Caspari, W.: Höhenklima und Bergwanderungen in ihrer Wirkung auf den Menschen. Berlin:Deutsches Verlagshaus, 1905.

Réserves d'énergie et utilisation des substrats dans les muscles au cours de l'effort physique

L'auteur traite des réserves d'énergie, des séries d'utilisation du combustible et du rendement comparatif de puissance au niveau moléculaire dans la cellule d'un muscle squelettique. L'utilisation de différents combustibles dans le métabolisme musculaire repose nettement sur l'intensité et la durée du travail: on peut consommer l'ATP jusqu'à 70 ou 80% et la CrP jusqu'à 20 ou 30% des valeurs au repos, lors d'un effort difficile entraînant l'épuisement; les réserves de glycogène dans la cellule peuvent être complètement épuisées au cours d'un effort physique de longue durée, le cas variant selon le type de fibre musculaire. Les triglycérides intramusculaires dans un muscle aérobie entraîné servent à empêcher l'hypoglycémie et à augmenter l'endurance, sans toucher aux réserves de glycogène.

Delivery and Uptake of Substrates

Philip D. Gollnick

The transport of substrates and the processes occurring at or in the membranes that are regulatory for their uptake are discussed with particular reference to glucose and free fatty acids as the principal energy compounds carried by the blood. It is shown that the transport capacity of the circulatory system to offer substrate to the working muscles exceeds their capacity to extract and oxidize the fuels. The rate-limiting step in the uptake of blood-borne fuels by skeletal muscle appears to lie in carrier-mediated transport systems contained within the plasma membrane. Such limitations are believed to represent self-protective mechanisms against overwork or an ill-advised expenditure of some of the body's stored energy reserves.

Introduction

During exercise large amounts of energy are released in skeletal muscle to support the contractile process. This energy comes from the oxidation of energy compounds either stored within the muscles or brought to them via the circulation. In this paper the dynamics of the delivery of substrates to and their uptake by skeletal muscle will be considered. Others have dealt with or will deal with the role of the liver, adipose tissue and skeletal muscle energy reserves. Since the bulk of the energy for exercise comes from stores of the liver, adipose and skeletal muscle, this presentation will cover only the transport of substrates and the processes occurring at or in the membranes that are regulatory for their uptake. Some overlap between authors is inevitable. Hopefully such overlap will result in differences that will stimulate discussion and result in additional experiments in this area.

Delivery of Substrates

The delivery of extramuscular substrates to muscle is via the blood. Since the principal energy compounds carried by the blood

Philip D. Gollnick, Department of Physical Education for Men, Washington State University, Pullman, Washington, U.S.A.

are glucose and free fatty acids (FFA), this presentation will be limited to a consideration of these two substrates. It is realized that there may be some contribution to the work metabolism from circulating triglycerides [21,], ketone bodies and glycerol, but these are probably of minor importance. The first question then is what is the capacity of the blood to transport glucose and FFA and is this limiting to work?

Glucose

At rest blood glucose concentration of normal man ranges from 4 to 6 mM with a mean of about 5 mM. Glucose is carried in blood in solution in the blood water. A blood glucose concentration of 5 mM does not represent a saturation of the blood water. This is apparent from the fact that in glucose tolerance tests and in untreated diabetics blood glucose levels three to five times normal are frequently observed.

During either prolonged endurance or short heavy exercise there is no remarkable change in blood glucose. Thus, the full glucose-carrying capacity of the blood is not used and this cannot be considered as a limiting factor to exercise. Occasional reports of elevated blood glucose levels during exercise can be found in the literature [10, 37]. These observations are most frequently made when the work was interrupted while blood samples were drawn. This probably is the result of a continued outpouring of glucose from the liver, whereas uptake by muscle has been significantly reduced or has stopped. The end result is a temporary imbalance between influx and efflux. It has been our observation that during endurance work when blood samples are taken from indwelling catheters, no major increase in blood glucose concentrations occurs [14, 15]. This is true for man and rats [2]. During the latter stages of prolonged exercise a drop in blood glucose occurs [20]. Values in man as low as 1.7 mM have been reported [20] at the end of exhaustive exercise for subjects whose total body carbohydrate stores had been depleted by prior exercise and a low carbohydrate diet. In rats we have observed that blood glucose is maintained at near normal levels until liver glycogen is nearly depleted [2]. With short heavy exercise there is no major change in blood glucose levels [14]. Training has no effect on the level of glucose in the blood either at rest or during exercise.

An uptake of glucose from the gut can occur during exercise [7, 12]. This should not be overlooked as an energy source during prolonged exercise such as cross-country skiing and so forth. However, at present the magnitude of the uptake and its importance to the total energy metabolism has not been fully elucidated.

Free Fatty Acids

Resting FFA levels in man range from .4 to .6 mEq/liter with the average being about .5 mEq/liter. FFA being insoluble in water are carried in the blood as a lipid-albumin complex. Thus, an upper limit exists for the amount of FFA that can be transported at any one time. This limit is a function of the albumin concentration of the blood and its FFA binding capacity. The normal albumin concentration of blood is about 40 gm/liter and the FFA binding capacity is between 5 and 7 moles of FFA per mole of albumin. With a molecular weight of about 68,000 daltons for albumin, the maximal FFA concentration in blood would be about 3.5 mEq/liter.

During exercise there is an initial decrease and then a progressive increase in plasma FFA. The initial decline has been attributed to an elevated extraction for FFA by the working muscle with a delay in either their release from adipose tissue or a temporary reduction in blood flow to the adipose tissue. The FFA level in blood during endurance exercise may increase to 2 mEq/liter or higher [15, 16]. This level is usually well below the total carrying capacity of the blood and would suggest that the total transport capacity of the blood for FFA is rarely fully utilized during exercise. This last statement must be interpreted with caution, since it is unknown whether the total binding capacity of albumin as observed in vitro studies is available under in vivo conditions.

Blood Flow and Substrate Availability

A second factor involved with the availability of substrates to muscle is the blood flow. Thus, a second question is what is the total substrate available as a consequence both of the concentrations in the blood and the total blood flow?

It is well established that cardiac output increases during exercise [33]. This increase is linear up to about 70% of the $\dot{V}O_2$max. Subsequent increases to maximal values occur at reduced rates. It is important that a large fraction of the cardiac output be diverted to the working muscle mass. Studies with in situ stimulation of dog muscle [6, 11, 24, 35] and with intact dogs [36] and man [22, 29, 34, 38] have demonstrated a large increase in blood flow to the working muscle during heavy exercise. Wharen and Jorfeldt [39] have measured blood flow through the legs at rest and during exercise using a dye dilution method. They found a blood flow of about 450 ml through the region of the leg supplied by the femoral artery and drained by the femoral vein. During exercise this flow increased linearly to about 3.0 liters per leg at a work load of 600 kpm (total body $\dot{V}O_2$ = 1.5 liters/min). Saltin et al [34] observed leg blood flow of above 6.0 liters/min for subjects exercising at 70% of their $\dot{V}O_2$max.

It is possible to calculate the total amount of substrate that is available (passes through) to the muscle each minute from the blood flow and the concentrations of energy compounds in the blood. Thus, at rest blood flow is about .450 liter/min, blood glucose concentration is 5 mM, and FFA is about .5 mEq/liter. Total glucose passing through one leg is 2.25 mmoles, whereas FFA is .124 mEq (plasma volume based on a hematocrit of 45%). This is equivalent to an O_2 uptake of 300 ml for glucose and 63 ml/min for FFA if all the substrate were extracted and oxidized. During exercise at 70% $\dot{V}O_2$max the blood flow per leg increased to about 6.0 liter/min (plasma flow about 3.3 liter/min). The glucose concentration in blood is largely unchanged, whereas plasma FFA increases to 2 mEq/liter or higher. Under these conditions 30 mmoles of glucose and 6.6 mEq of FFA enter the leg each minute. This energy pool is equal to an O_2 equivalent of 7.4 liter/min (4.0 and 3.4 liter/min, respectively, for glucose and FFA) for one leg.

From these calculations it is apparent that the energy reserves that pass through the muscle each minute during exercise exceed the delivery of oxygen. Measurement of A-V differences across the resting or working muscle has demonstrated that only a small fraction of the energy available to the muscle in the blood is actually taken up. For glucose this is probably a self-protective mechanism to insure that the carbohydrate supply for the central nervous system is not depleted. Thus, the major source of blood glucose, the 50-100 gm of glycogen in the liver, would be used in a matter of minutes if the muscles extracted all the glucose available in the blood. A similar danger would not exist for plasma FFA, since the body reserves are rather extensive.

The Role of Blood Glucose in
Rest and Exercise Metabolism

Since a relatively large amount of carbohydrate flows through skeletal muscle both at rest and during exercise, a logical question is just what is its contribution to the metabolism?

The relative importance of the uptake and oxidation of blood glucose to the resting and exercise metabolism has been the subject of several investigations. There is generally uniform agreement that blood glucose plays a relatively minor role in the resting metabolism of skeletal muscle [1, 3, 5, 6, 11, 16, 22, 24, 35, 40]. Disagreement does exist in the area of the role of the uptake and oxidation of blood glucose during exercise. Reports exist suggesting that blood glucose is not used during exercise [6], that it is used to a minor extent (10% to 15% of total $\dot{V}O_2$) [24, 31, 34] and that it may play a major role in prolonged submaximal exercise for the arms and legs [5, 22, 37, 38]. Our recent work [34] suggests that the oxidation of glucose taken up by the leg during one hour of bicycle exercise at 70% $\dot{V}O_2$ max could account for only about 10% of the total carbohydrate utilized. This was unaltered by either a sprint or an endurance training program.

The highest reported rate of glucose uptake by contracting skeletal muscle is 567 μmoles/kg/min [5]. If this value were extrapolated to a person using 20 kg of muscle, it would be a glucose uptake of 2 gm/min. At this rate a complete emptying of the liver glycogen reserves would occur in about 25 minutes. This value seems high. However, in intact man it is probably unlikely that a complete activation of the muscle occurs as was the case with the electrical stimulation used in the dog experiment.

We (Bagby, Green and Gollnick, unpublished data) have attempted to ascertain the role of blood-borne carbohydrates in the metabolism of exercising rats. For these experiments rats with indwelling carotid and jugular vein catheters were exercised from about one to four hours on a treadmill at a speed of 21 m/min. During the exercise, solutions of glucose, lactate, pyruvate, or physiological saline (all pH 7.4) were infused into the jugular vein at a rate equal to 1.51 kcal/hr. This infusion rate was selected from the work of Armstrong and co-workers [2] which showed that this was the rate of liver glycogen decline for rats with a constant blood glucose during exercise of similar intensity. One objective of the study was to determine whether infusion of an external glucose source at the rate of the normal decline in liver glycogen could retard the rate of liver glycogen depletion during exercise. A second objective was to study the ability of alternate substrates (lactate and pyruvate) to substitutes as carbohydrates during submaximal exercise.

Blood samples (0.1 ml) were drawn from the carotid artery at rest and at 30 minute intervals during the exercise. Samples were analyzed for glucose, lactate and pyruvate. At the end of the exercise the animals were killed by exsanguination. This final blood sample was analyzed for plasma FFA. At the time of death the liver and gastrocnemius and soleus muscles were rapidly exercised. These tissues were weighed and samples removed for glycogen determination.

The infusion of lactate and pyruvate depressed the endurance capacity of the rats by about 40%. This reduced exercise tolerance was manifest by severe symptoms of fatigue at the end of the run such as the development of rigor mortis almost immediately after death. In contrast, glucose-infused rats ran 40% longer than the physiological saline-infused group. There was no evidence of muscular rigor up to 10 to 15 minutes after death.

Blood glucose rose slightly in the lactate, pyruvate and physiological saline groups. No major changes occurred thereafter until near the termination of work when blood glucose was significantly lower in these groups. In the glucose-infused group blood glucose was elevated throughout the exercise. Blood lactate and pyruvate were unchanged throughout the exercise in all groups except those into which these compounds had been infused. In all cases, however, a sharp rise in blood lactate occurred at the end of the exercise.

A nearly linear decline in liver glycogen occurred in the physiological saline-, pyruvate- and lactate-infused groups. In the lactate- and pyruvate-infused rats exhaustion preceded the complete emptying of the liver glycogen reserves. In physiological saline-infused animals liver glycogen was near zero at exhaustion. Glucose infusion exerted a glycogen-sparing effect on the liver. This was most pronounced during the second and third hours of exercise. Thereafter, a sharp decline in liver glycogen occurred.

Declines in skeletal muscle glycogen were similar to those of liver glycogen. In all muscles examined an exceptionally sharp decline in the glycogen stores occurred in pyruvate- and lactate-infused rats. Glucose infusion had a glycogen-sparing effect. However, like the liver a rapid fall in muscle glycogen occurred in the final hour of exercise. This could be responsible for the final elevation in blood lactate levels.

Plasma FFA increased by 225% in physiological saline-infused animals. In glucose- and lactate-infused animals plasma FFA were about 28% below resting values. These latter data suggest that an inhibition of lipolysis occurred as a result of these infusions. An elimination of plasma FFA as an energy source could have been responsible for the early onset of fatigue in lactate- and pyruvate-infused animals.

Regulation of Glucose Uptake

It is apparent that a fairly large quantity of substrate passes through the skeletal muscles both at rest and during exercise. The question then is why isn't this energy reserve taken up and oxidized to support the energy requirements of the muscle cells?

A simple answer is that it would be unwise for the body to deplete its extramuscular carbohydrate reserves, since the central nervous system is almost totally dependent upon the blood for a constant glucose supply. Rapid exhaustion of liver glycogen would lead to disastrous effects for the total body.

The fact that glucose uptake by muscle is carrier-mediated [25] and not diffusion-limited serves to avoid rapid depletion of extramuscular carbohydrate reserves at rest and during work. Although the specific carrier has not been identified, some of the factors controlling it are well known. These factors include extracellular hormones such as insulin and epinephrine; intracellular substances such as ATP, G6P, citrate and FFA levels; and activities of enzymes such as hexokinase and phosphofructokinase.

Both insulin and epinephrine are known to stimulate glucose uptake by skeletal muscle [4, 19, 25]. This is true both at rest and during electrical stimulation [24]. However, it has been reported that during exercise a substance is released that results in an elevated glucose uptake in the absence of insulin [13]. This concept has been challenged by Berger et al [4] in a recent paper where they could not demonstrate a glucose uptake during electrical stimulation of muscle when insulin was absent. However, a depletion of liver and muscle glycogen does occur in untreated diabetic rats during exercise (C. D. Ianuzzo, personal communication).

One important regulator of glucose uptake is phosphorylation by hexokinase as it enters the cell. Hexokinase is known to be inhibited by G6P [8, 30, 32]. In the isolated perfused rat heart G6P levels drop and glucose entry into the myocardium increases during anoxia [27]. Increases in ventricular pressure also result in an enhanced glucose uptake [9, 26]. Elevated FFA levels, however, depress the rate of glucose uptake by the working heart.

The situation in skeletal muscle appears to be somewhat different from that of the heart. Here, both electrical stimulation and very heavy work result in increases in intracellular G6P [6, 23]. Under such conditions free glucose in the cell increases and a release of glucose may even occur (presumably resulting from the activity of the debranching enzyme) [38]. The rise in G6P would suggest an inhibition of hexokinase and a decrease in glucose uptake. The differences in control of glucose entry into the heart and skeletal muscle may be associated with their function and metabolic reserves. The heart must continue to function for survival of the organism. Its metabolism is primarily aerobic with little reliance on a rather limited glycogen store. Thus when oxygen is lacking, it will compensate by a rapid uptake of extracellular glucose. In contrast, skeletal muscle has a fairly large glycogen reserve. It can afford the luxury of depleting its energy reserve and if exhausted usually poses no internal threat to the total organism.

Levels of citrate and ATP may also be important, since they will result in either a stimulation or inhibition of phosphofructokinase which in turn affects intracellular G6P levels. Since all the factors relate to the metabolic rate and the availability of oxygen to meet the metabolic requirements, it is clear that the skeletal muscle is organized to control its metabolism without a great reliance upon extracellular glucose. This fact is clear even when at very heavy work loads the prime energy source is carbohydrate. Under these conditions there is an almost total dependence upon intracellular glycogen.

The Role of Plasma FFA in the
Resting and Exercise Metabolism

The respiratory quotient of resting muscle suggests that lipid is the primary fuel being oxidized [1, 3, 11, 16, 40]. Similarly, the uptake of FFA by resting leg or forearm can account for most of the CO_2 produced. However, most of the FFA taken up by resting muscle do not appear immediately as CO_2 [14]. This suggests that a continual cycling of FFA through the glyceride pool occurs in resting muscle.

During short heavy or even short light exercise, plasma FFA probably contribute little as metabolic fuels [28]. With prolonged submaximal exercise the rate of FFA oxidation increases and may account for as much as 30% of the metabolic fuel during prolonged heavy work [16-18].

Perhaps the clearest demonstration of the relative importance of FFA to exercise metabolism was the experiment of Pernow and Saltin [29] in which the one-leg model was employed. In these experiments the exercise capacity of each leg was tested on one day. This resulted in a glycogen depletion which was sustained until the second day through the consumption of a low carbohydrate diet. On the second day the work to exhaustion with each leg was determined before and after an inhibition of lipolysis induced by an infusion of nicotinic acid. Such an infusion resulted in a fall in plasma FFA and 50% reduction in work capacity.

Regulation of FFA Uptake by
Muscle at Rest and During Exercise

Overall, very little information exists concerning the mechanisms controlling the uptake of FFA by skeletal muscle. It has been postulated that a carrier-mediated transport system exists for the translocation of FFA across adipocyte membranes. Some membrane transport system probably also exists in skeletal muscle. However, it has not been well characterized nor have the factors controlling it been identified. It is known that the rate of FFA uptake and oxidation is dependent upon the concentration of FFA in the plasma. In exercise, however, the fractional extraction of FFA decreases even though plasma levels increase [18]. Under such conditions the increased uptake of FFA is the result of an increased plasma flow through the muscle. Undoubtedly, this area needs additional study.

References

1. Andres, R., Baltzan, M.A., Cader, G. and Zierler, K.L.: Effect of insulin on carbohydrate metabolism and on potassium in the forearm of man. J. Clin. Invest. 41:108-115, 1962.
2. Armstrong, R.B., Saubert, C.W. IV, Sembrowich, W.L. et al: Glycogen depletion in rat skeletal muscle fibers at different intensities and durations of exercise. Pflügers Arch. 352:243-256, 1974.
3. Baltzan, M.A., Andres, R., Cader, G. and Zierler, K.L.: Heterogeneity of forearm metabolism with special reference to free fatty acids. J. Clin. Invest. 41:116-125, 1962.
4. Berger, M., Hagg, S. and Reuderman, N.B.: Glucose metabolism in perfused skeletal muscle. Interaction of insulin and exercise on glucose uptake. Biochem. J. 146:231-238, 1975.
5. Chapler, C.K. and Stainsby, W.N.: Carbohydrate metabolism in contracting dog skeletal muscle in situ. J. Appl. Physiol. 215:995-1004, 1968.
6. Corsi, A., Midrio, M. and Granata, A.L.: In situ utilization of glycogen and blood glucose by skeletal muscle during tetanus. Am. J. Physiol. 216:1534-1541, 1969.
7. Costill, D.L., Bennett, A., Branam, G. and Eddy, D.: Glucose ingestion at rest and during prolonged exercise. J. Appl. Physiol. 34:764-769, 1973.
8. Crane, R.K. and Sols, A.: The association of hexokinase with particulate fractions of brain and other tissue homogenates. J. Biol. Chem. 203:273-292, 1953.
9. Crass, M.F., McCaskill, E.S. and Shipp, S.C.: Effect of pressure development on glucose and palmitate metabolism in perfused heart. Am. J. Physiol. 216:1569-1576, 1969.
10. Dill, D.B., Edwards, H.T. and Mead, S.: Blood sugar regulation in exercise. Am. J. Physiol. 111:21-30, 1935.

11. DiPrampero, P.E., Cerretelli, P. and Pipper, J.: O_2 consumption and metabolite balance in the dog gastrocnemius at rest and during exercise. Pflügers Arch. 309:38-47, 1969.
12. Fordtran, J.S. and Saltin, B.: Gastric emptying and intestinal absorption during prolonged severe exercise. J. Appl. Physiol. 23:331-335, 1967.
13. Goldstein, M.S.: Humoral nature of hypoglycemia in muscular exercise. Am. J. Physiol. 200:67-70, 1961.
14. Gollnick, P.D., Armstrong, R.B., Sembrowich, W.L. et al: Glycogen depletion pattern in human skeletal muscle fibers after heavy exercise. J. Appl. Physiol. 34:615-618, 1973.
15. Gollnick, P.D., Armstrong, R.B., Saubert, C.W. IV et al: Glycogen depletion patterns in human skeletal muscle fibers during prolonged work. Pflügers Arch. 344:1-12, 1973.
16. Havel, R.J., Naimark, A. and Borchgrevink, C.F.: Turnover rate and oxidation of free fatty acids of blood plasma in man during exercise: Studies during continuous infusion of palmitate-1-C^{14}. J. Clin. Invest. 42:1054-1063, 1963.
17. Havel, R.J., Carlson, L.A., Ekelund, L-G. and Holmgren, A.: Turnover rate and oxidation of different free fatty acids in man during exercise. J. Appl. Physiol. 19:618, 1964.
18. Havel, R.J., Pernow, B. and Jones, N.L.: Uptake and release of free fatty acids and other metabolites in the legs of exercising men. J. Appl. Physiol. 23:90-96, 1967.
19. Helmreich, E. and Cori, C.F.: Studies of tissue permeability. J. Biol. Chem. 224:663-679, 1957.
20. Hermansen, L., Hultman, E. and Saltin, B.: Muscle glycogen during prolonged severe exercise. Acta Physiol. Scand. 71:129-139, 1967.
21. Jones, N.L. and Havel, R.J.: Metabolism of free fatty acids and chylomicron triglycerides during exercise in rats. Am. J. Physiol. 213:824-828, 1976.
22. Jorfeldt, L. and Wahren, J.: Human forearm muscle metabolism during exercise. V. Quantitative aspects of glucose uptake and lactate production during prolonged exercise. Scand. J. Clin. Lab. Invest. 26:73-81, 1970.
23. Karlsson, J., Diamant, B. and Saltin, B.: Muscle metabolites during submaximal and maximal exercise in man. Scand. J. Clin. Lab. Invest. 26:385-394, 1971.
24. Karlsson, J., Rosell, S. and Saltin, B.: Carbohydrate and fat metabolism in contracting canine skeletal muscle. Pflügers Arch. 331:57-69, 1972.
25. Morgan, H.E., Regen, D.M. and Park, C.R.: Identification of a mobile carrier-mediated sugar transport system in muscle. J. Biol. Chem. 239:369-374, 1964.
26. Neely, J.R., Bowman, H. and Morgan, H.E.: Effects of ventricular pressure development and palmitate on glucose transport. Am. J. Physiol. 216:804-811, 1969.
27. Newsholme, E.D. and Randle, R.J.: Regulation of glucose uptake by muscle. Biochem. J. 93:641-651, 1964.
28. Pernow, B. and Wahren, J.: Lactate and pyruvate formation and oxygen utilization in the human forearm muscles during work of high intensity and varying duration. Acta Physiol. Scand. 56:267-285, 1962.
29. Pernow, B. and Saltin, B.: Availability of substrates and capacity for prolonged heavy exercise in man. J. Appl. Physiol. 31:416-422, 1971.

30. Regen, D.M., Davis, W.W., Morgan, H.E. and Park, C.R.: The regulation of hexokinase and phosphofructokinase activity in heart muscle. J. Biol. Chem. 239:43-49, 1964.
31. Reichard, G.A., Issekutz, B., Jr., Kimbel, P. et al: Blood glucose metabolism in man during muscular work. J. Appl. Physiol. 16:1001-1005, 1961.
32. Rose, I.A. and O'Connell, E.L.: The role of glucose 6-phosphate in the regulation of glucose metabolism in human erythrocytes. J. Biol. Chem. 239:12-17, 1964.
33. Rowell, L.B.: Human cardiovascular adjustments to exercise and thermal stress. Physiol. Res. 54:75-159, 1974.
34. Saltin, B., Nazar, K., Costill, D.L. et al: The nature of the training response; peripheral and central adaptations to one-legged exercise. Acta Physiol. Scand. 96:289-305, 1976.
35. Skinner, N.S. Jr., Costin, J.C., Saltin, B. and Vastogh, G.: Glucose uptake in contracting, isilateral in situ dog skeletal muscle. In Pernow, B. and Saltin, B. (eds.): Muscle Metabolism During Exercise. New York:Plenum Press, 1971, pp. 177-188.
36. Vatner, S.F., Higgins, C.B., White, S. et al: The peripheral vascular response to severe exercise in untethered dogs before and after complete heart block. J. Clin. Invest. 50:1950-1960, 1971.
37. Wahren, J.: Human forearm muscle metabolism during exercise. IV. Glucose uptake at different work intensities. Scand. J. Clin. Lab. Invest. 25:129-135, 1970.
38. Wahren, J., Ahlborg, G., Felig, P. and Jorfeldt, L.: Glucose metabolism during exercise in man. In Pernow, B. and Saltin, B. (eds.): Muscle Metabolism During Exercise. New York:Plenum Press, 1971, pp. 179-203.
39. Wahren, J. and Jorfeldt, L.: Determination of leg blood flow during exercise in man: An indicator-dilution technique based on femoral venous dye infusion. Clin. Sci. Mod. Med. 45:135-146, 1973.
40. Zierler, K.L. and Andres, R.: Carbohydrate metabolism in intact skeletal muscle in man during the night. J. Clin. Invest. 35:991-997, 1956.

Distribution et absorption des substrats

Examen du transport des substrats et des opérations qui se présentent au niveau des membranes qui règlent leur absorption, plus particulièrement du glucose et des acides gras libres qui sont les principaux composés énergétiques transportés par le sang. L'auteur montre que la capacité de transport de l'appareil circulatoire, qui vise à fournir des substrats aux muscles en action, dépasse la capacité de ces derniers d'extraire et d'oxyder le combustible. Les systèmes de transport dans la membrane plasmatique, qui sont aussi des supports interposés, semblent contenir le facteur limitant la vitesse avec laquelle les muscles squelettiques absorbent le combustible porté par le sang. On croit que de telles restrictions sont des mécanismes d'auto-protection contre le surmenage ou une dépense malavisée de certaines réserves d'énergie accumulées dans le corps.

Regulation of Carbohydrate Metabolism in the Liver During Rest and Exercise With Special Reference to Diet

Eric Hultman

The mechanisms of glucose production from the liver at rest and its mobilization during exercise by the pathways of glycogenolysis and of gluconeogenesis are presented and discussed at length; references are made to animal and human experiments, in conditions of normal feeding and of both CHO-poor and CHO-rich dietary conditions. It is suggested that the regulation of liver carbohydrate metabolism during exercise after different diets is dependent upon both hormonal influences and on the size of the glycogen store.

Introduction

The liver is generally recognized as the only significant source of blood glucose in the postprandial state. It is well known today that during increased energy demands as occur during exercise glucose mobilization from the liver is increased by the pathways of glycogenolysis and gluconeogenesis. The importance of these mechanisms for work performance capacity was demonstrated among others by Issekutz et al [21] who showed that dogs performing endurance exercise ceased to work as soon as the supply of newly released glucose from the liver became inadequate. Pronounced decreases of blood sugar during prolonged exercise, limiting the performance capacity, have also been observed in man [3].

Liver Glycogen Store at Rest

The liver glycogen store in normal man in the postabsorptive state after a normal mixed diet has been shown to be 270 mmol glucose units per kilogram liver (range of 87 to 460 mmol) (Fig.

Eric Hultman, Department of Clinical Chemistry, Stockholm, Sweden.
This work was supported by grants of the Swedish Medical Research Council (project no B76-19X-2647-O8B) and Idrottens Forskningsrad (IFR).

1) [18,27]. Assuming a normal liver weight of 1.8 kg this corresponds to a total of 490 mmol glucose units.

The size of the liver glycogen store, however, can be varied by the preceding diet and may be as high as 500 mmol/kg liver (or 900 mmol totally) after a carbohydrate (CHO)-rich diet and as low as 12 to 73 mmol/kg (or 20-120 mmol totally) after a CHO-poor diet (Table I).

Liver Glucose Production in Resting Man

After Normal Mixed Diet

The net rate of glucose production from the splanchnic area in normal man in the postabsorptive state has been determined in liver

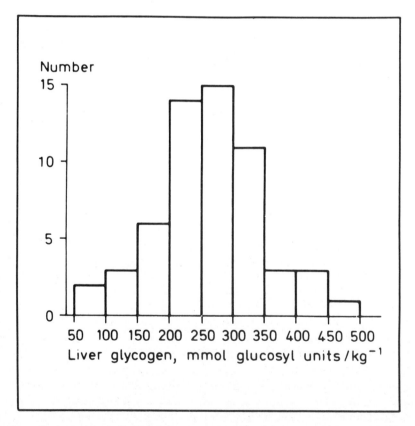

FIG. 1. Liver glycogen content in the postabsorptive state in normal man, determined in tissue obtained by percutaneous liver biopsy.

Table I. Glycogen Store and Glucose Metabolism in the Liver at Rest
in Relation to Preceding Diet. The Diet Period Before Determination
of Liver Glucose Metabolism Was 3-4 Days

| | Glycogen Content mmol/Kg | | Glucose Release mmol/Min | Glycogen-olysis Rate mmol Glucose/Min | Gluconeo-genesis Rate mmol Glucose/Min |
	Mean	Liver Range	Mean ± SE	Mean ± SE	
After mixed diet	270	87-460	0.87 ± 0.058*	0.54 ± 0.052†	0.31§
After CHO-poor diet, 1-10 days	37	12-73	0.30 ± 0.031*	0	0.30§
After CHO-rich diet, 1-5 days	467	267-624	0.95 ± 0.061	0.50‡	0.45‡

*From Nilsson et al [30].

†Determined by glycogen determination in liver biopsy samples [30].

‡Glycogenolysis rate calculated as difference between glucose release and gluconeogenesis rate, which was determined as uptake of lactate, pyruvate, glycerol and alanine by the splanchnic area.

§ Determined as gluconeogenesis (‡) using urea output by the liver as a measure of amino acid utilization [30].

vein catheterization studies and found to be 0.8 to 1.1 mmol glucose per minute, or approximately 1 mol per day. This amount of glucose is just sufficient to cover the energy needs of the brain and obligatory glycolytic tissues in the body [11]. If liver glycogen were the only source for blood glucose the store would be empty within eight hours.

In the postprandial state glucose is also produced by an additional mechanism, gluconeogenesis, in which lactate, pyruvate, glycerol and amino acids are utilized for glucose production. From studies of the uptake of gluconeogenic substrates by the splanchnic area it has been determined that approximately 25% to 30% of the glucose output may be derived from measured precursor substrates [28, 40], assuming that all the gluconeogenic substrates taken up were utilized for glucose production. Direct measurement of liver glycogen decrease by determination of glycogen content in repeatedly sampled tissue specimens showed a glycogen degradation rate of 0.54 mmol glucose units per minute. This corresponds to the remaining two thirds of the total glucose release from the liver [20, 29].

The amount of glycogen in the liver in the postabsorptive state is as a mean 270 mmol glucose units per kilogram but shows a large variation (Fig. 1). The liver glycogen content decreased during a

four-hour observation period of rest and starvation by a mean of
0.30 mmol glucose units per kilogram liver. The liver weight in a
normal man is about 1.8 kg, which means that the total liver
glycogen store is about 490 mmol glucose units and the glycogenolysis rate corresponds to 0.54 mmol glucose units per minute
(Fig. 2, Table II). This value of glycogen degradation rate in man is
of the same order of magnitude as those described for intact rats

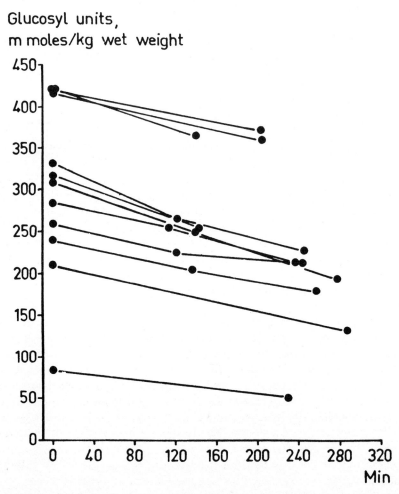

FIG. 2. Liver glycogen content during short-term starvation. Tissue samples
obtained in the morning in the postabsorptive state and after two and four hour
further rest and starvation.

Table II. Liver Glycogen Content During Short-Term Starvation.
Tissue Samples Obtained by Repeated Needle Biopsy

| | | *Glycogen, Glucosyl Units, mmol/Kg Wet Liver Tissue* | | |
| | | *Further Starvation* | | |
Subject	*Basal*	*Approx.* *2 hr.*	*Approx.* *4 hr.*	*Decrease* *Per Min*
BO	419	366	–	0.38
UT	316	254	–	0.43
GD	308	250	196	0.40
SS	284	257	212	0.30
TL	259	227	213	0.19
LT	210	–	133	0.27
BG	241	206	179	0.24
LR	420	–	374	0.23
GO	416	–	362	0.27
AA	335	265	229	0.43
KE	87	–	51	0.16
Mean	300			0.30
± SE	30.5			0.029

during diurnal fast [32] and similar to the rate of glucose release by the isolated liver of fed rats perfused with a glucose concentration of 6 to 7 mmol per liter [34].

From the figure on glycogenolysis rate it can be calculated that the mean glycogen store of the liver should last for 15 to 16 hours and should be completely empty after one day of starvation. This result was confirmed in two subjects, in whom liver biopsies were taken after 24 and 48 hours of starvation [29].

After Starvation or CHO-Poor Diet

In subjects maintained on a CHO-poor normocaloric diet the liver glycogen content was the same as after 24 hours of starvation. When this diet regimen (high fat and protein content) was continued for up to ten days, a low liver glycogen content was recorded during the whole observation period (12 to 73 mmol glucose units per kilogram liver or totally between 20 and 130 mmol/1.8 kg) (Fig. 3, Table III).

The rate of uptake of gluconeogenic substrates by the liver was studied in the postabsorptive state after a normal diet and after three to six days of CHO-poor diet. The results are presented in Table IV and show that the uptake of gluconeogenic substrates was unchanged. Since the liver glycogen content was close to zero after the CHO-poor diet, glycogenolysis is unlikely to occur and the result must be a decrease in total glucose production from the liver. This

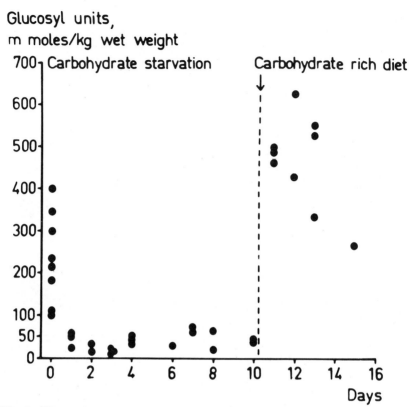

FIG. 3. Liver glycogen content during prolonged starvation or supply of CHO-poor diet followed by CHO refeeding.

was confirmed by direct measurement of glucose output from the splanchnic area (Table IV).

Despite a 70% decrease in the splanchnic glucose production no decrease in the blood glucose level was observed. This infers that a corresponding reduction of glucose uptake by extrahepatic tissue must have occurred. The decreased glucose uptake corresponds to the change from glucose to ketone body utilization by the brain [15, 16, 24, 31, 37, 42].

After CHO-Rich Diet

When a normocaloric CHO-rich diet was given after a period of a CHO-poor diet, an immediate increase in liver glycogen content was observed. After one day of CHO-refeeding liver glycogen content was as high as 469 to 513 mmol/kg. The hepatic glucose release under

Table III. Prolonged Starvation or Supply of Carbohydrate-Poor Diet Followed by Carbohydrate Refeeding. Liver Glycogen Content and Blood Glucose Levels

Glycogen, mmol Glucosyl Units/Kg Wet Liver Tissue

Subjects	Basal	Days of Total Starvation* or Carbohydrate-Poor Diet**										Days of Carbohydrate-Rich Diet				
		1	2	3	4	5	6	7	8	9	10	1	2	3	4	5
L.A.*	155	24	15	21	–	–	–	–	–	–	–	513	–	–	–	–
T.W.*	345	48	–	–	–	–	–	–	–	–	–	–	–	–	–	–
J.S.**	98	–	–	–	33	–	–	60	–	–	42	462	–	552	–	–
K.E.**	298	–	–	–	44	–	–	73	–	–	39	496	–	526	–	–
M.A.**	213	–	–	12	–	–	–	–	64	–	–	–	624	–	–	–
C.F.**	401	55	–	15	–	–	–	–	17	–	–	–	–	–	–	–
M.F.**	112	–	–	–	–	–	30	–	–	–	–	–	424	–	–	–
E.J.**	230	–	32	–	48	–	–	–	–	–	–	–	–	336	–	267
Mean	232	–	–	–	–	–	–	–	–	–	–	–	–	–	–	–
							Blood Glucose, mmol/l									
n	8	8	6	7	4	2	3	2	4	2	2	7	6	4	–	2
Mean	5.10	4.58	3.92	3.92	3.86	3.78	4.68	4.00	4.50	4.17	4.25	5.01	4.91	4.61	–	4.59
± SEM	0.115	0.149	0.223	0.144	0.190	–	–	–	0.451	–	–	0.227	0.105	0.190	–	–

Table IV. Calculated Glucose Production from Glycogenolysis
and from Gluconeogenesis. A Maximum Conversion Efficiency
of Urea and Gluconeogenic Substrates Was Assumed.
Values Given in mmol Per Min

From	Normal Diet	CHO-Poor Diet
Glycogenolysis*	0.54	0
Protein, calculated from urea production	0.15	0.13
Lactate	0.12	0.13
Glycerol	0.04	0.04
Total calculated glucose production	0.85	0.30
Directly determined glucose production	0.87	0.30

*Glycogenolysis value was taken from Nilsson and Hultman [29].

these conditions was higher than after the CHO-poor diet (Table I).
Measurement of gluconeogenic substrates showed increased hepatic
uptake of lactate and alanine and blood concentration of these
substrates higher after CHO-rich diet than after the CHO-poor (Table
V). The uptake of pyruvate, however, was very low after the
CHO-rich diet or in some cases was changed to a small production
from the liver. The increased gluconeogenesis rate at rest after
CHO-rich diet (Table I) was probably dependent upon increased
availability of lactate and alanine produced by extrasplanchnic
tissues.

Substrate Control of Hepatic Glucose Release

The role of the gluconeogenic substrates for hepatic glucose
release was studied in three healthy volunteers. They were given a

Table V. Arterial Concentrations of Glucose and
Gluconeogenic Substrates At Rest, After
CHO-Poor and CHO-Rich Diets

Arterial Concentration mmol/l	CHO-Poor Mean ± SE	CHO-Rich Mean ± SE
Glucose	4.29 ± 0.070	5.64 ± 0.063
Lactate	0.527 ± 0.013	0.861 ± 0.064
Pyruvate	0.036 ± 0.001	0.074 ± 0.009
Alanine	0.109 ± 0.012	0.327 ± 0.013
Glycerol	0.050 ± 0.010	0.042 ± 0.008

CHO-poor normocaloric diet for three days to empty the liver glycogen store. On the morning of day 4, liver vein catheterization was performed and liver blood flow as well as hepatic output of glucose and urea and uptake of lactate, pyruvate and glycerol was measured. After the basal period an amino acid solution with high alanine content was infused at a rate of 1.76 mmol/min (0.7 to 1.0 mmol alanine). After one hour of amino acid infusion tryptophan was given through a stomach tube (0.038 to 0.135 mmol/min).

The results (Table VI) showed that the rate of glucose production after the period with CHO-poor diet was 0.30 mmol/min. Glucose production was derived mainly from gluconeogenesis: 45% from amino acid degradation and 42% from lactate uptake. During amino acid infusion the rate of glucose release increased to 0.55 mmol/min. This increase was paralleled by increased release of urea from the liver. Assuming the carbon skeleton in the deaminated amino acids to be utilized as substrate for gluconeogenesis — the factor used for calculating maximum glucose production from urea was 0.769 [26] — the amino acids could account for 74% of the total glucose release.

When tryptophan was ingested during continued infusion of the amino acid solution, the rate of glucose production decreased to 0.14 mmol/min. This decrease was paralleled by decrease of both urea production and lactate uptake by the splanchnic organs. Only glycerol uptake was unchanged. In experiments with perfused liver, the effect of tryptophan is ascribed to an inhibition of phosphoenol pyruvate carboxykinase activity (PEPCK) [33].

Table VI. Glucose Release From the Liver After 3 Days of CHO-Poor Diet With and Without Amino Acid Infusion (1.76 mmol/min) and With Simultaneously Supplied Tryptophan (0.14 mmol/min) Given Through a Duodenal Tubing. Values in mmol Glucose/Min

Hepatic Glucose Production From	Before Infusion	During Amino Acid Infusion	Amino Acids + Tryptophan
Amino acids (urea)	0.14	0.39	0.06
Lactate	0.13	0.10	0.01
Glycerol	0.04	0.04	0.06
Total calculated	0.31	0.53	0.13
Determined by liver vein catheterization	0.30	0.55	0.14

Thus increased availability of gluconeogenic substrates may increase glucose production by the liver, whereas inhibition of key gluconeogenic enzymes decreased the glucose production. Both these observations were made in normal subjects after three days of CHO-poor diet.

Liver Glycogen Synthesis

The effect of carbohydrate ingestion on liver glycogen content is seen in Tables I and III. To study the synthesis rate from different sugars, a standardized infusion was given amounting to 5.6 mmol hexose per kilogram body weight per hour during four hours. The metabolic state of the liver in the postabsorptive resting state changed from one of glycogen degradation to that of glycogen synthesis. The glycogen synthesis rate during glucose infusion or during peroral administration of the same dose was 0.3 mmol glucose units per minute per kilogram liver during the four-hour observation period [30]. The synthesis rate was three times as high when fructose was given (Fig. 4). The rate of fructose conversion to glycogen was 1.1 mmol glucose units per kilogram liver per minute. This corresponds to the maximum rate of glucose conversion to glycogen in rat liver in situ reported by Krebs and co-workers [23] and to an estimated liver glycogen synthesis rate of 0.5 mmol glucose units per kilogram liver per minute [32] in intact rats during the feeding period. During fructose infusion at this rate (5.6 mmol/kg b.w./hr) a pronounced degradation of ATP in the liver was observed [6, 7, 18, 22, 25, 43]. The rapid intravenous infusion of fructose can thus give rise to a lack of high energy phosphates in the liver. At the same time lactate was produced during the fructose infusion. The rate of lactate formation was directly correlated to the fructose infusion rate [5].

Hepatic Glucose Production During Exercise
After Normal Mixed Diet

Experiments with ^{14}C glucose as well as with direct measurements of hepatic glucose output showed that the turnover rate of plasma glucose increases two- to threefold during exercise both in man and in dogs.

It has also been shown that glucose production from the liver increases with increasing workload and also with work time during the exercise period [3, 17, 19, 21, 35, 36, 39, 40].

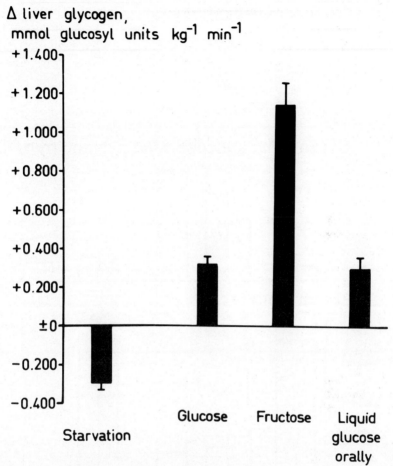

FIG. 4. Liver glycogen degradation or synthesis rate during a four-hour period with and without hexose infusion or peroral glucose administration. The amount hexose given was 5.6 mmol/kg body weight per hour.

Thus, the largest outputs of glucose from the liver are invariably found at the end of an exercise performed with a high workload (Fig. 5).

Total Hepatic Glucose Release During Exercise

In an early work from our laboratory [17] the hepatic production of glucose and the splanchnic uptake of lactate were studied during rest and exercise. The exercise was performed on a bicycle ergometer at a load of 75% of the subjects' maximum oxygen uptake

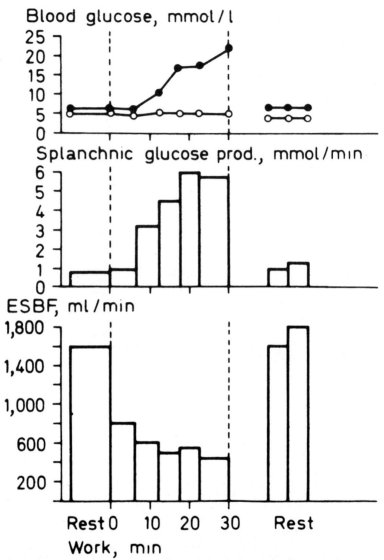

FIG. 5. Splanchnic blood flow and splanchnic glucose production at rest and during exercise at a work intensity of 85% of the subject's $\dot{V}O_2$ max.

capacity. The exercise was performed as repeated bouts of work of 20 minute duration with 10 minute rest between the periods. With this work schedule it was possible to almost completely empty the glycogen store in the quadriceps femoris muscles (Fig. 6). During

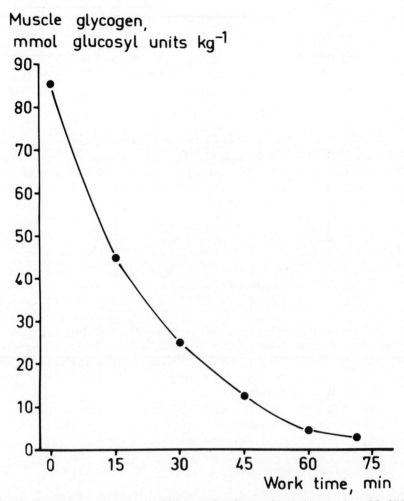

FIG. 6. Glycogen content in working muscles during dynamic exercise with 85% of $\dot{V}O_2$ max. Mean values of ten subjects working to exhaustion.

these exercise periods the output of glucose as well as the uptake of lactate by the splanchnic organs was measured.

It was found that the hepatic glucose output increased from 0.80 mmol/min at rest to 1.94 mmol during the first work period and to a mean of 3.13 mmol/min during the last period. During the total exercise period the mean glucose output was 2.36 mmol/min. The total carbohydrate consumption calculated from oxygen uptake and respiratory RQ was at rest 32% of the total energy expenditure,

71.5% during the first work period, 47% at the end of exercise and as a mean 61% during the whole work.

The hepatic glucose output, if burned completely to CO_2 and water, was responsible for 93.6% of the carbohydrate utilization at rest, 39% at the end of the work and 23% as a mean during the total exercise. Of the total energy substrates used hepatic glucose output accounted for 14% during the whole exercise period and for 19% at the end.

Similar but slightly higher figures for hepatic glucose utilization were reported by Wahren et al [40]. By a combination of direct determination of hepatic glucose output and uptake of glucose over exercising leg muscles they could calculate the fraction of carbohydrate utilized by the exercising legs which was derived from blood-borne glucose produced by the liver. They found at the end of an exercise with a high workload that 75% to 89% of the locally utilized carbohydrate was derived from hepatic glucose release. Of the total substrates oxidized by the muscle at this point 28% to 37% was derived from blood glucose.

At low work intensities the rate of glucose release from the liver is lower. In a study by Ahlborg et al [2] the hepatic glucose release at rest was 0.82 mmol/min. After 90, 180 and 240 minutes of exercise the amounts released were 1.85, 1.92 and 1.46 mmol/min, respectively. This glucose release, if oxidized by the working muscles, corresponded to 41%, 36% and 30%, respectively, of the total oxygen uptake by the muscles.

Thus, it seems undisputable today that during exercise the hepatic output of glucose is important as an energy source for the working muscles.

Glycogenolysis During Exercise

Direct measurements of the liver glycogen store were made by the percutaneous liver biopsy technique. A liver biopsy was taken in the morning in the postprandial state after one hour of bicycle exercise and the glycogen content in the tissue specimen was compared with liver tissue obtained from a similar group of subjects after one hour of rest in the postprandial state. As a mean the liver glycogen content was found to be 125 mmol lower per kilogram liver after exercise than after rest. This decrease would correspond to an output of glucose from the liver of 2.08 mmol per kilogram liver per minute from glycogenolysis. This value fits surprisingly well with data of total output of hepatic glucose during exercise found by measurement in liver vein catheterization studies, i.e., 2.4 to 3.1 mmol/min [17] and 2.2 to 3.8 mmol/min [40].

Gluconeogenesis During Exercise

Maximum gluconeogenesis during exercise was calculated from total uptake of gluconeogenic substrate (lactate, pyruvate, glycerol and amino acids) by the splanchnic area. The uptake after 30 to 40 minutes of exercise showed only marginal increases over the value at rest corresponding to 0.27 mmol glucose per minute at low loads and 0.22 mmol at high workload compared to 0.21 mmol at rest [39, 40]. In percent of total glucose output the gluconeogenesis could account for 16% and 6% during the exercise periods as compared to 25% at rest.

Of the gluconeogenic substrates taken up both at rest and during exercise lactate is quantitatively the dominating one. At rest and during exercise at low to moderate workloads about 50% of the gluconeogenesis was derived from lactate. At increasing workloads the dominance of lactate as gluconeogenic substrate increased [39, 40].

Other individual substrates are quantitatively of minor importance. Several amino acids are taken up by the splanchnic area, but only alanine showed a constant release from working muscle and a splanchnic uptake at all levels of work intensity. The splanchnic uptake of alanine during exercise exceeded that of all other amino acids [14]. However, at high workloads less than 1% of the splanchnic glucose production could be attributed to alanine uptake [39].

At low workloads, at which work periods of several hours' duration could be sustained, the uptake of gluconeogenic precursors is of quantitative importance. Thus, it was shown that after four hours of light exercise, the splanchnic uptake of gluconeogenic precursors increased two- to tenfold and was sufficient to account for 45% of the glucose release. The dominating substrates during the prolonged exercise were lactate and glycerol. The total amino acid uptake over the splanchnic organs could at a maximum account for 8% of the glucose production after four hours of exercise and the alanine uptake for only half of that.

Thus, the alanine shunt described by Felig and Wahren [14] is of quantitatively negligible importance as a provider of energy substrate during exercise, especially at moderate to high workloads. On the other hand, both alanine and glutamine function as transporters of amino groups from working muscles to the splanchnic organs and the kidneys.

Dietary Effects on Hepatic Glucose Release
During Exercise

In an earlier study made in our laboratory [3], it was found that of those subjects performing a standardized bicycle exercise after different diets (CHO-rich, mixed or CHO-poor) those receiving a CHO-rich diet were able to sustain the work longest. This was attributed to a greater amount of glycogen stored in the muscles after this diet. In those subjects receiving the CHO-poor diet, it was further noted that the blood glucose level frequently decreased to subnormal levels. In these subjects, who had a shorter work time than those on mixed diet, it seems probable that insufficient supply of blood-borne glucose to the muscles was limiting the exercise.

As is obvious from Tables I and III, the liver glycogen store is different after a CHO-rich and CHO-poor diet. This difference could be the reason for the inability to release sufficient amounts of glucose during hard muscular work. However, in an earlier study with liver vein catheterization in two subjects, one on a CHO-rich and one on a CHO-poor diet [19], it was observed that glucose release from the liver was only slightly lower in the subject exercising after the CHO-poor diet. The study showed that in this latter subject the hepatic glucose released was derived mainly from gluconeogenesis; 54% of the glucose released could be accounted for by lactate uptake by the splanchnic area. The corresponding value for hepatic glucose released by the subject pre-fed with the CHO-rich diet was 5.6%. These two subjects were both sedentary and showed a high lactate concentration in blood during the exercise. The extraction ratio over the splanchnic area for lactate, α-amino acids and glycerol was much higher in the subject pretreated with the CHO-poor diet (Fig. 7, Table VII).

To confirm whether this observation was valid also in well-trained subjects the study was repeated in five others all of whom exercised regularly (students at the College of Physical Education or active athletes). Eight experiments were performed with liver vein catheterization during exercise after pretreatment of the subjects during four days with a CHO-poor or a CHO-rich diet.

They all showed the same pattern with increased gluconeogenesis rate during exercise after the CHO-poor diet compared with earlier data on exercise after mixed diet [17, 40] or with the subjects receiving the CHO-rich diet.

Two of the subjects will be presented in detail. They both worked at a load of approximately 80% of their $\dot{V}O_2$ max, once after a CHO-poor and once after a CHO-rich diet.

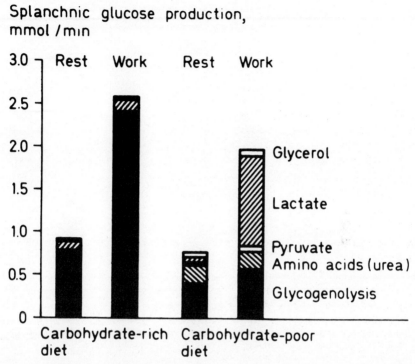

FIG. 7. Splanchnic glucose production at rest and during exercise. One subject was given CHO-rich diet for three days, the other CHO-poor. Total glucose production from the splanchnic area was measured as well as uptake of gluconeogenic substrates. Maximum glucose production from gluconeogenesis was calculated from uptake of substrates. The difference between maximum gluconeogenesis and total glucose production is depicted as glycogenolysis. For details, see Table VII.

The work schedule was the same; after liver vein catheterization and a rest period, a first work of 20-minutes duration was performed on a bicycle ergometer. This was followed by a ten-minute relative rest period with continued pedaling at a low workload. Thereafter, the work was resumed at the predetermined load until exhaustion.

Splanchnic blood flow, release of glucose and uptake of substrates were determined at five-minute intervals during the first rest period, as well as during the two work periods. Muscle biopsies for glycogen determination were obtained during the initial rest period and at the end of the first and second exercise periods. The blood levels of glucose and gluconeogenic substrates are presented in Figures 8 and 9.

Table VII. Splanchnic Carbohydrate Metabolism

Metabolite Shift Mean Values mmol/Min	Carbohydrate Rich Diet		Carbohydrate Poor Diet	
	Rest	Work	Rest	Work
Glucose production	0.92	2.59	0.77	1.99
Lactate uptake	0.25	0.29	0.13	2.14
Pyruvate uptake	0.02	0.02	0.03	0.11
Glycerol uptake	0.04	0.04	0.11	0.13
a-Amino acid uptake	0.61	0.07	0.80	0.50
Alanine uptake	0.13	0.04	0.18	0.14
Urea production	0	0.03	0.30	0.27
Oxygen uptake	2.43	2.70	2.44	4.46
Total glucose production mmol		57.55		49.50
Total uptake of metabolites mmol		9.0		72.2
Total calculated maximal gluconeogenesis mmol		4.5		36.1
Calculated glyco-genolysis mmol		53.0 (8.6 gm)		13.4 (2.2 gm)

Splanchnic metabolism during rest and exercise in subjects pretreated for four days with a CHO-rich diet, respectively (Fig. 7). Metabolite shifts were calculated as mean values (mmol/min) of three rest periods and four to six work periods in each subject. The total production of glucose and uptake of metabolites were calculated on the whole work period.

As can be seen the glucose, lactate, pyruvate and alanine levels in arterial blood at rest were higher after the CHO-rich than after the CHO-poor diet. The hepatic venous-arterial (Hv-A) glucose difference was greater especially during the second work period after the CHO-rich diet in subject TL and this work period was prolonged by 40 minutes (total work time increased from 43 to 83.5 minutes). At the end of the work the Hv-A glucose difference was 4 and 14 mmol/liter after the different diets, respectively. The splanchnic extraction ratio of lactate was near to zero after the CHO-rich diet and pyruvate was released instead of extracted. Similarly, alanine and glycerol uptakes were lower after the CHO-rich than after the CHO-poor diet (Fig. 8). There was a significant drop in arterial glucose concentration at the end of the exercise after the CHO-poor diet.

In subject SL the same pattern was seen with lower glucose release and higher extraction ratio of gluconeogenic substrates after the CHO-poor than after the CHO-rich diet. Also in this subject release of pyruvate from the liver at rest and during most of the

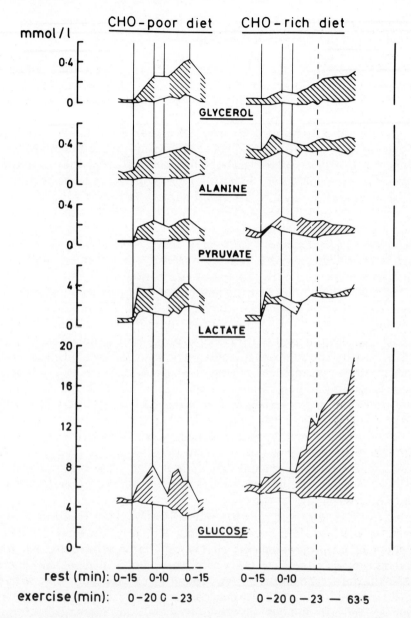

FIG. 8. Arterial and H-V contents of glucose and gluconeogenic substrates in subject TL working with the same workload (200 w) after CHO-poor and CHO-rich diet.

\\\\\\= hepatic extraction

///// = hepatic release

exercise period was seen after the CHO-rich diet, in contrast to the uptake after the CHO-poor diet (Fig. 9).

In Table VIII the total amount of carbohydrate utilized during exercise has been calculated. As may be seen the total amount utilized by exhaustion was in subject TL three times greater after the CHO-rich than after the CHO-poor diet. In subject SL the increase was smaller though still 70%.

After the CHO-poor diet the calculated total amount of liver glycogen used was 80.1 mmol glucose units in subject TL and 42.8 in subject SL. These values are of the same order as the total liver glycogen store measured in biopsy studies after the same period of CHO-poor diet, i.e., 12 to 73 mmol glucose units per kilogram liver, or totally 20 to 130 mmol (Tables I and III). It is thus reasonable to suppose that in these cases the liver glycogen store was completely depleted by exhaustion and may have been limiting to the performance capacity. An indication of this is the decrease in arterial glucose level seen in both subjects at exhaustion.

After the CHO-rich diet the amount of liver glycogen utilized was four to five times higher, i.e., 322.2 and 196.6 mmol glucose units, respectively. However, these figures do not exceed the expected initial glycogen content after this type of diet (Tables I and III). Thus, despite the increase in total work time and total utilization of carbohydrate, there is no reason to suspect that the liver glycogen store is limiting to performance. Significantly, the blood glucose level was not decreased at exhaustion in either subject after the CHO-rich diet.

As may be seen the muscle glycogen store was also increased by the CHO-rich diet. However, at exhaustion the muscle glycogen store was almost equally depleted after either diet. This suggests that it might be the muscle glycogen store which is limiting to performance capacity irrespective of the diet.

After the CHO-rich diet the rate of total CHO utilization during exercise was increased in both subjects. Similarly, the rate of hepatic glucose release was increased mainly due to an augmented hepatic glycogenolysis rate. Simultaneously, there was a decrease in gluco-neogenic rate. The opposite was found after CHO-poor diet with a lower rate of total CHO utilization, a lower rate of total hepatic glucose release and of glycogenolysis but an increased rate of gluconeogenesis (Table VIII). In Table IX the contribution of the different gluconeogenic substrates to glucose production from the splanchnic area after the two different diets is presented. After the CHO-poor diet the rate and total uptake of the different gluco-

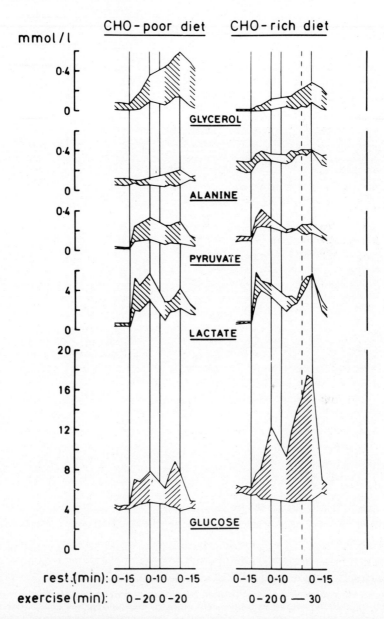

FIG. 9. Arterial and hepatic venous contents of glucose and gluconeogenic substrates in subject SL working with the same workload (205 w) after CHO-poor and CHO-rich diet.

\\\\\ = hepatic extraction

///// = hepatic release

Table VIII. Carbohydrate Metabolism During Exercise in Two Subjects
(TL and SL) Each Working Twice to Exhaustion at the Same Relative Work Load
After 4 Days With CHO-Poor and CHO-Rich Diet

	Subject TL		Subject SL	
	CHO-Poor Diet	CHO-Rich Diet	CHO-Poor Diet	CHO-Rich Diet
1. Total work time, min	43.1	89.5	42.0	52.0
2. Work load, watts	200	200	205	205
3. Rate of oxygen uptake, liter/min	2.83	2.65	3.00	2.84
4. Calculated total CHO oxidized:				
a. mmol glucose units	454.3	1343.0	364.4	593.2
b. % of oxygen uptake accounted for	50	80	37	58
5. Lactate accumulated at the end of exercise, mmol in total body water	94.5	81.8	85.2	177.0
6. Calculated total CHO utilized:				
a. mmol glucose units	501.6	1383.9	407.0	681.7
b. mmol glucose units/min	11.63	15.46	9.69	13.11
7. Calculated total CHO output from hepatic glycogenolysis:				
a. mmol glucose units	80.1	322.2	42.8	196.6
b. mmol glucose units/min	3.57	3.76	1.74	4.17
c. % of total CHO utilized	16.0	23.3	10.5	28.8
8. Glycogen content of *m. quadriceps femoris*				
a. before exercise, mmol glucose units/kg muscle	46.0	100.4	69.0	92.5
b. after exercise, mmol glucose units/kg muscle	6.8	10.1	14.8	20.4
9. Calculated CHO utilization from muscle glycogen:				
a. mmol glucose units	421.5	1061.2	364.2	485.1
b. mmol glucose units/min	9.8	11.9	8.7	9.3
c. % of total CHO utilized	84.0	76.7	89.5	71.2
10. Calculated amount of muscle depleted of glycogen by the end of exercise, kg	10.8	11.7	6.7	6.7

4. Calculated from O_2 uptake and RQ (in expired air).

5. Arterial concentration of lactate at the end of exercise multiplied by 60% of body weight.

6. Sum of 4a and 5.

7. Total hepatic glucose release minus uptake of gluconeogenic substrates.

8. Determined in biopsy specimens.

9. Calculated as 6 minus 7. The calculation infers that the only important sources for carbohydrate utilization during exercise are the glycogen stores in liver and muscle. Gluconeogenic substrates as lactate, pyruvate and part of alanine circulate between muscle and liver. Additional substrates contributing to the carbohydrate moiety are glycerol from triglycerides and some amino acids from muscle protein. The contributions of these substrates are quantitatively of minor importance (Table IX).

10. 9a/8a–8b.

Table IX. Splanchnic Carbohydrate Metabolism During Exercise
After Different Diets in Two Subjects, TL and SL.
Results Continued From Table VIII

Metabolite Shift Mean Values in mmol Glucose Equivalents Per Min	TL		SL	
	CHO-Poor Diet	CHO-Rich Diet	CHO-Poor Diet	CHO-Rich Diet
Glucose production	3.57	3.76	1.74	4.17
Lactate uptake	1.33	0.14	0.57	0.33
Pyruvate uptake or release	0.15	−0.03	0.02	−0.03
Glycerol uptake	0.13	0.05	0.08	0.03
Alanine uptake	0.09	0.03	0.05	0.03
Calculated maximum gluconeogenesis rate	1.71	0.09	0.73	0.36
Calculated glycogenolysis rate	1.86	3.60	1.02	3.78
Glycogenolysis in % of hepatic glucose release	52.1	95.7	58.6	90.6

neogenic substrates corresponded to 41% to 48% of hepatic glucose
release and was higher than observed in earlier studies after a mixed
diet during exercise with a corresponding workload [17, 40]. Again,
lactate was the dominating gluconeogenic substrate but the uptakes
of pyruvate, alanine and glycerol were also increased. A similar result
was found by Wahren et al [41] in diabetic patients deprived of
insulin.

After the CHO-rich diet the uptake of gluconeogenic precursors
corresponded to a maximum gluconeogenic rate of 0.1 to 0.36 mmol
glucose per minute or 4.4% to 9.4% of the total hepatic glucose
release. The remaining glucose was apparently derived from glycogenolysis. A low hepatic extraction was found for all the gluconeogenic precursors after this diet, and pyruvate was actually
released from the liver.

Thus, the observed differences in hepatic carbohydrate metabolism during exercise after the two diets are increased gluconeogenesis
rate after CHO-poor diet, as calculated from uptake of precursors,
predominantly lactate, and increased glucogenolysis rate after CHO-
rich diet with very low uptake of gluconeogenic precursors.

The reason for the difference in substrate utilization after the
two different diets could be of hormonal origin. It is known today
that glycogenolysis as well as gluconeogenesis is dependent upon the
relation between insulin and glucagon [38]: a low insulin-glucagon
quotient enhancing glycogenolysis and gluconeogenesis. It is also

known that the effect of starvation or CHO-free diet is to decrease insulin production and to increase that of glucagon [1, 10]. Such a bihormonal change would increase c-AMP in the liver. Increased c-AMP content in blood was also seen after glucagon administration in man [8, 9] and it was also shown that a dose response existed between the amount of glucagon given and the plasma content of c-AMP. In isolated rat liver the glucose content in the perfusate correlated well with the c-AMP content when glucagon was given [8, 9].

In the present study the c-AMP content in arterial and hepatic venous blood was determined at rest and during exercise. From Figure 10 it can be seen that along with the increased concentration of glucose in the hepatic venous blood there was also an increase in c-AMP content. The increase in c-AMP after the CHO-rich diet was lower in relation to glucose content than after the CHO-poor diet, but the absolute concentration of c-AMP at the end of exercise (which is concomitant with the highest content of Hv-glucose) was similar after the two diets.

An increase in glucagon with simultaneous decrease in insulin (for insulin see Table X) would stimulate gluconeogenesis [13] and could thus explain the augmented substrate uptake after the CHO-poor diet. This effect has been observed in rats after a diet with high protein and low carbohydrate content [13]. However, this would not explain the difference in glycogenolysis rate during exercise after the two different diets since the c-AMP content in hepatic venous blood was the same. Clearly, other factors must be operative, such as differences in the size of the liver glycogen store.

Table X. Plasma Insulin Concentration (mU/l) in Hv and Arterial Blood At Rest and At End of Exercise After Different Diets

Subject	Plasma	CHO-Poor Diet		CHO-Rich Diet	
		Rest	End of Exercise	Rest	End of Exercise
TL	Hv	4.50	3.52	10.49	6.22
	Arterial	4.13	2.76	7.98	5.25
SL	Hv	5.66	3.32	9.10	3.50
	Arterial	4.07	2.33	6.68	3.19

All values are mean of three to four plasma samples.

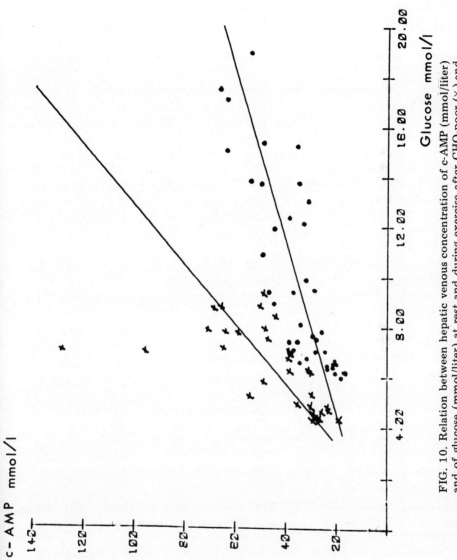

FIG. 10. Relation between hepatic venous concentration of c-AMP (mmol/liter) and of glucose (mmol/liter) at rest and during exercise after CHO-poor (×) and CHO-rich (•) diets.

Summary

The liver glycogen content *at rest* was shown to vary considerably with the diet. Thus, the normal glycogen store of 270 mmol glucose units per kilogram liver decreased after only one day of CHO-poor diet to 37 mmol/kg, and the liver glycogen store remained low during a continued period of CHO-poor diet.

Refeeding a CHO-rich diet increased the liver glycogen content within one day to high values (mean 467 mmol glucose units per kilogram).

The glycogenolysis rate decreased from a normal rate of 0.54 mmol/min to zero or close to zero after a CHO-poor diet.

The gluconeogenesis rate was normally 0.30 mmol/min and was unchanged after three to four days of CHO-poor diet. Consequently, the glucose release from the liver decreased by 66% during the CHO-poor diet period.

During exercise after normal diet the glycogenolysis rate in the liver increased three to four times releasing up to 3.8 mmol glucose per minute. Also, the gluconeogenesis rate increased during exercise but only marginally after normal diet intake. During exercise with high workloads, the uptake of gluconeogenic substrates could maximally correspond to 6% to 11% of the total hepatic glucose release measured at the end of the work period.

After a CHO-poor diet resulting in a low glycogen store in the liver, the glycogenolysis rate during exercise was lower, but still a high rate of glucose release from the liver was observed due to an enhanced uptake of gluconeogenic substrates. Gluconeogenesis in this situation was responsible for 40% to 70% of the hepatic glucose release during the exercise. Quantitatively the dominating gluconeogenic substrate was lactate.

The amount of liver glycogen utilized during the exercise was of the same order as the total glycogen store found in the liver after a similar period of CHO-poor diet. Thus, it seems probable that the preformed glycogen store in the liver could be limiting to exercise performance time. A decrease in arterial glucose concentration at the end of exercise was also observed.

After a CHO-rich diet with a high liver glycogen store the glycogenolysis rate during exercise was increased compared to a similar exercise after a CHO-poor diet.

Parallel with the increase in glycogenolysis rate a decrease in gluconeogenesis was observed.

The uptake of lactate was low, pyruvate was actually released from the liver, and also the uptakes of alanine and glycerol were lower than after the CHO-poor diet. Total gluconeogenesis could maximally account for 3% to 9% of the hepatic glucose release during the exercise after the CHO-rich diet.

Glycogenolysis, although showing a rate increase of four- to fivefold compared with the rate after the CHO-poor diet, did not seem to be limited by lack of substrate since the observed glycogen content in the liver after this type of diet exceeded the calculated amount released during the exercise. No decrease in blood sugar was seen during the prolonged exhaustive exercise after the CHO-rich diet.

It seems probable that the regulation of liver carbohydrate metabolism during exercise after different diets is dependent upon both hormonal influences and on the size of the glycogen store.

References

1. Aguilar-Parada, E., Eisentraut, A.M. and Unger, R.H.: Diabetes 18:717, 1969.
2. Ahlborg, G., Felig, P., Hagenfeldt, L. et al: J. Clin. Invest. 53:1080, 1974.
3. Bergström, J., Hermansen, L., Hultman, E. and Saltin, B.: Acta Physiol. Scand. 71:140, 1967.
4. Bergström, J., Hultman, E. and Roch-Norlund, A.E.: Scand. J. Clin. Lab. Invest. 29:127, 1972.
5. Bergström, J., Hultman, E. and Roch-Norlund, A.E.: Acta Med. Scand. 184:359, 1968.
6. Bode, C., Schumacher, H., Goebell, H. et al: Horm. Metab. Res. 3:289, 1971.
7. Bode, C., Zelder, O., Rumpelt, H.J. and Wittkamp, U.: Europ. J. Clin. Invest. 3:436, 1973.
8. Broadus, A.E., Kaminsky, N.I., Hardman, J.G. et al: J. Clin. Invest. 49:222, 1970.
9. Broadus, A.E., Kaminsky, N.I., Northcutt, R.C. et al: J. Clin. Invest. 49:2237, 1970.
10. Cahill, G.F. Jr., Herrera, M.G., Morgan, A.P. et al: J. Clin. Invest. 45:1751, 1966.
11. Cahill, G.F. and Owen, O.E.: In Dickens, F., Randle, P.J. and Whelan (eds.): Carbohydrate Metabolism and Its Disorders. Vol. 1. New York:Academic Press, 1968, p. 497.
12. Danforth, W.H.: J. Biol. Chem. 240:558, 1968.
13. Eisenstein, A.B., Strack, I. and Steiner, A.: Metabolism 23:15, 1974.
14. Felig, P. and Wahren, J.: J. Clin. Invest. 50:2703, 1971.
15. Flatt, J.P., Blackburn, G.L., Randers, G. and Stanbury, J.B.: Metabolism 23:151, 1974.
16. Gottstein, U., Müller, W., Berghoff, W. et al: Klin. Wschr. 49:406, 1971.
17. Hultman, E.: Scand. J. Clin. Lab. Invest. 19 Suppl. 94, 1967.
18. Hultman, E. and Nilsson, L.H:son: Nutr. Metab. 18 Suppl. 1:45, 1975.
19. Hultman, E. and Nilsson, L.H:son: In: Keul, J. (ed.): Limiting Factors of Physical Performance. Int. Symp. at Gravenbruch 1971. Stuttgart:Georg Thieme Publishers, 1973, p. 113.

20. Hultman, E. and Nilsson, L.H:son: *In*: Pernow, B. and Saltin, B. (eds.): Advances in Experimental Medicine and Biology. Vol. 11. New York: Plenum, 1971, p. 143.
21. Issekutz, B., Issekutz, A.C. and Nash, D.J.: Appl. Physiol. 29:691, 1970.
22. Kekomäki, M., Raivio, K.O. and Mäenpää, P.H.: Acta Anaesth. Scand. Suppl. 27:114, 1970.
23. Krebs, H.A., Cornell, N.W., Lund, P. and Hems, L.R.: *In* Lundquist, F. and Tygstrup, N. (eds.): Regulation of Hepatic Metabolism. Copenhagen: Munksgaard, 1974, p. 549.
24. Krebs, H.A., Williamson, D.H., Bates, M.W. et al: Adv. Enzyme Regul. 9:387, 1971.
25. Mäenpää, P.H., Raivio, K.O. and Kekomäki, M.P.: Science 161:1253, 1968.
26. Marliss, E.B., Aoki, T.T., Pozefsky, T. et al: J. Clin. Invest. 50:814, 1971.
27. Nilsson, L.H:son: Scand. J. Clin. Lab. Invest. 32:317, 1973.
28. Nilsson, L.H:son, Fürst, P. and Hultman, E.: Scand. J. Clin. Lab. Invest. 32:331, 1973.
29. Nilsson, L.H:son and Hultman, E.: Scand. J. Clin. Lab. Invest. 32:325, 1973.
30. Nilsson, L.H:son and Hultman, E.: Scand. J. Clin. Lab. Invest. 33:5, 1974.
31. Owen, O.E., Morgan, A.P., Kemp, H.G. et al: J. Clin. Invest. 46:1589, 1967.
32. Potter, V.R. and Ono, T.: Cold Spring Harbor Symp. Q. Biol. 26:355, 1961.
33. Ray, P.D., Foster, D.O. and Lardy, H.A.: J. Biol. Chem. 241:3904, 1966.
34. Ross, B.D., Hems, R., Freedland, R.A. and Krebs, H.A.: Biochem. J. 105:869, 1967.
35. Rowell, L.B.: *In* Pernow, B. and Saltin, B. (eds.): Advances in Experimental Medicine and Biology. Vol. 11. New York:Plenum, 1971, p. 127.
36. Rowell, L.B., Masoro, E.J. and Spencer, M.J.: J. Appl. Physiol. 20:1032, 1965.
37. Sugden, P.O. and Newsholme, E.A.: Biochem. J. 134:97, 1973.
38. Unger, R.H.: Metabolism 23:581, 1974.
39. Wahren, J., Ahlborg, G., Felig, P. and Jorfeldt, L.: *In* Pernow, B. and Saltin, B. (eds.): Advances in Experimental Medicine and Biology. Vol. 11. New York:Plenum, 1971, p. 189.
40. Wahren, J., Felig, P., Ahlborg, G. and Jorfeldt, L.: J. Clin. Invest. 50:2715, 1971.
41. Wahren, J., Hagenfeldt, L. and Felig, P.: Israel J. Med. Sci. 11:551, 1975.
42. Williamson, D.H., Bates, M.W. and Krebs, H.A.: Biochem. J. 121:41, 1971.
43. Woods, H.F., Eggleston, L.V. and Krebs, H.A.: Biochem. J. 119:501, 1970.

Régulation du métabolisme des hydrates de carbone dans le foie, au repos ou pendant l'effort, et importance du régime alimentaire

Examen de la production de glucose dans le foie au repos et sa mobilisation, pendant l'effort, par la réalisation de la glycogénolyse et de la gluconéogénèse; l'auteur fait état d'expériences sur des humains et sur des animaux, dans des conditions d'alimentation normales et dans des conditions d'alimentation pauvres ou riches en hydrates de carbone. On suppose que la régulation du métabolisme des hydrates de carbone dans le foie pendant l'effort physique, après différents régimes, dépend des influences hormonales et du volume des réserves de glycogène.

Sources of Fatty Acids for Oxidation During Exercise

L. B. Oscai, J. A. McGarr and J. Borensztajn

The major sources of the fatty acids oxidized during exercise
are described as the free fatty acids originating from the
adipocytes, the plasmatriacylglycerols and the intramuscular
triacylglycerol stores. Data obtained on animals are presented
and discussed relative to the effects of endurance training on
the levels of activity of the enzyme responsible for the
hydrolysis of triacylglycerols in adipocytes and on the enzyme
responsible for removing the triacylglycerols from circulation
by muscle. Evidence is provided to the fact that the lipolytic
activity of adipocytes is sufficiently large to meet the
increased demands for FFA imposed by vigorous exercise. It is
shown that regularly performed endurance exercise can
increase the levels of activity of lipoprotein lipase in fast-
twitch red, fast-twitch white and slow-twitch red fibers of
rodent skeletal muscle.

Introduction

Numerous studies are available to show that fat can serve as the
major energy source for skeletal muscle metabolism during prolonged
exercise [15, 18, 25, 26, 43, 44, 53]. The amount of fat oxidized
during exercise appears to vary with the individual's level of physical
training. Exercise-trained men and animals derive more of their
energy from fatty acid oxidation than do untrained during exercise
of submaximal intensity [3, 15, 31]. This difference in fat utilization
may be explained in part by the observation that exercise-training
can increase by twofold the capacity of skeletal muscle to oxidize
fat [38]. Fatty acids oxidized during exercise are thought to be
derived from three major sources: free fatty acids originating from
adipocytes, plasma triacylglycerols [34] and intramuscular triacyl-

---

L. B. Oscai, J. A. McGarr and J. Borensztajn, Department of Physical
Education, University of Illinois at Chicago Circle, Chicago, and Department of
Pathology, Pritzker School of Medicine, University of Chicago, Illinois, U.S.A.
This work was supported by Public Health Research Grants AM-17357,
AM-16831 and HL-17296 and by the Chicago and Illinois Heart Association.

glycerol stores [28]. A paucity of data exists regarding the extent, if any, to which exercise-training can result in an increased capacity of adipose tissue to mobilize fatty acids and of muscle to utilize triacylglycerols found in circulation or stored in its cells. In our initial studies dealing with these problems, an attempt was made to examine the effects of regularly performed endurance exercise on the levels of activity of the enzyme responsible for the hydrolysis of triacylglycerols in adipocytes (hormone-sensitive lipase) and on the enzyme responsible for removal of triacylglycerols from circulation by muscle (lipoprotein lipase). The present discussion deals with the progress we have made in these areas.

Methods

Our studies were conducted on male rats of a Wistar strain (specific pathogen-free CFN rats from Charles River). The animals were divided into three groups. An exercising group was trained to run on a Quinton Instruments 42-15 rodent treadmill and exercised five days per week [27]. The speed and duration of the run were progressively increased over 12 weeks until the animals were running continuously for 120 minutes at 31 m/min, up an 8° incline, with 12 intervals of running at 42 m/min, each lasting 30 seconds, spaced 10 minutes apart through the exercise sessions. They were maintained at this work level until they were sacrificed. The exercising rats were fed ad libitum.

A paired-weight sedentary group had its food intake restricted so as to maintain its rate of weight gain at approximately that of the exercisers. A freely eating sedentary group was provided with food ad libitum. These two groups of sedentary animals were not subjected to treadmill running.

Glycerol release was determined by the method of Garland and Randle [22].

Procedures for incubation, extraction and measurement of free fatty acid release have been previously described [11].

Effect of Exercise on Lipolysis in Adipocytes

In exercise-trained rats, sacrificed immediately after their last bout of work, lipolysis was significantly higher than that in freely eating sedentary controls, when the results were expressed per gram adipose tissue (P <0.001; Table I). Since the diameter of the cells in the epididymal fat pads of the treadmill runners was significantly reduced compared to that of the sedentary controls (68.7 ± 2.7 μ vs.

Table I. Glycerol Released From Adipocytes of Physically Trained Rats
Sacrificed Immediately After a Two Hour Treadmill Run*

Group	Glycerol Released μmol/hr per gm		Glycerol Released μmol/hr per cell × 10^6	
	+ Epinephrine	– Epinephrine	+ Epinephrine	– Epinephrine
Exercising (9)	7.54 ± 0.77	6.42 ± 0.99	1.27 ± 0.10	1.04 ± 0.08
Sedentary, freely eating (11)	2.96 ± 0.22	2.04 ± 0.26	1.11 ± 0.07	0.76 ± 0.09

*Data from McGarr [36].
Values are means ± SE; number of animals per group is given in parentheses.

82.0 ± 2.7 μ; P <0.01), the increase in lipolysis could have been a reflection of difference in cell size. A reduction in the diameter of adipocytes has been a consistent finding in epididymal pads of highly trained rats [2, 40, 42]. As a result, it appeared to us that expressing the values on a per cell basis was the most meaningful reference when relating the lipolytic capacity of adipose tissue cells to their levels of enzyme activity. Viewed in this context, Table I shows that glycerol release remained significantly elevated (P <0.05) in adipocytes of the trained animals sacrificed immediately after their last bout of work. When the tissue was incubated in the presence of epinephrine, lipolysis was stimulated in adipocytes of both the exercise-trained and sedentary control animals, but to a greater extent in adipocytes of control animals so that the difference in glycerol release between the two groups was no longer apparent (Table I). In animals sacrificed 24 hours after exercise, glycerol release from adipocytes of physically trained rats was essentially the same as that of freely eating sedentary controls (Table II). Although the underlying reason for an increase in lipolysis in tissue not exposed to epinephrine from animals sacrificed immediately after exercise remains unclear, two possibilities can be advanced. One possibility is that in addition to measuring the amount of glycerol released from the fat cells as a result of lipolysis during incubation, we were also measuring a significant amount of glycerol that might have accumulated in adipocytes as a result of triacylglycerol hydrolysis during the two-hour exercise session. This possibility seems unlikely, however, because glycerol release under all experimental conditions was found to be linear with time over the incubation period. A more likely possibility is that the adipocytes of the animals killed immediately after exercise were already stimulated by sufficient amounts of epinephrine as a result of the treadmill run to cause a significant increase in lipolysis during incubation. In this context, it is of

Table II. Glycerol Released From Adipocytes of Physically Trained Rats
Sacrificed 24 Hours After Exercise*

	Glycerol Released $\mu mol/hr$ per gm		Glycerol Released $\mu mol/hr$ per cell $\times$ 10^6	
	+ Epinephrine	- Epinephrine	+ Epinephrine	- Epinephrine
Exercising	6.62 ± 0.71 (12)	3.41 ± 0.65 (10)	1.25 ± 0.11 (12)	0.65 ± 0.14 (10)
Sedentary, paired-weight	2.80 ± 0.25 (13)	1.49 ± 0.16 (9)	1.14 ± 0.14 (13)	0.63 ± 0.09 (9)
Sedentary, freely eating	2.70 ± 0.15 (12)	1.81 ± 0.21 (12)	1.16 ± 0.15 (12)	0.67 ± 0.09 (12)

*Data from McGarr [36].
  Values are means ± SE; number of glycerol release determinations per group is given in
  parentheses.

interest that catecholamine levels in the blood increase markedly in
response to a bout of prolonged vigorous exercise [24, 39, 51] while
the concentration of insulin, which has an antilipolytic effect, is
markedly lowered [47]. The above results suggest, therefore, that
when adipocytes are stimulated maximally, tissues from exercise-
trained as well as untrained animals are able to mobilize equivalent
amounts of fatty acids. These results could help to explain the
observation that free fatty acid levels in plasma of trained men and
animals are actually lower than those of untrained counterparts
during exercise of submaximal intensity [32, 33, 47, 52]. This is true
because exercise training results in an increased capacity to oxidize
fat. It appears, therefore, that during exercise, hormone-sensitive
lipase activity is markedly elevated, presumably in response to
catecholamine stimulation, to account for the increased free fatty
acid mobilization seen with a single bout of work [7, 49], but
returns to preexercise levels shortly after work.

Effect of Exercise on Lipoprotein Lipase Activity

The removal of triacylglycerols from circulation by muscle, as
well as other extrahepatic tissues, is regulated by lipoprotein
lipase [48]. This enzyme hydrolyzes plasma triacylglycerols from
chylomicrons and very low density lipoproteins on the lumenal
surface of the endothelial cells of the capillaries and the fatty acids
released are then taken up by tissue to be oxidized or stored [48].

Three distinct fiber types have been identified in rodent skeletal
muscle. These fiber types, classified according to their metabolic and

mechanical characteristics, are fast-twitch red (high oxidative, high glycogenolytic, high myosin ATPase activity), fast-twitch white (low oxidative, high glycogenolytic, high myosin ATPase activity) and slow-twitch red (intermediate oxidative, low glycogenolytic, low myosin ATPase activity) [1, 6, 16, 23, 45]. Our results [10] show that marked differences in lipoprotein lipase (LPL) activity exist among the three muscle fiber types in sedentary animals (Table III). LPL activity in slow-twitch red fibers was approximately 14- to 20-fold higher than that in white fibers and approximately 2-fold higher (P <0.001) than that in fast-twitch red. Since the uptake of triacylglycerols from circulation in a variety of tissues such as adipose, muscle and the mammary gland appears to be directly related to their levels of lipoprotein lipase activity [21, 37, 48], the finding that the highest levels of LPL activity are in red muscle compared to that in white suggests that the major portion of plasma triacylglycerols is taken up by slow-twitch red and fast-twitch red fibers. In contrast, white fibers may have a much reduced capacity to take up triacylglycerols due to their extremely low levels of LPL activity. This interpretation is consistent with the observation that of the three fiber types only fast-twitch white has a low oxidative capacity [4].

Exercise training clearly resulted in a marked increase in LPL activity in the three fiber types (Table III). The largest increase occurred in fast-twitch red fibers. These fibers in the trained animals contained approximately three times the LPL activity as that found in sedentary freely eating animals. In contrast, LPL activity in slow-twitch red and fast-twitch white fibers increased approximately

Table III. Levels of Lipoprotein Lipase Activity in Skeletal Muscle
From Fasted Exercise-Trained and Sedentary Animals*

	Quadriceps		Soleus
Group	Fast-twitch Red	Fast-twitch White	Slow-twitch Red
		U/g Wet Wt.	
Sedentary, freely eating	11 ± 0.7 (13)	1.1 ± 0.2 (11)	21 ± 2 (12)
Sedentary, paired-weight	7 ± 0.4 (14)	1.3 ± 0.2 (10)	17 ± 1 (12)
Runners	31 ± 2.0 (14)	2.2 ± 0.2 (11)	35 ± 4 (12)

*Data from Borensztajn et al [10].
   One unit represents 1 μmole of free fatty acids released per hour incubation per
   gram wet weight tissue. Values are means ± SE. The number of LPL determinations
   per group is given in parentheses.

twofold in response to the program of treadmill running. These results provide suggestive evidence that the contribution of plasma triacylglycerols to the total oxidizable fatty acid pool is also increased. In this context, it is of interest that exercise can result in a reduction in plasma triacylglycerols [13, 20, 29, 35, 41].

Our results described above indicating that exercise training can cause marked increases in skeletal muscle LPL activity were observed in fasted rats. On the basis of evidence obtained from cardiac muscle and the diaphragm, it has been shown that LPL activity is considerably lower in fed rats than in fasted animals [8, 9, 50]. It was thought, therefore, that the decrease in LPL activity seen with feeding might mask the marked increase in enzyme activity seen in response to exercise training. As shown in Tables III and IV, LPL activity was lower in fast red (P <0.001) and slow red muscle fibers of fed animals than in those of fasted rats. Nevertheless, feeding did not prevent an approximate 2- to 2.5-fold rise in LPL activity as a result of exercise training. The finding that LPL activity in the red muscle of the fed exercisers (Table IV) was essentially the same as that of the fasted sedentary controls (Table III) indicates that exercise can counteract the effects of feeding on the levels of skeletal muscle LPL activity.

Levels of LPL activity in our experiments were routinely measured in fresh tissue homogenates of whole muscle. It should be pointed out that results from studies with whole homogenates of heart from starved rats have shown that the myocardium contains a functional and a nonfunctional LPL fraction [8]. The functional

Table IV. Levels of Lipoprotein Lipase Activity
in Skeletal Muscle From Fed Exercise-Trained
and Sedentary Animals

Group	Quadriceps Fast-twitch Red	Soleus Slow-twitch Red
	U/g Wet Wt.	
Sedentary, freely eating	6 ± 0.1 (10)	16 ± 1.5 (11)
Runners	16 ± 1.8* (11)	24 ± 1.1* (9)

*Runners vs. sedentary, freely eating, P < 0.001.

Following an overnight fast, animals were force-fed 3 ml of a 50% solution of dextrose and sacrificed three hours later.

One unit represents 1 μmole of free fatty acids released per hour incubation per gram wet weight tissue. Values are means ± SE. The number of LPL determinations per group is given in parentheses.

LPL fraction is present at the lumenal surface of the endothelial cells of the capillaries and is the enzyme fraction responsible for the hydrolysis of plasma triacylglycerols [48]. From the results of our work, it is not clear whether the significant increases in skeletal muscle LPL activity seen with exercise represent increases in the functional or nonfunctional enzyme. Further studies will be necessary to clarify this point.

The factors which participate in the regulation of LPL activity in skeletal muscle of treadmill runners remain to be investigated. Exercise is accompanied by an increased secretion of glucagon in the plasma [12, 17]. In skeletal muscle, however, elevated plasma glucagon levels may not have been responsible for the increase in LPL activity in the runners for two reasons. First, the animals were permitted to rest at least 24 hours after the last bout of exercise. Second, heart enzyme activity for the runners (88 ± 5 U/g wet wt) was approximately the same as that for the freely eating sedentary controls (92 ± 4 U/g wet wt) [10].

Conclusions

Lipids oxidized during exercise are thought to be derived from free fatty acids originating from adipocytes, plasma triacylglycerols [34] and intramuscular triacylglycerol stores [28]. Previously, it has been shown that between 25% and 50% of the fat oxidized during exercise comes from plasma free fatty acids [25, 30]. If an exercise-induced increase in the capacity to mobilize fatty acids from adipocytes were to occur, then a corresponding increase in the levels of activity of hormone-sensitive lipase would be expected. Our results provide evidence that the lipolytic capacity of adipocytes of normal, untrained rats is sufficiently large to meet the increased demand for free fatty acids imposed by a program of vigorous exercise without the need for an adaptive increase in enzyme activity.

In sedentary animals, it appears that mainly slow-twitch red and fast-twitch red fibers are capable of taking up plasma triacylglycerols. Regularly performed endurance exercise can increase, by two- to threefold, the levels of activity of LPL in the three fiber types of rodent skeletal muscle. The increase in LPL activity in response to treadmill running suggests that exercise increases the capacity of these fibers to take up and oxidize plasma triacylglycerols.

Intramuscular triacylglycerols appear to contribute significantly to the energy needs of muscle during prolonged endurance exer-

cise [5, 14, 19, 46]. The proportion of the contribution of
endogenous triacylglycerols, however, is unclear at the present time.

Acknowledgments

The authors express their appreciation to Ms. Suzan Bertucci for
assistance in the preparation of this manuscript.

References

1. Ariano, M.A., Armstrong, R.B. and Edgerton, V.R.: J. Histochem. Cytochem. 21:51, 1973.
2. Askew, E.W., Huston, R.L., Plopper, C.G. and Hecker, A.L.: J. Clin. Invest.
   56:521, 1975.
3. Åstrand, P.-O.: Fed. Proc. 26:1772, 1967.
4. Baldwin, K.M., Klinkerfuss, G.H., Terjung, R.L. et al: Am. J. Physiol.
   222:373, 1972.
5. Baldwin, K.M., Reitman, J.S., Terjung, R.L. et al: Am. J. Physiol.
   225:1045, 1973.
6. Barnard, R.J., Edgerton, V.R., Furukawa, T. and Peter, J.B.: Am. J. Physiol.
   220:410, 1971.
7. Basu, A., Passmore, R. and Strong, J.A.: Q. J. Exp. Physiol. 45:312, 1960.
8. Borensztajn, J. and Robinson, D.S.: J. Lipid Res. 11:111, 1970.
9. Borensztajn, J., Otway, S. and Robinson, D.S.: J. Lipid Res. 11:102, 1970.
10. Borensztajn, J., Rone, M.S., Babirak, S.P. et al: Am. J. Physiol. 229:394,
    1975.
11. Borensztajn, J., Samols, D.R. and Rubenstein, A.H.: Am. J. Physiol.
    223:1271, 1972.
12. Böttger, I., Schlein, E. M., Faloona, G.R. et al: J. Clin. Endocrinol. Metab.
    35:117, 1972.
13. Carlson, L.A. and Fröberg, S.O.: Gerontologia 15:14, 1969.
14. Carlson, L.A., Ekelund, L.-G. and Fröberg, S.O.: Eur. J. Clin. Invest. 1:248,
    1971.
15. Christensen, E.H. and Hansen, O.: Skand. Arch. Physiol. 81:160, 1939.
16. Close, R.I.: Physiol. Rev. 52:129, 1972.
17. Felig, P., Wahren, J., Hendler, R. and Ahlborg, G.: N. Engl. J. Med.
    287:184, 1972.
18. Friedberg, S.J., Sher, P.B., Bogdonoff, M.D. and Estes, E.H. Jr.: J. Lipid
    Res. 4:34, 1963.
19. Fröberg, S.O.: Metabolism 20:714, 1971.
20. Fröberg, S.O.: Metabolism 20:1044, 1971.
21. Garfinkel, A.S., Baker, N. and Schotz, M.C.: J. Lipid Res. 8:274, 1967.
22. Garland, P.B. and Randle, P.J.: Nature 196:987, 1962.
23. Gauthier, G.F. In Briskey, E.J., Cassens, R.G. and Marsh, B.B. (eds.): The
    Physiology and Biochemistry of Muscle as a Food, ed. 2. Madison:
    University of Wisconsin Press, 1970, p. 103.
24. Häggendal, J., Hartley, L.H. and Saltin, B.: Scand. J. Clin. Lab. Invest.
    26:337, 1970.
25. Havel, R.J., Carlson, L.A., Ekelund, L.-G. and Holmgren, A.: J. Appl.
    Physiol. 19:613, 1964.

26. Havel, R.J., Naimark, A. and Borchgrevink, C.F.: J. Clin. Invest. 42:1054, 1963.
27. Holloszy, J.O.: J. Biol. Chem. 242:2278, 1967.
28. Holloszy, J.O. and Booth, F.W.: Ann. Rev. Physiol. 38:273, 1976.
29. Holloszy, J.O., Skinner, J.S., Toro, G. and Cureton, T.K.: Am. J. Cardiol. 14:753, 1964.
30. Issekutz, B. Jr. and Paul, P.: Am. J. Physiol. 215:197, 1968.
31. Issekutz, B. Jr., Miller, H.I. and Rodahl, K.: Fed. Proc. 25:1415, 1966.
32. Johnson, R.H. and Walton, J.L.: Q. J. Exp. Physiol. 57:73, 1972.
33. Johnson, R.H., Walton, J.L., Krebs, H.A. and Williamson, D.H.: Lancet 2:452, 1969.
34. Jones, N.L. and Havel, R.J.: Am. J. Physiol. 213:824, 1967.
35. Lopez-s, A., Vial, R., Balart, L. and Arroyave, G.: Atherosclerosis 20:1, 1974.
36. McGarr, J.A., Oscai, L.B. and Borensztajn, J.: Am. J. Physiol. 230:385, 1976.
37. Mendelson, C.R. and Scow, R.O.: Am. J. Physiol. 223:1418, 1972.
38. Molé, P.A., Oscai, L.B. and Holloszy, J.O.: J. Clin. Invest. 50:2323, 1971.
39. Muir, G.G., Chamberlain, D.A. and Pedoe, D.T.: Lancet 2:930, 1964.
40. Oscai, L.B., Babirak, S.P., McGarr, J.A. and Spirakis, C.N.: Fed. Proc. 33:1956, 1974.
41. Oscai, L.B., Patterson, J.A., Bogard, D.L. et al: Am. J. Cardiol. 30:775, 1972.
42. Palmer, W.K. and Tipton, C.M.: Am. J. Physiol. 224:1206, 1973.
43. Paul, P.: In Pernow, B. and Saltin, B. (eds.): Muscle Metabolism During Exercise. New York:Plenum Press, 1971, p. 225.
44. Paul, P. and Issekutz, B. Jr.: J. Appl. Physiol. 22:615, 1967.
45. Peter, J.B., Barnard, R.J., Edgerton, V.R. et al: Biochemistry 11:2627, 1972.
46. Reitman, J., Baldwin, K.M. and Holloszy, J.O.: Proc. Soc. Exp. Biol. Med. 142:628, 1973.
47. Rennie, M.J., Jennett, S. and Johnson, R.H.: Q. J. Exp. Physiol. 59:201, 1974.
48. Robinson, D.S.: In Florkin, M. and Stotz, E.H. (eds.): Comprehensive Biochemistry. Amsterdam:Elsevier, Vol. 18, 1970, p. 51.
49. Rodahl, K., Miller, H.I. and Issekutz, B. Jr.: J. Appl. Physiol. 19:489, 1964.
50. Rogers, M.P. and Robinson, D.S.: J. Lipid Res. 15:263, 1974.
51. Vendsalu, A.: Acta Physiol. Scand. Suppl. 173:57, 1960.
52. Winder, W.W., Baldwin, K.M. and Holloszy, J.O.: Can. J. Physiol. Pharmacol. 53:86, 1975.
53. Zierler, K.L., Maseri, A., Klassen, G. et al: Trans. Assoc. Am. Physicians 81:266, 1968.

Sources des acides gras pour l'oxydation pendant l'effort physique

Description des sources principales des acides gras oxydés au cours de l'effort physique comme étant des acides gras libres qui tirent leur origine des adipocytes, du plasmatriacylglycérol et des réserves intramusculaires de triacylglycérol. Présentation de données relatives aux animaux et commentaires concernant les effets de l'entraînement en endurance organique sur les niveaux d'activité de l'enzyme responsable de l'hydrolyse du triacylglycérol dans les adipocytes et sur l'enzyme qui permet au muscle d'extraire le triacylglycérol de la circulation sanguine. On montre que l'activité lipolitique des adipocytes peut répondre aux demandes accrues en AGL lors d'un effort vigoureux. On explique que l'entraînement régulier de type endurance organique peut élever les niveaux d'activité de la lipoprotéinelipase dans les fibres rouges et pâles à contraction rapide et dans les fibres rouges à contraction lente dans les muscles squelettiques chez le rat.

Electrolytes and Water: Changes in Body Fluid Compartments During Exercise and Dehydration

David L. Costill

The water and electrolyte contents of intra- and extramuscular compartments are presented and discussed in conditions of dehydration and with reference to prolonged exercise at various temperatures. The fluid and muscle concentrations, the retention and excretion rates of Na^+, K^+, Cl^- and Mg^{++} are discussed as well as observable alterations in resting membrane potentials. Data are presented that fail to support the belief that heavy exercise on repeated days will threaten the muscle and plasma K^+ stores. From the discussion of experimental data on sweat loss and the distribution of water and electrolytes between various fluid compartments, it appears unlikely that prolonged exercise and/or dehydration can induce sufficient disturbances in body electrolyte balance to impair exercise performance.

Introduction

Since the early work of Adolph [1] numerous studies have examined the effects of dehydration and exercise on the alterations in water and electrolyte content of various body fluid compartments [16, 24, 41]. These fluid reservoirs furnish a medium to support the internal activities of the cell and provide a vehicle for transporting nutrients to the active muscles, eliminating waste products and dissipating excessive body heat. Disturbances in the volume and distribution of body water and electrolytes pose a significant threat to exercise performance.

The following discussion is intended to provide a description of the impact of body fluid loss on (1) the distribution of water and

David L. Costill, Director, Human Performance Laboratory, Ball State University, Muncie, Indiana, U.S.A.

This research was supported by research grants from the National Institutes of Health (AM 17083-02) and the Ball State University Faculty Research Committee.

electrolytes in extra- and intramuscular compartments, (2) body electrolyte deficits during repeated days of dehydration and (3) physical work capacity and heat tolerance.

Water and Electrolyte Losses in Sweat

Before discussing the topic of body water and electrolyte distribution, it seems appropriate to consider the magnitude of possible water and electrolyte losses in the sweat of subjects exposed to prolonged exercise and/or heat. Sweat losses in excess of 6 liters have been observed among marathon runners competing in air temperatures of 20 to 24 C (23% to 31% relative humidity) [13]. Such water deficits constitute a body weight reduction of 8% to 10%. Since the body is roughly 60% water, a 6-liter sweat loss may decrease a 65 kg runner's body water content by about 15%.

Several methods have been used to collect samples of sweat for analysis, but most limit sampling to a small area of the skin [41]. This makes it impossible to estimate accurately the ions lost in the total body sweat. A body wash method, however, permits relative accuracy ($\pm$ 1%) in determining the total ion losses in sweat during prolonged exercise and/or heat exposure [41].

The ionic concentration of sweat may vary markedly between individuals and is strongly affected by the rate of sweating and the subject's state of heat acclimatization. In general, however, the Na^+, K^+, Cl^- and Mg^{++} concentrations in sweat are similar to those listed in Table I. When compared to electrolyte concentrations in cellular and extracellular fluids, it is apparent that sweat is hypotonic and that the principal ions lost are those from the extracellular compartments.

As shown in Table II, Na^+ and Cl^- constitute the major ionic losses in sweat. The most severe level of dehydration (4.11 liters or 5.8% of body weight) produced deficits in body Na^+ and Cl^- of

Table I. Electrolyte Concentrations and Osmolality (Osm)
in Sweat, Muscle and Plasma [6]

| | Electrolytes (mEq/liter) | | | | |
	Na^+	Cl^-	K^+	Mg^{++}	Osm. (mOsmol/l)
Sweat	40 – 60	30 – 50	4 – 5	1.5 – 5	80 – 185
Plasma	140	101	4	1.5	302
Muscle	9	6	162	31	302

Table II. Total Body Electrolyte Losses With Varied Volumes of Sweat [9].
Estimates of the Percentage of Total Body Losses (% TBL) Are Based
on the Body Contents for Subjects Weighing 72 kg [10]

Sweat Volume (Liters)	Sweat Loss (mEq)				% TBL			
	Na^+	K^+	Cl^-	Mg^{++}	Na^+	K^+	Cl^-	Mg^{++}
1.38	60.5	5.4	53.3	4.5	2.0	0.2	2.6	0.4
2.99	97.6	11.5	104.4	8.7	3.3	0.3	5.2	0.8
4.11	154.8	15.9	136.6	12.6	5.2	0.5	6.7	1.2

roughly 5% to 7%. At the same time, total body K^+ and Mg^{++}, two ions principally confined to the intracellular space, decreased very little (<1.2%). Urine electrolyte losses during these periods are usually small as a result of decreased urine formation and increased renal Na^+ reabsorption [7]. This decreased urinary loss of electrolytes may continue for 12 to 18 hours after exercise and/or until a body water-electrolyte balance has been reestablished. Thus, it is apparent that during acute bouts of heavy sweating, the only ionic deficits of major concern are those of the extracellular compartment (Na^+ and Cl^-).

Distribution of Water and Electrolytes
Between Body Fluid Compartments:
Acute Exercise and Dehydration

· In an effort to examine the changes in water and electrolyte contents of extra- and intracellular compartments during and following large sweat losses, two methods have been used. First, their distribution in muscle biopsy samples was determined by the chloride method previously described by Bergström [4]. The second method used to determine the changes in water and electrolytes from extra- and intracellular spaces is based on calculations of the total loss of chloride in urine and sweat and assumes proportionate losses of Cl^- from both the vascular and interstitial fluids [8].

Traditionally, studies of the effect of heavy sweating on body water and electrolytes have been limited to measurements of plasma. Thus, an obvious question to be answered: How do these extracellular measurements compare to muscle water and electrolyte contents following varied levels of dehydration? In an effort to answer this question we studied eight men before and after weight losses of 2.2, 4.1 and 5.8% [8]. Sweating was promoted by continuous cycling exercise at 60% to 70% of $\dot{V}O_2$ max in an environmental chamber maintained at 39 C with a relative humidity of 25%. Blood (venous) and muscle (vastus lateralis) samples were always obtained after the subjects had rested for 30 minutes. Sweat electrolytes were determined by a "total body washdown" method. The electrolyte concentrations in sweat, blood, urine and muscle were determined by standard methods [4, 41]. Plasma and red cell volumes were measured with sodium chromate 51, while changes in plasma volume were computed from measurements of hemoglobin and hematocrit [15].

Since the major ions lost in sweat and urine were those of the extracellular compartment, it is not surprising to observe a disproportionately larger loss of water from plasma and interstitial spaces than from the intracellular compartment. While plasma and interstitial water declined approximately 2.5% for each percent of dehydration, the intracellular water decreased only 1.1% for each percent of dehydration. The absolute loss of water from these compartments, however, was quite evenly distributed between the extra- and intracellular spaces (Fig. 1). It is interesting to note that at all stages of dehydration, plasma water accounts for 10% to 11% of the total body water loss. Except for the 2.2% stage of dehydration, intracellular fluids contribute roughly half of the water lost.

In keeping with previously mentioned calculations of the change in intracellular water, muscle water declined steadily with dehydration (Table III). The change from 341 to 318 ml per 100 gm fat-free solids (FFS) constitutes a 6.8% decrease in muscle water, which is similar to the change in intracellular water (−6.5%) determined by the loss of Cl^- in urine and sweat. The values reported in Table III for muscle Na^+, K^+, and Cl^- content were not statistically significant at any stage of dehydration. Only muscle Mg^{++} content showed a significant change, decreasing 12% following the final stage of dehydration (−5.8%).

Table III. Muscle Water, Electrolytes and Glycogen Content
Before and After Varied Degrees of Dehydration

			Per 100 g Fat-Free Solids			
Dehydration	H_2O_m (ml)	Na^+_m (mEq)	K^+_m (mEq)	Cl^-_m (mEq)	Mg^{++}_m (mEq)	Glycogen (mmoles/kg)
0	341	9.9	46.3	6.1	9.0	115
−2.2%	329	10.4	47.4	6.6	8.3	76
−4.1%	324	11.1	47.0	8.3	8.1	61
−5.8%	318	9.6	47.8	6.2	7.9	48

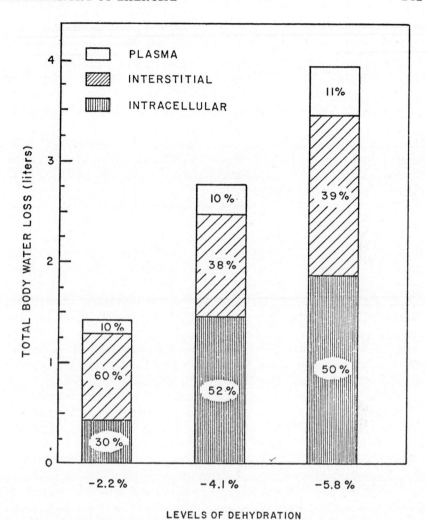

FIG. 1. Distribution of water lost from plasma, interstitial and intracellular compartments during varied levels of dehydration [8.]

Since these values are computed on the basis of the FFS weight of the tissue, they do not reflect the concentration of the ions in muscle water. Based on the Cl^- method [4], however, we have calculated the Na^+, K^+ and Mg^{++} concentrations in intramuscular water. As a result of the decline in muscle water, the ions present in the tissue samples were concentrated. Thus, the K_i^+ increased significantly, but Mg_i^{++} and Na_i^+ remained unchanged.

Based on the preceding data and the equation by Hodgkin and Horowicz [20], it is possible to estimate the effects of dehydration on the muscle's resting membrane potential (RMP). Before dehydration the RMP averaged -91.4 mV, which is similar to previously reported values in the leg muscles of man [14, 21]. Since the concentrations of intra- and extracellular K^+ and Na^+ increased somewhat proportionately with dehydration, the RMP remained relatively constant. Although such methods of computing the RMP must be viewed cautiously, these calculations confirm our earlier studies and suggest that dehydration does not alter the excitability of the muscle cell membrane [12].

Thus, this series of observations demonstrate that body water lost during exercise in the heat is attributed to relatively larger water losses from extracellular than from intracellular compartments. However, in terms of absolute losses, both intra- and extracellular volumes contribute similar quantities of water to account for the total fluid losses. Although muscle Mg^{++}, K_i^+ and H_2O_i all demonstrate significant changes following dehydration, calculations of the RMP suggest that dehydration has little effect on the excitability of the muscle cell membrane. However, one should not overlook the fact that these measurements were made following 30 minutes of recovery from the heat-exercise exposure, and muscle samples were obtained only from heavily exercised muscles.

Thus, subsequent studies were undertaken to demonstrate the interaction between active and inactive muscles to determine the relative distribution of water and ions during exercise and dehydration. Subjects were studied before, during and after two hours of exercise at roughly 60% $\dot{V}O_2$ max. Muscle biopsies were obtained from exercising (vastus lateralis) and nonexercising (deltoid) muscles before, at 10 and 120 minutes of cycling, and after 30 minutes of recovery from the activity. Venous blood was sampled before and after 10, 30, 60, 90 and 120 minutes of exercise. Muscle and blood specimens were subsequently analyzed for water and electrolytes as previously described [8].

The combined loss of body water via sweating, respiration and urination produced a 3.2% reduction in body weight. Electrolyte excretion (sweat plus urine) during this period averaged 92.6 mEq Na^+, 22.3 mEq K^+, 94.8 mEq Cl^- and 4.6 mEq Mg^{++}. These values are similar to those observed during the study of varied levels of dehydration and confirm the fact that relatively little K^+ and Mg^{++} is lost during prolonged exercise.

At the onset of exercise plasma volume decreased 4.4%. This loss of water from plasma is apparently the result of a transcapillary fluid flux in the exercising muscle. Muscle tissue taken from the thigh showed a 6.8% increase in water content, while the water in the inactive muscle remained unchanged. The mechanism behind this transcapillary fluid flux into exercising muscles was studied by Kjellmer [22], who arrived at the conclusion that it was solely due to filtration caused by increased capillary hydrostatic pressure. More recent studies by Mellander et al [27] suggest that muscle tissue hyperosmolality may also be involved. In any event, the loss of water from plasma in the first few minutes of exercise results in a marked difference in the water content of active and inactive muscle. This difference persists throughout the two-hour exercise bout despite a gradual decline in plasma volume. Thirty minutes after the exercise, some fluids appear to return to the plasma from the active muscles, leaving plasma 4% below the pre-exercise volume. At this point, both the exercise and nonexercise muscle water contents were similar to the pre-exercise values.

At the onset of exercise, there is a small but significant decrease in active muscle K^+ content with a concomitant rise in plasma K^+ content. This response is similar to previous reports which suggest that in the early minutes of muscular activity, there is an efflux of K^+ from the cell [22, 28]. Subsequently, exercise-dehydration seems to have little effect on the plasma K^+ content, while K^+ appeared to reenter the active muscles. The K^+ in the deltoid muscle, on the other hand, did not change at any time during exercise, but decreased roughly 5% after 30 minutes of recovery. However, due to individual variability, this decline was not statistically significant ($P > 0.05$).

The exercising muscle appears to slowly increase its Mg^{++} content, which is paralleled by a gradual decline in plasma Mg^{++}. Although we can only speculate, it is possible that these Mg^{++} shifts into contracting muscle are a function of increased metabolic need. Unfortunately, these data do not permit us to detail mechanisms responsible for this change or its physiological significance.

Apparently the ionic and water shifts which occur at the onset of exercise have little effect on the RMP. At the end of the two hours of cycling, however, the calculated RMP showed a 6 mV increase in the working muscle, but returned to the pre-exercise value (90 mV) after 30 minutes of recovery. The RMP of the inactive muscle was unaffected by either exercise or dehydration. The Cl^- method used in calculating the intra- and extramuscular water content assumes that the RMP remains constant and that 95% of the Cl^- in the biopsy specimen is extracellular. In light of these RMP calculations, it seems that these assumptions may not be valid during prolonged exercise, thereby falsely describing the distribution of muscle water between the extra- and intracellular compartments.

In any event, it appears that there are marked differences between active and inactive muscles with regard to their water and ionic contents during both short-term and prolonged exercise. After 30 minutes of recovery, however, these constituents are redistributed so that both tissues have similar water and electrolyte contents. Therefore, muscle tissue sampled from a single site can be used to estimate the effects of dehydration on muscle water and electrolytes, provided the subject has been inactive for 30 minutes. These observations also suggest that attempts to calculate the distribution of muscle water and ions during exercise by the chloride method are probably invalidated due to a shift in the membrane potential.

Changes in Body Water and Electrolytes
During Repeated Days of Exercise
in the Heat

Thus far our discussion has been limited to the effects of exercise and large sweat losses on muscle fluids. Although we have observed some marked changes in muscle ions and water during exercise, acute dehydration's principal effect is in reducing muscle water with little influence on the muscle Na^+, K^+, Cl^- and Mg^{++} contents. As a result, we are led to conclude that aside from the temporary loss of body water, ions lost in sweat probably have little effect on the functional capacity of muscle. However, in the absence of information concerning the subcellular ion distribution following exercise and dehydration, caution should be used in speculating on the effects of even small ionic changes on the dynamics of muscular contraction.

It has been suggested that individuals who perform heavy exercise and sweat profusely on repeated days may accumulate large deficits of selected ions, principally K^+ [23, 32]. Despite many accusations, only measurements of plasma K^+ have been offered to substantiate these claims.

In 1973 we attempted to gain some insight into this problem by studying 12 subjects (ten men, two women) during five successive days of dehydration [9]. Although the subjects were permitted to eat and drink ad libitum, the total water, K^+, Na^+, Cl^- and caloric intake was closely monitored. Likewise, the daily excretion of water and ions in sweat and urine was accurately measured. These body water and electrolyte exchange data revealed that repeated days of exercise-dehydration induced a renal conservation of Na^+ with a small decline in urine K⁺. As a result, the subjects tended to store Na⁺ (392 mEq/5 days), while total body K⁺ increased roughly 100 mEq during the five days of these observations. The relatively large gains in Na⁺ were accompanied by a proportionate increase in extracellular water. This is well documented by the expansion of plasma volume illustrated in Figure 2. It is interesting to note that 48 to 72 hours were required for the elimination of this "excess" water and extracellular ion.

The mechanism apparently responsible for this Na⁺-conserving response to successive days of dehydration is an increase in mineral corticoid function. Exposure to heat, exercise and/or dehydration results in arterial hypovolemia and relative renal ischemia. Both factors are known to be responsible for increased aldosterone

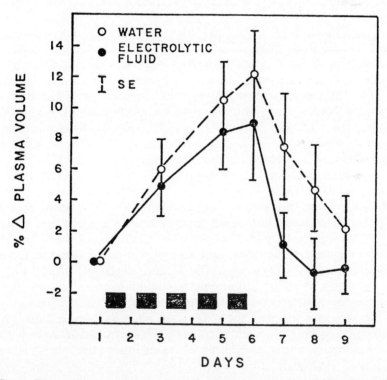

FIG. 2. Percentage change in plasma volume during five days of repeated dehydration (−3% per day). During one series the subjects were only permitted to drink water, while in the second treatment thirst was satisfied by ad libitum ingestion of an electrolyte drink [9].

production and renal sodium reabsorption [3, 7, 19]. This point is documented by changes in plasma renin and aldosterone concentrations following a single bout (one hour) of exercise [7]. Despite ad libitum water intake, plasma aldosterone remains elevated for nearly 12 hours following such exercise.

Thus, despite the sweat and urinary losses incurred during dehydration, men and women can maintain a positive Na^+, K^+ and Cl^- balance via dietary intake and renal conservation of these ions, provided food and drink are provided ad libitum. Nevertheless, it has been suggested that under some occupational and athletic situations it is possible for persons to lose more than 6% to 8% of body weight by heavy sweating, with Na^+ and K^+ losses in excess of 200 and 40 mEq/24 hours, respectively [23]. Although such losses provide strong stimuli for renal Na^+ conservation, it is possible that the kidney may continue to excrete K^+ despite a serious body potassium deficit.

In 1972 Knochel et al [23] observed that six men undergoing intensive physical training in a hot climate developed a mean K^+ deficit of 349 mEq in the first four days of exercise. This deficit, estimated from measurements of ^{42}K, occurred despite a K^+ intake of 100 mEq/day. Unfortunately, the balance of K^+ intake and excretion (sweat, urine and feces) was not adequately monitored to validate the ^{42}K calculations. If, in fact, heavy sweating and exercise on repeated days can induce such large body K^+ deficits, then such changes should be detectable in muscle biopsy specimens.

For that reason, we recently conducted an investigation to determine the effects of low dietary K^+ and repeated days of heavy exercise on muscle water and electrolytes. Eight men exercised sufficiently on four successive days to achieve a mean body weight loss of 3.1 kg/day (4.2% of body weight). This protocol was followed under two dietary regimens. One diet sequence provided 25 mEq of K^+ daily (low K^+ diet), while the second contained 80 mEq of K^+ per day (high K^+ diet). Both experimental diets included 180 mEq of Na^+ per day with an average daily caloric content of 2880 kcal.

In response to the four days of exercise-dehydration, urine production decreased from a control value of approximately 1300 ml/24 hours to a low of 600 ml/24 hours during the low K^+ dietary sequence. Although urine volume was depressed in both experimental treatments, the low K^+ diet elicited a significantly greater reduction than did the high K^+ diet. At the same time, there was a marked reduction in urine Na^+ excretion, which also seemed to be more pronounced during the low K^+ experiment. As a matter of fact, some individuals excreted less than 10 mEq of Na^+ in a 24-hour period. These patterns of reduced renal water and Na^+ excretion are similar to our earlier observations and suggest that dietary K^+ may be influential in the renal Na^+-water conservation during repeated days of heavy exercise [9].

Of greater interest was the rate of body K^+ lost in urine and sweat during the exercise and dietary regimens. We observed substantially less K^+ excreted in urine during the low K^+ diet than when the men consumed the 80 mEq of K^+ daily. Changes in dietary K^+ intake had no effect on sweat K^+ content. If this lower renal K^+ excretion were a function of the reduced urine volume, then we would expect to see a decreased K^+ excretion in both dietary treatments and no change in the concentration of K^+ in urine. Urine K^+ concentration, however, decreased significantly during the low K^+ intake, but remained relatively constant during the high K^+ treatment. Thus, with a reduced K^+ intake and repeated days of dehydration, there is a selective reduction in renal K^+ excretion. The mechanism responsible for this apparent K^+ conservation is not easily explained, but may simply reflect the lower K^+ entry into plasma following the low K^+ diet.

Given the dietary intake and losses (urine and sweat) of Na^+ and K^+, it is possible to calculate the average daily change in body Na^+ and K^+ content. Despite heavy sweating and relatively normal urine K^+ losses, the subjects were able to remain in positive K^+ balance with an intake of 80 mEq/day. When the diet contained only 25 mEq of K^+ per day, however, the subjects incurred a body K^+ deficit of about 17 mEq/day (-68 mEq/4 days). If we assume that these men had total body K^+ contents of 3450 mEq (42 mEq/kg), then the deficits incurred in this study were roughly 2% of the body K^+ stores [31].

As anticipated, the subjects showed a positive Na^+ balance during both dietary-exercise regimens, with the low K^+ diet producing a significantly greater increase in body Na^+ content than was observed in the high K^+ treatment (Table IV). In light of these findings we are inclined to speculate that when combined with chronic exercise a low K^+ intake results in a greater aldosterone response followed by an increased rate of Na^+ and water retention.

This concept is supported by the fact that there was a significantly greater increase in plasma volume during the low K^+ diets than when the subjects consumed 80 mEq of K^+ each day. Muscle biopsy samples obtained at rest on the first, third and fifth days of the experiments revealed an increase in muscle water content

Table IV. Average Daily Na^+ and K^+ Balance During
Successive Days of Dehydration

	Intake (mEq/day)	Loss (mEq/day) Urine	Loss (mEq/day) Sweat	Balance (± mEq/day)
K^+ (High K^+ Diet)	79.9 (±2.8)	−67.1 (±4.1)	−11.5 (±0.7)	+ 1.3
(Low K^+ Diet)	25.0 (±0.1)	−31.7 (±3.5)	−10.4 (±0.6)	−17.1
Na^+ (High K^+ Diet)	179.0 (±5.7)	−92.6 (±12.2)	−84.0 (±9.7)	+ 2.4
(Low K^+ Diet)	181.2 (±7.2)	−69.0 (±14.0)	−82.7 (±7.7)	+29.5

(H_2O_m) during both dietary conditions. In keeping with the plasma volume and Na^+ balance data, H_2O_m increased significantly more during the low K^+ diet than with the high K^+ intake.

Since the subjects showed little change in body K^+ content (+5 mEq/4 days) during the high K^+ treatment and a 2% body K^+ deficit in the low K^+ experiment, it is surprising to note that muscle K^+ content increased significantly. At the present time we are unable to explain this response, but we have observed similar patterns among competitive cyclists who performed 100 km rides on four successive days. This increase in K_m^+ is probably isolated to the heavily exercised muscle and does not represent the K_m^+ content of all body tissues. In any event, these studies fail to support the concept that heavy exercise on repeated days will threaten the muscle and plasma K^+ stores.

Some investigators have suggested that athletes engaged in heavy training may be more susceptible to heat stress injuries as a result of depleted body K^+ stores [32, 36]. Before and after our experiments with low and high K^+ diets and repeated days of exercise, the subjects performed a 90-minute heat tolerance test. Aside from excreting a more dilute sweat, all thermal (skin and rectal temperatures) and circulatory parameters were unaffected by the experimental treatments. It should be remembered, however, that these men experienced little change in body K^+ despite efforts to alter K^+ storage.

Effects of Water and Electrolyte Losses
on Exercise Performance

In the past 30 years numerous studies have examined the effects of rapid dehydration on muscular performance. Although some early studies [18] showed slight improvements in both strength and speed following acute weight losses of 0.9 to 6.1 kg, it is generally observed that dehydration of up to 10% of body weight has no effect on strength, speed or reaction time [17, 29, 37, 42]. On the other hand, endurance-type activities which impose severe demands on the cardiovascular system are markedly impaired as a result of large sweat losses [11, 34].

Saltin [35] noted that after a 5.2% reduction in body weight by thermal dehydration, plasma volume declined up to 25%. As a result, during submaximal work the subjects' stroke volume decreased while heart rates increased to maintain the cardiac output. When the severity of the exercise was increased, the subjects' maximal stroke volume, heart rates and cardiac output were found to be similar to maximal measurements made prior to dehydration. Despite a reduction in maximal exercise time, the subjects' oxygen uptake capacities during cycling were decreased only a few percent with dehydration.

In the full upright position (treadmill running) dehydrated subjects seem less tolerant of both submaximal and maximal exercise (unpublished). This point is illustrated in Figure 3. When plasma volume (PV) was reduced 10% to 19% with a diuretic drug, the subjects' heart rate during exercise at 75% $\dot{V}O_2$ max was approximately 15 beats per minute higher. Since body weight had been reduced 2.8 kg as a result of the urine loss, it is not surprising to see that the absolute $\dot{V}O_2$ was also less (-6.7%). If we assume that the ratio of oxygen consumed to heart rate (O_2 pulse) reflect changes in stroke volume (SV), then it would seem that the exercising SV may have decreased roughly 10% as a consequence of the loss of PV.

In terms of maximal treadmill exercise, a diuretic-induced body weight loss results in a lower oxygen uptake capacity (Fig. 4). Unlike the cycling data reported by Saltin, plasma-depleted subjects performing maximal treadmill work showed a 6% to 7% decrease in $\dot{V}O_2$ max. The discrepancy between the present data and Saltin's findings may be the result of a lesser capacity to redistribute blood from capacitance vessels and less active tissues during full upright exercise than during sitting and supine cycling.

Previous studies have shown that dehydrated men and women are less tolerant of exercise in the heat [5, 30, 38]. As can be seen in Figure 5, both muscle and rectal temperatures are significantly elevated when diuretically dehydrated (-3% of body weight) subjects exercise (35% $\dot{V}O_2$ max) in the heat [5]. At the same time, mean skin temperature ($\overline{T}_s$) is substantially lower in the dehydrated condition. This suggests that a strong sympathetic outflow has reduced both skin and muscle blood flow during dehydration. It was found that only highly trained, heat acclimatized subjects (group II)

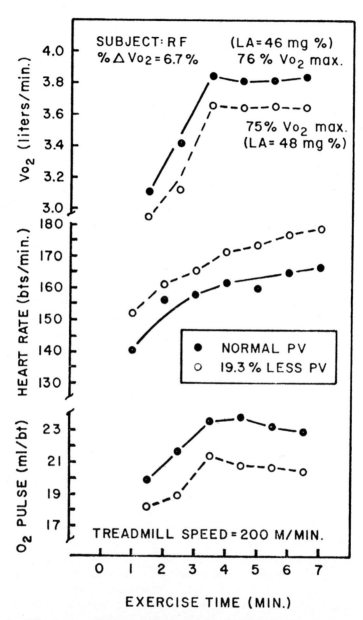

FIG. 3. Effects of diminished plasma volume (PV) on oxygen consumption ($\dot{V}O_2$), heart rate and oxygen pulse during submaximal exercise ($\sim$ 75% $\dot{V}O_2$ max). The % $\dot{V}O_2$ max values shown in the upper panel have been computed from the $\dot{V}O_2$ max values measured during the normal PV and 19.3% less PV trials, respectively.

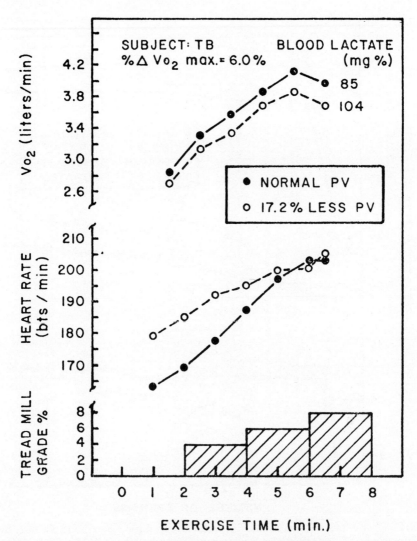

FIG. 4. Continuous measurements of oxygen consumption and heart rates during treadmill exercise to exhaustion. Plasma volume was reduced with a diuretic drug (4-chloro-N-furfuryl-5-sulfamoyl-anthranilic acid).

were able to complete a two-hour exercise bout when dehydrated. The less fit individuals who comprised group I experienced heat syncope and were unable to exercise beyond 55 to 60 minutes when dehydrated. Since one's endurance exercise capacity and heat tolerance depend upon the ability to divert a large fraction of the

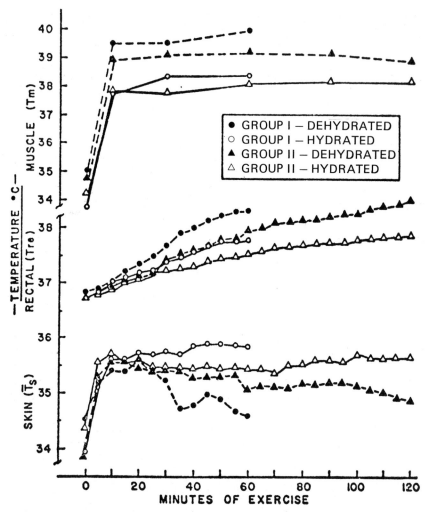

FIG. 5. Mean muscle, rectal and skin temperatures during exercise in the heat for two groups of subjects under hydrated and dehydrated conditions. The subjects in group I experienced heat syncope after 55 to 60 minutes of exercise when dehydrated [5].

cardiac output to both the skin and working muscles, dehydration impairs the subjects' thermoregulation and exercise performance.

With respect to the effects of body electrolyte deficits on muscular performance, it is unfortunate that little information is available on normal, active subjects. Data from clinically abnormal patients have too often been used to predict the influence of profuse sweating on muscular performance of active humans. As previously mentioned, the electrolyte concentration of sweat is lower than that of the extracellular fluids. During heavy sweating, therefore, the total body electrolyte content is decreased, but the concentration of extracellular sodium and chloride tends to increase. This water-electrolyte imbalance is relatively small (<2% to 3%) and seems of little physiological significance. From our preceding discussions on sweat losses and the distribution of water and electrolytes between various body fluid compartments, it is unlikely that prolonged exercise and/or dehydration can induce sufficient disturbances in body electrolyte balance to impair exercise performance.

Numerous attempts have been made to describe the effects of ingesting selected ions on neuromuscular fatigue [26, 38, 40]. Taylor et al [40] studied the effects of three salt intake levels (6, 15 and 30 gm/day) on selected physiological variables during three days of exposure to a hot, dry environment. While sweat rates varied from 5 to 8 liters/day, the intake of 6 gm of NaCl per day caused heat syncope. There was no difference between the 15 and 30 gm/day groups, but both experienced fewer symptoms of heat exhaustion than the 6 gm/day treatment.

Although several studies [2, 33, 39] have suggested that aspartate (potassium and magnesium salts of aspartic acid) may serve to reduce fatigue at the neuromuscular level, more recent studies by Consolazio et al [6] have shown no beneficial effects of prolonged (five weeks) administration of Mg^{++} and K^+ salts of aspartic acid (2 gm/day). In light of these conflicting results, it seems that more definitive studies are needed to establish the value of supplemental electrolyte intake on physical exercise capacity and resistance to fatigue.

Conclusion

The preceding discussion has described the effects of prolonged exercise and dehydration on the distribution of body water and electrolytes and has defined the effects of large body fluid losses on exercise performance. In summary, these studies demonstrate the body's capacity to minimize electrolyte losses during acute and repeated bouts of exercise and dehydration. Although there are marked shifts in water and selected ions in the exercising muscle, only during prolonged exertion is the ratio of intra- to extramuscular K^+ significantly altered, suggesting that some modifications of the muscle cell membrane may occur. Muscle tissue not engaged in the exercise seems unaffected by the sweat lost during prolonged activity, but relinquishes intracellular water shortly after work is terminated. Blood, muscle, sweat and urine measurements before and following varied levels of dehydration demonstrate that body water lost during exercise in the heat is accomplished at the expense of larger water losses from extracellular than from intracellular compartments. Moreover, the loss of ions in sweat and urine has little effect on the K^+ content of either plasma or muscle.

With repeated days of dehydration and heavy exercise, plasma volume increases in proportion to an increase in body Na^+ storage. At this point some mention should be made concerning the effect of this increased plasma water on the concentration of blood constituents. Since red blood cell and hemoglobin are confined to the vascular space, both may decrease significantly as a function of hemodilution induced by repeated days of exercise and dehydration. This may in part explain the apparent anemia reported by sports physicians among athletes undergoing intensive training. It is also possible that such hemodilution may produce low concentrations of plasma K^+, which might be falsely interpreted as suggestive of a hypokalemic state. In any event, some caution should be used in the clinical interpretation of plasma concentrations of various constituents among endurance-trained athletes.

With regard to the question of possible body K^+ depletion during repeated days of heavy exercise, calculations of K^+ balance (intake minus excretion) and measurements of plasma and muscle K^+ content fail to confirm the large deficits previously reported by Knochel et al [23]. Despite low dietary K^+ intake, we observed little change in total body K^+ (<2% change) and an increase in muscle K^+ content. In the presence of a low K^+ intake there are strong suggestions that the kidneys were selectively conserving K^+.

While current knowledge enables us to anticipate the impairments of dehydration on exercise performance, little empirical information is available to show the effects of ionic losses on neuromuscular function. Only data from clinical patients and in vitro preparations are available to demonstrate the abnormal response of muscle deficient in selected ions. These findings may have little application to normally healthy subjects who perform intense physical exercise.

References

1. Adolph, E.F.: Heat exchange of man in the desert. Am. J. Physiol. 123:486-499, 1938.

2. Agersborg, H.P.K. and Shaw, D.L.: Presented at the American College of Sports Medicine Meeting, Norristown, Pa., 1961.

3. Bartter, F.C. and Gann, D.S.: On the hemodynamic regulation of the secretion of aldosterone. Circulation 21:1016-1021, 1960.

4. Bergström, J.: Muscle electrolytes in man. Determination by neutron activation analysis on needle biopsy specimens. A study on normal subjects, kidney patients, and patients with chronic diarrhea. Scand. J. Clin. Lab. Invest. 18:16-20, 1962.

5. Claremont, A.D., Costill, D.L., Fink, W. and Van Handel, P.: Heat tolerance following diuretic induced dehydration. Med. Sci. Sports. (In press.)

6. Consolazio, C.F., Nelson, R.A., Matoush, L.O. and Isaac, G.J.: J. Appl. Physiol. 19:257-261, 1961.

7. Costill, D.L., Branam, G., Fink, W. and Nelson, R.: Exercise induced sodium conservation: Changes in plasma renin and aldosterone activities. Eur. J. Appl. Physiol. (In press.)

8. Costill, D.L., Coté, R. and Fink, W.: Muscle water and electrolytes following varied levels of dehydration in man. J. Appl. Physiol. 40:6-11, 1976.

9. Costill, D.L., Coté, R., Miller, E. et al: Water and electrolyte replacement during repeated days of work in the heat. Aviat. Space. Environ. Med. 46(6):795-800, 1975.

10. Costill, D.L. and Fink, W.J.: Plasma volume changes following exercise and thermal dehydration. J. Appl. Physiol. 37:521-525, 1974.

11. Costill, D.L., Kammer, W.F. and Fisher, A.: Fluid ingestion during distance running. Arch. Environ. Health 21:520-525, 1970.

12. Costill, D.L. and Saltin, B.: Muscle glycogen and electrolytes following exercise and thermal dehydration. In Howald, H. and Poortmans, J.R. (eds.): Metabolic Adaptation to Prolonged Physical Exercise. Basel:Verlag Birkhäuser, 1975.

13. Costill, D.L. and Sparks, K.E.: Rapid fluid replacement following thermal dehydration. J. Appl. Physiol. 34:299-303, 1973.

14. Cunningham, J.N., Carter, N.W., Rector, F.C. and Seldin, D.W.: Resting membrane potential difference of skeletal muscle in normal subjects and severely ill patients. J. Clin. Invest. 50:49-59, 1971.

15. Dill, D.B. and Costill, D.L.: Calculation of percentage changes in volumes of blood, plasma, and red cells in dehydration. J. Appl. Physiol. 37:247-248, 1974.

16. Dill, D.B., Hall, F.G. and van Beaumont, W.: Sweat chloride concentration: Sweat rate, metabolic rate, skin temperature, and age. J. Appl. Physiol. 21(1):99-106, 1966.

17. Edwards, J.B.: A Study of the Effect of Semi-starvation and Dehydration on Strength and Endurance With Reference to College Wrestling. Master's thesis. University of North Carolina, 1951.

18. Gillum, O.C.: The Effects of Weight Reduction on the Bodily Strength of Wrestlers. Master's thesis. Ohio State University, Columbus, Ohio, 1940.

19. Hartroft, P.M. and Hartroft, S.: Regulation of aldosterone secretion. Br. Med. J. 1:1171-1179, 1961.

20. Hodgkin, A.L. and Horowicz, P.: The influence of potassium and chloride ions on the membrane potential of single muscle fibers. J. Physiol. (Lond.) 148:127-160, 1959.

21. Johns, R.J.: Microelectrode studies of muscle membrane potential in man. Neurol. Disorders 38:704-713, 1960.

22. Kjellmer, I.: The effect of exercise on the vascular bed of skeletal muscle. Acta Physiol. Scand. 62:18-30, 1964.
23. Knochel, J.P., Dotin, L.N. and Hamburger, R.J.: Pathophysiology of intense physical conditioning in a hot climate. I. Mechanisms of potassium depletion. J. Clin. Invest. 51:242-255, 1972.
24. Kozlowski, S. and Saltin, B.: Effect of sweat loss on body fluids. J. Appl. Physiol. 19:1119-1124, 1964.
25. Kuno, Y.: Human Perspiration. Springfield, Ill.:Thomas, 1956, pp. 190-192.
26. Ladell, W.S.S.: The effects of water and salt intake upon performance of men working in hot and humid environments. J. Physiol. 127:11-46, 1955.
27. Mellander, S., Johansson, B., Gray, S. et al: The effects of hyperosmolarity on intact and isolated vascular smooth muscle. Possible role in exercise hyperemia. Angiologica 4:310-322, 1967.
28. Miller, H.C. and Darrow, D.C.: Relation of serum and muscle electrolytes, particularly potassium to voluntary exercise. Am. J. Physiol. 132:801-807, 1941.
29. Nichols, H.: The Effects of Rapid Weight Loss on Selected Physiological Responses of Wrestlers. Doctoral dissertation. University of Michigan, Ann Arbor, Michigan.
30. Pitts, G.C., Johnson, R.E. and Consolazio, F.C.: Work in the heat as affected by intake of water, salt and glucose. Am. J. Physiol. 142:253-270, 1944.
31. Pitts, R.F.: Physiology of the Kidney and Body Fluids. Chicago:Year Book Medical Publishers, 1968, pp. 36-37.
32. Rose, K.D.: Warning for millions: Intense exercise can deplete potassium. Physician Sports Med. 3:26-29, 1975.
33. Rosen, H.A., Blumenthal, A. and Agersborg, H.P.K.: J. Pharm. Sci. 51:592-593, 1962.
34. Saltin, B.: Aerobic work capacity and circulation at exercise in man with special reference to the effect of prolonged exercise and/or heat exposure. Acta Physiol. Scand. suppl. 230, 1964.
35. Saltin, B.: Circulatory responses to submaximal and maximal exercise after thermal dehydration. J. Appl. Physiol. 19:1125-1132, 1964.
36. Schamadan, J.L. and Snively, W.D., Jr.: Potassium depletion as a possible cause for heat stroke. Ind. Med. Surg. 36:785-788, 1967.
37. Singer, R.N. and Weiss, S.A.: Res. Q. 39:361-369, 1968.
38. Snellen, J.W.: Mean body temperature and the control of thermal sweating. Acta Physiol. Pharm. 14:99-108, 1966.
39. Taylor, B.B.: West. Med. 2:535, 1961.
40. Taylor, H.L., Henschel, A., Michelsen, O. and Keys, A.: The effect of the sodium chloride intake in the work performance of man during exposure to dry heat and experimental exhaustion. Am. J. Physiol. 140:439-451, 1943.
41. Vellar, O.D.: Studies on sweat losses of nutrients. I. Iron content of whole body sweat and its association with other sweat constituents, serum iron levels, hematological indices, body surface area and sweat rate. Scand. J. Clin. Lab. Invest. 21:157-167, 1968.
42. Williams, W.R., Blyth, C.S. and Jamerson, R.E.: Proceedings of the AAHPER Convention, Dallas, Texas, 1965.

Electrolyte et eau: changements dans les compartiments contenant les liquides du corps pendant l'effort et la déshydratation

L'auteur examine le volume de l'eau et des électrolytes dans les compartiments intra et extramusculaires pendant la déshydratation, en particulier lors d'un effort soutenu à différentes températures. Examen des teneurs et des taux de rétention et d'excrétion des ions Na^+, K^+, Cl^- et Mg^{++} dans les fluides et dans les muscles, ainsi que des modifications observables dans le potentiel au repos de la membrane. Il présente des données qui ne peuvent confirmer la croyance selon laquelle l'effort vigoureux, pendant plusieurs journées consécutives, mettrait en danger les réserves en K^+ des muscles et du plasma. Il ressort de la présentation de données expérimentales sur la transpiration et sur la distribution de l'eau et des électrolytes dans les divers compartiments, qu'il est peu probable que l'effort soutenu ou la déshydratation puisse causer, dans l'équilibre des électrolytes du corps, un trouble pouvant compromettre l'exécution de l'effort.

Protein Turnover During Exercise

Jacques R. Poortmans

Muscle is presented as an extremely versatile tissue capable of acute and chronic adaptations to a wide range of work requirements. Because of the importance of the mass of muscular tissue in humans (about 50% of the body weight in male subjects) it is obvious that muscle plays a significant role in metabolism. Since about 80% of the dry weight of muscle consists of protein, the latter do indeed serve a number of important purposes in the maintenance of homeostasis. An extensive review is made of the control of amino acid transport, of their use in energy balance, of protein synthesis in muscle, of protein degradation and of regulation of protein metabolism, with particular reference to the acute and chronic effects of exercise, in both animals and humans.

Introduction

The effect of exercise on striated muscle fibers has been an accepted fact for many years. In 1895, Morpurgo found that strenuous exercise could cause the cross-sectional area of the sartorius muscle to increase without altering the total number of muscle fibers [1]. He attributed fiber hypertrophy to an increase in the sarcoplasm rather than the myofibrils. More recent biochemical studies made by Helander in 1961 clearly indicate that hypertrophy is usually associated with a large increase in the myofibrillar material of the fiber [2]. Since these two princeps papers, numerous physiologists and biochemists have repeatedly confirmed that the size of skeletal and cardiac muscle is affected by the pattern of muscular activity.

It is common knowledge that muscle is an extremely versatile tissue capable of acute adaptation to a wide range of work requirements. One of the best examples of intensive exercise is weight-lifting which was found to be very effective in producing fiber hypertrophy. On the contrary, athletes who practice endurance training leave the size of the musculature relatively unchanged,

Jacques R. Poortmans, Chimie physiologique, Institut supérieur d'éducation physique et de kinésithérapie, Université libre de Bruxelles, Bruxelles, Belgique.

although endurance produces biochemical changes that lead to greater maximum capacities to perform work and to consume oxygen.

Because of the great mass of this tissue, being about 50% of body weight in male subjects [127], it can be assumed that this tissue must play a significant role in metabolism. About 80% of the dry weight of muscle consists of protein which serves a number of purposes in maintenance of homeostasis. Surprisingly little attention has been focused on the cellular mechanisms and regulation of muscle adaptation to exercise.

In this review, "protein turnover" will refer strictly to the control of amino acid transport including their use in the energy balance, increased synthesis of proteins and nucleic acids, hydrolysis of intracellular proteins and the regulation of protein metabolism.

Control of Amino Acid Transport

Intramuscular Amino Acids

The use of amino acids as precursors of proteins is the central fact dominating any consideration of amino acid metabolism. Skeletal muscle, the largest tissue in the body, is the major site of free amino acid deposition, often accounting for more than half the total amount in the whole animal [3]. In contrast, the plasma contains a very small proportion of the total free amino acid pool, varying from 0.2% to 6% for individual amino acids. Intracellular free amino acid concentration in human muscle tissue has been investigated by Bergström et al [4]. Of the total pool of free amino acids the eight essential amino acids represent only 8.4% whereas glutamine constitutes 61%, glutamic acid 13.5% and alanine 4.4%. In fact, an uptake of glutamate and a production of glutamine in human muscle has been observed by Marliss et al [5]. These data suggest that muscle is a major site of glutamine synthesis in man.

Besides the gradient between intracellular and plasma concentration, several authors have demonstrated that in normal man in the postabsorptive state there is a net release of amino acids from skeletal muscle tissue, as reflected in negative arteriovenous differences [5-9]. The output of alanine and glutamine exceeds that of all other amino acids and accounts for over 50% of total alpha amino acid nitrogen release [5, 7]. The heart also shows an even greater predominance in the output of alanine than in skeletal muscle, accounting for 80% of total amino acid release [10].

Moreover, recent evidence has become available which suggests that circulating blood cells [11], and presumably erythrocytes [9], in man play an important role in amino acid transport. With whole blood, the arteriovenous difference in skeletal muscle indicates again a net release of several amino acids, the greatest values being that of alanine and glutamine which accounted for 35% and 21%, respectively, of the measured amino acid output. These data clearly implicate the blood cells as important carriers in the net flux of various amino acids between skeletal muscle and liver in normal humans at rest.

The rate of entry of essential amino acid into muscle has been shown by Baños et al to be directly proportional to its blood concentration over the physiological range [12]. However, the situation is less clear with the entry rate of other amino acids which failed to increase in proportion to their concentration in the blood, or even showed evidence of intramuscular metabolic inter-relationship. They conclude that skeletal muscle provides a quantitatively important storage system which helps to maintain the concentration of amino acids in the bloodstream within normal limits under changing conditions. Short-term needs can be met by the passage of free amino acids into blood, while long-term needs can be met by the breakdown of muscle protein.

Amino Acid Uptake by Stimulated Muscle

The effect of exercise on plasma amino acid levels has been investigated with rats and humans. It has been shown that amino acid metabolism varies with the duration and intensity of activity. Studying the metabolism of the isolated levator ani muscle of the rat, Arvill has reported that electrical stimulation of this muscle in vitro causes increased uptake of the nonmetabolized amino acid analog, alpha-aminoisobutyric acid (AIB), within minutes [13]. This observation has been confirmed on the frog sartorius [14, 19], on papillary muscle [15] and on rat diaphragm [16]. Figure 1 indicates that the increase in transport is a function of the amount and pattern of stimulation. Thus the number of contractile responses in the muscle appears to determine the rate of AIB uptake. In addition, the aforementioned experiments suggested that a given number of stimuli had greater effects if they occurred over a shorter period of time [16]. Supporting this assumption, the basal rate of AIB uptake has been shown to vary in different muscles of the body [16, 21]. The continuously active dark muscles, such as the heart or soleus, accumulated AIB from blood more rapidly and achieved a higher intracellular to extracellular concentration ratio than the pale muscles, such as the extensor digitorum longus or plantaris [16]. Uptake of labeled glycine, alanine, methionine and serine also

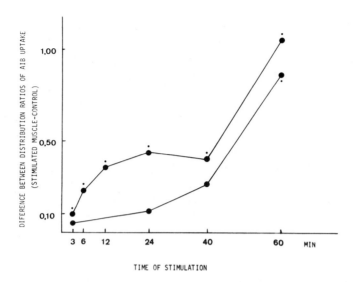

FIG. 1. Effect of electrical stimulation on ^{14}C-AIB uptake by rat diaphragm. One hemidiaphragm was stimulated at 2.5 (*lower curve*) and 10 (*upper curve*) pulse · sec^{-1} for the indicated time. The contralateral muscle served as control. Following stimulation, the diaphragms were incubated in medium containing ^{14}C-AIB and their total AIB was measured after 45 minutes. The distribution ratio was taken as the ratio of the total AIB content to that in the medium. The difference between distribution ratios (stimulated muscle control) is plotted in ordinate. Significance (P < 0.05) was determined by paired analysis (·). (From Goldberg et al [16].)

increases following repeated contractions, but the magnitude of the response is smaller than with AIB [17]. By contrast, repeated electrical stimulation does not increase the uptake of branched-chain amino acids, e.g., leucine, isoleucine and valine. Thus in muscle these different transport systems for the amino acids appear to be regulated in different fashions which still remain unclear. However, Goldberg et al have provided evidence that changes in AIB uptake do not depend upon gene expression, since stimulation increased uptake by the rat diaphragm even when protein or RNA synthesis is inhibited by over 90% with cycloheximide or actinomycin D [16].

Additional experiments carried out by the same laboratory strongly suggest that some biochemical consequence of the contractile process, and not a neural event or an electrical effect in the postsynaptic membrane, affects the transport process [17]. Goldberg et al showed that the uptake of AIB by muscle is an uphill process, dependent upon the presence of external Na^+ and a functioning Na^+ pump [16]. In addition, the results of Narahara and Holloszy suggest that electrical stimulation enhances the penetration of amino acids into muscles by altering the organization of the cell membrane [19]. Isometric contractions of muscles enhance the uptake of the AIB more rapidly than muscles contracting against no load or stimulated controls. Surprisingly, the effects of electrical stimulation are greater if the muscle is stretched 10% to 15% beyond its resting length. Therefore, isometric exercise appears most effective though the biochemical reasons are yet to be resolved.

The distribution of amino acids in cell fractions remains poorly understood. However, it appears in rat cells that there is an apparent division of total lysine pool of the tissue into at least two smaller compartments, one in the cytoplasm and another in the mitochondrial fraction [20].

Once in the intracellular pool, amino acids are subjected to a variety of metabolic reactions including protein synthesis, oxidation, transamination and synthesis of nonprotein nitrogenous compounds. In fact, Gan and Jeffray have shown that the turnover time in rat muscle is between four and seven hours [18].

Amino Acid Catabolism

The effect of exercise on plasma amino acid levels has been investigated with rats and humans. Muscular activity leads to an increase of total amino-N in plasma which varies with the duration and intensity of exercise. However, the primacy of alanine in amino acid outflow from peripheral protein depots is indicated by the fact that the arteriovenous difference for alanine in skeletal [8] and heart muscle [10] is far in excess of that of other amino acids. The existence of a glucose-alanine cycle, proposed initially by Felig and Wahren [8], involving muscle and liver has been confirmed by further studies [22, 23]. During exercise the increased availability of pyruvate and amino acid groups in muscle results in augmented peripheral synthesis and greater release of alanine into the circulation. The importance of alanine synthesis may be related to amino acid oxidation with alanine serving as a vehicle for the transfer of nitrogen in nontoxic form from muscle to liver. In this respect, it is relevant to quote that Holloszy et al have observed that rats submitted to a training program enhanced their content of muscle alanine aminotransferase [24]. The carbon skeleton of the alanine synthesized by muscle is undoubtedly pyruvate derived from glucose.

The transamination of pyruvate, catalyzed by glutamate-pyruvate aminotransferase, is a reversible reaction with the Km of the enzyme for both glutamate and pyruvate being within the range of their concentration in the muscle cell [27]. Ruderman and Lund have demonstrated in rat muscle that the alpha-amino nitrogen of the alanine released was largely derived from the catabolism of other amino acids [25]. These include valine, leucine and isoleucine [25, 31] and possibly some other amino acids which may be deaminated to some extent in muscle [25]. However, experiments undertaken by Odessey et al [26] showed that only leucine, isoleucine and valine appeared to be physiologically important sources of amino acids for alanine synthesis. Muscle indeed possesses a high activity of the aminotransferase which catalyzes the transfer of amino-N of branched-chain amino acids to alpha-ketoglutarate, whose intra-muscular concentration is close to the Km of the transaminase. The glutamate formed in this way can then be used for synthesis of alanine. Thus, the aforementioned experiments of Odessey et al [26] suggest that the release of the branched-chain amino acids by liver and muscle may be an important determinant of the rate of alanine synthesis by muscle. A recent study of Buse et al suggests branched-chain amino acid oxidation in muscle may be regulated by alpha-ketoglutarate at two points: as an amino-group acceptor by accelerating transamination and by accelerating the oxidation of the resulting branched-chain alpha-keto acid.

In terms of ATP production the glucose-alanine cycle, like the Cori cycle, can contribute to the energy demands of the muscle without any net consumption of glucose carbon. The glucose-alanine cycle appears more efficient than the Cori cycle, since the conversion of 1 mole of glucose to alanine provides 8 moles of ATP instead of only 2 moles for the conversion to lactate. Furthermore, the findings of Odessey and Goldberg [28] on rat skeletal muscle suggest that this tissue is the major site of leucine oxidation accounting for about 50% of leucine catabolism of the body. In addition, there seems to be no significant difference in the oxidation of leucine by the soleus, which contains predominantly dark fibers and by the extensor digitorum longus, which contains primarily pale fibers. In fact, in a subsequent study, these authors have demonstrated that leucine, isoleucine, valine, alanine, glutamate and aspartate are primarily oxidized in isolated skeletal muscle [29].

Since skeletal muscle represents the major site of catabolism of the branched-chain amino acids in the body, the complete oxidation of leucine, isoleucine and valine would give, respectively, an additional 42, 43 and 32 ATP per mole. This means that the glucose-branched-chain amino acid-alanine cycle could provide up to 25 times more ATP than the glucose-lactate cycle. In human muscle, a figure of 14% of the total energy has been calculated to originate from the branched-chain amino acids when they are burned to CO_2. Thus, the branched-chain amino acid oxidation could provide a noncarbohydrate energy source for muscle to one extent which remains to be determined during muscular activity.

Protein Synthesis in Muscle

Normal Muscle

Early works gave rise to the general impression that muscle protein has a relatively low turnover, as compared with the protein of an organ such as the liver. Millward [33, 34] and Gan and Jeffray [18] have observed that in rat the myofibrillar proteins turn over more slowly than the sarcoplasmic proteins. These last years, it has been demonstrated that among the myofibrillar components, myosin, actin, tropomyosin and the troponins have different rates of turnover and do not degrade as a unit [35-37]. Koizumi has estimated the turnover of structural proteins of rabbit skeletal muscle by incorporation of five amino acids, namely, glycine, leucine, valine, lysine and alanine [38]. The results showed that the troponins turn over much more rapidly than myosin or actin. However, Rabinowitz using the double isotope technique of Schimke et al [132] showed that the $^3H/^{14}C$ ratio gives an essentially identical half-life for myosin, actin, tropomyosin and troponin [57]. Therefore, this question still remains open for further evidence.

Goldberg also provided evidence that the average half-lives of skeletal muscle proteins, both soluble and myofibrillar, vary in different muscles and are smaller in the tonic muscles than in the phasic ones [21]. Moreover, recent experiments in man suggested that the rate of sarcoplasmic protein synthesis was more than double of the myofibrillar protein synthesis [127].

The incorporation of amino acids into normal skeletal muscle protein has been studied by various labeled compounds, e.g., ^{14}C-Na_2CO_3 [33], ^{14}C-glycine [38], ^{14}C-aspartate [43], ^{15}N-lysine [127], ^{14}C-lysine [18, 39-41], ^{14}C-leucine [21, 122, 126], ^{14}C-tyrosine [18, 39, 42, 129] and ^{15}N-ammonium acetate [123]. Such studies have generally utilized intact animals and are prone to a variety of difficulties and possible artifacts. For example, the reported average half-lives of muscle protein vary over a wide range, presumably because of methodological problems. In 1975 Goldberg's laboratory described a simple method for the study of overall rates of protein synthesis in isolated skeletal muscle [42]. L-(U-^{14}C)tyrosine was chosen since it rapidly equilibrates between intracellular pools and the medium and it is neither synthesized nor degraded by this tissue. Their experiments have shown that various factors are important for muscle growth. Insulin stimulated amino acid transport [19, 42, 44] and promoted protein synthesis [42]. This latter effect was greater when glucose and oxidizable non-carbohydrate substrates were also present in the medium [42, 128]. The addition of the three branched-chain amino acids at plasma concentrations promoted protein synthesis. The circulating levels of leucine, isoleucine and valine vary under different physiological conditions and thus may influence protein turnover in muscle in vivo. However, Millward et al recently suggested that the regulation of protein content in rat skeletal muscle is achieved through alterations of the synthesis rate as the primary response by mechanisms that are unlikely to involve the branched-chain amino acids [163].

Investigations in humans led to the conclusion that the amino acid pool which is in immediate continuity with the protein synthesis sites equilibrates rapidly with the extracellular amino acid pool [126]. Reutilization of amino acids released at protein degradation has a competitive advantage for incorporation as compared with extra- and intracellular free amino acids. In skeletal muscle, Hider et al [131] have presented evidence for direct incorporation of amino acids into protein from the extracellular space. This mechanism would bypass the intracellular pool of amino acids, presumably by a yet unidentified membrane-bound carrier.

Finally, total muscle protein synthesis in normal man was calculated to account for 53% of total body protein turnover, establishing the quantitative importance of muscle protein synthesis in protein metabolism of the whole body [127].

Work-induced Modifications of Muscular Tissue

Numerous studies have investigated work-induced modifications on isolated muscle and in vivo preparation: hyperactivation of intact animal (forced exercise), electrical and specific stimulation, compensatory hypertrophy induced by tenotomy of the synergistic muscle, cross-innervation, passive stretch of muscle and isometric exercise.

The first work on the influence of muscular activity on the protein composition of skeletal muscle is that of Helander, in 1961, who concluded that guinea pig muscle adapts itself by a higher myofilamental protein content [2]. In 1967, Gordon et al concluded that red and white fiber size must be determined differentially since trends may be opposite and give apparently contradictory conclusions regarding hypertrophy of muscle [117]. Increased incorporation of labeled amino acids into proteins has been observed by several investigators in both skeletal muscle [14, 45, 47, 49, 52] and cardiac muscle [46, 48, 50-53]. Interestingly, incorporation of ^{3}H-leucine into sarcoplasmic and myofibrillar fractions increased in parallel [45]. Unlike the growth of muscle that occurs during postnatal development, experiments on hypophysectomized [49], alloxan-diabetic [54] male and female rats [55] indicate that work-induced growth does not require pituitary growth hormone, thyroid hormones, insulin or androgens.

Hypertrophy. As pointed out earlier, hypertrophy is one form of muscle modification induced by exercise. The increase in muscle mass represents an increase in tissue protein which is already demonstrable a few hours after induction of hypertrophy [17].

Histological observations and biochemical studies have shown that hypertrophy of cardiac muscle and adaptation of skeletal muscle to strength exercise consist of hypertrophy of muscle cells and hyperplasia of connective tissue cells. The same situation also occurs after tenotomy of the synergistic muscle [45, 118, 119, 130]. In addition, Gonyea and Ericson showed that weight-lifting exercise training on cats induces an increase in the diameter of the three fiber types [162].

Myocardial protein may increase by 20% to 50% within 48 hours after constriction of the ascending aorta in rats. Short periods of heart hypertrophy caused large increases in the rate of amino acid incorporation into the isolated mitochondria [59]. Rabinowitz has observed that increased synthesis of cytochrome c appears 24 hours after aortic constriction [58], earlier than other cardiac cell constituents. However, studies of Dart and Holloszy [60] clearly suggest that after 7.5 weeks of hypertrophy, cardiac mitochondria increased in parallel with the other components of the myocardial cell. It appears that the capacity for regenerating ATP, both aerobically and anaerobically, expressed either per gram of heart or per milligram of myocardial protein, is unchanged in the nonfailing, hypertrophied heart.

Endurance exercise. As shown by Holloszy [61], if exercise is of the endurance type, such as long-distance running or swimming, adaptative increases occur in the maximum capacity to perform work and to consume oxygen. There is no muscle hypertrophy but, instead, an increase in the capacity for aerobic metabolism. The biochemical adaptations to endurance exercise suggest that skeletal muscle tends to become more like heart muscle in its enzyme pattern.

Sprint exercise. High intensity training (three weeks) of short term (45 sec) exercise was investigated in rats by Staudte et al [62]. No hypertrophy occurred but, as far as the investigated enzymes can be regarded as representing distinct metabolic pathways, it appeared that only enzyme activities of phosphorylation, glycogen breakdown, glycolysis and citric acid cycle were enhanced after short-term, high-intensity training. Furthermore, there were fewer changes in the rectus femoris muscle than in the soleus muscle. This observation might indicate that the latter muscle has acquired to a certain degree properties of the fast muscle.

Similar investigations have been performed with humans. It has been found that strength-trained athletes have higher total LDH [120], myosin ATPase, myokinase and phosphorylcreatine kinase activities [121] than untrained or endurance trained subjects.

Electrical stimulation and cross-innervation. We have seen that electrical stimulation of muscles in vitro increases AIB transport. However, Goldberg et al [17] were unable to observe increased protein synthesis in isolated muscles electrically stimulated. Further experiments are needed to determine whether some additional factor lacking in the in vitro experiments is required to induce greater synthesis under the influence of electrical stimulation.

In vivo electrical stimulation of rabbit muscles conducted Pette et al to a very interesting finding [63]. The authors used intermittent long-term (four weeks) stimulation of fast rabbit muscles with a frequency pattern resembling that of a slow muscle. Besides a reduction of the speed of contraction and an increase of tetanic tension, the activities of key enzymes were also altered after only four days. An increase of activity levels of hexokinase and key enzymes of aerobic oxidative metabolism is concomitant with a decrease of glycogenolytic and glycolytic enzymes. This rearrangement of the enzyme activity pattern corresponds to a change in the metabolic type of the fast muscle into that of a slow muscle [63]. The same results have been recently found by the group of Gergely [64].

These changes are similar to metabolic changes observed in cross-innervation experiments [65-67]. During the last two years, several laboratories have investigated the effect of cross-innervation on properties of myofibrillar proteins. Analysis of myosin ATPase [68], myosin light chains [64, 69, 70, 75] and heavy chains [71], intact myosin [72] and troponin I [73] after cross-innervation showed essentially complete conversion of fast to slow and vice-versa. Thus, it seems likely that the metabolic and structural changes occurring in cross-innervation are induced by the particular pattern of neuronal activity [63, 74].

Increased Synthesis of DNA and RNA

Gordon et al [76] and Hamosh et al [47] have shown that growth of skeletal muscle is associated with that of DNA. Cardiac enlargement produced by a variety of experimental procedures invariably also leads to an increase in DNA content [77, 78, 124]. These changes reflected an increase in DNA synthesis as demonstrated by the enhanced incorporation of ^{3}H-thymidine into nuclear DNA [84]. Although the mitochondrial DNA of myocardial cells increases in heart enlargement [79, 80], it is present in relatively small amounts (1% to 2% of total DNA) to contribute to the observed increases in total cardiac DNA in hypertrophy.

The increased rate of protein synthesis during hypertrophy also appears to be related primarily to an increase in RNA content in rats [34, 81, 83, 90]. In human skeletal muscle, Bylund et al confirm the correlation between RNA concentration and incorporation rate of leucine carbon into proteins [86]. Quantitatively, ribosomal RNA comprises 80% to 85% of total cellular RNA, transfer RNA 10% to 20% and messenger RNA 1% to 2%. The increase in RNA content in hypertrophy is predominantly due to ribosomal RNA [81, 82]. An increase in ^{3}H-uridine labeling of polyribosome profiles has been reported by Schreiber et al [85] and interpreted to indicate an increase in synthesis of mRNA. Likewise, an increase in synthesis of tRNA accompanying cardiac work overload has been presented by Stringfellow et al [87]. Unfortunately, these suggestions were not confirmed by later studies [82, 88, 96]. In addition, hypertrophy of cardiac muscle is not attributable to aminoacyl-synthetase or aminoacyl-transferring enzymes [106] enhancement.

Recently, Buresova et al studied the protein synthetic capacity of ribosomes in cell-free systems of cross-innervated muscles [89]. They found that cross-innervation of rat soleus resulted in an increase of capacity of ribosomes for protein synthesis into that of the fast muscle type. Polysomal aggregates are associated with the synthesis of heavy chains and light chains of myosin [91, 92]. The results showed that the light chains were synthesized on the size class of polyribosomes containing 4 to 9 ribosomes whereas the heavy chains were synthesized separately on a much larger size class of poly-ribosomes containing 60 to 80 ribosomes. Hjalmarson and Isaksson have revealed that aggregation of the ribosomal subunits to ribo-somes goes together with an increase in protein synthesis in in vitro rat heart submitted to workload [93].

It is apparent that increased synthesis of RNA probably precedes and accompanies the increased protein synthesis in hypertrophying tissue. The enzyme RNA polymerase, which synthesizes cellular RNA, was also found to increase its activity as a consequence of enlargement in skeletal muscle [94] and heart muscle [95]. A feature unique to eucaryotes is the presence of three types of RNA polymerases, one for each type of RNA. Nair et al [96] have studied the RNA polymerase activities programmed for rRNA and mRNA synthesis in cardiac hypertrophy. It is clear from their data that only the rRNA polymerase activity is increased in this case.

Most of the RNA metabolism mentioned above provides evidence that new RNA synthesis is an essential prerequisite for work-induced growth of skeletal muscle and cardiac muscle fibers. However, autoradiographs prepared from both types of tissue labeled by incubation in a medium containing tritiated thymidine, uridine or orotic acid show that most of the developed grains are located in interstitial cells [97] and connective tissue cells [98, 99] and not in the muscle fibers (Fig. 2). Thus, most of the new RNA is probably not directly involved in the increased synthesis of muscle proteins. Jablecki et al have observed that the radioactivity associated with the RNA is concentrated in a distal part of the hypertrophied muscle adjacent to the tendon [99]. In addition, the incorporation of thymidine into DNA and ^{3}H-leucine into protein was slightly greater in the distal portion of the muscle [17]. We do not have an explanation for this proliferation of interstitial cells and collagenous matrix. Meanwhile, it appears that this material may be involved in the transmission of contractile force. Further observations are needed to indicate clearly an intimate relationship between the contractile and interstitial cells within the muscle.

Protein Degradation

Proteins are continually degraded and replaced. Accumulation of a protein can represent either increased synthesis or reduced breakdown. Goldberg has considered that the increase in amino acid incorporation during hypertrophy is too small to account entirely for the gain in muscle weight [45]. During work-induced growth, the

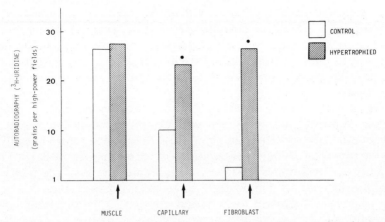

FIG. 2. Autoradiography of soleus muscle of rat labeled in vivo with ^{3}H-uridine two days after unilateral tenotomy. Control and hypertrophied soleus muscles were injected with thymidine and ^{3}H-uridine. Specimens for autoradiography were taken from the middle of control and hypertrophied muscles. The frequency of the grains over muscle cells, capillaries and fibroblasts was determined by examination of ten high-power fields (magnification × 1,600) of each sample. Statistical difference is significant (P <0.05) between the hypertrophied and control grain counts for the capillary cells and fibroblasts (•). No significant difference was observed between the labeling of muscle cells and the hypertrophied muscle. (From Jablecki et al [99].)

average rates of protein catabolism are decreased in skeletal muscle [16, 100] and heart muscle [101]. The degradation of sarcoplasmic proteins decreased more markedly than that of myofibrillar proteins, resulting in a relative increase in the sarcoplasmic proteins during compensatory growth [100].

Studies of protein degradation, however, are limited by methodological artifacts [102, 103]. In order to overcome potential difficulties, Fulks et al [42] have determined rates of degradation by measuring the release of ^{14}C-tyrosine from protein of muscles incubated in the presence of cycloheximide. Under these conditions, the tyrosine release may be used as a measure of degradation. With the aid of this technique, Goldberg and his associates have demonstrated that the dark soleus released tyrosine from protein more rapidly than the pale extensor digitorum longus [16]. These in vitro results are in concordance with their previous experiments with intact animal which also indicated that the basal rate of protein turnover is more rapid in the slow muscle than in the fast muscle. In vitro electrical stimulation also showed that the rate of protein degradation depends upon the level of muscular activity [16].

Subsequently, passive tension and active contraction appeared to have additive effects in delaying breakdown (Fig. 3). Eventually, a number of factors can directly alter rates of catabolism in muscles in vivo and in vitro [104]. Among these factors it is relevant to quote that insulin, glucose and branched-chain amino acids reduce protein catabolism.

In hypertrophying muscles, the increased amino acid transport, protein synthesis and the decreased protein degradation should all have compensatory effects in promoting net muscle growth [84].

Factors controlling degradation of proteins are still not well established. Lysosomes represent a candidate but they are relatively few and difficult to demonstrate in heart and skeletal muscle [105]. The pathway of protein degradation appears to be dependent upon proteolytic enzymes of lysosomal origin. Of these enzymes cathepsin-D is thought to be of major importance [107] and a correlation between the incorporation rate of leucine into protein and the cathepsin-D activity has been found in human skeletal muscles [108]. Recently, the degree of reutilization of amino acids

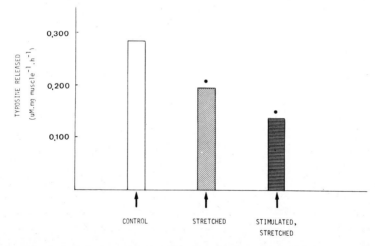

FIG. 3. Effect of stimulation and passive tension on protein degradation in rat soleus. Soleus muscles were removed and stimulated for one hour at 5 pulse·sec^{-1} in a medium containing glucose and amino acids. When stretched, the muscles were approximately 20% longer than that of their resting lengths. The change in protein degradation upon stimulation and/or passive stretch was calculated as the difference in net loss of tyrosine from muscle protein as described by Fulks et al [42]. Statistical significance ($P < 0.05$) was determined by paired analysis (·). (From Goldberg et al [16].)

from protein degradation for protein synthesis was observed to be 10% to 15% in human skeletal muscles [108]. However, in heart hypertrophy, lysosomal enzyme activities have been reported to remain unchanged [88, 109]. It is also noteworthy that ammonia appears to inhibit, at least in the liver, endogenous protein degradation [110]. Knowing that ammonia production during muscular activity is proportional to the work done [111], it should be tempting to stimulate experiments in this direction.

Concerning specific protein degradation we only have few data on cytochrome c and on myosin. Studies of Terjung et al revealed that both in skeletal muscle [112, 113] and in cardiac muscle [114], a decrease in the rate of degradation plays the major role in accounting for the adaptive increase in the concentration of cytochrome c that occurs in muscle in response to exercise. Studies of myosin synthesis and degradation during cardiac hypertrophy, however, remain inconclusive since degradation rate of myosin is increased for some authors [115] and unchanged for others [116].

Regulation of Protein Metabolism

At the molecular level, metabolic control is affected by two different mechanisms: (a) by regulation of enzyme activity and (b) by regulation of protein synthesis. Regulation of enzyme activity may involve kinetic effects of substrates, cofactors, products and physical parameters. This mechanism is rapidly effective, within seconds or minutes, and enables the organism to adapt to acute physiological circumstances. The second mechanism mentioned above, involving genetically directed formation of new protein, might necessarily require hours or longer. This process which affects the amount of protein available would likely increase the ultimate capacity of an organism for muscular work.

The regulation of protein synthesis in muscle is complex and poorly understood. Much of our information in this area has come from bacteria where most of the regulation of gene expression operates through regulatory genes. The latter ones have never been found with high confidence in eucaryotes. Meanwhile, several steps of regulation are available in higher organisms [133].

General Outline in Eucaryotic Cells

Protein synthesis is known to be controlled at the nuclear level and at the cytoplasmic level. All the DNA in eucaryote chromosomes exists as a complex of one-third DNA, one-third histone proteins (five components) and one-third nonhistone proteins [134]. One believes that the histone proteins play a part in the regulation of protein synthesis by inhibiting RNA synthesis from DNA templates. Thus, they act as repressors. The nonhistone proteins function in either the replication or transcription of DNA, as well as in the respective control processes governing DNA and RNA synthesis. These proteins play a fundamental part in displacing the inhibition of histone proteins toward RNA [125]. Among these de-repressors one found protein kinases, DNA polymerase and RNA polymerases. After transcription, most mRNA molecules are modified by the addition of a guanine nucleotide in 5'-5' linkage and at their 3' ends by the addition of adenine nucleotides (Poly A). Unlike procaryotic mRNAs, eucaryotic mRNAs have only one ribosome binding site and therefore always code for only single polypeptide chains. The monocistronic mRNA molecule is subsequently broken down into smaller chains, each of which functions as a separate protein.

Specific inhibitors of protein synthesis are known to be present in the cytoplasm [133]. These molecules are able to combine with mRNA and thus block their translation. Eucaryotic cells have 80S ribosomes with 60S and 40S subunits. At the ribosomal level, proteins are made in almost exactly the same way in both procaryotes and eucaryotes.

Mitochondria contain their own unique species of DNA from which mitochondrial rRNA, mRNA, 12 tRNAs and Poly-A-containing RNAs are transcribed. However, most of the proteins in mitochondria, more than 85% [114], including mitochondrial ribosomal proteins, the initiation and elongation factors involved in the synthesis of mitochondrial DNA and RNA are synthesized outside the mitochondria on cytoplasmic ribosomes with information derived from the nuclear genome.

Overall Gene De-repression During Muscle Hypertrophy

It seems likely that work-induced hypertrophy in skeletal and cardiac muscles would obey to de-repression of the whole gene expression mechanisms. Biochemical characterization of hypertrophied nonfailing rat heart has conducted Dart and Holloszy to suggest that the process leading to the development of cardiac hypertrophy involves the de-repression of all the genetic material normally present in this tissue [60]. Therefore, hypertrophy does not result from induction of specific protein, but instead seems to involve the reactivation of growth of the whole cardiac cell. It looks obvious that most of the biochemical changes implicated in hypertrophy are secondary events rather than initiating factors in compensatory muscle growth.

It is recognized that mechanical factors which produce pressure overloading of the heart lead to greater degrees of cardiac hypertrophy than that of those which produce volume overloading [53]. Tension development and the degree of fiber shortening have been identified as major mechanical determinants of myocardial oxygen consumption [135, 136]. However, myocardial protein and nucleic acid synthesis does not change so rapidly in response to alterations in mechanical stimuli as does oxygen consumption [137].

Several examples of stretch resulting in enhancement of muscle growth have been described [17, 138-143]. Passive stretch of muscle stimulates AIB transport and reduces protein degradation [16]. Denervation of a rat hemidiaphragm results initially in its hypertrophy, presumably because it is passively stretched by the contralateral hemidiaphragm [144, 145]. Elimination of the stretch stimulus by denervation of both diaphragms prevents the hypertrophy [144]. These observations indicate that passive stretch can directly affect protein balance in vivo as well as in vitro. Because of the stretch reflex and the anatomical limits set by the muscle's origin and insertion, it is suggested that increased tension in the muscle resulting from the passive stretch or from normal contractions is the crucial factor inducing hypertrophy [17]. However, the mechanisms coupling tension development to the metabolic events of contractile work remain to be elucidated.

The chemical linkage between mechanical factors and activation of synthetic processes presumably involves changes in membrane function and changes in the levels of metabolites derived from muscular activity. Increased stretch may be translated into protein synthesis by altering the properties of the plasma membrane in order to enhance the transport of precursors of protein and RNA synthesis. Cyclic-AMP has been shown to be involved in the regulation of mammalian cell in culture [146]. Though levels of cAMP have not been reported in heart and muscle after workload, it is tempting to postulate their intervention since the molecule appears to be a potent activator of RNA and protein synthesis. In this context, an increased rate of synthesis of polyamines, such as spermidine, spermine and putrescine, has been shown to occur in a variety of rapidly growing tissues [147]. Caldarera et al have reported a rapid increase in the myocardial content of polyamines during the early phase of cardiac enlargement [148]. Gibson and Harris have studied the in vitro and in vivo effects of polyamines on cardiac protein biosynthesis [149]. Moreover, they have observed that after a transient ATP concentration decrease, ornithine decarboxylase, an enzyme which controls polyamine synthesis, increases in activity within two hours of aortic constriction [160]. They add that the polyamines do not increase rates of protein synthesis in the heart by any direct effect on aminoacyl-tRNA synthetase activity, aminoacyl-tRNA transferring enzyme activity, or on the properties of the ribosomal system. These results may be interpreted as showing that polyamines increase myocardial protein synthesis, probably not by any effect on the cytoplasmic protein synthetic system, but by a modification of the cell wall membrane in such a way as to facilitate the entry of amino acids into the cell [149].

Adenine nucleotides are one of the immediate precursor substances of RNA. Accelerated biosynthesis of de novo adenine nucleotides in the hypertrophying heart accompanies the increase in protein synthesis [150, 151]. In trying to explain the increased rates of adenine nucleotide synthesis, one has to consider that the activities of certain enzymes of the pentose phosphate shunt [83, 152] were shown to be increased in the hypertrophying heart. The resulting ribose-5-phosphate which is formed by this cycle would become available for the adenine nucleotide synthesis. However, this speculation needs further investigations to prove its validity.

Other factors have been proposed to lead to muscle hypertrophy. Recently, Ingwall et al have shown, on breast muscle from chick embryos [153, 154] and on heart muscle from fetal mice [155], that creatine stimulates selectively the rate of synthesis of actin and myosin heavy chain, while the activities of glycolytic and lysosomal enzymes were unaffected [155]. This role of creatine in the regulation of myofibrillar proteins, however, has not been observed with the soleus muscle from young rats [17]. Therefore, the stimulatory effect of creatine appears to be restricted to embryonic muscle. David and Avi-Dor [156] observed that glucose accelerates the incorporation of labeled amino acids into the polypeptide chain by acting presumably at the initiation and elongation sites. Nevertheless this effect of glucose on the rate of protein synthesis was already maximal when the glucose concentration was above 2 mM. Obviously, the stimulatory effect of glucose should not have an appreciable action on muscle hypertrophy.

Recently Källfelt et al [158, 159] showed that in vitro and in vivo catecholamines exert a direct stimulatory effect on heart protein synthesis within one hour after administration. The rather high levels of circulating catecholamines found during hard muscular exercise should be in the future correlated to the development of muscle hypertrophy.

Eventually, the concentration of leucine in muscle cells or a compartment thereof has been suggested to play a part in regulating the turnover of muscle proteins [157]. Studying isolated rat hemi-diaphragms, several authors observed that their data are compatible with the hypothesis that leucine [42, 157], isoleucine and valine [42] inhibit protein degradation and promote protein synthesis in skeletal muscle. Once more, no definite explanation may today shed light on this regulation.

To conclude, one could synthesize the above information on a general view (Fig. 4).

Our knowledge of the basic processes involved in the control of protein synthesis in the development of muscle hypertrophy is far from complete.

Specific Biosynthetic Process of Endurance Exercise

Skeletal muscle adapts to endurance exercise with an increase in the capacity of aerobic metabolism [61]. Underlying this increase in the ability to produce more ATP is the increase in both the size and the number of mitochondria. In addition, an alteration in mito-

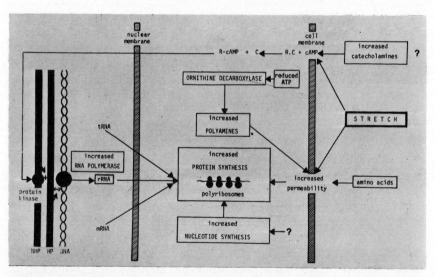

FIG. 4. Tentative hypothesis for increased protein synthesis during muscle hypertrophy. The stretch of the cell increases the permeability of the membrane resulting in enhanced amino acid transport. A transient reduced ATP concentration induces the ornithine decarboxylase which increases the rate of synthesis of polyamines. The latter ones also facilitate the entry of amino acids into the cell. Unidentified factors promote nucleotide synthesis. Cyclic AMP would promote protein kinase (R.C.) activity which removes the inhibition of rRNA polymerase. The resulting effects of the changes mentioned above lead to the aggregation of ribosomes subunits into polyribosomes and subsequent increased protein synthesis.

chondrial composition also occurs. As a result of biochemical adaptations, skeletal muscle tends to become more like heart muscle in its enzyme pattern [61]. Unfortunately, almost no research has shed light on the mechanism by which adaptations of individual protein metabolism are mediated. The only study in this direction is the evidence that the exercise-induced increase in cytochrome c in skeletal muscle is the result of both an increase in the rate of synthesis and a decrease in the rate of degradation [112]. Therefore, once more, the only possibility today is to speculate in reasonable terms.

When an organism is subjected to endurance training its heart undergoes hypertrophy while its legs do not change in weight. On the contrary, the capacity of the respiratory chain doubles in leg muscles and remains constant in the myocardium. These facts suggest that the increase in the maximum capacity to consume oxygen (and correspondingly to produce more ATP) prevents the development of hypertrophy. This metabolic adaptation entails the sequential reprogramming of gene expression that is manifested in an integrated and ordered pattern of enzyme production. The trained individual derives a greater percentage of his energy from fat oxidation than the untrained during submaximal exercise. This situation compels the citric acid cycle to increase its activity level. Indeed, it is well known that $\dot{V}O_2$ max is higher in trained subjects than in the untrained ones; therefore, at the same relative work rate, the former ones do more work and oxidize more substrates than the latter ones.

Control mechanisms may operate through regulatory genes. Pleiotropic genes act as integrative genes to coordinate simultaneously at the biochemical phenotype a series of opposing and competing key enzymes in a number of opposing and competing metabolic pathways [161]. These genes seem to be at least partially involved in our situation. There are results which clearly demonstrate a decrease in activity of enzymes, subsequent to endurance training. Indeed, Baldwin et al have observed a consistent decrease of approximately 20% in the levels of key enzymes of the glycolytic cycle in fast-twitch red fibers while an increase in the respiratory capacity was found in the same fibers [164]. The same conclusion was obtained by other researchers on rabbit [63, 165] and on human [166, 167] skeletal muscles.

One knows that the increase of oxidative enzyme concentration in skeletal muscles depends upon the relative percent of utilization of the $\dot{V}O_2$ max. It can be assumed that this percent averages 80% to 85% of the maximum capacity of trained individuals. Endurance training leads to a preferential utilization of free fatty acids as a fuel instead of carbohydrates. The stimulus to fatty acid mobilization could be the increasing catecholamine release by nerve activity [119] and the increase in growth hormone concentration [169] which occur under the influence of muscular activity. The raised fatty acid level provides the necessary signal for muscular tissue to oxidize these fatty acids.

The question arises by what mechanisms and at what cytological levels is regulation capable of accomplishing a reprogramming of gene expression. At the present stage it is not possible to pinpoint how and where the level of the pleiotropic regulation is exerted.

To conclude, one may cite a sentence of a French biologist, Albert Delaunay, who said: "Le but à atteindre est encore loin mais il nous semble distinguer déjà sa pâle et fascinante lumière" [170].

References

1. Morpurgo, B.: Arch. Sci. Med. 19:327, 1895.
2. Helander, E.A.S.: Biochem. J. 78:478, 1961.
3. Munro, H.N.: Mammalian Protein Metabolism, vol. IV. New York:Academic Press, 1970, p. 299.
4. Bergström, J., Fürst, P., Norée, L.-O. and Vinnars, E.: J. Appl. Physiol. 36:693, 1974.
5. Marliss, E.B., Aoki, T.T., Pozefsky, T. et al: J. Clin. Invest. 50:814, 1971.
6. London, D.R., Foley, T.H. and Webb, C.G.: Nature 208:588, 1965.
7. Felig, P., Pozefsky, T., Marliss, E. and Cahill, C.F. Jr.: Science 167:1003, 1970.
8. Felig, P. and Wahren, J.: J. Clin. Invest. 50:2703, 1971.
9. Felig, P., Wahren, J. and Räf, L.: Proc. Nat. Acad. Sci. USA 70:1775, 1973.
10. Carlsten, A., Hallren, B., Jagenburg, R. et al: Scand. J. Lab. Clin. Invest. 13:418, 1961.
11. Aoki, T.T., Müller, W.A., Brennan, M.F. and Cahill, C.F. Jr.: Diabetes 22:768, 1973.
12. Baños, G., Daniel, P.M., Moorhouse, S.R. and Pratt, O.E.: J. Physiol. 235:459, 1973.
13. Arvill, N.: Acta Endocrinol. 122 (suppl. 27): 1967.
14. Kendrick-Jones, J. and Perry, S.V.: Nature 213:406, 1967.
15. Lesch, M., Gorlin, E. and Sonnenblick, E.H.: Circ. Res. 27:445, 1970.
16. Goldberg, A.L., Jablecki, C. and Li, J.B.: Ann. N.Y. Acad. Sci. 228:190, 1974.
17. Goldberg, A.L., Etlinger, J.D., Goldspink, D.F. and Jablecki, C.: Med. Sci. Sports 7:248, 1975.
18. Gan, J.C. and Jeffray, H.: Biochim. Biophys. Acta 252:125, 1971.
19. Narahara, H.T. and Holloszy, J.O.: J. Biol. Chem. 249:5435, 1974.
20. Portugal, F.H., Elwyn, D.H. and Jeffray, H.: Biochim. Biophys. Acta 215:339, 1970.
21. Goldberg, A.L.: Nature 216:1219, 1967.

22. Keul, J., Doll, E. and Keppler, D.: Energy Metabolism in Human Muscle. Basel:Karger, 1972.
23. Poortmans, J., Siest, G., Galteau, M.M. and Houot, O.: Eur. J. Appl. Physiol. 32:143, 1974.
24. Mole, P.A., Baldwin, K.M., Terjung, R.L. and Holloszy, J.O.: Am. J. Physiol. 224:50, 1973.
25. Ruderman, N.B. and Lund, P.: Israel J. Med. Sci. 8:295, 1972.
26. Odessey, R., Khairallah, E.A. and Goldberg, A.L.: J. Biol. Chem. 249:7623, 1974.
27. Barman, T.E.: Enzyme Handbook. Berlin:Springer-Verlag, 1969.
28. Odessey, R. and Goldberg, A.L.: Am. J. Physiol. 223:1376, 1972.
29. Goldberg, A.L. and Odessey, R.: Am. J. Physiol. 223:1384, 1972.
30. Krebs, H.A.: *In* Munro, H.N. (ed.): Mammalian Protein Metabolism, vol. 1. New York:Academic Press, 1964, p. 125.
31. Buse, M.C., Biggers, J.F., Friderici, K.H. and Buse, J.F.: J. Biol. Chem. 247:8085, 1972.
32. Buse, M.G., Jursinic, S. and Reid, S.S.: Biochem. J. 148:363, 1975.
33. Millward, D.J.: Clin. Sci. 39:577, 1970.
34. Millward, D.J., Garlick, P.J., James, W.P.T. et al: Nature 241:204, 1973.
35. Velick, S.F.: Biochim. Biophys. Acta 20:228, 1956.
36. Funabiki, R. and Cassens, R.G.: Nature 236:249, 1972.
37. Funabiki, R. and Cassens, R.G.: J. Nutr. Sci. Vitaminol. 19:361, 1973.
38. Garlick, P.J.: Nature 223:61, 1969.
39. Gan, J.C. and Jeffray, H.: Biochim. Biophys. Acta 148:448, 1967.
40. Waterlow, J.C. and Stephen, J.M.L.: Clin. Sci. 35:287, 1968.
41. Arnal, M., Fauconneau, G. and Pech, R.: C.R. Acad. Sc. Paris 267:1016, 1968.
42. Fulks, R.M., Li, J.B. and Goldberg, A.L.: J. Biol. Chem. 250:290, 1975.
43. Rourke, A.W.: J. Cell. Physiol. 86:353, 1975.
44. Riggs, T.R. and McKirahan, K.J.: J. Biol. Chem. 248:6450, 1973.
45. Goldberg, A.L.: J. Cell. Biol. 36:653, 1968.
46. Gudbjarnason, S., Telerman, M. and Bing, R.J.: Am. J. Physiol. 206:294, 1964.
47. Hamosh, M., Lesch, M., Baron, J. and Kaufmann, S.: Science 159:935, 1967.
48. Moroz, L.: Circ. Res. 11:449, 1967.
49. Goldberg, A.L.: Am. J. Physiol. 312:1193, 1967.
50. Meerson, F.Z.: Circ. Res. 10:250, 1962.
51. Schreiber, S.S., Oratz, M. and Rothschild, M.: Am. J. Physiol. 211:314, 1966.
52. Zimmer, H.G. and Gerlach, E.: *In* Keul, J. (ed.): Limiting Factors of Physical Performance. Stuttgart:Thieme, 1973, p. 102.
53. Hjalmarson, A. and Isaksson, O.: Acta Physiol. Scand. 86:126, 1972.
54. Goldberg, A.L.: Endocrinology 83:1071, 1968.
55. Mackova, E. and Hnik, P.: Physiol. Bohemoslov. 21:9, 1972.
56. Goldberg, A.L. and Goodman, H.M.: Am. J. Physiol. 216:1111, 1969.
57. Rabinowitz, M.: Am. J. Cardiol. 31:202, 1973.
58. Albin, R., Dowell, R.T., Zak, R. and Rabinowitz, M.: Biochem. J. 136:629, 1973.
59. Hamberger, A., Gegson, N. and Lehninger, A.L.: Biochim. Biophys. Acta 186:373, 1969.

60. Dart, C.H. and Holloszy, J.O.: Circ. Res. 25:245, 1969.
61. Holloszy, J.O.: Med. Sci. Sports 7:155, 1975.
62. Staudte, H.W., Exner, G.U. and Pette, D.: Pflüger Arch. 344:159, 1973.
63. Pette, D., Smith, M.E., Staudte, H.W. and Vrbova, G.: Pflügers Arch. 338:257, 1973.
64. Sréter, F.A., Luff, A.R. and Gergely, J.: J. Gen. Physiol. 66:811, 1975.
65. Prewitt, M.A. and Salafsky, B.: Am. J. Physiol. 218:69, 1970.
66. Dubowitz, V.: J. Physiol. 193:481, 1967.
67. Guth, L., Watson, P.K. and Brown, W.C.: Exp. Neurol. 20:52, 1968.
68. Barany, M. and Close, R.I.: J. Physiol. 213:455, 1971.
69. Sréter, F.A., Gergely, J. and Luff, A.L.: Biochem. Biophys. Acta Res. Comm. 56:84, 1974.
70. Weeds, A.G., Trentham, D.R., Kean, C.F.C. and Buller, A.J.: Nature 247:135, 1974.
71. Jean, D.H., Guth, L. and Albers, R.W.: Exp. Neurol. 38:458, 1973.
72. Hoh, J.F.Y.: Biochemistry 14:742, 1975.
73. Amphlett, G.W., Perry, S.V., Syska, H. et al: Nature 257:602, 1975.
74. Perry, S.V.: J. Neurol. Sci. 12:289, 1971.
75. Medugorac, I., Kämmereit, A. and Jacob, R.: Hoppe-Seyler's Z. Physiol. Chem. 356:1161, 1975.
76. Gordon, E.E., Kowalski, K. and Fritts, M.: Am. J. Physiol. 210:1033, 1966.
77. Morkin, E. and Ashford, T.P.: Am. J. Physiol. 215:1409, 1968.
78. Grimm, A.F., de la Torre, L. and LaPorta, M.: Circ. Res. 26:45, 1970.
79. Laguens, R.P. and Gomez Gumm, C.L.: Experientia 24:163, 1968.
80. Meerson, F.Z. and Pomoinitsky, V.Z.: J. Mol. Cell. Cardiol. 4:571, 1972.
81. Fanburg, B.L. and Posner, B.I.: Circ. Res. 23:123, 1968.
82. Koide, T. and Rabinowitz, M.: Circ. Res. 24:9, 1969.
83. Meerson, F.Z.: Circ. Res. 25 (suppl. II), 1969.
84. Goldberg, A.L.: In Alpert, N.R. (ed.): Cardiac Hypertrophy. New York: Academic Press, 1971, p. 301.
85. Schreiber, S.S., Oratz, M., Evans, C. et al: Am. J. Physiol. 215:1250, 1968.
86. Bylund, A.C., Holm, J., Lundholm, K. and Schersten, T.: Enzyme 21:39, 1976.
87. Stringfellow, C. and Brachfeld, N.: J. Mol. Cell. Cardiol. 1:221, 1970.
88. Martin, A.F., Reddy, M.K., Zak, R. et al: Circ Res. 34 and 35 (suppl. III):32, 1974.
89. Buresova, M., Hanzlikova, V. and Gutmann, E.: Pflügers Arch. 360:95, 1975.
90. Blake, C.A. and Hazelwood, R.L.: Proc. Soc. Exp. Biol. Med. 136:632, 1971.
91. Low, R.B., Vournakis, J.N. and Rich, A.: Biochemistry 10:1813, 1971.
92. Sarkar, S. and Cooke, P.H.: Biochem. Biophys. Res. Comm. 41:918, 1970.
93. Hjalmarson, A. and Isaksson, O.: Acta Physiol. Scand. 86:342, 1972.
94. Sobel, B.E. and Kaufmann, S.: Arch. Biochem. Biophys. 137:469, 1970.
95. Nair, K.G., Cutilletta, A.F., Zak, R. et al: Circ. Res. 23:451, 1968.
96. Nair, K.G., Umali, T. and Potts, J.: Circ. Res. 34 and 35 (suppl. II):33, 1974.
97. Schiaffino, S., Bormioli, S.P. and Aloisi, M.: Virchows Arch. Abt. B. Zellpath. 11:268, 1972.
98. Morkin, E.: In Alpert, N.A. (ed.): Cardiac Hypertrophy. New York: Academic Press, 1971, p. 259.

99. Jablecki, C.K., Heuser, J.E. and Kaufmann, S.: J. Cell. Biol. 57:743, 1973.
100. Goldberg, A.L.: J. Biol. Chem. 244:3217, 1969.
101. Zak, R., Aschenbrenner, V. and Rabinowitz, M.: J. Clin. Invest. 50:102A, 1971.
102. Schimke, R.T.: In Munro, H.N. (ed.): Mammalian Protein Metabolism, vol. IV. New York:Academic Press, 1970, p. 178.
103. Goldberg, A.L. and Dice, J.F.: Ann. Rev. Biochem. 43:835, 1974.
104. Goldberg, A.L., Howell, E.M., Li, J.B. et al: Fed. Proc. 33:1112, 1974.
105. Travis, D.F. and Travis, A.: J. Ultrastruct. Res. 39:124, 1972.
106. Gibson, K.: In: Les surcharges cardiaques. Paris:INSERM, 1972, p. 299.
107. Hajek, J., Gutmann, E. and Syrovy, I.: Physiol. Bohemoslov. 14:481, 1965.
108. Lundholm, K. and Schersten, T.: Exp. Geront. 10:155, 1975.
109. Stoner, C.D., Bishop, S.P. and Sirak, H.D.: J. Molec. Cell. Cardiol. 5:171, 1973.
110. Seglen, P.O.: Biochem. Biophys. Res. Comm. 66:44, 1975.
111. Parnas, J.K., Mozolowski, W. and Lewinskiw, W.: Biochem. Z. 188:15, 1927.
112. Terjung, R.L., Winder, W.W., Baldwin, K.M. and Holloszy, J.O.: J. Biol. Chem. 248:7404, 1973.
113. Terjung, R.L.: Biochem. Biophys. Res. Comm. 66:173, 1975.
114. Rabinowitz, M. and Zak, R.: Circ. Res. 36:367, 1975.
115. Morkin, E., Kimata, S. and Skillman, J.J.: Circ. Res. 30:690, 1972.
116. Schreiber, S.S., Oratz, M., Evans, C. et al: Am. J. Physiol. 224:338, 1973.
117. Gordon, E.E., Kowalski, K. and Fritts, M.: Arch. Phys. Med. Rehab. 48:296, 1967.
118. Margreth, A. and Salviati, G.: Biochem. J. 124:669, 1971.
119. Gutmann, E. and Hajek, I.: Physiol. Bohemoslov. 20:205, 1971.
120. Karlsson, J., Sjödin, B., Thorstensson, A. et al: Acta Physiol. Scand. 93:150, 1975.
121. Thorstensson, A., Sjödin, B. and Karlsson, J.: Acta Physiol. Scand. 94:313, 1975.
122. Strohman, R.C., Cerwinsky, E.W. and Holmes, D.W.: Exp. Cell Res. 35:617, 1964.
123. Fürst, P., Jonsson, A., Josephson, B. and Vinnars, E.: J. Appl. Physiol. 29:307, 1970.
124. Leclercq, J.F. and Swynghedauw, B.: Eur. J. Clin. Invest. 6:27, 1976.
125. Frenster, J.H. and Herstein, P.R.: N. Engl. J. Med. 288:1224, 1973.
126. Lundholm, K. and Schersten, T.: Acta Physiol. Scand. 1975.
127. Halliday, D. and McKeran, R.O.: Clin. Sci. Mol. Med. 49:581, 1975.
128. Rannels, D.E., Hjalmarson, A.C. and Morgan, H.E.: Am. J. Physiol. 226:528, 1974.
129. James, W.P.T., Garlick, P.J. and Sender, P.M.: Clin. Sci. Mol. Med. 46:8P, 1974.
130. Schiaffino, S. and Bormioli, S.P.: Exp. Neurol. 40:126, 1973.
131. Hider, R.C., Fern, E.B. and London, D.R.: Biochem. J. 114:171, 1969.
132. Schimke, R.T., Ganschow, R., Doyle, D. and Arias, I.M.: Fed. Proc. 27:1223, 1968.
133. Kruh, J.: In: Synthèse normale et pathologique des protéines chez les animaux supérieurs. Paris:INSERM, 1973, p. 45.
134. Watson, J.D.: Molecular Biology of the Gene. London:W. A. Benjamin Inc., 1976.

135. Mitchell, J.H., Hefner, L.L. and Monroe, R.G.: Am. J. Med. 53:481, 1972.
136. Sonneblick, E.H., Ross, J. Jr. and Braunwald, E.: Am. J. Cardiol. 22:328, 1968.
137. Morkin, E.: Circ. Res. 34 and 35 (suppl. II):37, 1974.
138. Sola, O.M., Christensen, D.L. and Martin, A.W.: Exp. Neurol. 41:76, 1973.
139. Csapo, A., Erdos, T., De Mattos, C.R. et al: Nature 207:1378, 1965.
140. Gutmann, E., Schiaffino, S. and Hanzlikova, V.: Exp. Neurol. 31:451, 1971.
141. Buresova, M., Gutmann, E. and Kliepera, M.: Experientia 25:144, 1969.
142. Schiaffino, S. and Hanzlikova, V.: Experientia 26:152, 1970.
143. Schiaffino, S.: Experientia 30:1163, 1974.
144. Feng, T.P. and Lu, D.X.: Sci. Sinica(Pékidg) 14:1772, 1965.
145. Zak, R., Grove, D. and Rabinowitz, M.: Am. J. Physiol. 216:647, 1969.
146. Sheppard, J.R.: Nature (New Biology) 236:14, 1972.
147. Snyder, S.H., Kreuz, D.S. and Medina, V.J.: Ann. New York Acad. Sci. 171:749, 1970.
148. Caldarera, C.M., Casti, A., Rossoni, C. and Visioli, O.: J. Mol. Cell. Cardiol. 3:121, 1973.
149. Gibson, K. and Harris, P.: Cardiovasc. Res. 8:668, 1974.
150. Zimmer, H.G., Trendelenburg, C. and Gerlach, E.: J. Mol. Cell. Cardiol. 4:279, 1972.
151. Zimmer, H.G.: Personal communication.
152. Valadares, J.E.R., Singhal, R.L., Parnlekar, M.R. and Beznak, M.: Can. J. Physiol. Pharmacol. 47:388, 1969.
153. Ingwall, J.S., Morales, M.F. and Stockdale, F.E.: Proc. Natl. Acad. Sci. USA 69:2250, 1972.
154. Ingwall, J.S., Weiner, C.D., Morales, M.F. et al: J. Cell Biol. 63:145, 1974.
155. Ingwall, J.S. and Wildenthal, K.: J. Cell Biol. 68:159, 1976.
156. David, M. and Avi-Dor, Y.: Biochem. J. 150:405, 1975.
157. Buse, M.G. and Reid, S.S.: J. Clin. Invest. 56:1250, 1975.
158. Källfelt, B.J., Hjalmarson, A.C. and Isaksson: Personal communication.
159. Källfelt, B.J., Hjalmarson, A.C., Waldenström, A.P. and Sourander, P.: Personal communication.
160. Gibson, K.: Personal communication.
161. Weber, G., Trevisani, A. and Heinrich, P.C.: Adv. Enz. Regul. 12:11, 1974.
162. Gonyea, W.J. and Ericson, G.C.: J. Appl. Physiol. 40:630, 1976.
163. Millward, D.J., Garlick, P.J., Nnamyelugo, D.O. and Waterlow, J.C.: Biochem. J. 156:185, 1976.
164. Baldwin, K.M., Winder, W.W., Terjung, R.L. and Holloszy, J.O.: Am. J. Physiol. 225:962, 1973.
165. Cotter, M., Hudlicka, O., Pette, D. et al: J. Physiol. 230:34P, 1973.
166. Morgan, T.E., Cobb, L.A., Short, F.A. et al: In Pernow, B. and Saltin, B. (eds.): Muscle Metabolism During Exercise. New York:Plenum, 1971, p. 187.
167. Moesch, H. and Howald, H.: In Howald, H. and Poortmans, J. (eds.): Metabolic Adaptation to Prolonged Physical Exercise. Basel:Birkhäuser, 1975, p. 463,
168. Häggendal, J.: In Pernow, B. and Saltin, B. (eds.): Muscle Metabolism During Exercise. New York:Plenum, 1971, p. 119.
169. Hartley, L.H.: Med. Sci. Sports 7:34, 1975.
170. Delaunay, A.: Journal d'un biologiste, Plon 1959, p. 250.

Cycle des protéines pendant l'effort physique

L'auteur présente le muscle comme un tissu très polyvalent pouvant s'adapter de façon rapide et chronique aux nombreuses exigences du travail. Etant donné l'importance de la masse du tissu musculaire chez l'être humain (environ 50% du poids du corps chez le mâle), il est clair que le muscle joue un rôle important dans le métabolisme. Puisque environ 80% du poids du muscle est constitué de protéines, ces dernières servent à nombre d'usages importants dans le maintien de l'homéostasie. Etude approfondie du contrôle du transport des acides aminés, de leur emploi dans l'équilibre énergétique, de la synthèse des protéines dans les muscles, de la dégradation des protéines et de la régulation du métabolisme des protéines, et en particulier les effets aigus et chroniques de l'effort physique, tant chez l'être humain que chez l'animal.

Individual Scientific Contributions

Communications scientifiques individuelles

Response of Serum Enzymes to Intermittent Work

M. E. Houston, M. R. Waugh, H. J. Green
and E. G. Noble

Introduction

The response of serum enzymes to various stresses has been well documented. Cold, heat, hypoxia, myocardial infarction and physical exercise result in sometimes dramatic alterations in both the qualitative and quantitative pattern of enzymes in the blood. The increases in serum enzyme activities during and following physical exercise have been shown to be derived from both liver and skeletal muscle. Although the exact cause of the increased release of certain enzymes from liver and muscle during exercise is unknown, it is generally agreed that this is due to altered permeability of the muscle fiber and hepatocyte membranes.

Much speculation concerning the nature of the exercise stress and the serum enzyme response is evident upon examination of the literature. Shapiro et al and Hunter and Critz have shown that exercise intensity is the major factor, whereas Gardner et al, Fowler et al and Sanders and Bloor report that the duration of the exercise stress is the factor most responsible for elevating serum enzyme activities. Despite these aforementioned divergent views it is well documented that training significantly reduces the exercise-induced elevations in serum enzyme activities.

The types and concentrations of metabolic substrates and products are also decisively influenced by the intensity and duration of an exercise stress. This can be best illustrated by the reciprocal relationship exhibited by blood FFA and lactate levels during brief continuous high intensity versus prolonged low intensity exercise.

The aim of this investigation was to study the response of selected serum enzymes to three conditions of high intensity intermittent exercise, an area not previously studied. All conditions

M. E. Houston, M. R. Waugh, H. J. Green and E. G. Noble, Department of Kinesiology, University of Waterloo, Waterloo, Ontario, Canada.

were run at a maximal load with work to rest durations arranged so that a low lactate, moderate lactate and high blood lactate response would be elicited.

Methods

Six moderately trained male subjects ($\dot{V}O_2$ max 50-60 ml $\times$ kg^{-1} $\times$ min^{-1}) between 21 and 24 years of age served as subjects in this study. On the basis of the individually derived relationship between oxygen uptake and treadmill running intensity, a grade and speed was selected for each subject to represent 100% of the subject's $\dot{V}O_2$ max. The intermittent running schedules, designated as 0.5/0.5, 1.5/1.5 and 3/3, consisted of running for 0.5, 1.5 and 3 minutes, with intervening rest periods of the same duration, for one hour. Blood was sampled from an antecubital vein prior to exercise, early in the exercise (7 to 9 minutes, depending upon the condition) at the mid-point (30 minutes) and at the end of exercise (60 minutes). The serum enzymes assayed were glutamine oxalo-acetic transaminase (GOT), glutamic pyruvate transaminase (GPT), lactate dehydrogenase (LDH) and creatine phosphokinase (CPK). In addition blood glucose, lactate, pyruvate and FFA were measured.

Results

Lactate

In general, there was significant positive relationship, as expected, between the duration of each intermittent work bout and the venous lactate concentration. Elevations over the pre-exercise values were found at all sampling times, and although there was a tendency for the lactate level to decrease at the end of exercise, this was not significant.

Glucose

Venous glucose levels were significantly greater than rest levels at the midpoint of work. While a similar trend to the lactate levels was apparent, there was no statistically significant difference between the three intermittent work conditions. An interesting trend was the decline in blood glucose levels in the two longer exercise conditions from 30 to 60 minutes.

Pyruvate

Blood pyruvate levels revealed a similar pattern with lactate levels in that the increase in pyruvate was related with the increased work

Table I. Serum Enzyme and Blood Metabolite Levels During
Three Different Forms of Intermittent Treadmill Running

Intermittent Exercise Condition	Before Exercise	Blood Sampling Time		
		Early in Exercise	Mid-point of Exercise	Post Exercise
		GPT (units/ml)		
0.5/0.5	16.8 ± 4.7	17.7 ± 6.4	21.0 ± 7.5	21.3 ± 5.6
1.5/1.5	16.0 ± 2.9	16.8 ± 3.3	20.2 ± 5.0	22.0 ± 4.8
3.0/3.0	17.8 ± 4.4	18.5 ± 3.8	21.8 ± 7.0	24.8 ± 7.1
		GOT (units/ml)		
0.5/0.5	23.8 ± 5.8	23.5 ± 6.3	23.7 ± 6.9	30.8 ± 8.9
1.5/1.5	21.2 ± 6.0	23.3 ± 5.3	28.3 ± 7.5	32.7 ± 9.8
3.0/3.0	22.3 ± 6.9	24.8 ± 5.1	32.7 ± 6.2	39.2 ± 7.3
		LDH (I.U.)		
0.5/0.5	44.1 ± 8.6	45.6 ± 7.1	46.8 ± 5.4	49.3 ± 11.1
1.5/1.5	46.5 ± 7.4	45.7 ± 6.5	46.4 ± 10.6	49.0 ± 6.1
3.0/3.0	46.3 ± 6.7	48.3 ± 4.1	47.2 ± 6.6	47.0 ± 6.3
		CPK (I.U.)		
0.5/0.5	32.4 ± 7.3	35.7 ± 5.9	39.7 ± 8.0	42.3 ± 11.2
1.5/1.5	33.7 ± 5.9	33.4 ± 6.0	39.5 ± 7.1	46.5 ± 9.7
3.0/3.0	31.6 ± 7.1	35.0 ± 5.0	47.8 ± 7.8	51.2 ± 10.9
		Blood Lactate (mg%)		
0.5/0.5	10.5 ± 1.3	18.5 ± 2.0	20.3 ± 2.9	17.7 ± 3.1
1.5/1.5	17.6 ± 3.8	33.0 ± 4.5	42.5 ± 5.6	38.0 ± 4.0
3.0/3.0	12.2 ± 1.6	60.9 ± 7.2	72.6 ± 7.9	67.7 ± 8.6
		Plasma FFA (μmol/ml)		
0.5/0.5	0.94 ± 0.15	0.60 ± 0.13	1.05 ± 0.10	1.41 ± 0.21
1.5/1.5	0.53 ± 0.18	0.49 ± 0.06	0.60 ± 0.09	1.27 ± 0.23
3.0/3.0	0.87 ± 0.24	0.58 ± 0.14	0.61 ± 0.07	1.14 ± 0.16

time in each exercise bout. Between exercise conditions, significant differences were found at all sampling times for the 0.5/0.5 and 3/3 conditions, whereas significance was found only at the last two sampling times when the 0.5/0.5 and 1.5/1.5 conditions were compared.

Free Fatty Acids

Variations in free fatty acids did not significantly differ between conditions, but only over time. In general, an initial transient decline was observed early in exercise, followed by progressive increases throughout each of the exercise conditions. The most pronounced increase occurred for the condition with the shortest work bout duration.

Serum Enzymes

Serum GPT and CPK activities were significantly greater than the pre-exercise values for the last two sampling times for all three intermittent exercise conditions. Serum GOT levels were similarly significantly elevated for 1.5/1.5 and 3/3 conditions, but significance was only found for the GOT activity at the end of exercise. Serum LDH showed no significant exercise-related effect. Between conditions significance was observed for CPK and GOT only.

Summary and Conclusions

The results of this study indicate that the blood concentrations of both pyruvate and lactate increase in proportion to the length of the intermittent work bouts. In all conditions the major change in these blood metabolites occurred early in work. These response patterns are similar to those reported in previous investigations and appear to reflect differential degrees of glycolytic involvement in energy metabolism. Due to the lag in oxygen uptake at the start of exercise both the anaerobic splitting of the phosphagens ATP and CP plus the aerobic metabolism associated with myoglobin-bound oxygen can contribute significantly to energy delivery early in exercise. However, the capacity of these as energy sources is limited, and a rapid and increasingly important reliance on glycolytic metabolism has been shown to exist if heavy exercise is continued beyond 20 seconds or more. This can be illustrated by the differences in glycogen depletion observed in a related experiment utilizing two of the intermittent exercise programs of the present study.

Previous studies on exercise-induced alterations in serum enzyme activities have used widely different exercise types, durations, intensities and subject fitness levels. This has produced some remarkably different enzyme responses, making comparisons with the data in the present study both risky and tenuous. However, some comparisons may be justified.

The effect of increasing duration of intermittent exercise revealed a time-dependent increase in three of the enzymes, namely, GOT, GPT and LDH. LDH showed no significant response compared to rest values for all sampling periods during exercise. Prolonged running in the studies of Rose et al and Magazanik et al showed significant increases in CPK and LDH and CPK and GOT, respectively. The percent increases in CPK activity were greater than those reported here, but the running durations were considerably longer.

LDH has shown puzzling variations with prolonged work. Some investigations have observed large increases during prolonged exercise, whereas others have shown no change and, in one case, a decline. Further investigation of this consistency appears warranted.

Cunningham and Critz and Shapiro et al have reported that the intensity of the exercise stress is the more dominant factor in altering serum enzyme levels than durations. Other studies do not show this same effect. In the present study exercise intensity was fixed for all three intermittent conditions. However, it is noteworthy that the responses of the enzymes CPK and GOT bore a relationship to the degree of anaerobic stress as determined by venous lactate concentrations. It has been widely assumed that relative muscle hypoxia is a primary factor in elevating serum enzymes during work. The results of the present investigation seem to bear this out.

An examination of the sources of the serum enzymes and their exercise-induced responses presents some interesting relationships. CPK is believed to be primarily of muscle origin, whereas GPT has been shown to increase in hepatic venous blood during exercise. Serum GOT is considered to be derived from a number of tissues, including muscle. Since only the muscle-derived CPK and partially muscle-derived GOT showed any variations with the duration of the work bouts, further support for the hypothesis of relative muscle hypoxia is evident.

Bibliography

Bedrak, E.: Blood serum enzyme activity of dogs exposed to heat stress and muscular exercise. J. Appl. Physiol. 20:587-590, 1965.

Fojt, E., Ekelund, L.-G. and Hultman, E.: Enzyme activities in hepatic venous blood under strenuous physical exercise. Pflügers Arch. 361:287-296, 1976.

Forssell, G., Nordlander, R., Nyquist, O. et al: Creatine phosphokinase after submaximal physical exercise in untrained individuals. Acta Med. Scand 197:503-505, 1975.

Fowler, Jr., W.M., Gardner, G.W., Kazerunian, H.H. and Lauvstad, W.A.: The effect of exercise on serum enzymes. Arch. Phys. Med. Rehabil. 49:554-565, 1968.

Gardner, G.W., Bratton, R., Chowdhury, J.R. et al: Effect of exercise on serum enzyme levels in trained subjects. J. Sports Med. 4:103-110, 1964.

Hunter, J.B. and Critz, J.B.: Effect of training on plasma enzyme levels in man. J. Appl. Physiol. 31:20-23, 1971.

Ladue, J., Wroblewski, F. and Karman, A.: Serum glutamic oxaloacetic transaminase activity in human transmural myocardial infarction. Science 120:497-499, 1954.

Magazanik, A., Shapiro, Y., Meytes, D. and Meytes, J.: Enzyme blood levels and water balance during a marathon race. J. Appl. Physiol. 36:214-217, 1974.

Meltzer, H.Y.: Plasma creatine phosphokinase activity, hypothermia, and stress. Am. J. Physiol. 221:896-901, 1971.

Nelson, B.D.: Hepatic lysosomes and serum enzymes in rats exposed to high altitude. Am. J. Physiol. 211:651-655, 1966.

Rose, L.I., Bousser, J.E. and Cooper, K.H.: Serum enzymes after marathon running. J. Appl. Physiol. 29:355-357, 1970.

Sanders, T.M. and Bloor, C.M.: Effects of repeated endurance exercise on serum enzyme activities in well-conditioned males. Med. Sci. Sports 7:44-47, 1975.

Schmidt, E. and Schmidt, F.W.: Enzyme modifications during activity. In Poortman, J.R. (ed.): Biochemistry of Exercise. Medicine and Sport Vol. 3. New York:Karger, 1969, pp. 216-238.

Schwartz, P.L., Carroll, H.W. and Douglas, Jr., J.S.: Exercise-induced changes in serum enzyme activities and their relationship to max VO_2. Int. Z. Angew. Physiol. 30:20-33, 1971.

Shapiro, Y., Magazanik, A., Sohar, E. and Reich, C.B.: Serum enzyme changes in untrained subjects following a prolonged march. Can. J. Physiol. Pharmacol. 51:271-276, 1973.

Serum Enzyme Response to Exercise Bouts of Varying Intensity and Duration

Russell R. Pate, Patricia Palmieri,
David Hughes and Thomas Ratliffe

Introduction

Previous research has demonstrated that strenuous exercise produces an elevation of the serum enzyme activities in man [19]. Isoenzyme studies have shown the predominant source of these enzymes to be skeletal muscle [8, 14, 15], and histopathologic observations of exercised skeletal muscle have led to the conclusion that postexercise serum enzyme elevations can result from passage of enzymes across the intact muscle cell membrane [9]. Several investigators have hypothesized that postexercise serum enzyme elevations in humans are due to increased cell membrane permeability [4, 8, 19]. Among the factors suggested as possible causes for an increase in membrane permeability have been local muscle hypoxia [3, 8, 10], catecholamines [5, 13], decreased blood glucose [8], increased serum potassium [8] and anaerobiosis [8].

Recently reported evidence suggests that efflux of enzyme from intact cells is due to increased membrane permeability secondary to decreased intracellular levels of adenosine triphosphate (ATP) [21-23]. During exercise ATP concentration in muscle is inversely related to the relative intensity of work [16]. Consequently, if depressed intracellular levels of ATP are responsible for efflux of enzyme into the circulation, the magnitude of the efflux should be well related to the intensity of the work. Duration of work, particularly at workloads requiring relatively low percentages of the maximum aerobic power, should be of lesser importance.

Russell R. Pate, Patricia Palmieri, David Hughes and Thomas Ratliffe, Human Performance Laboratory, College of Health and Physical Education, University of South Carolina, Columbia, S.C., U.S.A.

Supported by a grant from the University of South Carolina, Committee on Research and Productive Scholarship.

193

Previous studies have drawn conflicting conclusions regarding the relative importance of intensity and duration of work in the exercise-induced serum enzyme increases [4, 8]. The present study was designed specifically to test the hypothesis that changes in serum enzyme activities are related to both intensity and duration of exercise.

Methods

Subjects for this study were four well-trained male distance runners (ages 24 to 47). Three of the subjects were competitive marathon runners and the fourth participated regularly in 5 to 10 mile road races. At the time of the investigation the subjects were running 40 to 60 miles per week. Maximal oxygen uptake ($\dot{V}O_2$max) for the group was 64.5 ± 1.8 ml/kg/min (mean ± SEM).

Each subject completed the $\dot{V}O_2$max test and five long duration treadmill runs. In testing $\dot{V}O_2$max we employed the continuous treadmill running protocol described by Åstrand [2]. Intensity and duration of the long duration runs were as follows: (1) 60% of the individual's $\dot{V}O_2$max, 60 min; (2) 60%, 90 min; (3) 60%, 120 min; (4) 70%, 60 min; (5) 80%, 60 min. These workloads were selected so as to provide three runs of varying duration at 60% of $\dot{V}O_2$max and three runs of equal duration with intensity varying from 60% to 80% of $\dot{V}O_2$max. The order in which the subjects completed the runs was randomized. All runs were completed within an eight-week period and a minimum of seven days separated successive runs. During each long duration run $\dot{V}O_2$ was monitored for the last 3 minutes of each 15-minute period. A standard open circuit procedure, using a Parkinson-Cowan CD4 gasometer, was employed for measurement of expired air volume and collection of expired air samples. Oxygen analyses were performed using a Beckman E2 oxygen analyzer which was regularly calibrated with gases of known oxygen content as established by Haldane analysis.

Venous blood samples were drawn from a cubital vein before and three minutes after each exercise bout. Whole blood samples were analyzed for hematocrit (Hct) and for hemoglobin concentration (Hb) using the cyanmethemoglobin method [6]. Postexercise samples were assayed for lactate concentration using an enzymatic procedure [11]. Sera were assayed for hemoglobin concentration (SHb) and creatine phosphokinase (CPK), lactic dehydrogenase (LDH), glutamic-oxalacetic transaminase (GOT) and glutamic-pyruvic transaminase (GPT) activities. Ultraviolet spectro-photometric techniques were used in all serum enzyme assays (Sigma assay kits). Transaminase and LDH units were defined as the activity which caused a decrease in OD_{340} of 0.001 per minute in a 3 ml reaction mixture. CPK activity was expressed in International milli-units. All serum enzyme assays were performed at 25 C using a Beckman Model 25 recording spectrophotometer.

Preexercise (T1) and postexercise (T2) means for each variable were compared using the correlated t-test for paired observations. A repeated measures ANOVA procedure was utilized to examine the relation of the change in each variable (T2-T1) to intensity and duration of work.

Results

Table I presents the pre- to postexercise changes which occurred in each serum enzyme due to each of the six treatments. Significant ($p < .10$) increases were observed in CPK for each exercise bout excepting No. 2. LDH was increased significantly after each of the three most strenuous long duration runs, Nos. 3, 4, and 5. Runs 1 and 4 produced significant increases in GOT. None of the treatments resulted in significant changes in GPT. The expected exercise hemoconcentration was observed as indicated by significantly increased Hb following each run. Hct was increased significantly only after the $\dot{V}O_2$max test. No significant alterations in SHb were observed.

As shown in Figure 1 the mean changes in CPK and LDH increased with increasing intensity of work. Changes in GOT and GPT showed no consistent pattern of response. Statistical analysis, using the repeated measures ANOVA procedure, yielded a significant F-ratio only for the changes in CPK activity ($p < .025$). Application of the Duncan Multiple Range Test as a post hoc treatment revealed that all possible differences between mean changes in CPK were significant excepting that between runs 4 and 5. Changes in Hb, Hct and SHb were not related to work intensity.

Figure 2 displays the data collected in runs 1, 2 and 3 and demonstrates that there was no apparent linear trend in the response of any of the serum enzymes to work bouts of varying duration. Statistical analysis confirmed that none of the changes in serum enzyme activity were significantly related to duration of exercise. Likewise, changes in Hb, Hct and SHb were unrelated to duration of work.

Postexercise mean blood lactate concentrations remained essentially at resting levels (10.5 to 13.4 mg%) following all runs at 60% and 70% of $\dot{V}O_2$max. Run 5, conducted at 80% of the $\dot{V}O_2$max,

Table I. Pre- to Postexercise Changes in Serum Enzyme Activities
and Hemoglobin Concentration (Mean ± SEM)

		VO2max Test	1.60%,60'	2.60%,90'	3.60%,120'	4.70%,60'	5.80%,60'
CPK	Pre	8.67±3.35	12.14±2.88	12.60±4.16	11.47±3.07	13.06±4.98	9.91±3.15
	Post	10.60±3.64	13.16±2.89	17.72±7.34	15.67±4.42	16.39±5.16	14.16±3.17
	Δ	1.93±0.33	1.02±0.26	5.12±3.45	4.20±1.74	3.33±1.15	4.25±0.29
	%Δ	22.3	8.4	40.6	36.3	25.5	42.9
	Signif	.05	.05	NS	.10	.10	.01
LDH	Pre	311.7±42.7	353.0±79.4	362.3±17.3	302.0±20.3	308.8±31.8	300.8±20.0
	Post	311.3±38.6	356.3±26.8	353.0±25.8	371.3±31.5	379.0±30.6	384.8±26.2
	Δ	-0.4±9.3	3.3±57.4	-9.3±20.9	69.3±17.5	70.2±10.0	84.0±6.9
	%Δ	-0.1	0.9	-2.6	22.9	22.7	27.9
	Signif	NS	NS	NS	.05	.01	.01
GOT	Pre	44.7±14.7	42.0±8.4	48.0±7.3	46.5±9.4	38.3±3.1	54.3±10.4
	Post	49.0±8.0	47.5±7.2	48.0±3.2	41.3±4.3	44.3±3.5	61.7±12.5
	Δ	4.3±3.4	5.5±1.3	0.0±4.1	-5.2±5.8	6.0±1.7	7.5±8.0
	%Δ	9.6	13.1	0.0	-11.2	15.7	13.8
	Signif	NS	.05	NS	NS	.05	.01
GPT	Pre	31.5±4.5	44.0±3.9	44.3±8.8	40.8±2.9	54.0±10.2	49.0±3.1
	Post	44.0±1.0	52.0±10.4	38.5±7.2	51.0±11.7	45.8±3.5	54.5±3.7
	Δ	12.5±5.5	8.0±8.1	-5.8±6.8	10.2±11.1	-8.2±8.0	5.5±4.5
	%Δ	39.7	18.2	-13.1	25.0	-15.2	11.2
	Signif	NS	NS	NS	NS	NS	NS
Hb (g%)	Pre	15.85±0.28	15.65±0.33	15.53±0.15	15.83±0.06	15.55±0.23	15.75±0.26
	Post	16.55±0.26	16.68±0.40	16.40±0.41	16.65±0.03	16.63±0.27	16.68±0.27
	Δ	0.70±0.04	1.03±0.25	0.87±0.29	0.82±0.06	1.08±0.09	0.93±0.24
	%Δ	4.4	6.6	5.6	5.2	6.9	5.9
	Signif	.01	.05	.10	.01	.01	.05

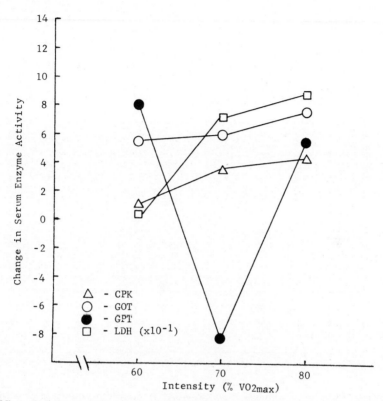

FIG. 1. Relation of changes in serum enzyme activities to intensity of work.

elevated mean blood lactate to 36.6 ± 12.6 mg%. These data indicate that the anaerobic threshold for this group fell between 70% and 80% of the $\dot{V}O_2$max. Mean blood lactate following the $\dot{V}O_2$max test was 89.1 ± 11.2 mg%.

Discussion

Serum enzyme response to exercise is known to depend, in part, upon the species of animal observed [17], training state of the subjects [7, 8, 12] and characteristics of the specific enzymes [19]. Therefore, this discussion will focus primarily on the exercise response of serum CPK, LDH, GOT and GPT in trained humans. Of these four enzymes CPK has been most consistently observed to increase in activity with acute exercise in trained subjects [5, 12, 15]. Sanders and Bloor have concluded that of the commonly observed serum enzymes, CPK is the most sensitive to exercise stress

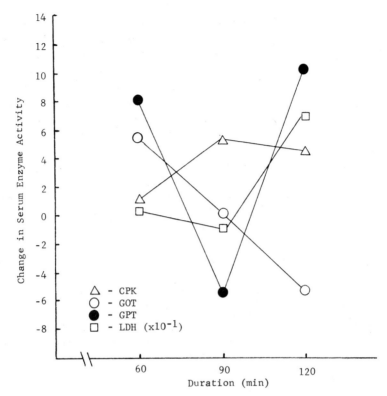

FIG. 2. Relation of changes in serum enzyme activities to duration of work.

in trained individuals [18]. Our data are in agreement with these findings. We observed increases in CPK for all exercise exposures and these increases were statistically significant in five of six cases. In contrast, our LDH data showed significant increases only following the more strenuous long duration runs. Little or no change ($<3\%$) in LDH activity followed $\dot{V}O_2$max testing or 60 and 90 minutes of running at 60% of $\dot{V}O_2$max. These observations are in basic accord with the literature which indicates that substantial LDH increases are observed in trained subjects only when the exercise treatment is severe. Generally, increases in LDH have been observed following very long duration activity [15] and relatively intense exercise [3], but no changes have followed exercise of short duration and/or moderate intensity [3, 12, 18]. These data may indicate that relatively low intensity and/or short duration work causes no increase in LDH efflux or, possibly, that any increases in efflux are at least balanced by an increased clearance rate. However, it does appear that if the magnitude of exercise stress reaches a certain critical level, the rate of LDH efflux will exceed the rate of clearance.

Our data reflect responses in GOT and GPT which are less readily interpreted than those of CPK and LDH. In the present study GOT was increased significantly following the 60% and 70% runs of 60-minute duration, but failed to show significant changes with work bouts of either greater duration or greater intensity. Most other investigators have observed increases in GOT with submaximal and maximal exercise [8, 10, 12, 18], although Critz and Merrick have reported decreased GOT in track athletes who participated in a time trial [5]. These data may indicate that rate of GOT clearance increases more than the rate of GOT efflux as duration and/or intensity of work increases. The studies of Schmidt and Schmidt [19] suggest that this may be the case for GOT in work of very long duration. In the present study GPT was unchanged in all cases. While some other investigators have observed increases in GPT with acute exercise [8, 10], this finding has not been consistent. For instance, Sanders and Bloor, whose subjects and exercise treatments were similar to ours, found no change in GPT [18].

Overall our data on the response of serum enzymes to acute exercise seem internally consistent when viewed with respect to the concentration in skeletal muscle of the enzymes observed. In muscle CPK activity > LDH > GOT > GPT [19]. Thus our finding that CPK increased significantly in five of six cases, LDH in three, GOT in two and GPT in one is consistent with the belief that skeletal muscle is the origin of most of the increased serum enzyme observed after exercise.

Our primary purpose was to evaluate the validity of the hypothesis that postexercise serum enzyme activity changes are directly related to both intensity and duration of exercise. While the literature clearly supports the contention that increases in serum enzymes are related to intensity of work, the relationship with duration of exercise is not well established. Several authors, including Schmidt and Schmidt in their extensive review [19], have concluded that both intensity and duration are of significant importance. Fowler and co-workers have suggested that of the two factors, duration is of greater significance [8]. However, Cerny and Haralambie [4], in the only previously reported study designed to look specifically at the relative importance of intensity and duration, concluded that intensity of work is the more important factor. Our finding that serum enzyme activity changes were unrelated to duration of work supports the conclusion of Cerny. The untrained subjects in Cerny's study were exposed to four work bouts of 60-

and 100-minute duration at 50% and 80% of $\dot{V}O_2$max. No significant differences in serum enzyme activities were found between the 60- and 100-minute work bouts at either intensity. Furthermore, larger increases were found for the 80%, 60-minute bout than for the 50%, 100-minute exposure. Our treatment and observations regarding the effects of duration closely parallel those of Cerny. The contrasting conclusion of Fowler and co-workers was based primarily on their observation that serum enzymes increased more on an 8-mile (one hour duration) training run than during a 15-minute exhaustive treadmill run. Comparison of our data with those of Fowler et al is difficult since in their study the intensity, in terms of $\dot{V}O_2$max, of the 8-mile run was not indicated. However, if the assumption is made that Fowler's subjects ran at a minimum of 70% of their $\dot{V}O_2$max, then our data are in substantial agreement. At 70% and 80% of $\dot{V}O_2$max we observed greater percentage increases in CPK, LDH and GOT than were observed with $\dot{V}O_2$max testing. In interpreting these findings we conclude that regardless of intensity, some critical duration of work is necessary to induce sizable serum enzyme changes. To this extent serum enzyme efflux from muscle must be related to duration of work. Current evidence would suggest that the critical duration is a function of intensity, decreasing as intensity increases. However, if intensity of work is held constant at between 50% and 80% of $\dot{V}O_2$max, serum enzyme changes are not well related to duration of work between 60 and 120 minutes. The data of Schmidt and Schmidt [19] indicate that if duration of work exceeds two hours, serum enzyme activities may show a secondary, duration-related increase.

Our data showed progressively greater increases in serum LDH and CPK with increasing intensity of work. These findings are comparable to those reported by other investigators [3, 8] and are particularly similar to those of Cerny [4] who found that serum enzyme increases were greater following either 60 or 100 minutes of exercise at 80% of $\dot{V}O_2$max than at 50%. We conclude that if duration of work is held constant between 60 and 120 minutes, increases in CPK and LDH are directly related to intensity of work. We would expect similar responses in other enzymes which are found in high concentrations in skeletal muscle. Our intensity-related increases in CPK and LDH did not follow a pattern of response similar to that of either lactate or Hb. We observed no elevation in lactate below 80% of $\dot{V}O_2$max, yet serum enzyme increases were found at lower intensities of exercise. Increases in Hb did not vary with intensity of work and consequently the elevations in CPK and LDH were not due to a progressive hemoconcentration.

The mechanism of the release of enzymes from skeletal muscle into the circulation is not fully understood. Several investigators have suggested that the enzymes pass across the intact muscle cell membrane due to an exercise-induced increase in permeability [4, 8, 19], and it has been hypothesized that increased membrane permeability may result from decreased availability of ATP for maintenance of normal membrane structure and function [12, 19]. Our observation that changes in serum CPK and LDH were directly related to intensity of work but unrelated to duration is consistent with this hypothesis. It has been shown that intracellular ATP levels in skeletal muscle decrease with increasing intensity of exercise [16]. The recently reported study of Thomson and co-workers [22] has demonstrated an inverse relation between intracellular ATP and enzyme efflux from cat skeletal muscle. Also it seems possible that efflux of enzyme from cells may be, at least in part, due to release of enzymes from their normal intracellular locations. Arnold and Pette [1] have shown that aldolase is bound to actin and have suggested that all glycolytic enzymes may be bound to structural protein, perhaps as multienzyme complexes. Furthermore, their findings indicate that the binding of glycolytic enzymes to structural proteins is dependent upon ionic strength and may be affected by variations in metabolite concentrations. Thus, it seems possible that efflux of enzyme from muscle cells is a consequence of decreased intracellular ATP levels and variations in metabolite concentrations. During strenuous work enzymes may be released from their structural protein binding locations becoming free to contact a cell membrane which is itself more permeable due to a loss of microstructural integrity. Confirmation of this hypothesis must await further experimental testing.

References

1. Arnold, H. and Pette, D.: Binding of glycolytic enzymes to structure proteins of the muscle. Eur. J. Biochem. 6:163-171, 1968.
2. Åstrand, P.-O. and Rodahl, K.: Textbook of Work Physiology. New York:McGraw-Hill, 1970.
3. Bratton, R.D., Chowdhury, S.R., Fowler, W.M. et al: Effect of exercise on serum enzyme levels in untrained males. Res. Q. 33:182-193, 1962.
4. Cerny, F.J. and Haralambie, G.: Exercise intensity vs. duration as related to loss of muscle enzymes into serum. Abstracts of 22nd Annual Meeting, American College of Sports Medicine. Med. Sci. Sports 7:65, 1975.
5. Critz, J.B. and Merrick, A.W.: Serum glutamic-oxalacetic transaminase levels after exercise in men. Proc. Soc. Exp. Biol. Med. 109:608-610, 1962.
6. Eilers, R.J.: Notification of final adoption of an international method and standard solution for hemoglobinometry: Specifications for preparation of standard solution. Am. J. Clin. Pathol. 47:212, 1967.

7. Fowler, W.M., Chowdhury, S.R., Pearson, C.M. et al: Changes in serum enzyme levels after exercise in trained and untrained subjects. J. Appl. Physiol. 17:943-946, 1962.
8. Fowler, W.M., Gardner, G.W., Zazerunian, H.H. and Lauvstad, W.A.: The effect of exercise on serum enzymes. Arch. Phys. Med. 49:554-565, 1968.
9. Garbus, J., Highman, B. and Altland, P.D.: Serum enzymes and lactic dehydrogenase isoenzymes after exercise and training in rats. Am. J. Physiol. 207:467-472, 1964.
10. Gardner, G.W., Bratton, R., Chowdhury, S.R. et al: Effect of exercise on serum enzyme levels in trained subjects. J. Sports Med. Phys. Fit. 4:103-110, 1964.
11. Henry, R.J.: Clinical Chemistry — Principles and Technics. New York: Harper and Row, 1968.
12. Hunter, J.B. and Critz, J.B.: Effect of training on plasma enzyme levels in man. J. Appl. Physiol. 31:20-23, 1971.
13. Raven, P.D., Conners, T.J. and Evonuk, E.: Effects of exercise on plasma lactic dehydrogenase isozymes and catecholamines. J. Appl. Physiol. 29:374-377, 1970.
14. Rose, L.I., Lowe, S.L., Carroll, D.R. et al: Serum lactate dehydrogenase isoenzyme changes after muscular exertion. J. Appl. Physiol. 28:279-281, 1970.
15. Rose, L.I., Bousser, J.E. and Cooper, K.H.: Serum enzymes after marathon running. J. Appl. Physiol. 29:355-357, 1970.
16. Saltin, B. and Karlsson, J.: Muscle ATP, CP, and lactate during exercise after physical conditioning. In Pernow, B. and Saltin, B. (eds.): Muscle Metabolism During Exercise. New York:Plenum Press, 1971, pp. 395-399.
17. Sanders, T.M. and Bloor, C.M.: Effects of endurance exercise on serum enzyme activities in the dog, pig and man. Proc. Soc. Exp. Biol. Med. 148:823-828, 1975.
18. Sanders, T.M. and Bloor, C.M.: Effects of repeated endurance exercise on serum enzyme activities in well-conditioned males. Med. Sci. Sports 7:44-47, 1975.
19. Schmidt, E. and Schmidt, F.W.: Enzyme modifications during activity. In Poortmans, J.R. (ed.): Biochemistry of Exercise. Baltimore, Md.:University Park Press, 1968, pp. 216-238.
20. Sigel, P. and Pette, D.: Intracellular localization of glycogenolytic and glycolytic enzymes in white and red rabbit muscle. J. Histochem. Cytochem. 17:225-235, 1969.
21. Sweetin, J.C. and Thomson, W.H.S.: Enzyme efflux and clearance. Clin. Chim. Acta 48:403-411, 1973.
22. Thomson, W.H.S., Sweetin, J.C. and Hamilton, I.J.D.: ATP and muscle enzyme efflux after physical exertion. Clin. Chim. Acta 59:241-245, 1975.
23. Wilkinson, J.H. and Robinson, J.M.: Effect of ATP on release of intracellular enzymes from damaged cells. Nature 249:662-663, 1974.

Evolution of Plasma Cortisol During Short-Time Exercises

R. Leclercq and J. R. Poortmans

Introduction

Considerable controversial data concerning the adrenal cortical response to muscular exertion were obtained [1-3, 8, 10]. Furthermore, the question of the qualitative or quantitative relation between cortisol secretion and exercise remains unanswered, since a possible threshold of work seems to be necessary to induce a systematic increment in plasma cortisol levels, simultaneously with an acceleration of the half-disappearance time of cortisol ([4] confirmed by J. P. Foulliot et al, personal communication). However, a frequent but not systematic response was often elicited by a lower level of work of various durations [7].

Short-time exercises were seldom studied in this aspect [11]. However, they could provide an answer to a part of the question concerning the relation between muscular work and cortisol secretion. The attempt of the present study was to compare peripheral cortisol levels after two different short-time exercises, both felt as exhaustive, in the same subjects, to confirm the weak relation (if present) between cortisol secretion and intensity of work in short-time exercises, already observed in long-lasting steady-state works [7].

Material, Method and Subjects

Subjects

Twelve well-trained university students in physical education, aged 21 to 25, agreed to participate in the study. In a preliminary stage, max $\dot{V}O_2$ was determined for each subject.

R. Leclercq, Laboratoire de biologie clinique, I.M.C. Anderlecht, Bruxelles, Belgique and J. R. Poortmans, Laboratoire de chimie physiologique générale et spéciale, Institut supérieur d'éducation physique et de kinésithérapie, Université libre de Bruxelles, Belgique.

Protocol

The 12 subjects were divided into two groups and were investigated in two afternoon sessions in November 1975. An indwelling plastic needle was inserted in a forearm vein just before the initiation of the work. Heparinized blood samples were obtained immediately before the exercise, at its end and 5, 10, 15 and 30 minutes later. The first group of six subjects performed work at 75% of their respective max $\dot{V}O_2$ in apnea until exhaustion followed 30 minutes later by one minute's work at 140% of their max $\dot{V}O_2$. The six others performed first the heavier exercise, followed at the same time interval by the exercise in apnea. Averaged performances asked were 194 w in apnea and 360 w in aerobia.

Method

Plasma cortisol was determined by an original radioimmunoassay [5] using a highly specific antibody obtained after rabbit's immunization with 3-CMO-BSA conjugate.

Main steps of this assay were as follows:
1. Alkaline denaturation of plasma proteins [12]
2. Chlorhydric neutralization of the basic reagent
3. Addition of tritiated cortisol and antibody
4. Dextran-coated charcoal separation of free and antibody-bound radioactivity.

Results

Mean basal values were completely comparable in both exercises (13.0 ± 1.8 $\mu g/100$ ml in apnea; 13.1 ± 1.4 in aerobia: mean $\pm$ SEM; this difference was not significant: *t* test for paired differences: t = 0.1441). A significant increase in plasma cortisol was observed at the end of the work in all but two tests. This increase ranged from 1.0 to 11.3 $\mu g/100$ ml (mean 4.3). There was no difference between the first and the second part of the test.

The maximum level of cortisol was obtained during the first 15 minutes in all but two tests where it was only reached at the 30th minute.

In all subjects after either type of work, a significant increase was observed; furthermore, this increase as a mean was statistically significant at all times (except +30 min after the aerobic work) (Table I).

Comparing the responses obtained after both types of work, no difference could be evidenced, nor in mean responses at any time, nor when the maximum increments above the basal values were compared in each subject (Tables I and II).

Discussion

University students in physical education, despite good physical fitness, cannot be compared to athletes. In this type of population, exhaustive work is much more limited than in the literature.

When disregarding the type of work performed, and only looking to the chronology, it is obvious that a remnant effect of the first work was observed on the basal level of the second proof. This increase in basal level was however limited (2.9 ± 0.8 μg/100 ml) and its effect can be neglected, since half of the subjects performed first the work in apnea, the six others beginning with the aerobic work.

One interesting point is the constancy of the responses we obtained. In our experience, a systematic increase in plasma cortisol was observed only in exhaustive works or in competitive trials [7]. This is an argument in favor of the exhaustive nature of the exercises performed. Also noteworthy is the fact that the level of work performed at these levels does not influence the amplitude of the cortisol response. We already observed this absence of relation during long-lasting nonexhaustive exercises [7]. This may not be true for other types of subjects and/or levels of work [4].

Table I. Mean Levels of Peripheral Plasma Cortisol (μg/100 ml; Mean ± SEM)

	Base	End	+5 min	+10 min	+15 min	+30 min
				Time		
Anaerobia (75% $\dot{V}O_2$ max) paired *t* test vs.	13.0 ± 1.7	17.2 ± 2.2	16.6 ± 2.4	17.8 ± 2.0	16.8 ± 1.8	15.5 ± 1.7
basal level		3.97	2.92	3.44	4.22	3.00
Aerobia (140% $\dot{V}O_2$ max) paired *t* test vs.	13.1 ± 1.4	18.6 ± 0.9	16.0 ± 1.4	16.5 ± 1.9	19.8 ± 1.9	15.4 ± 1.6
basal level		4.95	3.30	2.60	4.10	1.20

Table II. Increases in Plasma Cortisol Above Basal Levels

	End	+5 min	+10 min	+15 min	+30 min	Maximum
Anaerobia	3.9 ± 1.1	3.1 ± 1.1	4.3 ± 1.2	4.2 ± 1.0	2.6 ± 0.8	6.0 ± 1.0
Aerobia	3.7 ± 0.8	2.8 ± 0.9	3.4 ± 1.3	5.9 ± 1.4	1.4 ± 1.2	6.4 ± 1.1

The practically constant increase in plasma level of cortisol from the first minute is difficult to explain by ACTH action alone. Indeed, even in the case of isolated adrenal quarters incubated in vitro, ACTH addition results in a measurable increase in adrenal corticosteroid content after only three to five minutes and in the perfusion medium this increase becomes evident only five to seven minutes after ACTH addition [6]. These times must be corrected for the better vascularization of the glands in vivo, but the circulatory time alone accounts for one fourth of the delay observed. It seems thus unlikely to imagine that this increase could be due to ACTH action only. Furthermore, the intravenous injection of physiological-like doses of β^{1-24}ACTH in man does not induce a measurable increase in plasma cortisol after five minutes in five out of eight tests (unpublished data). Thus, the regulatory mechanism involved in the adrenocortical response to physical exercise could be due to other determinants than the usual pituitary-adrenal pathway. A possible local role of catecholamines inducing an abrupt release of corticosteroids could explain this type of cortisol pattern, as we suggested previously [8]. It seems also unlikely to invoke a de-adsorption mechanism as suggested for insulin [9], since the cortisol molecule is much smaller than insulin and, on the other hand, its solubility in lipids would evidently limit the amount of cortisol adsorbed on the vascular walls. Finally, a dissociation of the transcortin-cortisol or albumin-cortisol complexes could not explain the observed phenomenon, since the cortisol levels measured by this radioimmunoassay represent the total cortisol and not the only free fraction.

Summary

As already seen during different types of muscular work, the adrenocortical reaction to exercise is not proportionally related to the level of work achieved nor to its duration, but well to the environmental rather unspecific stress induced by the exhaustion, which is not markedly influenced by the state of apnea.

References

1. Bellet, S., Roman, L. and Barham, F.: Metabolism 18:484, 1969.
2. Cornil, A., De Coster, A., Copinschi, G. and Franckson, J.R.M.: Acta Endocrinol. (Kbh) 48:163, 1965.
3. Crabbe, J., Riondel, A. and Mach, E.: Acta Endocrinol. (Kbh) 22:119, 1956.
4. Few, J.D.: J. Endocrinol. 62:341, 1974.
5. Leclercq, R. and Leclercq-Meyer, V.: To be published.

6. Leclercq, R., Lutz, B. and Mialhe-Voloss, C.: Excerpta Med. 210:113, 1970.
7. Leclercq, R. and Poortmans, J.R.: *In* Klotz, H.P. (éd.): Problèmes Actuels d'Endocrinologie et de Nutrition. Paris:Expansion Scientifique Francaise, 1975, vol. 1, p. 153.
8. Leclercq, R. and Poortmans, J.R.: *In* Siest, G. (éd.): Reference Values in Human Chemistry. Basel:Karger, 1972, vol. 1, p. 264.
9. Rasio, E.: *In* Passage capillaire de l'Insuline. Paris:Maloine, 1971, vol. 1, p. 79.
10. Raymond, L.W., Sode, J. and Tucci, J.R.: Acta Endocrinol. (Kbh) 70:73, 1972.
11. Viru, A.: Endokrinologie 59:61, 1972.
12. Wong, W.H.: Clin. Chem. 21:216, 1975.

Metabolic Controls of Human Growth Hormone (HGH) in Trained Athletes Performing Various Workloads

Guy Métivier, J. Poortmans and R. Vanroux

Introduction

The role which human growth hormone (HGH) plays during physical work has attracted the attention of various work physiologists in the last decade. This hormone also has been compared and contrasted with insulin since both seemed at first to play a major role in regulating fuel for muscular work. Insulin, however, has been shown to be concerned mostly with submaximal work whereas growth hormone seemed to be quite ineffective at that intensity.

In untrained subjects given a relatively short work bout plasma growth hormone was shown to rise significantly while insulin values either remained unchanged or fell slightly [8]. It was also demonstrated that epinephrine administration did *not* stimulate the release of growth hormone [8].

It has become evident that HGH is related to the degree of physical fitness. There is some evidence to show that in physically fit subjects HGH returned to basic levels within 30 minutes following a work bout of 30 minutes in contrast to the unfit group which took another hour before decreasing [10]. With submaximal workloads (40% of W 170) only the unfit subject produced a rise in HGH level. The same investigators suggested that it is the lactate liberated from muscles as a result of anoxia which caused the release of HGH in the unfit subjects after exercise and which resulted in a delayed return of HGH to basic levels in the unfit subjects compared with the rapid return in the fit ones.

Some investigators [9] have also postulated that in untrained subjects GH rise starts almost immediately at the beginning of the

Guy Métivier, School of Human Kinetics and Leisure Studies, University of Ottawa, Ottawa, Ontario, Canada; J. Poortmans, Chimie physiologique, Institut supérieur d'éducation physique, Université libre de Bruxelles; and R. Vanroux, Service des fonctions pulmonaires, Hôpital civil de Charleroi, Charleroi, Belgique.

exercise both in obese and in normal weight individuals. Growth hormone in normal subjects is a graded response to exercise and corresponds to the work done and under strenuous conditions is not blocked by glucose in blood [2]. Peak values for HGH occur in blood in about 25 minutes from the start of the exercise [1] and during prolonged moderate exercise it seems to be secreted in a series of bursts [6].

In fully trained athletes growth hormone's release has been shown to be lesser following a controlled work bout [3] than previous to the training period. Also in trained athletes there appears to be a threshold level of exercise after which HGH is secreted. Is this threshold level related to lactic acid concentration or other factors related thereof?

The hypothesis tested in the present experiment was of significant changes in HGH, lactic acid and blood oxygen saturation (PaO_2) in the arterial blood of trained athletes working at 50% and 66% of max $\dot{V}O_2$ for a period of 30 minutes.

Method

The 11 male subjects were chosen for the experiment on the basis of their superior physical fitness levels. The mean oxygen uptake for the group was calculated by a Fleisch metabograph while the subjects performed work on a Fleisch ergocycle. Each subject was tested twice for his maximal oxygen consumption and a mean value recorded.

Following these preliminary evaluations the same individuals were scheduled to appear in a basal state one morning in the laboratory. At that time while the subject was under local anesthesia a (Cournand) needle was inserted in the humeral artery and he was made to rest on a bed for one hour. Blood samples were collected at 9:00 and 9:30 a.m. while the subject was resting. The subject was then weighed and made to sit comfortably on the Fleisch ergocycle. Subsequently he worked at a fixed workload which would produce an oxygen consumption equivalent to 50% of his original maximal calculated value.

During the 30 minutes work bout blood samples were collected at 9:50, 9:55 and 10:00 o'clock. Thereafter the subject was again weighed and made to rest on a bed while additional blood samples were collected at 10:30 and 11:30. Each subject was rescheduled 15 days later where the same procedures were followed except that the workload was adjusted this time to produce an energy expenditure equivalent to 66% of max $\dot{V}O_2$. Growth hormone was determined by radioimmunoassay technique using a charcoal-dextran separation procedure [11]. Lactic acid was determined by the enzymatic method of Hohorst [5]. Blood oxygen saturation was measured by means of the Astrup technique. Analysis of variance and the Scheffe test for significance of F values was applied to the results.

Results

In Table I are the results of mean differences between time series of HGH during work performed at 50% and 66% of max $\dot{V}O_2$. The values of the Scheffe test necessary to render the results significant are also indicated. As may be observed, for the work period performed at 50% of max $\dot{V}O_2$, significant differences were recorded between mean values from time series: 1-7; 2-7; 5-7. According to this table there is no significant rise in the hormone during the 30 minutes of physical work, but there appeared a significant decrease of this hormone in blood following exercise. During more demanding energy output (66% max $\dot{V}O_2$) significant changes were evident between time series: 3-7; 4-7; 5-7. These changes signify a greater change in the hormone during the more severe work session than the milder form of exercise.

During the work period at 50% max $\dot{V}O_2$ there were no significant changes at any time series in blood oxygen saturation. Therefore, there was reason for not computing the Scheffe values (Table II). At the more strenuous work level significant changes were recorded in oxygen saturation between time series: 1-3; 1-4; 3-7; 4-7. Accordingly, it was clear that during this 30-minute effort a significant overall decrease in blood oxygen saturation occurred.

Lactic acid increased significantly during both exercise periods (Table III), but the greatest increases were recorded during the more strenuous exercise.

Discussion

According to our results it was clear that HGH was secreted during exercise in trained athletes only when the workload exceeded at least 50% of the maximal oxygen uptake. In athletes who are well trained HGH secretions seemed to be proportional to the work output level, but any work output lesser than 50% max $\dot{V}O_2$ was not sufficient to elicit the HGH secretion. In contrast unfit individuals do show increases in this hormone at lesser levels such as workloads of 40% of W 170 [10]. Since growth hormone takes at least ten minutes to be secreted during physical work and its maximal time for

Table I. Mean Differences Between Time Series of HGH in Trained Athletes
During Workloads Equivalent to 50% and 66% of Max $\dot{V}O_2$

MVO₂ 50%

	1	2	3	4	5	6	7
1		1.74	2.11	2.29	1.32	3.01	5.00*
2			.37	.54	.42	1.27	3.26+
3				.18	−.73	.90	2.89
4					−.97	.72	2.71
5						1.69	3.68*
6							1.99
7							

SCHEFFE	
P < .05	3.12
P < .01	3.68

MVO₂ 66%

	1	2	3	4	5	6	7
1		2.51	−4.76	−4.84	−6.23	4.57	9.97
2			−7.27	−7.35	−8.74	2.06	7.46
3				−.078	−1.46	9.33	14.73*
4					−1.39	9.41	14.81*
5						10.8	16.2*
6							5.4
7							

SCHEFFE	
P < .05	11.06
P < .01	13.07

Mean value of HGH at individual time series (Ng/ml)

	1	2	3	4	5	6	7
MVO₂66	12.31	9.8	17.07	17.15	18.54	7.74	2.34
MVO₂50	6.42	4.67	4.31	4.13	5.10	3.41	1.42

* P = < .01
+ P = < .05

Table II. Mean Differences Between Time Series of O_2 Saturation of Arterial Blood (PaO_2) in Trained Athletes During Workloads Equivalent to 50% and 66% of Max $\dot{V}O_2$

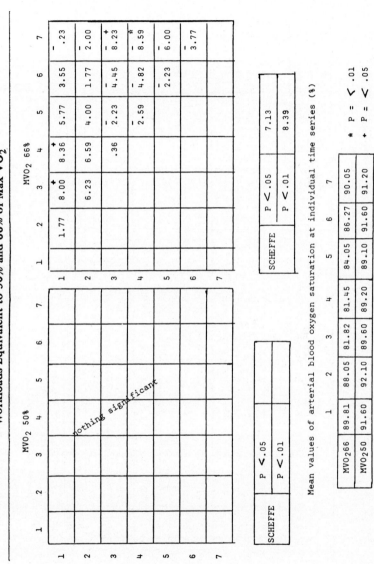

MVO_2 50%

nothing significant

SCHEFFE	
P < .05	
P < .01	

MVO_2 66%

	1	2	3	4	5	6	7
1		1.77	+ 8.00	+ 8.36	5.77	3.55	- .23
2			6.23	6.59	4.00	1.77	- 2.00
3				.36	- 2.23	- 4.45	+ 8.23
4					- 2.59	- 4.82	-* 8.59
5						- 2.23	- 6.00
6							- 3.77
7							

SCHEFFE	
P < .05	7.13
P < .01	8.39

Mean values of arterial blood oxygen saturation at individual time series (%)

	1	2	3	4	5	6	7
$MVO_2$66	89.81	88.05	81.82	81.45	84.05	86.27	90.05
$MVO_2$50	91.60	92.10	89.60	89.20	89.10	91.60	91.20

* P = < .01
+ P = < .05

Table III. Mean Differences Between Time Series in Lactic Acid of Arterial Blood in Trained Athletes During Workloads Equivalent to 50% and 66% of Max VO_2

MVO_2 50%

	1	2	3	4	5	6	7
1		.76	−7.77+	−8.24*	−11.92*	.55	1.55
2			−8.53*	−9.00*	−12.68*	.21	.79
3				.48	−4.16	8.32*	9.32*
4					−3.68	8.49*	9.79*
5						12.47*	13.44*
6							1.00
7							

SCHEFFE	
P < .05	6.06
P < .01	7.33

MVO_2 66%

	1	2	3	4	5	6	7
1		.16	−16.89+	−17.61*	−17.91*	3.16	.25
2			−17.05*	−17.76*	−18.08*	3.33	.41
3				.73	1.03	13.73*	16.64*
4					−.30	14.45*	17.36*
5						14.75*	17.66*
6							2.91
7							

SCHEFFE	
P < .05	9.17
P < .01	9.69

Mean values of arterial blood lactic acid at individual time series (mg/100 ml)

	1	2	3	4	5	6	7
$MVO_2$66	13.09	12.92	29.98	30.70	31.00	16.25	13.34
$MVO_2$50	12.78	12.02	20.55	21.02	24.70	12.23	11.23

* P = < .01
\+ P = < .05

optimal secretion is on the order of 30 minutes [1], we are quite prepared to suggest that in our experiment if HGH would have been necessary for this physical work it would have been secreted before the end of the work bout. In accordance with this statement we do suggest that if lipolysis was needed other systems such as the nervous system [4] permitted it.

We are somewhat convinced that lactic acid was not the stimulus for the enhanced secretion of this hormone because during both periods of exercise there were significant rises in lactic acid (Fig. 1) but in only one case (66% max $\dot{V}O_2$) was there a significant rise in HGH.

In both work periods the significant drop in secretion occurred at the termination of the exercise. This phenomenon could have been attributed to an increased hormonal degradation.

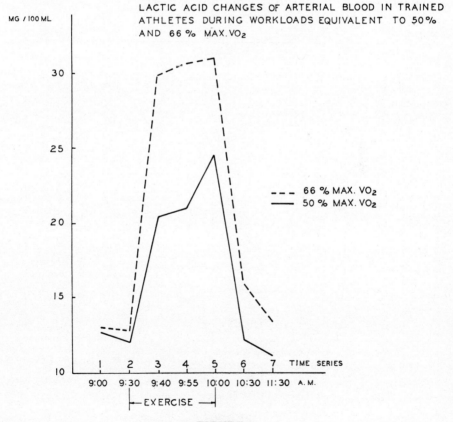

FIGURE 1.

There was a very close relationship however between oxygen saturation in the blood during the more intense work bout and growth hormone (Figs. 2 and 3). The changes in blood oxygen saturation during 50% max $\dot{V}O_2$ work period did not vary significantly nor did the HGH levels; however, at the 66% max $\dot{V}O_2$ level as blood O_2 saturation decreased to very low levels, HGH increased to very high levels. Accordingly it would seem that PaO_2 (blood oxygen saturation) was a more logical stimulus for HGH release than was lactic acid. These results confirm those previously recorded [3], but furthermore it gives the relative importance between lactic acid and PaO_2 in the control of HGH release. We are tempted to suggest that in highly trained athletes there is a threshold work output value for the stimulation of HGH and that this value lies between 50% and 66% of max $\dot{V}O_2$. If lipolysis is needed to carry out the work before this point is reached, the nervous system may be directly implicated in carrying out this process.

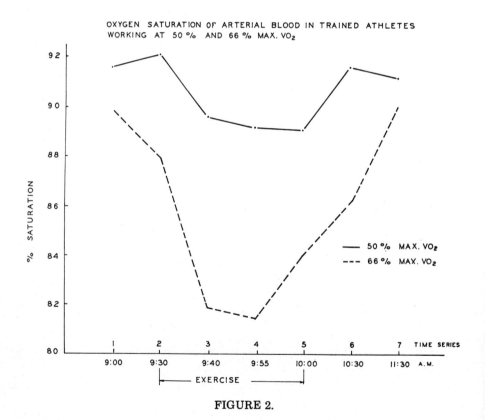

OXYGEN SATURATION OF ARTERIAL BLOOD IN TRAINED ATHLETES
WORKING AT 50 % AND 66 % MAX. VO₂

FIGURE 2.

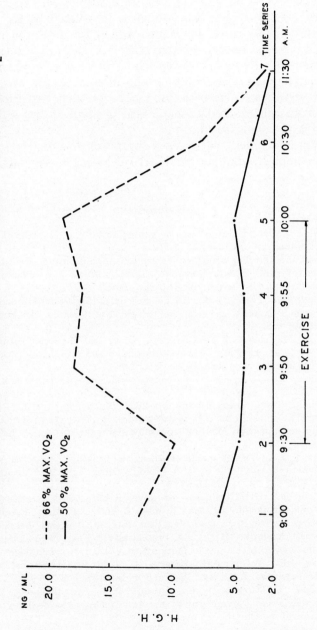

PLASMATIC HUMAN GROWTH HORMONE CHANGES IN ARTERIAL BLOOD DURING VARIOUS WORK LOADS EQUIVALENT TO 50 % AND 66 % MAX. VO$_2$

FIGURE 3.

Summary

HGH seems to be related to the state of physical fitness. Also the secretory control mechanism seems to be related to the workload and there appears to be in trained athletes a threshold level. This threshold level has been associated with lactic acid production.

In trained athletes who were made to work at 50% and 66% of their relative max $\dot{V}O_2$, only at the more difficult workload was there a significant increase in HGH. In this experiment HGH secretion was not related to lactic acid production but rather to the arterial blood oxygen saturation.

It was concluded that oxygen saturation in blood seemed to be the more logical stimulus for HGH release than was lactic acid in trained athletes.

References

1. Buckler, J.M.H.: Exercise as a screening test for growth hormone release. Acta Endocrinol. 69:219-229, 1972.
2. Hansen, Aa. P.: The effect of intravenous glucose infusion on the exercise induced serum, growth hormone rise in normals and juvenile diabetics. Scand. J. Clin. Lab. Invest. 28:195-205, 1971.
3. Hartley, L.H., Mason, J.W., Hogan, R.P. et al: Multiple hormonal responses to graded exercise in relation to physical training. J. Appl. Physiol. 33(5):602-606, 1972.
4. Hartog, M., Havel, R.J., Copinschi, G. et al: The relationship between changes in serum levels of growth hormone and mobilization of fat during exercise in man. Q. J. Exp. Physiol. 52:86-96, 1967.
5. Hohorst, H.J.: L. — (+) Lactate determination with lactic dehydrogenase and DPN. In Bergmeyer, H.V. (ed.): Methods of Enzymatic Analysis. Weinheim:Verlag Chemie, 1965, pp. 266-270.
6. Hunter, W.M., Fonseka, C.C. and Passmore, R.: The role of growth hormone in the mobilization of fuel for muscular exercise. Q. J. Exp. Physiol. 50:40-16, 1965.
7. Pruett, E.D.R.: Plasma insulin levels during prolonged exercise. In Advances in Experimental Medicine and Biology. New York and London:Plenum Press, Vol. 11, 1971, pp. 165-175.
8. Schalch, D.S.: The influence of physical stress and exercise on growth hormone and insulin secretion in man. J. Lab. Clin. Med., February, 1967.
9. Schwarz, F., Ter Haar, D.J., Van Riet, H.G. and Thijssen, J.H.H.: Response of growth hormone (GH), JFA, blood sugar and insulin to exercise in obese patients and normal subjects. Metabolism Vol. 18, No. 12 (December) 1969.
10. Sutton, J.R., Young, J.D., Lazarus, L. et al: The hormonal response to physical exercise. Aust. Ann. Med. 18:84-90, 1969.
11. Virasoro, E., Copinschi, G., Bruno, O.D. and Leclercq, R.: Radioimmunoassay of human growth hormone using a charcoal-dextran separation procedure. Clin. Chem. Acta 31:234-297, 1971.

Plasma Growth Hormone, Aldosterone, Cortisol and Insulin Changes in a 100-Kilometer Run

G. von Glutz, U. Lüthi and H. Howald

Introduction

Muscular work of high intensity and extremely long duration is controlled by the nervous system on the one hand and humoro-endocrine factors on the other. The latter are primarily responsible for the energy supply to the working muscle by regulating the mobilization, the membrane transport and the intracellular utilization of substrates. Some 20 years ago, it was postulated that exhaustion would be characterized by a breakdown of hormone production in the adrenals, while even in severe fatigue this would not be the case [6]. This hypothesis was based on measurements of urine electrolytes, since a direct determination of hormones was not possible at this time. More recent studies showed controversial results in this respect, as in some cases there was a decrease [2, 8] and in others an increase [3, 7] in plasma concentrations of adrenal hormones after exercise in animals and man. The present study was designed to further evaluate the hormonal response of the human pituitary gland, the adrenal cortex and the pancreas to a severe and extremely prolonged workload.

Methods

Blood samples from seven healthy male subjects were analyzed by radioimmunoassay for growth hormone, aldosterone, cortisol and insulin concentration before, immediately after and one day after a 100-km run. All assays were performed using standard kits from the CEA-IRE-SORIN association without special purification steps in the plasma, except the aldosterone determination in which the hormone was primarily separated by chromatography on silica gel [1]. The

G. von Glutz, U. Lüthi and H. Howald, Research Institute of the Swiss School for Physical Education and Sports, Magglingen, Switzerland.

219

run took place at about 15 to 20 C and lasted from 10 p.m. to the next morning. The participants ingested varying amounts of fluid and food with unknown contents of carbohydrates, fat and electrolytes during the run. Statistical analysis of the data was performed using the paired t-test.

Results

The mean age of the subjects was 33.3 ± 3.5 years (s_x), they weighed 72.7 ± 4.9 kg and their maximum oxygen uptake was 59.9 ± 4.9 ml/min $\cdot$ kg. The mean running time was 10.69 ± 1.42 hours (range: 7.90 to 11.92 hours). Despite the fluid ingestion the loss in body weight averaged 2.66 ± 1.08 kg. Nevertheless, no hemoconcentration could be demonstrated, hematocrit and plasma protein concentration showing no significant changes.

The plasma hormone changes are graphically represented in Figure 1. We found a significant ($2 \, p < 0.05$) increase in blood concentration of *human growth hormone* (HGH) from 1.0 ± 1.0 ng/ml before the run to 7.1 ± 5.1 ng/ml after the run, with a total recovery on the next day (1.1 ± 1.0 ng/ml). The observed increase is in agreement with the results of other studies with shorter endurance performances in trained subjects [4].

For *cortisol* there was a significant increase from 9.59 ± 5.80 μg/100 ml before the run to 28.41 ± 6.80 μg/100 ml immediately after and a total recovery to 3.47 ± 4.03 μg/ml on the next day. Our values are again comparable to the ones of other authors dealing with performances of shorter duration.

Plasma *aldosterone* concentration increased significantly from 26 ± 21 pg/ml to 795 ± 346 pg/ml with a still significantly elevated level of 360 ± 191 pg/ml on the next day. This result is in agreement with other studies on prolonged heavy exercise, although our absolute values after the run and on the next day seem to be extremely high. To make sure that we did not have to deal with a measuring artefact, we had another laboratory control our results. These values agreed with the ones measured by us within the 10% methodological error.

No significant changes in plasma *insulin* could be detected. Normally, a decrease of immunoreactive insulin is observed after work at 50% to 70% of $\dot{V}O_2$ max, an intensity which was also estimated in a similar study for subjects running the 100 km at about the same speed [5].

To investigate whether all the observed hormonal changes would depend upon a common stress factor, we calculated correlations

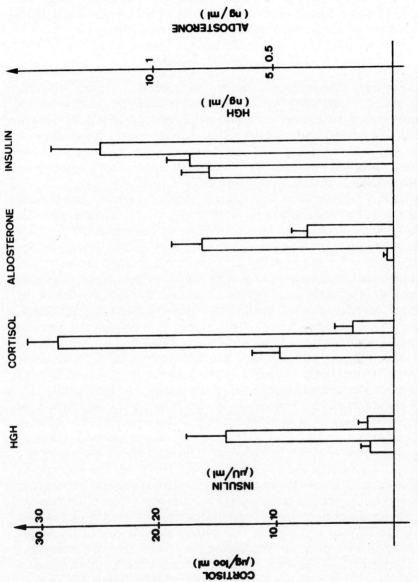

FIG. 1. Plasma levels of human growth hormone (HGH), cortisol, aldosterone and insulin before, immediately after and one day after the 100-km run (means ± standard error of the means).

between the individual increments in the different hormones. The highest coefficient of correlation was found for the changes in plasma cortisol and plasma aldosterone: $r = 0.71$, $p < 0.1$ (Fig. 2). The coefficients for HGH and aldosterone on the one hand and HGH and cortisol on the other were 0.1 and 0.48, respectively.

Discussion and Conclusions

Measuring plasma concentrations of hormones implies the difficulty that one cannot differentiate whether the observed changes are a consequence of altered secretion or excretion, or if they simply reflect a modified distribution in the different body pools. Despite these limitations, our results may nevertheless demonstrate some valuable information about the hormonal response due to extremely prolonged and heavy muscular work in man.

Growth hormone is thought to control normal growth and regulation of protein turnover, neither of which is important in the physiological adjustments to work. However, mobilization of FFA induced by growth hormone may considerably contribute to the energy supply for the working muscles. The stimulus influencing the hypothalamus to increase the growth hormone production or release by the pituitary gland is not fully known for the conditions of physical exercise. Several possibilities are discussed: hypoglycemia, hyperaminoacidemia, stress and others. A very special growth hormone response was found in an 82-year-old man not included in the present group, who finished the 100-km run after 19.65 hours and who was the only subject to show a decrease of plasma growth hormone concentration at the end of the run (6.3 to 4.5 ng/ml).

Four factors are known to be involved in the regulation of aldosterone secretion: the renin angiotensin system, the adrenocorticotropic hormone (ACTH), and the serum concentration of potassium and probably of sodium. Unfortunately, we could not measure the plasma renin concentration. However, the increase in plasma cortisol suggests a rise in ACTH output, particularly since it has been found that angiotensin II, the effector of the renin system, inhibits cortisol production. The correlation between the increments in plasma cortisol and plasma aldosterone also indicates that ACTH in part may be a common stimulator for these hormones under our conditions of investigation. The mineralocorticoid aldosterone is responsible for the electrolyte balance by stimulating the sodium retention and the potassium excretion. The glucocorticoid cortisol enhances the rate of gluconeogenesis, the mobilization of amino

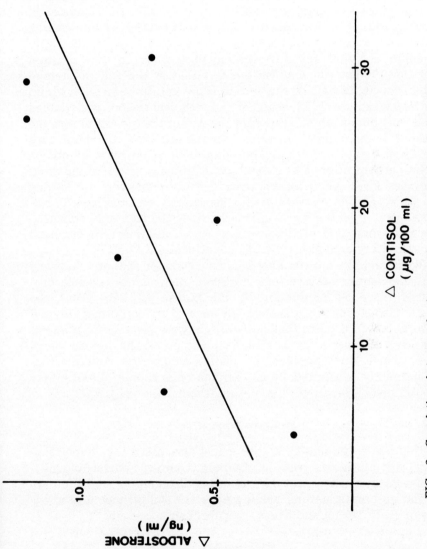

FIG. 2. Correlation between the increments in plasma cortisol and plasma aldosterone during the 100-km run. The regression line is defined by the following equation: △ aldosterone = (0.0235 · △ cortisol) + 0.3328.

acids and of free fatty acids, thus increasing the supply of energy-rich substrates to the different organs during exercise.

Insulin is considered to be an important regulatory hormone during exercise. Its plasma concentration is normally described to decrease during exercise, probably in part because of a decrease in insulin secretion by the pancreas and in part because of an increased removal of insulin out of the blood [9]. A possible explanation why we could not find any difference in plasma insulin concentration after the 100-km run may be the fact that at the end of exercise plasma concentrations of this hormone are known to increase within two to ten minutes [11], while out of technical reasons, we sampled blood only about ten minutes after the end of the run. Moreover, the repeated carbohydrate ingestion throughout the run may have stimulated insulin secretion. The absence of an increase of plasma insulin concentration is in clear contrast to the response of the other hormones investigated in the present study. However, the lacking increase in plasma insulin does not necessarily mean an insufficient glucose supply to the working muscle, since the manyfold enhanced muscular blood flow during exercise would allow for an increased insulin delivery even at low plasma concentrations [10].

To summarize our results it may be concluded that even in heavy physical exercise of very long duration, there is no evidence of a reduced hormone production by the human pituitary gland, the adrenal cortex and the pancreas. In view of the hypothesis quoted above, this would mean that our subjects were severely fatigued but in no way completely exhausted. With respect to the adrenal gland, the extremely high postexercise plasma aldosterone concentration was indirectly confirmed by an extreme renal sodium retention (to be published), which would also exclude exhaustion [6].

Acknowledgments

The results presented in this paper are part of a cooperation study with Dr. Keul's group in Freiburg, German Federal Republic, and Dr. Poortman's laboratory in Brussels, Belgium.

The authors gratefully acknowledge the skillful technical assistance of Ruth Dienel and Theres Appenzeller.

References

1. Buhler, F.R., Sealey, J.E. and Laragh, J.H.: Radio immunoassay of plasma aldosterone. In Laragh, J.H. (ed.): Hypertension Manual. New York:Yorke Medical Books, Dun-Donnelley, 1974, pp. 655-669.

2. Cornil, A., Decoster, A., Copinschi, G. and Franckson, J.: Effect of muscular exercise on the plasma level of cortisol in man. Acta Endocrinol. 48:163-168, 1965.
3. Hartley, L., Mason, J., Hogan, R. et al: Multiple hormone responses to prolonged exercise in relation to physical training. J. Appl. Physiol. 33:607-610, 1972.
4. Métivier, G.: The effects of long lasting physical exercise and training on hormonal regulation. In Howald, H. and Poortmans, J.R. (eds.): Metabolic Adaptation to Prolonged Physical Exercise. Basel:Birkhäuser, 1975, pp. 276-292.
5. Oberholzer, F., Claassen, H., Moesch, H. and Howald, H.: Ultrastrukturelle, biochemische und energetische Analyse einer extremen Dauerleistung (100 km-Lauf). Schweiz. Z. Sportmed. 24:71-98, 1976.
6. Schönholzer, G.: Ermüdung, Erschöpfung, Tod. Schweiz. Z. Sportmed. 5:65-80, 1957.
7. Sundsfjord, J.A., Stromme, S.B. and Aakvaag, A.: Plasma aldosterone (PA), plasma renin activity (PRA) and cortisol (PF) during exercise. In Howald, H. and Poortmans, J.R. (eds.): Metabolic Adaptation to Prolonged Physical Exercise. Basel:Birkhäuser Verlag, 1975, pp. 308-314.
8. Viru, A. and Akke, H.: Effects of muscular work on cortisol and corticosterone content in the blood and adrenals of guinea pigs. Acta Endocrinol. 62:385-390, 1969.
9. Vranic, M., Kawamori, R. and Wrenshall, G.A.: The role of insulin and glucagon in regulating glucose turnover in dogs during exercise. Med. Sci. Sports 7:27-33, 1975.
10. Vranic, M., Kawamori, R., Pek, S. et al: The essentiality of insulin and the role of glucagon in regulating glucose utilization and production during strenuous exercise in dogs. J. Clin. Invest. 57:245-255, 1976.
11. Wahren, J., Felig, P. and Hendler, R.: Glucose and amino acid metabolism during recovery after exercise. J. Appl. Physiol. 34:838-845, 1973.

Testosterone Production Rate During Exercise

John R. Sutton, M. J. Coleman and J. H. Casey

Introduction

Physical exercise results in the elevation of serum levels of a number of hormones, including catecholamines [10], glucagon [1], cortisol [5] and growth hormone [4]. The most striking changes occur with growth hormone, where increases of twenty- to fortyfold above basal concentrations are frequently noted [8, 9]. In a previous study, we found that athletes during competition were also seen to have increases in plasma levels of serum androgens [7].

In Figure 1, the increase in the serum androgens in a group of seven male swimmers from 1,000 ng/100 ml to almost 1800 ng/100 ml is seen following a maximal 800-meter swim. In order to investigate the possible mechanisms of this rise in the plasma level of androgens, we sought evidence for the normal control mechanisms involved in testosterone secretion usually considered to be under the influence of pituitary luteinizing hormone (LH).

We studied four normal males, aged 20-24 years, with average cardiorespiratory fitness levels. They exercised at 900 kpm/min for 20 minutes on a cycle ergometer. This represented between 75% and 90% of their $\dot{V}O_2$ max. There was a significant rise in serum androgen levels (Fig. 2). However, examining the luteinizing hormone changes, there was no significant difference throughout the rest of the exercise period. Thus, the elevation of serum androgens seen in this study was independent of serum luteinizing hormone.

Since the change we observed is more than a 40% to 50% rise in serum androgens, any change in plasma volume, while contributing, cannot explain the total change in serum androgens.

Since the elevation of serum androgens was independent of LH, was it possible that the source of the androgens was adrenal and not

John R. Sutton,* M. J. Coleman and J. H. Casey, Garvan Institute of Medical Research, St. Vincent's Hospital, Sydney, N.S.W., Australia.

*Present address: Department of Medicine, McMaster University Medical Centre, Hamilton, Ontario, Canada.

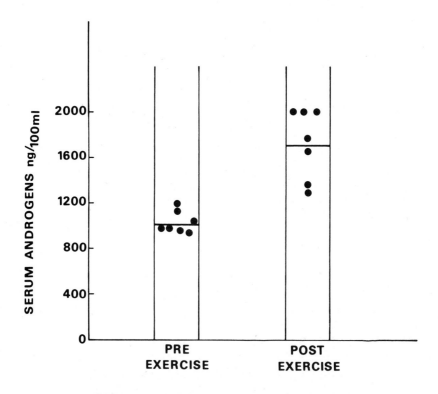

SERUM ANDROGENS IN MALE SWIMMERS
BEFORE AND AFTER MAXIMAL EXERCISE

FIG. 1. Serum androgens in seven young swimmers before and following an 800-meter maximal swim.

testicular, and if so, under the influence of ACTH? We studied this possibility by suppressing ACTH secretion during exercise by the administration of 10 mg betamethasone 30 minutes before exercise. Complete suppression of the serum cortisol response to exercise was achieved; however, the elevation of serum androgens remained unaltered [6].

Possible factors which might be responsible for an elevation in serum androgens during exercise are listed:

1. an increased production
2. an altered protein binding
3. a decreased metabolic clearance
4. some combination of the above factors

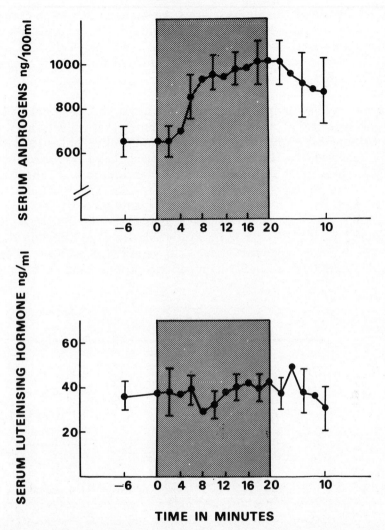

FIG. 2. Serum androgens and serum luteinizing hormone before, during and following exercise at 900 kpm/min for 20 minutes on a cycle ergometer.

In a previous study [7], we measured the percentage of testosterone protein bound and found no change from rest to exercise. Thus, to examine which of possibilities 1, 3 or 4 was important, it was necessary to perform more detailed studies.

Methods

To investigate these possibilities, we studied testosterone production rates during exercise in three normal male subjects. We used tritiated testosterone and gave an intravenous bolus of 12.5 μc at time zero as a priming dose. Twenty minutes later, we commenced a constant intravenous infusion in which 37.5 μc was given over the subsequent 105 minutes. This was infused by a Harvard constant infusion syringe pump. (Figure 3 illustrates this protocol.) Blood samples were taken at 80, 90 and 100 minutes, at which stage it was hoped that a steady state of infused radioactive testosterone had been achieved. At 105 minutes, the subjects began to exercise on a cycle ergometer at a power output of 900 kpm/min. At the 10, 15 and 20 minute marks of the exercise, further blood samples were taken and it was hoped that a new steady state of testosterone metabolism would have occurred. Total serum androgens were measured as the 17 beta hydroxysteroids by a modification of the protein binding technique of Horton et al [2]. Testosterone itself was measured by a similar competitive protein binding technique

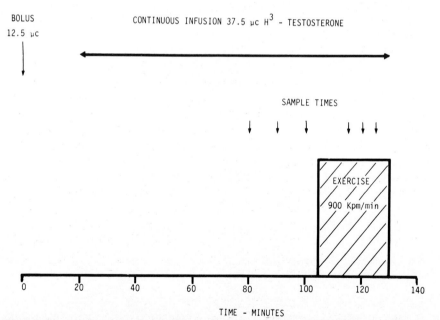

FIG. 3. Protocol used in the metabolic clearance rate studies in which a bolus of 12.5 μc of H^3-Testosterone was given at time 0, followed by a constant infusion of 37.5 μc of H^3-Testosterone which commenced 20 minutes later and continued until the exercise was completed.

after chromatography of the serum extract on Sephadex L.H. 20. The method used for the metabolic clearance rate studies was based on the work of Horton and Tait [3]. We used thin layer chromatography in the initial separation from plasma in our clearance rate determinations with alumina thin layer (300 μ thick) on glass plates, with the system benzine, ethylacetate 3:2 developed in a single direction. This thin layer chromatography with alumina will separate testosterone from epitestosterone. It will also separate androstanediol and androstandione from andosterone and etiocholanolone. The capacity of the system allows the use of an ether extract of 50 ml plasma as a 1 cm streak with adequate resolution of these steroids in two hours.

The second chromatography system in the clearance work was a modified bush A system (stationary phase — methanol water system). This system was equilibrated for 5 hours and developed for 12 hours. The carrier steroids were located by their absorption of ultraviolet light at 254 mμ.

The combination of these two systems separated the testosterone from all expected metabolites.

All counting was performed with a nuclear Chicago liquid scintillation counter.

Samples of the infusate were obtained from both the syringe and from the tubing and blood was immediately centrifuged and the plasma removed and coated immediately. Fifty micrograms of carrier steroid C-14 labeled was mixed with the plasma in a 125 ml separatory funnel and the steroids were extracted twice with 2 vol of cold ether. The ether was then washed twice with 1/10th volume water and the extract dried in vacuo and spread on the alumina thin layer plate. After running in this system in one dimension, the carrier steroids were located under a 254 mμ ultraviolet lamp, marked and aspirated under low vacuum into a pipette packed with glass wool. The inverted pipette was then eluded with 10 ml of ethanol and the eluate taken into dryness. This extract was next streaked over a 2 cm line on Whatman 2 paper and run in the Bush A system for 12 hours. The area was then cut out and eluted with 10 ml of ethanol. The dried extract was then transferred to counting vials.

Calculations

Metabolic clearance rate is defined as the volume of blood cleared completely and irreversibly of steroid in unit time. Under the conditions of the experiment, we have assumed steady-state conditions apply; therefore, the rate of testosterone entering the blood endogenously is equal to the rate of testosterone leaving the blood. The same argument also applies to the labeled testosterone. In the calculation of metabolic clearance rate (MCR) by the constant infusion technique, we use the rate of the radioactive infusion, divided by the plasma radioactivity per liter, corrected for the recovery and measured specifically as the same steroid as that infused.

$$MCR = \frac{\text{Infusion rate}}{\text{Radioactive concentration } H^3 \text{ testosterone}}$$

Production rate (PR) is the product of metabolic clearance rate, multiplied by endogenous plasma concentration.

$$PR = MCR \times \text{Serum Testosterone}$$

Results and Discussion

Figure 4 illustrates the results of the endogenous plasma levels, the specific activity and the disintegration per milliliter of plasma in one of the three subjects. From rest to exercise, there is an increase in the plasma concentration of testosterone; there is also an increase

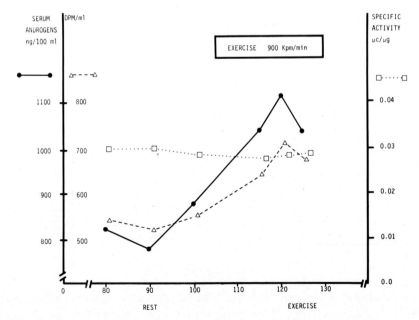

FIG. 4. Serum androgens, serum radioactivity and specific activity at rest and during exercise in one subject.

in the radioactivity of the plasma testosterone. Therefore, in calculating the specific activity in microcuries per nanogram of testosterone, it can be seen that the specific activity is essentially unchanged from rest to exercise. This implies that there has been no addition of cold or endogenous testosterone to the system. Otherwise, we would have noted a fall in the specific activity of testosterone, i.e., there has been no increase in the production rate of testosterone to account for the increase in the plasma level.

The mean results of the group of three subjects, showing the increase in the serum concentration of testosterone from rest to exercise, are seen in Figure 5. These are graphed as mean ± 1 SEM. It illustrates that the radioactivity of serum also increases; however, the MCR decreases while the production rate is virtually unchanged. Thus, the elevation of serum testosterone during exercise is a result of a decreased metabolic clearance with no increase in production. This is most likely to be the result of a reduced hepatic metabolism of testosterone which may be related to the reduced hepatic blood flow, which has been demonstrated to occur with exercise [11].

Summary

1. Physical exercise results in an elevation of serum androgens, principally testosterone.

2. The elevation is related to the intensity of the exercise.

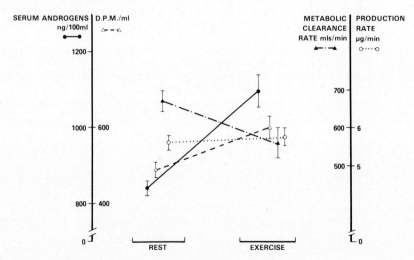

FIG. 5. Mean data showing serum androgens, serum radioactivity, metabolic clearance rate and production rate of testosterone at rest and during exercise.

3. It is independent of pituitary luteinizing hormone.

4. The androgens probably are testicular in origin, since there is no contribution from the adrenal glands.

5. There is no alteration in the plasma protein binding of testosterone during exercise.

6. The elevation of serum androgens results from a decreased metabolic clearance of the hormone and not from increased production.

References

1. Bottger, I., Schlein, E.M., Faloona, G.L. et al: The effect of exercise on glucagon secretion. J. Clin. Endocrinol. 35:117, 1972.
2. Horton, R., Kato, T. and Sherins, R.: A rapid method for the estimation of testosterone in male plasma. Steroids 10:245, 1967.
3. Horton, R. and Tait, J.F.: Androstenedione production and interconversion rates measured in peripheral blood and studies on the possible site of its conversion to testosterone. J. Clin. Invest. 45:301, 1966.
4. Roth, J., Glick, S.M., Yalow, R.S. and Berson, S.A.: Secretion of human growth hormone: Physiologic and experimental modification. Metabolism 12:577, 1963.
5. Sutton, J.R. and Casey, J.H.: The adrenocortical response to competitive athletics in veteran athletes. J. Clin. Endocrinol. 40:135, 1975.
6. Sutton, J., Coleman, M.T. and Casey, J.H.: Adrenocortical contribution to serum androgens during physical exercise. Med. Sci. Sports 6:72, 1974.
7. Sutton, J.R., Coleman, M.J., Casey, J.H. and Lazarus, L.: Androgen responses during physical exercise. Br. Med. J. 1:520, 1973.
8. Sutton, J.R., Jones, N.L. and Toews, C.J.: Growth hormone secretion in acid-base alterations at rest and during exercise. Clin. Sci. Mol. Med. 50:241, 1976.
9. Sutton, J.R., Young, J.D., Lazarus, L. et al: The hormonal response to physical exercise. Aust. Ann. Med. 18:84, 1969.
10. Vendsalu, A.: Studies on adrenaline and noradrenaline in human plasma. Acta Physiol. Scand. 49 (Suppl. 173):1, 1960.
11. Wahren, J., Felig, P., Ahlborg, G. and Jorfeldt, L.: Glucose metabolism during leg exercise in man. J. Clin. Invest. 50:2715, 1971.

Metabolic Profile of Skeletal Muscle During Recovery

William B. McCafferty, Dee W. Edington, Roger P. Farrar,
Thomas N. Pearce and Michael J. Welch

Introduction

The metabolic state of the muscle is changed during recovery from acute exercise stress. Since even brief periods of exercise affect muscle metabolism, measurement of substrate levels in the cell may provide information on how the muscle recovers from muscular work.

Measurement of absolute changes of substrate levels during both short-term [9] and long-term [8] recovery has suggested that muscle metabolism is changed for a long time following muscular exercise. Metabolic differences probably exist until glycogen levels are replenished. Muscle stimulation is characterized by decreased levels of ATP, creatine phosphate (CP), and glycogen, and increased levels of glucose, glucose 6-phosphate and lactate. Recovery following muscular exercise is characterized by an apparent oscillation of substrate levels with substrates returning toward resting levels at different rates [8, 9]. An apparent supercompensation of creatine phosphate stores was observed during early recovery which may influence the shift from an exercise metabolism to a recovery metabolism. Glucose and glucose 6-phosphate appeared to remain elevated during recovery, while lactate returned to rest with 30 minutes of recovery [9].

While suggestions of metabolic changes have been made on the basis of absolute changes in substrate levels, it has been suggested by McGilvery [10] and others that the relative change in substrate concentration may be of greater significance than the absolute change. Metabolic profiles of relative substrate changes in the muscle

William B. McCafferty,* Dee W. Edington, Roger P. Farrar, Thomas N. Pearce and Michael J. Welch, Department of Exercise Science, University of Massachusetts, Amherst, Mass., U.S.A.

*Current address: Institute of Environmental Stress, University of California, Santa Barbara, Calif., U.S.A.

may therefore provide more information on substrate control in skeletal muscle during and following exercise.

Methods

Metabolic profiles have been obtained from substrate measurements observed at rest, following ten minutes of electrical stimulation and during several recovery periods. Young adult male rats (Sprague-Dawley) were employed as subjects, and all studies were conducted in conformance with the "Guiding Principles in the Care and Use of Animals" of the American Physiological Society.

Following anesthesia with ether, the gastrocnemius-plantaris muscle group was surgically exposed and the subject animal placed on a stimulation machine. The muscle group was then quick frozen with tongs precooled in liquid nitrogen either at rest, following 10 minutes of electrical stimulation, or at 30 seconds, 60 seconds and 2, 5, 10, 15 and 30 minutes of recovery. The muscles were then prepared for substrate analysis as previously described [8, 9]. Substrate levels were measured through the use of pyridine nucleotide enzymatically coupled reactions [2, 8, 9]. Substrates measured include adenosine triphosphate (ATP), adenosine diphosphate (ADP), adenosine monophosphate (AMP), creatine phosphate (CP), glucose 1-phosphate (GIP), glucose, glucose 6-phosphate (GGP), fructose 6-phosphate (FGP), fructose 1,6-diphosphate (FDP), dihydroxyacetone phosphate (DHAP), alpha-glycerophosphate (AGP), glyceraldehyde phosphate (GAP), pyruvate and lactate. Glycogen determinations were done by modification of the method of DuBois and co-workers [1]. Metabolic profiles were then measured by plotting the percent change from resting levels for each substrate at the various time periods.

Results

The percent change in substrate concentration compared to rest is a good indication of the relative change in each substrate. While a change in substrate concentration may appear small, the relative change rather than the absolute change may be the important factor, since it may be the amount of change rather than the absolute concentration which is of importance (Figs. 1 and 2).

Percent changes at ten minutes of stimulation indicate that the highest change was in the concentration of glucose 6-phosphate, increasing approximately fourfold. A 26% decrease in ATP was accompanied by a 29% increase in AMP. Pyruvate and lactate changed in a similar manner.

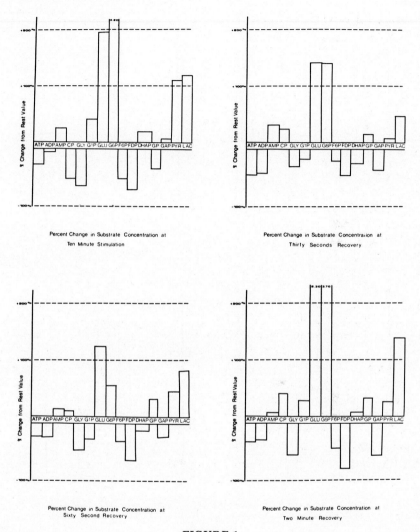

Percent Change in Substrate Concentration at
Ten Minute Stimulation

Percent Change in Substrate Concentration at
Thirty Seconds Recovery

Percent Change in Substrate Concentration at
Sixty Second Recovery

Percent Change in Substrate Concentration at
Two Minute Recovery

FIGURE 1.

Short-term recovery changes were characterized by continued low concentration in ATP and increased concentration of AMP, although the magnitude of these changes was less. The changes in glucose and glucose 6-phosphate during 30- and 60-second recovery were not as great as during stimulation or later recovery. The pattern of substrate changes further along the pathway was similar for early recovery periods, with lactate remaining high while pyruvate percent change values were not as great.

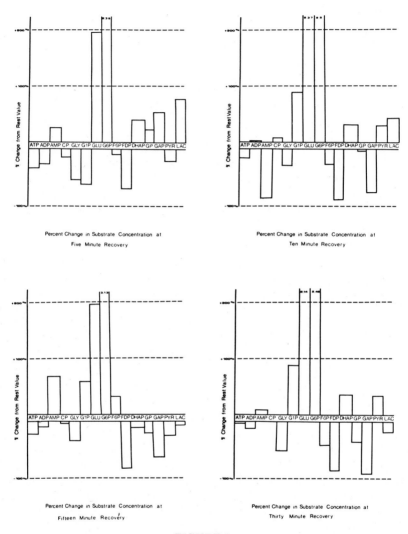

FIGURE 2.

Five-minute recovery changes show that most percent changes from rest were less than during two minutes of recovery, with changes in glucose, glucose 6-phosphate and lactate toward smaller percent values evident.

Percent changes in the profiles during long-term recovery present an interesting picture. The substrate changes past the phospho-fructokinase step were predominantly negative, especially at 15 minutes of recovery, while the intermediates prior to the above step were characterized by positive changes. This trend continues until 30 minutes of recovery, and percent change values at this time indicate that most substrate levels are still not similar to resting with the exception of the high energy phosphates.

Discussion

By looking at the metabolic profile of the muscle during either stimulation or recovery, an interesting picture of the metabolic state of the muscle may be observed (Fig. 3). With exercise, the profiles show increasing pyruvate and lactate concentrations, as well as glucose and glucose 6-phosphate. Observed increases in AMP and decreases in ATP and CP are in agreement with previous work involving skeletal muscle [2, 12, 13]. The decrease in ATP and CP and increase in AMP would increase activity of phosphofructokinase (PFK). ATP, for example, is inhibitory to PFK [11] and the decrease observed may be the stimulus for the increased rate of glycolytic activity. While absolute concentrations of ADP did not show appreciable differences, percent profile data indicate that ADP increases with stimulation and returns toward resting levels with recovery. It has been emphasized recently [10, 11] that it is the fractional change in substrates which is important for the response of the glycolytic enzymes. This is reflected in the large changes observed in the profiles for ATP, ADP and AMP.

Creatine phosphate decreases with stimulation, in agreement with the work of Edington and co-workers [2]. This decrease may activate pyruvate kinase, since CP acts as an inhibitor of both pyruvate kinase and phosphofructokinase [4, 6]. Substrate control may also be working in the upper pathway through effects on the enzyme hexokinase. Since this enzyme is inhibited by ADP and GGP [5], this may partially explain the high glucose levels observed following stimulation.

During recovery, substrate fluctuations as seen in the metabolic profiles appear to operate to insure sufficient substrate for the resynthesis of glycogen (Fig. 4). Recovery profiles indicate that during recovery a shift in metabolism takes place, reversing the exercise trend of substrates to build up at the lower end of the pathway. Comparison of substrate profiles during the different recovery periods indicates there is a large amount of substrate oscillation as the muscle returns to a resting state. The observed increases of ATP and CP are important to metabolic control in the muscle. The increase of CP during recovery may act to slow the rate

Proposed Control During Stimulation

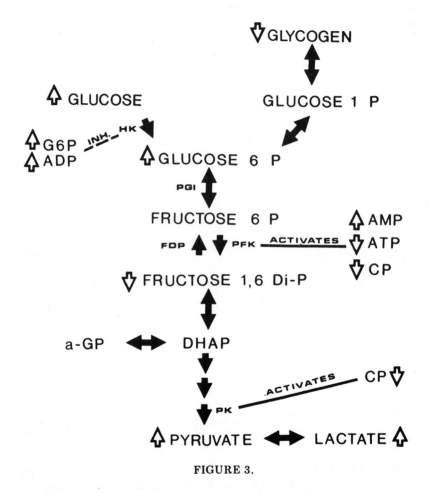

FIGURE 3.

of glycolysis since it acts as an inhibitor of both phosphofructokinase and pyruvate kinase. Increased glucose 6-phosphate during recovery may also slow the rate of glycolysis through substrate effects on PFK. At the same time PFK is inhibited, the reverse reaction catalyzed by the enzyme fructose diphosphatase is stimulated by increased ATP and CP and decreased AMP [3, 7]. At the same time pyruvate and lactate concentrations decrease, glycogen levels begin to increase.

Proposed Control During Recovery

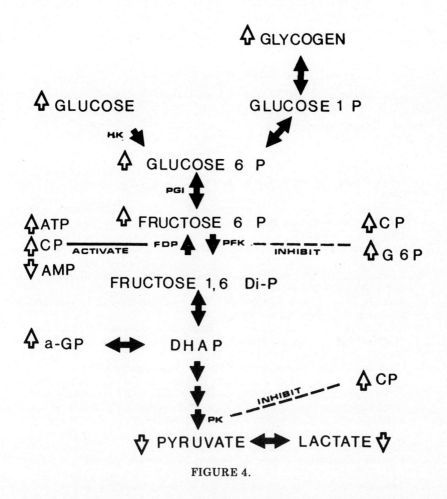

FIGURE 4.

Recovery, then, may be a time of the muscle changing from an exercise metabolism, directed toward production of energy, to a recovery metabolism, where it is directed toward the resynthesis of muscle energy stores. Substrate fluctuations appear to indicate that the enzyme phosphofructokinase is rate limiting for glycolysis both during exercise and recovery. While there is a buildup of metabolites during recovery prior to the phosphofructokinase step, below this step the substrates decrease and are probably transferred out of the cell as lactate. At the same time this enzyme limits the flow of substrate out of the cell during recovery, the reverse reaction is activated through substrate effects on the enzyme fructose diphosphatase. The metabolic environment, as evidenced in the profile data for recovery, favors the return of substrates to the upper pathway and thus appears to insure sufficient substrate for the resynthesis of glycogen.

Acknowledgments

The authors would like to acknowledge the very capable assistance of Ms. Kathryn McDonald, Ms. Patricia Ledger and Ms. Margie Cho in this work.

References

1. DuBois, M., Gilles, K., Hamilton, J. et al: Colometric method for determination of sugars and related substances. Anal. Chem. 28:350-356, 1956.
2. Edington, D.W., Ward, G. and Saville, W.: Energy metabolism of working muscle: Concentration profiles of selected metabolites. Am. J. Physiol. 224:1375-1380, 1973.
3. Fu, J. and Kemp, R.: Activation of muscle fructose, 1,6 diphosphatase by creatine phosphate and citrate. J. Biol. Chem. 248:1124-1125, 1973.
4. Kemp, R.G.: Inhibition of muscle pyruvate kinase by creatine phosphate. J. Biol. Chem. 248:3963-3967, 1973.
5. Keul, J., Doll, E. and Keppler, D.: Energy Metabolism of Human Muscle. Baltimore:Univ. Park Press, 1972.
6. Krzahowski, J. and Matchinsky, F.: Regulation of phosphofructokinase by phosphocreatine and phosphorylated glycolytic intermediates. Biochem. Biophys. Res. Comm. 34:816-823, 1969.
7. Lehninger, A.: Biochemistry. New York:Worth Publishers, 1975.
8. McCafferty, W.B. and Edington, D.W.: The effects of prolonged direct muscle stimulation and recovery on biochemicals associated with glycolysis in rat skeletal muscle. In Howald, H. and Poortmans, J. (eds.): Metabolic Adaptation to Prolonged Physical Exercise. Basel:Birkhauser Verlag, 1975.
9. McCafferty, W.B., Farrar, R.P., Pearce, T.N. and Edington, D.W.: Measurements of selected glycolytic intermediates during early recovery from electrical stimulation of skeletal muscle in the male rat. Med. Sci. Sports 7:88, 1975 (abstract).
10. McGilvery, R.W.: The use of fuels for muscular work. In Howald, H. and Poortmans, J. (eds.): Metabolic Adaptation to Prolonged Physical Exercise. Basel:Birkhauser Verlag, 1975.
11. Newsholme, E. and Start, C.: Regulation in Metabolism. New York:J. Wiley and Sons, 1972.
12. Sacktor, B. and Hurlbut, E.: Regulation of metabolism in working muscle in vivo. II. Concentrations of adenine nucleotides, arginine phosphate, and inorganic phosphate in insect flight. J. Biol. Chem. 241:632-634, 1966.
13. Sacktor, B., Wormser-Shavit, E. and White, J.: Diphosphopyridine nucleotide linked cytoplasmic metabolites in rat leg muscle in situ during contraction and recovery. J. Biol. Chem. 240:2678-2681, 1965.

Enzymatic Changes Following Prolonged Heavy Exercise

S. B. Stromme, B. Tveit and H. E. Refsum

Introduction

Several authors have demonstrated increases in serum enzyme levels following physical exertion [1, 2, 4, 5, 8, 11-14, 19, 22]. Most investigations have been carried out in connection with exercise of relatively short duration, and little seems to be known about the enzymatical changes taking place during the period of recovery after heavy exercise of several hours' duration.

The purpose of this presentation is to report on the alterations in serum enzyme levels in a group of well-trained subjects over a two-week period, during which they participated in two long distance cross-country skiing competitions, 90 and 70 km, respectively, one week apart. The following enzymes were examined: *creatine kinase = CK* (creatine phosphokinase = CPK), *aspartate aminotransferase = ASAT* (glutamic-oxaloacetic transaminase = GOT), *alanine aminotransferase = ALAT* (glutamic-pyruvic transaminase = GPT), *lactate dehydrogenase = LD* (LDH), *LD isoenzymes = LD-1 to LD-5* and *ornithine carbamyltransferase = OCT*.

Methods

Sixteen men, aged 21 to 58 years (mean 38 years), weighing 67 to 102 kg (mean 76.5 kg), served as subjects.

In the first competition they covered a distance of 90 km in an average of 6.26 hours (5.37 to 8.06). In the second competition seven days later, they covered 70 km in an average of 5.47 hours (5.02 to 6.52). During both events they were allowed to drink what they wanted of liquids with known amounts of sugar, but no salts, at seven and six places, respectively, which were almost equally spaced along the tracks. The average net weight loss was 2.70 kg (1.5 to 4.3)

S. B. Stromme, B. Tveit and H. E. Refsum, Laboratory of Physiology, Norwegian College of Physical Education and Sport, the Central Laboratory and the Institute for Respiratory Physiology, Ulleval Hospital, Oslo, Norway.

after the first race and 3.05 kg (1.9 to 4.3) after the second. At both races the air temperature at start was about −5 C. During the last part of the 70-km race the participants were exposed to relatively warm sunshine. The subjects did not engage in heavy exercise during the week between the races.

Blood for determination of the serum enzyme activities was taken from the antecubital vein on the day prior to each race, immediately after the races and on the first, second and fourth day after each race. In connection with the 90-km race, blood was also withdrawn two hours after the race.

Enzymatic Methods

ASAT and ALAT were determined by the method of Karmen [9] and LD according to Wroblewski and LaDue [23], with reagent kits from Kabi. The activity was recorded on an LKB Reaction Rate Analyzer. OCT was determined by a modification of the isotope technique of Reichard and Reichard [16]. CK was determined essentially according to Rosalki [17], employing Calbiochem's reagent kits. Details have been described previously [20]. LD isoenzymes were measured after electrophoretic separation on agarose gel; the method is modified from Van der Helm [21].

Reference values are based on studies of 190 healthy persons, aged 20 to 90 years. LD: 150 to 300 U/l 35 C (<50 years), 150 to 350 U/l 35 C (> 50 years); ASAT: 10 to 30 U/l 35 C; ALAT: 10 to 35 U/l 35 C; CK: 0 to 110 U/l 35 C; and OCT: 0 to 0.15 U/l 37 C. For LD isoenzymes reference values have been established with 30 medical students: LD-1: 24% to 34%; LD-2: 32% to 40%; LD-3: 24% to 32%; LD-4: 3% to 9%; LD-5: 1% to 3% of total LD.

Results

Figure 1 shows the changes in serum enzyme levels during the observation period of 13 days. Following both the 90- and 70-km race significant rises were observed in CK, ASAT and total LD, whereas only minor changes were noted in ALAT and OCT. The rise in total LD was due to increase in LD-4 and -5, LD-1, -2 and -3 being essentially unchanged. The percentage changes in CK, ASAT and total LD are presented in Figure 2.

Immediately after the 90-km race the average increase in CK was 186%; two hours later the increase was 240%, and the next day it was further increased to 297%, approximately four times the initial level. CK remained elevated during the following days and returned

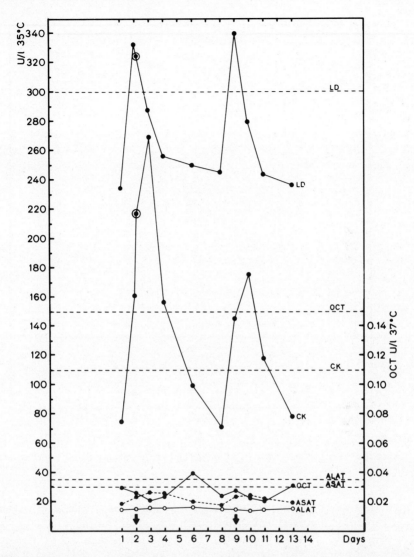

FIG. 1. Changes in serum enzyme levels during the observation period of 13 days. The arrows at day 2 and 9 indicate the 90- and 70-km race, respectively. The dotted vertical lines denote the upper limits for the reference values. In connection with the 90-km race, the blood sample taken two hours after the race is marked with a circle.

to pre-race level on the fourth day after the race. An analogous, but less pronounced rise in CK was observed after the 70-km race. Immediately after the competition CK increased to 160%; on the

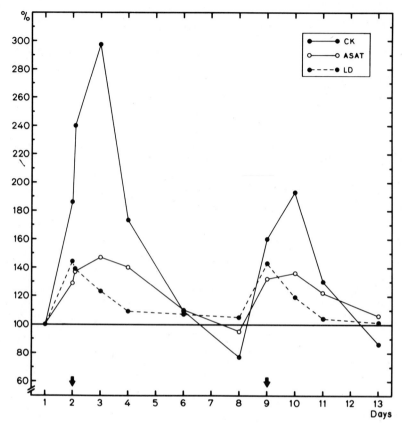

FIG. 2. The percentage changes in serum levels of CK, ASAT and total LD during the observation period of 13 days. The arrows at day 2 and 9 indicate the 90- and 70-km race, respectively.

next day to 193%, approximately three times the initial level. Again, CK remained elevated until the fourth day after the race.

Similarly, after both the 90- and the 70-km race ASAT reached peak values on the day after the race, being 147% and 136%, respectively, and did not return to the initial level until the fourth day after the races. Two hours after completion of the 90-km race ASAT had risen from 129% to 137% of the initial level.

At completion of the 90-km race total LD was increased to 144% of the pre-race level; two hours later it was slightly decreased to 139% and was back at the initial level on the second day after the competition. Almost exactly the same pattern was observed after the 70-km race.

The half-life of CK and ASAT, as estimated from the fall in serum activity after the recorded peak values, was of the order of 24 to 36 hours.

The serum osmolality remained essentially the same during the observation period, being an average of 294 before and 299 mOsm/l after the 90-km race.

Discussion

The main source of CK is skeletal and cardiac muscle, whereas OCT and ALAT originate in liver, and ASAT and LD in all three types of tissues. Since only minor changes were observed in OCT and ALAT, and in the isoenzyme fractions originating in cardiac muscle, erythrocytes, kidney and lung (LD-1, -2, -3), it seems reasonable to infer that striated muscle was the major source of enzyme release.

The fact that the peak values of CK and ASAT were found more than 24 hours after the physical exertion and the disappearance rate was slow indicates that an increased enzyme leakage out of the muscle cells has been going on for a prolonged period after the exercise, probably for several days. This suggests that the concerned muscles are not fully restituted until at least three to four days after this type of severe physical exertion. The lower peak values of CK observed after the second race may possibly be due to the previous, recent exertion, but the data allow no conclusions with regard to this.

None of the enzymes determined in this study give a specific answer as to which of the cellular structures or functions are affected by the exercise, and the mechanism by which the muscle enzyme activity in serum increases during and after exercise is still unclear. The increase in creatinine production observed during this type of prolonged heavy exercise [15] may suggest increased muscle tissue breakdown and a consequent increase in outflow of cellular enzymes. Haralambie [7] has demonstrated that muscle hyperexcitability and the prolonged elevation in serum CK after exercise are coincidental, strongly suggesting that fatigued (or recovering) muscle has a modified membrane permeability, causing both an increased loss of cytoplasmic enzymes and a disturbance of the ion distribution, leading to enhanced irritability. It has been postulated that an increased membrane permeability in active skeletal muscles may be due to insufficient oxygen supply. However, the intensity of the muscular work during long distance cross-country skiing and marathon running is not so high that anaerobic metabolism is brought into play to a major extent. This is further supported by the observations of Cunningham and Critz [3] that the pattern of postexercise serum enzyme changes is not significantly influenced whether test subjects are breathing low or high oxygen gas mixtures during exercise.

Some authors have suggested that the magnitude of increase in serum enzyme levels after exercise depends upon the physical condition of the subjects and that the training may prevent muscle enzyme release [1, 8, 10, 13]. This seems to be in contrast with the present observations and the results of Rose et al [18], showing that highly trained as well as moderately trained cross-country skiers and marathon runners had marked increases in serum enzyme levels after exertion. Furthermore, Misner et al [11] were unable to find any reduction in the exercise-induced enzyme increase in a group of subjects, who participated in progressive distance running three times per week for 15 weeks. The possibility that a large muscle mass per se is causing an elevated CK level has been suggested by Garcia [6] on the basis of observations of football players. However, his subjects were studied only under resting conditions. The fiber composition of the involved muscle mass may also be a factor of importance. Fast-twitch fibers are known to contain more CK than slow-twitch fibers, and the pattern of muscle contractions in different types of exercise might therefore influence the exertional enzyme release and make comparisons of data from studies with different experimental conditions difficult.

Although the large and prolonged liberation of muscle enzymes after exercise may be regarded as a normal physiological response, it should be taken into account during physical training. Thus, it seems reasonable to recommend only light physical training during the first three to four days of recovery after heavy exercise of long duration.

References

1. Ahlborg, B. and Brohult, J.: Immediate and delayed metabolic reactions in well-trained subjects after prolonged physical exercise. Acta Med. Scand. 182:41-54, 1967.
2. Critz, J.B. and Cunningham, D.A.: Plasma enzyme levels in man after different physical activities. J. Sports Med. 12:143-149, 1972.
3. Cunningham, D.A. and Critz, J.B.: Effect of hypoxia and physical activity on plasma enzyme levels in man. Int. Z. Angew. Physiol. 30:302-308, 1972.
4. Fojt, E., Ekelund, L.-G. and Hultman, E.: Enzyme activities in hepatic venous blood under strenuous physical exercise. Pflügers Arch. 361:287-296, 1976.

5. Fowler, W.M., Gardner, G.W., Kazerunian, H.H. and Lauvstad, W.A.: The effect of exercise on serum enzyme. Arch. Phys. Med. Rehab. 49:554-565, 1968.
6. Garcia, W.: Elevated creatine phosphokinase levels associated with large muscle mass. JAMA 228:1395-1396, 1974.
7. Haralambie, G.: Neuromuscular irritability and serum creatine phosphate kinase in athletes in training. Int. Z. Angew. Physiol. 31:279-288, 1973.
8. Hunter, J.B. and Critz, J.B.: Effect of training on plasma enzyme levels in man. J. Appl. Physiol. 31:20-23, 1971.
9. Karmen, A.: A note on the spectrophotometric assay of glutamic-oxaloacetic transaminase in human blood serum. J. Clin. Invest. 34:131-133, 1955.
10. Maqazanik, A., Shapiro, Y., Meytes, D. and Meytes, I.: Enzyme blood levels and water balance during a marathon race. J. Appl. Physiol. 36:214-217, 1974.
11. Misner, J.E., Massey, B.H. and Williams, B.T.: The effect of physical training on the response of serum enzymes to exercise stress. Med. Sci. Sports 5:86-88, 1973.
12. Nerdrum, H.J. and Berg, K.J.: Changes of serum glutamic-oxaloacetic transaminase and serum lactic dehydrogenase on physical exertion. Scand. J. Clin. Lab. Invest. 16:624-629, 1964.
13. Nuttall, F.Q. and Jones, B.: Creatine kinase and glutamic oxaloacetic transaminase activity in serum: Kinetics of change with exercise and effect of physical conditioning. J. Lab. Clin. Med. 71:847-854, 1968.
14. Rasch, P.J. and Schwartz, P.L.: Effect of amateur wrestling on selected serum enzymes. J. Sports Med. 12:82-86, 1972.
15. Refsum, H.E. and Stromme, S.B.: Urea and creatinine production and excretion in urine during and after prolonged heavy exercise. Scand. J. Clin. Lab. Invest. 33:247-254, 1974.
16. Reichard, H. and Reichard, P.: Determination of ornithine carbamyl transferase in serum. J. Lab. Clin. Med. 52:709-717, 1958.
17. Rosalki, S.B.: An improved procedure for serum creatine phosphokinase determination. J. Lab. Clin. Med. 69:696-705, 1967.
18. Rose, L.I., Bousser, J.E. and Cooper, K.H.: Serum enzymes after marathon running. J. Appl. Physiol. 29:355-357, 1970.
19. Schwartz, P.L., Carroll, H.W. and Douglas, J.S. Jr.: Exercise-induced changes in serum enzyme activities and their relationship to max $\dot{V}O_2$. Int. Z. Angew. Physiol. 30:20-33, 1971.
20. Tveit, B. and Runde, I.: The effect of enzyme concentration and serum concentration on initial rate measurements of serum enzymes. Scand. J. Clin. Lab. Invest. 27:161-167, 1971.
21. Van der Helm, H.J.: A simplified method of demonstrating lactic dehydrogenase isoenzymes in serum. Clin. Chim. Acta 7:124-128, 1968.
22. Vejjajiva, A. and Teasdale, G.M.: Serum creatine kinase and physical exercise. Br. Med. J. 1:1653-1654, 1965.
23. Wroblewski, F. and LaDue, J.S.: Lactic dehydrogenase in blood. Proc. Soc. Exp. Biol. Med. 90:210-213, 1955.

Loss of Potassium and Sodium After Long-Lasting Exercise: An Experiment in its Substitution

Dieter Böhmer and Reinhard Böhlau

Introduction

An adequate concentration of potassium in the cell is an important condition for the optimal functioning of the neuromuscular system.

The potassium content of the muscular cell is closely related to the glucose level and it is known to decrease during physical strain in a fashion that parallels the decrease in glucose. In fact, during physical performance, the level of potassium in the serum tends to increase. This occurrence is accompanied by the development of an acidosis.

With the help of the mechanism of aldosterone, the kidneys augment the secretion of potassium just as does the mechanism of perspiration.

During long-lasting exercise, a reduction of the total potassium of the organism obviously occurs. The clinical signs of this reduction are a loss of myogenic tonus, hyporeflexia, arrhythmia, tachycardia and hypotension [2, 5].

At best, both the magnitude and the duration of the potassium loss can only be estimated. It is only in conditions of normal acid base and water balance that one can evaluate from serum and urine determinations the real changes that have occurred in the muscular system. Muscle biopsies have indeed added much to our knowledge of what happens to potassium as a consequence of exercise. However, it should be noted that it has added to our knowledge of the reactions of potassium in that particular tissue only.

Methodology

With a view of gaining more insight on the loss of potassium during long-lasting physical strain, we measured before, immediately

Dieter Böhmer and Reinhard Böhlau, Department of Sportsmedicine, University of Frankfurt/Main, Frankfurt/Main, Federal Republic of Germany.

after and 24 hours after an exercise bout (three hours at 100 watt on a bicycle ergometer) the following variables:

> total body potassium measured by the K^{40} method (human body counter)
>
> K^+ and Na^+ ions in the serum
>
> sodium, potassium and creatinine clearance
>
> hematocrit, total body weight and urine volume

In our first series of tests, we examined 13 fairly well-trained male subjects; their mean age was 21 ± 4 years and their mean weight was 68.5 ± 5.0 kg. After the performance, the food ingested was kept low in potassium content.

Before and after performing 1½ hours of the 3-hour exercise, the subjects of the second series received 200 ml of an electrolyte sugar solution containing the following: sodium, 20 mval; potassium, 10 mval; magnesium, 5 mval; oligosaccharide, 120 K cal. The subjects of the second group differed slightly from those of the first group; their number was 14, they were also fairly well trained; their average age and weights were 20 ± 4 years and 72 ± 10 kg, respectively.

Results

The weight loss of the first group ranged from 1.4 to 1.9 kg per person, as compared to a range of 1.2 to 1.6 kg for the second group. The lesser weight loss of the second group is apparently related to their intake of 400 ml of fluid. The weight losses observed must be interpreted with caution since the outdoor temperatures were higher during the testing session of the second group.

In the first group (not fed a potassium substitute) the potassium content was seen to decrease markedly 24 hours after the performance by 0.07 gm/kg body weight (from a level of 2.00 ± 0.18 gm/kg of body weight, it decreased to a level of 1.93 ± 0.18).

With respect to the total body weight, the potassium content decreased from a mean of 137.0 ± 8.0 gm/body weight to a value of 131.0 ± 7.1 gm/body weight, for a loss of 153.0 mval potassium (Fig. 1). It can be seen from Figure 1 that immediately after the performance, the value reached for the first group was 134.9 gm/body weight, i.e., a loss of potassium of the order of 53.6 mval.

In the group that was fed potassium before and during the performance, the decrease was markedly less, namely, from a level of 1.97 ± 0.21 to one of 1.96 ± 0.25, the total potassium content of the body for the second group decreased during the experiment from a mean of 140.4 ± 10.6 to a mean of 138.0 gm/body weight (Fig. 1).

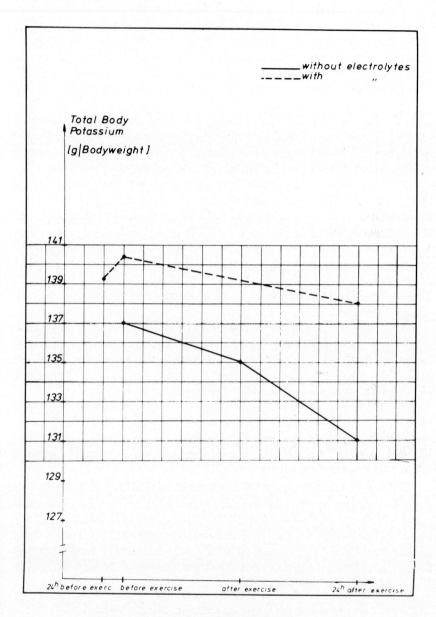

FIG. 1. Loss of total body potassium content after an exercise lasting three hours on a bicycle ergometer.

Figure 1 clearly indicates that 24 hours after the performance, the potassium balance has not returned to normal. The same observation has been made with animals; it implies that the so-called easily exchangeable potassium is not so readily taken up by the cells [1]. In 1942, Hevesy had come to the conclusion that the uptake of potassium into the cells was indeed a slow process [3]. Making use of radioactive potassium in rabbits, Nadell et al have shown that the intake of potassium into cells lasts about 40 hours [4]; only then can a complete restitution be expected. In our experiment, we were able to confirm this fact by our measurements of the hematocrit and of both sodium and potassium clearance.

In accordance with other investigations, the hematocrit in our study was observed to increase slightly from a mean of 45.8% before the performance to a mean of 47.5% after; the values returned to the starting levels soon after.

The level of sodium changed only slightly in both our groups. Figure 2 shows that the sodium clearance decreased after the performance, but increased slightly between the 4th and 6th hour after performance with a new decrease during the period between the 6th and the 24th hour.

By contrast, we have noted a slight increase of the potassium level and a remarkable increase of the potassium clearance immediately after the performance in both our groups (Fig. 3). It can be seen in Figure 3 that the potassium clearance was not normalized for our first group 24 hours after the performance.

In our group which was fed the electrolytic drinks, the trend observed was the same but not so marked. The aldosterone mechanism appears fully operative in this case. In the period between the 6th and the 24th hour after performance, the measured clearance levels returned to normal.

With due consideration of the intake of 400 ml of fluid by the subjects of the second group, the difference in the 24-hour urine volume before and after the performance was less for the second group as compared to the first group; the decrease was from a mean of 1290 ± 469 ml to a mean of 918 ± 349 ml for the second group, by comparison to values decreasing from a mean of 1650 ± 757 ml to 824 ± 166 ml, for the first group.

Summary and Conclusions

Our measurements of total body potassium before and after a performance lasting three hours on a bicycle ergometer showed a loss of potassium even 24 hours after the exercise. The loss of potassium,

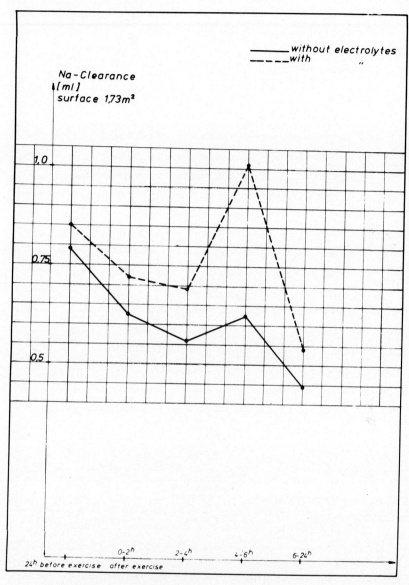

FIG. 2. Sodium clearance after the exercise (three hours).

resulting from a marked increased potassium clearance after the performance, is about twice as great as the daily requirement.

It appears from our results that during strenuous physical activity, not only the intake of fluid but also the intake of

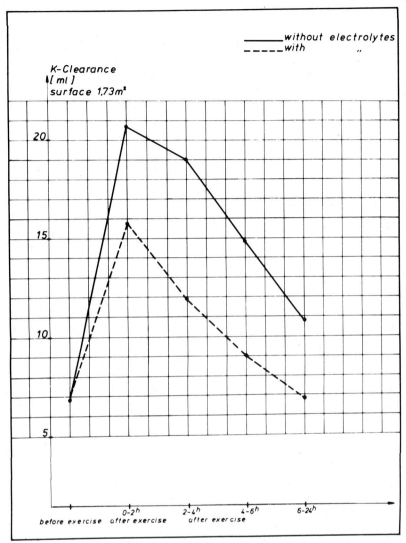

FIG. 3. Potassium clearance after the exercise (three hours).

electrolytes rich in potassium is recommendable, since it speeds up its restitution, especially on the day after the performance.

References

1. Bervenmark, H., Eriksson, G., Lingberg, S. and Paalzow, L.: Acta Pharm. Suec. 3:45, 1966.
2. Dahl, L.K., Leitle, G. and Heine, M.: Int. Exper. Med. 136:318, 1972.
3. Hevesy, G.: Acta Physiol. Scand. 3:123, 1941-1942.
4. Nadell, I., Sweet, N.I. and Edelmann, I.S.: Int. Clin. Invest. 35:512, 1956.
5. Schleusing, G.J.: Nöcker Med. Welt 31:1579, 1960.

Effects of Training, Rest and Renewed Training on Skeletal Muscle in Sedentary Men

J. E. Orlander and K.-H. Kiessling

Introduction

It is now widely accepted that physical training induces an increased metabolic capacity in skeletal muscle. The functional adaptation includes increased activity of several enzymes, all of which are involved in aerobic energy metabolism [12]. Structurally, this mitochondrial adaptation is reflected by increased volume fractions of mitochondria in skeletal muscle of rats [9, 11] and young men [17, 18, 20, 25], but not in middle-aged men [19, 20].

Prolonged moderate training in order to produce a better physical fitness is often interrupted by bad weather, shortness of time, colds and so on, and consequently becomes more or less irregular. Therefore, the present investigation was undertaken to see if a period of physical training has persisting effects in skeletal muscle during subsequent inactivity and to evaluate the effects of renewed training. This paper will deal with the functional state of the energy metabolism, measured as in vitro activities of representative enzymes. Also included are some preliminary results from structural studies, performed by means of quantitative electron microscopy.

Material and Methods

Twenty-four healthy, previously sedentary men volunteered to participate in the investigation. Eight subjects withdrew for various reasons, while 16 completed the training regimen. Only the latter are included in the results. Their age was 35 ± 1 years (mean $\pm$ SE), range 25 to 43, their height and weight 181 ± 2 cm (173 to 194) and 76.6 ± 3.1 kg (64.1 to 108.7), respectively.

J. E. Orlander and K.-H. Kiessling, Institute of Zoophysiology, University of Uppsala, and Department of Animal Nutrition, Swedish University of Agriculture, Forestry and Veterinary Medicine, Uppsala, Sweden.

The training program consisted of two seven-week periods of moderate training separated by an eight-week inactivity period. During a week of training, the subjects ran or walked 3 to 8 km twice, swam once and engaged in calisthenics once. Before and after each training period, muscle biopsies were taken from the musculus vastus lateralis with the needle technique described by Bergström [7]. The first two biopsies were taken from the left leg and the remaining two from the right. The muscle specimens were divided into three parts: one for the assay of enzyme activities, one for electron microscopy and one for histochemistry.

Maximal Oxygen Uptake

During maximal running, the expired air was collected in Douglas bags and subsequently analyzed for oxygen content by the Haldane technique.

Enzyme Assays

The activities of six different enzymes, each representing a subsystem in energy metabolism, were measured. The enzymes and subsystems were phosphofructokinase (PFK; E.C. 2.7.1.11) — glycolysis; lactate dehydrogenase (LDH; E.C. 1.1.1.27) — lactate formation; 3-hydroxyacyl-CoA-dehydrogenase (HAD; E.C. 1.1.1.35) — fatty acid; β-oxidation, citrate synthase (CS; E.C. 4.1.3.7) — TCA cycle; cytochrome oxidase (cytox; E.C. 1.9.3.1) — respiratory chain; and mitochondrial α-glycerophosphate dehydrogenase (m-GPD; E.C. 1.1.99.5) — α-glycerophosphate shuttle.

The biopsy specimens (15 to 50 mg) were homogenized with 19 times (w/v) the amount of ice-cold potassium bicarbonate buffer, 62.5 mM, pH 7.4, containing 0.15 M KCl and 6 mM EDTA in a small, ice-cooled, all-glass Potter-Elvehjem homogenizer. The homogenization was performed by hand in six periods of 30 s with 30 s intervals to avoid rises in temperature. The resulting crude homogenate was kept on ice and was used either directly or diluted five times to determine the enzyme activities.

Phosphofructokinase activity was determined spectrophotometrically according to Shonk and Boxer [29]. The activities of lactate dehydrogenase and 3-hydroxyacyl-CoA-dehydrogenase were estimated by the methods of Bass et al [4], citrate synthase as described by Srere [31] and cytochrome oxidase polarographically according to Whereat et al [35]. Mitochondrial α-glycerophosphate dehydrogenase activity was estimated by two different methods: The first two biopsies were analyzed polarographically, using a Clark oxygen electrode and a reaction mixture containing 50 mM potassium phosphate; pH 7.5, 20 μM cytochrome c, 4.5 mM DL-α-glycerophosphate, 1 μM rotenone and 100 μl homogenate in a final volume of 2 ml. The remaining two biopsies were assayed according to Bass et al [4] as modified by Peter et al [28]. The first method was abandoned, because it gave very low values, which could be suspected to be affected by nonspecific oxygen consumption in the assay system. However, since the second method showed a similar effect of training on the enzyme, the values from the first training period were included.

The spectrophotometrical assays were performed at 23 C in a Beckman model 25 recording double beam spectrophotometer. Polarographic assays were made at 28 C.

The muscle protein content was estimated according to Lowry et al [21].

Electron Microscopy

Small pieces of muscle tissue were fixed in ice-cold osmium tetroxide as described by Caulfield [8], washed, dehydrated in ethanol and propylene oxide, and embedded in Epon 812. Longitudinal sections, approximately 70 to 80 nm thick, were cut in an ultramicrotome (LKB Ultrotome, type I), stained with uranyl acetate and lead citrate and examined in an electron microscope (Siemens Elmiskop 101 or Hitachi HU-11E-1).

Eleven to sixteen micrographs per subject were taken at random and analyzed stereologically according to Weibel [33, 34]. The number of mitochondria per unit volume was estimated by the formula $N_v = K/\beta \sqrt{N_A^3/V_v}$ [33], with $K = 1.07$ and $\beta = 1.6$ (the latter value refers to spheroids with an axial ratio of 2). This of course gives only rough estimates of the true mitochondrial number, since skeletal muscle mitochondria are very irregularly shaped. For comparative purposes, however, the method is applicable.

Histochemistry

The muscle specimen was frozen in isopentane cooled by liquid nitrogen. Transverse sections (10 μm) were cut in a cryostat at -20 C and mounted on cover glasses for histochemical staining. Identification of muscle fiber types was based on the staining intensity of myofibrillar ATP:ase, according to Padykula and Herman [27].

Statistics

The significance of differences between means was tested with Student's *t* test.

Results

Maximal Oxygen Uptake

Maximal oxygen uptake was 3.32 ± 0.13, 3.58 ± 0.12, 3.49 ± 0.13 and 3.62 ± 0.15 liter/min (means $\pm$ SE) on the four test occasions, respectively. The differences are not statistically significant.

Fiber Composition

The percentage of slow twitch-oxidative fibers was 42.7 ± 4.5, 35.5 ± 4.7, 36.2 ± 3.7 and 39.5 ± 2.5 (means $\pm$ SE) on the four biopsy occasions, respectively. The differences are nonsignificant. This indicates that the training regimen had no effect on the relative contents of slow-twitch and fast-twitch fibers.

Enzyme Activities

The activities of the six enzymes before and after the two training periods are shown in Figure 1.

The first training period resulted in significant increases in the activities of HAD and LDH, representing fatty acid oxidation and lactate formation capacity, respectively. No significant changes in PFK, CS, cytox or m-GPD activities were observed.

During the inactivity period, a drop in HAD activity was the only significant change.

The second training period did not produce any rise in HAD activity. Unlike the first period, there was a significant 50% rise in cytochrome oxidase. Furthermore, the activities of CS and LDH were elevated as compared to before the first training period.

Muscle Protein

The muscle protein concentrations on the four biopsy occasions were 11.4 ± 0.5, 13.4 ± 0.9, 11.6 ± 0.6 and 14.1 ± 0.7 (percent of wet weight, means $\pm$ SE), respectively. The concentration was significantly higher after the second training period than before the first period ($p < 0.01$) and second ($p < 0.05$) periods.

Electron Microscopy

Data on volume fraction, number per unit volume and mean volume of mitochondria before and after the first training period, are given in Table I. Also included are volume fractions of intracellular lipid droplets.

No changes in mitochondrial volume or number were observed during this training period. The intracellular fat content, however, almost doubled.

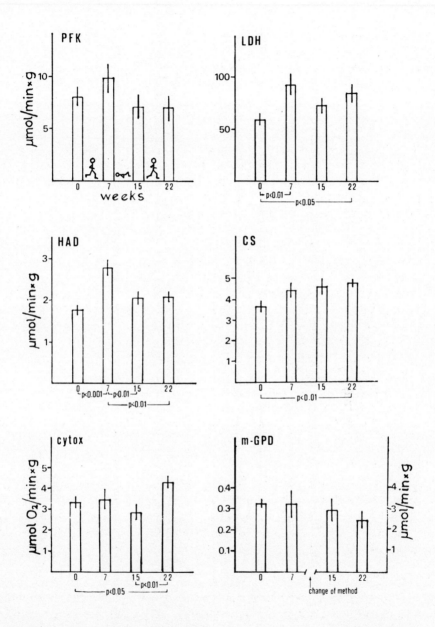

FIG. 1. Enzyme activities in skeletal muscle on the four biopsy occasions. Columns with vertical bars denote means ± SE. Significant differences are indicated below each diagram.

Table I. Ultrastructural Features in Skeletal Muscle Before and After the First Training Period. Values are means ± SE

	No. of Subjects	Mitochondria						Volume Fraction of Lipid Droplets (%)
		Fibrillar Space			Subsarcolemma Space			
		Volume Fraction (%)	Number (μm^{-3})	Mean Volume (μm^3) × 10^2	Volume Fraction (%)	Number (μm^{-3})	Mean Volume (μm^3) × 10^2	
Before training	16	4.67 ± 0.34	1.30 ± 0.12	5.05 ± 0.64	30.6 ± 3.2	5.44 ± 0.80	7.39 ± 1.63	0.82 ± 0.13
After training	15	4.80 ± 0.36	1.23 ± 0.10	4.84 ± 0.46	26.3 ± 2.6	4.74 ± 0.49	6.08 ± 0.57	1.56 ± 0.30
		n.s.	n.s.	n.s.	n.s.	n.s.	n.s.	$p < 0.05$

Note: Numbers and mean volumes of mitochondria refer to spheroid mitochondria with an axial ratio of 2. This means that the given figures are only estimates of the true values.

Discussion

Maximal Oxygen Uptake

The nonsignificant changes in maximal oxygen uptake in response to training and inactivity indicate that the kind of training employed in this investigation is insufficient to produce major changes in overall oxygen uptake capacity.

Enzyme Activities

However, the training intensity was high enough to induce significant metabolic changes in the m. vastus lateralis. The pattern of adaptation differed considerably between the two periods of training, a fact that implicates a difference in starting-point, possibly due to persisting effects from the first period.

The rise in HAD activity during the first training period is consistent with results from studies by Baldwin et al [2], Moesch and Howald [22] and Molé et al [23, 24] all showing an increased fatty acid oxidation in skeletal muscle after training. The lack of a corresponding increase during the second training period suggests a supercompensation during the first period.

The activity of lactate dehydrogenase is usually not influenced by moderate training [10]. The increases observed in the present study are probably due to the unusually low initial LDH activities. Similarly, very low LDH activities have been found by Bass et al in the thigh muscles of women, especially in obese individuals [5, 6].

The increase in citrate synthase, although becoming significant only after the second training period, apparently lingered during inactivity (Fig. 1). This may be interpreted as a persisting effect of the first training period. A similar, but shorter persisting effect has been demonstrated for hexokinase in guinea pigs by Barnard and Peter [3].

Cytochrome oxidase is not affected by the first seven weeks of training, but rises significantly during the second training period. This is in remarkable accordance with a previous study [19], where the cytox activity increased only 9% during eight weeks of moderate training, whereas seven additional weeks produced a further 65% increase. These results strongly suggest the necessity of a rather long period of moderate training to produce changes in mitochondrial oxygen consumption capacity.

During the lag period, changes in favor of an increased aerobic metabolism may occur. These changes, which may include improved blood supply, increased local oxygen supply by a rise in myoglobin content, and increased substrate supply by elevated fatty acid β-oxidation, must possibly occur before a rise in cytochrome oxidase activity will be induced. If this is true, these changes must have persisted during the inactivity period.

Muscle Protein

The observed increase in muscle protein concentration in response to training is contradictory to results by Askew et al [1] and Winder et al [36], who saw no such increase in rats. However, as training produces increases in mitochondrial protein [13, 14, 16, 25], cytochrome c [2, 14, 15, 23, 32] and myoglobin [12], increased amounts of metabolic enzymes and, possibly, rises in contractile proteins, these factors could account for the elevated protein level.

Ultrastructure

The lack of ultrastructural effects on the mitochondria during the first training period may be explained in two ways: (1) The training may have been too mild to stimulate mitochondrial growth or proliferation or (2) the subjects may have surpassed the age where major increases in mitochondrial volume are no longer possible. The existence of such an age effect is strongly implicated by results from previous studies [20].

Intracellular lipid stores almost doubled during the training period. This supports results by Howald [17], Askew et al [1] and Short et al [30], who all found increased triglyceride levels in muscle after training. Thus both ultrastructural and enzymatic results (the rise in HAD, Fig. 1) give strong evidence in favor of an increased role for fatty acids in skeletal muscle metabolism after training.

Acknowledgments

This investigation was supported by grants from the Research Council of the Swedish Sports Federation (Grants no 9/73 and 34/75). We are indebted to Drs. Björn Ekblom and Jan Karlsson, Gymnastikoch idrottshögskolan, Stockholm, for their helpful cooperation, and to Miss Gun-Britt Jönsson and Miss Maria Ahlberg for skillful technical assistance.

References

1. Askew, E.W., Huston, R.L. and Dohm, G.L.: Metabolism 22:473-480, 1973.
2. Baldwin, K.M., Klinkerfuss, G.H., Terjung, R.L. et al: Am. J. Physiol. 222:373-378, 1972.

3. Barnard, R.J. and Peter, J.B.: J. Appl. Physiol. 27:691-695, 1969.
4. Bass, A., Brdiczka, D., Eyer, P. et al: Eur. J. Biochem. 10:198-206, 1969.
5. Bass, A., Vondra, K., Rath, R. and Vitek, V.: Pflügers Arch. 354:249-255, 1975.
6. Bass, A., Vondra, K., Rath, R. et al: Pflügers Arch. 359:325-334, 1975.
7. Bergström, J.: Scand. J. Clin. Lab. Invest. 14, suppl. 68, 1962.
8. Caulfield, J.B.: J. Biophys. Biochem. Cytol. 3:827, 1957.
9. Gollnick, P.D., Ianuzzo, C.D. and King, D.W.: In Pernow, B. and Saltin, B. (eds.): Muscle Metabolism During Exercise. New York and London:Plenum Press, 1971, pp. 69-86.
10. Gollnick, P.D. and Hermansen, L.: Exerc. Sport. Sci. Rev. 1:1-43, 1973.
11. Gollnick, P.D. and King, D.W.: Am. J. Physiol. 216:1502-1509, 1969.
12. Holloszy, J.O.: Exerc. Sport Sci. Rev. 1:45-71, 1973.
13. Holloszy, J.O.: J. Biol. Chem. 242:2278-2282, 1967.
14. Holloszy, J.O. and Oscai, L.B.: Arch. Biochem. Biophys. 130:653-656, 1969.
15. Holloszy, J.O., Oscai, L.B., Don, I.J. and Molé, P.A.: Biochem. Biophys. Res. Commun. 40:1368-1373, 1970.
16. Holloszy, J.O., Oscai, L.B., Molé, P.A. and Don, I.J.: In Pernow, B. and Saltin, B. (eds.): Muscle Metabolism During Exercise. New York and London:Plenum Press, 1971, pp. 51-61.
17. Howald, H.: In Howald, H. and Poortmans, J.R. (eds.): Metabolic Adaptation to Prolonged Physical Exercise. Basel:Birkhäuser, 1975, pp. 372-383.
18. Kiessling, K.H., Piehl, K. and Lungquist, C.G.: In Pernow, B. and Saltin, B. (eds.): Muscle Metabolism During Exercise. New York and London:Plenum Press, 1971, pp. 97-101.
19. Kiessling, K.H., Pilström, L., Bylund, A.C. et al: Scand. J. Clin. Lab. Invest. 33:63-69, 1974.
20. Kiessling, K.H., Pilström, L., Karlsson, J. and Piehl, K.: Clin. Sci. 44:547-554, 1973.
21. Lowry, O.H., Rosebrough, N.J., Farr, A.L. and Randall, R.J.: J. Biol. Chem. 193:265-275, 1951.
22. Moesch, H. and Howald, H.: In Howald, H. and Poortmans, J.R. (eds.): Metabolic Adaptation to Prolonged Physical Exercise. Basel:Birkhäuser, 1975, pp. 463-465.
23. Molé, P.A. and Holloszy, J.O.: Proc. Soc. Exp. Biol. Med. 134:789-792, 1970.
24. Molé, P.A., Oscai, L.B. and Holloszy, J.O.: J. Clin. Invest. 50:2323-2330, 1971.
25. Morgan, T.E., Cobb, L.A., Short, F.A. et al: In Pernow, B. and Saltin, B. (eds.): Muscle Metabolism During Exercise. New York and London:Plenum Press, 1971, pp. 87-96.
26. Morgan, T.E., Short, F.A. and Cobb, L.A.: Biochem. Exerc. Med. Sport vol. 3, Basel and New York:Karger, 1969, pp. 116-121.
27. Padykula, H.A. and Herman, E.: J. Histochem. Cytochem. 3:170, 1955.
28. Peter, J.B., Barnard, R.J., Edgerton, V.R. et al: Biochemistry 11:2627-2633, 1972.
29. Shonk, C.E. and Boxer, G.E.: Cancer Res. 24:709-724, 1964.
30. Short, F.A., Ross, R., Cobb, L.A. and Morgan, T.E.: J. Clin. Invest. 49:88a-89a, 1970.

31. Srere, P.A.: Methods in Enzymology, vol 13. New York:Academic Press, 1969, pp. 3-11.
32. Terjung, R.L., Winder, W.W., Baldwin, K.M. and Holloszy, J.O.: J. Biol. Chem. 248:7404-7406, 1973.
33. Weibel, E.R.: Int. Rev. Cytol. 26:235-302, 1969.
34. Weibel, E.R., Kistler, G.S. and Scherle, W.F.: J. Cell. Biol. 30:23-38, 1966.
35. Whereat, A.F., Orishimo, M.W., Nelson, J. and Phillips, S.J.: J. Biol. Chem. 23:6498-6506, 1969.
36. Winder, W.W., Baldwin, K.M. and Holloszy, J.O.: Eur. J. Biochem. 47:461-467, 1974.

Effects of Endurance Training on the Fiber Area and Enzyme Activities of Skeletal Muscle of French-Canadians

A. W. Taylor, S. Lavoie, G. Lemieux, C. Dufresne,
J. S. Skinner and J. Vallée

Introduction

Since the advent of the Bergstrom muscle biopsy technique [1], a renewed interest has been shown in skeletal muscle fiber distribution and enzyme analysis of samples from healthy subjects. Numerous cross-sectional studies have been carried out [4, 8], but few training experiments using human subjects have been reported [6, 7, 18] and, in particular, none using female subjects. It was the purpose of the present study to compare the effects of regular endurance exercise upon fiber area and substrate-linked enzyme activities of skeletal muscle of healthy male and female subjects.

Methods and Procedures

Sixteen male and 21 female subjects were studied (see Tables I and II for physical characteristics). All were active in intramural sports but none were engaged in regular endurance training. Thirteen females and eight males participated in the training program and the others served as controls. Prior to the training regimen, maximal oxygen consumption ($\dot{V}O_2$ max) was determined and muscle biopsy samples were taken from the vastus lateralis, after an informed consent was obtained.

The subjects trained on the bicycle ergometer for 16 weeks for one hour per day, five days per week at a load requiring 75% of their maximal aerobic power. Pedal resistance was adjusted each week for

A. W. Taylor, S. Lavoie, G. Lemieux, C. Dufresne, J. S. Skinner and J. Vallée, Department of Physical Education, Université de Montréal and Centre hospitalier Maisonneuve-Rosemont, Montréal, Québec, Canada.

Supported in part by CAFIR grants #075-16-618 and 619; also, #075-16-633.

every subject to obtain the heart rate associated with 75% of their $\dot{V}O_2$ max.

Biopsy samples were also taken at rest and after an exhaustive 60-minute exercise, prior to and at the completion of the training program. Maximal oxygen uptake tests were done on the bicycle ergometer using a leveling-off criteria. Expired air was collected and analyzed with a Beckman E2 oxygen and LB2 carbon dioxide analyzer [3].

The muscle samples were divided into two sections. One portion was used for fiber area and distribution and histochemical analysis. The portion was mounted onto a chuck in OCT embedding medium (Ames Tissue-Tek) and frozen in liquid freon. The other portion was used for SDH and PFK activities and glycogen content with the methods of Cooperstein et al [2], Shank and Boxer [17] and Lo et al [11].

Serial sections 10μ thick were cut in a cryostat (American Optical Co.) at -30 C and mounted on cover slips. Myosin adenosine triphosphatase (ATPase), reduced diphosphopyridine nucleotide-diaphorase, (DPNH-diaphorase) and alpha-glycerophosphate dehydrogenase (αGPD) activities were estimated by the methods of Padykula and Herman [14], Novikoff et al [13], and Wattenberg and Leong [22], respectively. Glycogen content in another serial section (10 μ) was estimated for the periodic acid-schiff (PAS) reaction as described by Pearse [15]. Muscle fibers were identified as ST and FT, as described by Gollnick et al [8]. Area was determined by direct planimetry and a Zeiss particle counter on photographs of the DPNH stains.

Results

Anthropometric data for the subjects are presented in Tables I and II. Increases in $\dot{V}O_2$ max (16% for males and 11% for females) were noted after the training program. Mean SDH activity in the vastus lateralis increased approximately 112% (P < 0.01) in male and female subjects. PFK activity increased approximately 40% (P < 0.05) during training in the male subjects and 46% in the female subjects (Table III).

Oxidative capacity appeared to increase in both ST and FT fibers in both male and female muscle samples, as indicated by the more intense histochemical DPNH stains. Glycolytic capacity, as indicated by the αGP stain, appeared more intense in only the female FT skeletal muscle samples (Figs. 2 and 3).

Table I. Anthropometric Data for French-Canadian Female Subjects

Groups	Age (yr)	Ht (in)	Wt (kg)	$\dot{V}O_2$ max (l/min)	$\dot{V}O_2$ (ml/kg/min)
Sedentary (8)	22	64.49 ±2.51	56.66 ±8.91	2.26 ±.138	39.82 ±2.75
Exercised (13) pretraining	20	64.10 ±1.97	59.21 ±6.85	2.42 ±.261	40.79 ±2.92
Exercised (13) posttraining	20	–	59.07 ±6.87	2.87* ±.310	48.55* ±7.28

*Significantly different from sedentary at the .01 level.
Number of subjects are in parentheses.
Values are $\overline{X}$ ± SEM.

Table II. Anthropometric Data for French-Canadian Male Subjects

Groups	Age (yr)	Ht (in)	Wt (kg)	$\dot{V}O_2$ max (l/min)	$\dot{V}O_2$ (ml/kg/min)
Sedentary (8)	21	68.7 ±3.3	66.4 ±8.8	3.26 ±.34	49.4 ±3.6
Exercised (8) pretraining	24	68.9 ±4.5	70.8 ±6.4	3.45 ±.41	48.7 ±4.2
Exercised (8) posttraining	24	69.3 ±4.7	69.6 ±8.1	3.87* ±.31	55.6* ±4.9

*Significantly different from sedentary at the .01 level.
Number of subjects are in parentheses.
Values are $\overline{X}$ ± SEM..

Table III. Mean Enzyme Activities and Muscle Glycogen Concentration in Male and Female Subjects Before and After Training

Subjects	SDH Activity μmoles $g^{-1}min^{-1}$		PFK Activity μmoles $g^{-1}min^{-1}$		Glycogen mg/100 g wet wt. tissue	
	B	A	B	A	B	A
Female (13)	4.38	9.29*	14.21	20.75*	1.12	1.84*
Male (8)	5.12†	11.23‡	19.83†	27.37‡	1.32†	2.35‡

B – before training.
A – after training.
Number of subjects in parentheses.
*Before vs. after training (P < 0.01).
†Male vs. Female Subjects (P < 0.05).
‡Both before and after and male and female.

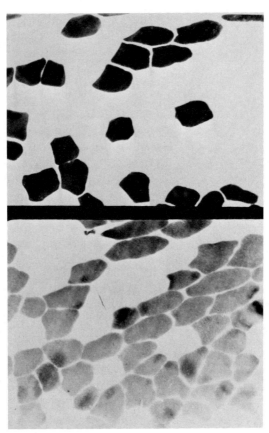

FIG. 1. Micrograph of an ATPase stain from male subject. Top: 1 = basic pH 10.3; Bottom: 2 = acid pH 4.35 (× 100).

The glycogen content of ST and FT fibers was similar (Fig. 4) and increased with training in both male and female muscle samples, whether measured histochemically by the PAS stain or biochemically (Table III). It is clear, however, that the glycogen content of the muscle sample in the male is greater than that found in the female (Fig. 5). With exercise to fatigue, glycogen depletion patterns appear similar for male and female samples (Figs. 6 and 7). The training program did not significantly alter the fiber distribution (ST/FT) (Table IV).

The mean ST fiber area for male and female samples prior to the training regimen was $7362\mu^2$ and $7290\mu^2$, respectively. The endurance training program resulted in significant increases in ST fiber area to $9092\mu^2$ and $8800\mu^2$, respectively. Prior to training, FT fiber areas

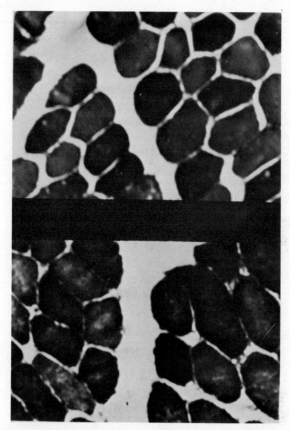

FIG. 2. Photomicrograph of muscle (× 100) stained for DPNH from one female subject before and after training.

were significantly greater (P < 0.01) in male fibers. The training elicited significant increases only in the female FT fiber areas; the FT fiber area in the male was still greater after the training program (Fig. 1 and Table V).

Discussion

The increases (16% for males and 11% for females) in maximal oxygen uptake due to the training program are similar to those found previously in this laboratory [20] and others [5, 7] and are indicative that the endurance ergometer training was of sufficient intensity to bring about substantial gains in aerobic capacity. The magnitude of the increases (112%) in muscle SDH activity following

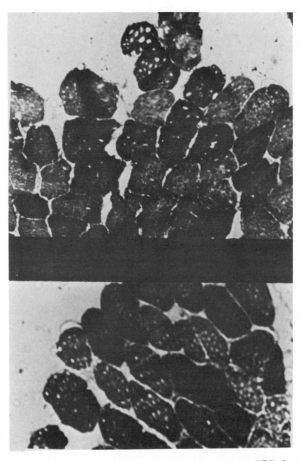

FIG. 3. Photomicrograph of muscle (× 100) stained for αGPD from one female subject before and after training.

training was similar to the increased oxidative capacity reported by Holloszy et al [9] for endurance trained rats and by Gollnick et al [8] for male subjects trained at a similar workload. Skeletal muscle from female subjects seems to react to endurance exercise in a manner similar to male skeletal muscle, demonstrating similar increases in SDH activity after training. As well, the increased staining intensity for DPNH diaphorase appears similar for both groups. It must be noted, however, that both the staining intensity and the absolute biochemical values for SDH are higher before and after training in the male muscle samples. This would probably be indicative of the greater activity level of our sample population.

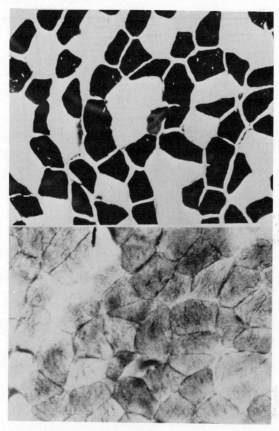

FIG. 4. Photomicrograph of muscle (× 100) of ATPase stain and glycogen (PAS) content in ST and FT fibers of a male subject.

The activity of PFK, a glycolytic marker-enzyme, increased by 46% in the female muscle samples, compared to 38% in the male samples. This change is much lower than that seen by Gollnick et al [7] for a similar training program and may be related to the high variability of the methodology. The increased staining intensity for αGP was found mainly in the FT fibers. These two findings would suggest that the glycolytic capacity of the FT fibers increased due to the training regimen. The workload obviously consumed a great deal of glycogen, as can be observed in Figures 5, 6 and 7. Obviously, an increased glycolytic capacity would be beneficial for the degradation of glycogen. The elevated posttraining glycogen values in both male and female subjects are lower than values previously shown for

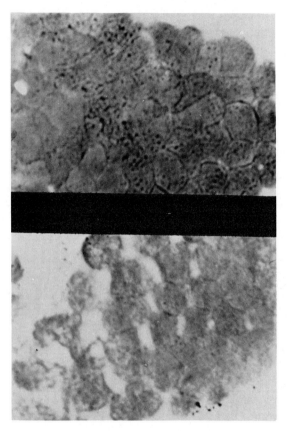

FIG. 5. Photomicrograph of muscle (× 100) stained for glycogen (PAS) comparing male and female samples pretraining.

high-trained endurance athletes [8], but similar to values reported for semi-active subjects [19, 21].

As expected, the fiber distribution of the vastus lateralis muscle was not altered by the endurance training program. However, there was a significant increase in the fiber area of both the ST and the FT fibers. The increase of 29% in area of the ST fibers of both male and female muscle samples demonstrates that the ST fibers were used extensively during the training program. The finding that pretraining ST fibers were smaller than FT fibers but that they were larger posttraining is further evidence of the predominant recruitment of ST fibers in this training regimen. However, although FT area did not increase in male skeletal muscle, an 18% increase was found in female

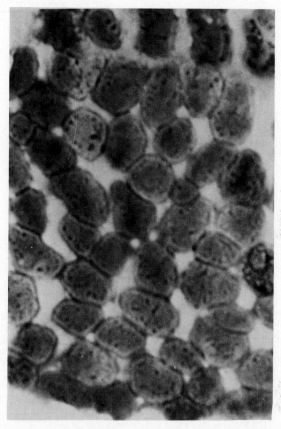

FIG. 6. Photomicrograph of muscle (× 100) stained for glycogen (PAS) before a fatiguing exercise on the bicycle ergometer.

samples. This would indicate that a greater recruitment of FT fibers was necessary for the female subjects to perform the training program and the final fatiguing exercise on the bicycle ergometer. The large increases (38% to 46%) in PFK activity and the increased staining intensity would further suggest that more of this activity was located in the FT fibers and that it is a response to greater utilization of FT fibers in the female subjects.

The results of this study demonstrate that endurance training greatly increases the oxidative and glycolytic capacity of skeletal muscle of male and female subjects. However, the higher absolute levels of oxidative (SDH) and glycolytic enzymes (PFK), as well as the substrate glycogen concentration found in the male muscle

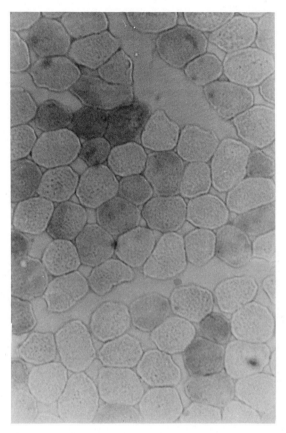

FIG. 7. Photomicrograph of muscle (× 100) stained for glycogen (PAS) after a fatiguing exercise bout. (Note: this is the same subject as in Figure 6.)

Table IV. Vastus Lateralis Fiber Distribution
in Nontrained and Trained Male and Female French-Canadian Subjects

| | ST(%) | |
	Pre	Post
Male	45	48
Female	49	51

samples, would suggest that some of the differences in work capacity between male and female subjects are related to substrate availability and substrate-linked enzyme activity. Furthermore, the finding that the FT area of the male subjects was always larger than that found in

Table V. Vastus Lateralis Fiber Area in Nontrained
and Trained Male and Female French-Canadian Subjects

| | ST (μ^2) | | | FT (μ^2) | | |
	Pre		Post	Pre		Post
Male	7362	29%†	9092	8224	7.0%*	8800
Female	7290	29%†	9003	7252	18.0%†	8557

*Significantly different (P < 0.05).
†Significantly different (P < 0.01).

the female muscle samples may prove to be one of the reasons that the differences in results between male and female subjects for explosive events are relatively greater than that found for endurance events.

References

1. Bergstrom, J.: Muscle electrolytes in man. Scand. J. Clin. Lab. Invest. Suppl. 68, 1962.
2. Cooperstein, S.J., Lazarow, A. and Kurfess, N.J.: A micro spectrophotometric method for the determination of succinic dehydrogenase. J. Biol. Chem. 186:129-139, 1950.
3. Corcoran, P.J. and Brengelmann, G.C.: Oxygen uptake in normal and handicapped subjects, in relation to speed of walking beside a velocity-controlled cart. Arch. Phys. Med. Rehab. 51:78-87, 1970.
4. Edstrom, L. and Ekblom, B.: Differences in sizes of red and white muscle fibres in vastus lateralis of musculus quadriceps femoris of normal individuals and athletes. Relation to physical performance. Scand. J. Clin. Lab. Invest. 30:175-181, 1972.
5. Ekblom, B.: Effect of physical training on oxygen transport system in man. Acta Physiol. Scand. Suppl. 328, 1969.
6. Eriksson, B.D., Gollnick P.D. and Saltin, B.: Muscle metabolism and enzyme activities, after training in boys 11-13 years old. Acta. Scand. Physiol. 87:485-497, 1973.
7. Gollnick, P.D., Armstrong, R.B., Saltin, B. et al: Effect of training on enzyme activity and fibre composition of human skeletal muscle. J. Appl. Physiol. 34:107-111, 1973.
8. Gollnick, P.D., Armstrong, R.B., Saubert, C.W., IV, et al: Enzyme activity and fibre composition in skeletal muscle of untrained and trained men. J. Appl. Physiol. 33:312-319, 1972.
9. Holloszy, J.O., Oscai, L.B., Molé, P.A. and Don, I.J.: Biochemical adaptations to endurance exercise in skeletal muscle. In Pernow, B. and Saltin, B. (eds.): Muscle Metabolism During Exercise. N.Y.:Plenum Co., 1971, pp. 51-61.
10. Hultman, E.: Studies on muscle metabolism of glycogen and active phosphate in man with special reference to exercise and diet. Scand. J. Lab. Clin. Invest. Suppl. 358, 1969.

11. Lo, S., Russell, J.C. and Taylor, A.W.: Determination of glycogen in small tissue samples. J. Appl. Physiol. 28:234-236, 1970.
12. Moore, M.J., Rebeiz, J.J., Holden, M. and Adams, R.D.: Biometric analyses of normal skeletal muscle. Acta Neuropath. 19:51-69, 1971.
13. Novikoff, A.B., Shin, W. and Drucker, J.: Mitochondrial localization of oxidation enzymes: Staining results with two tetrazoliam salts. J. Biophys. Biochem. Cytol. 9:47-61, 1961.
14. Padykula, H.A. and Herman, E.: The specificity of the histochemical method of adenosine triphosphatase. J. Histochem. Cytochem. 3:170-195, 1955.
15. Pearse, A.G.E.: Histochemistry — Theoretical and Applied. Boston:Little, Brown & Co., 1961, p. 832.
16. Saltin, B.: Metabolic fundamentals in exercise. Med. Sci. Sports 5:137-146, 1973.
17. Shonk, C.E. and Boxer, G.E.: Enzyme patterns in human tissue. I. Methods for the determination of glycolytic enzymes. Cancer Res. 24:709-724, 1964.
18. Taylor, A.W.: The effects of exercise and training on the activities of human glycogen cycle enzymes. In Howald, H. and Poortmans, J. (eds.): Metabolic Adaptation to Prolonged Physical Exercise. Basel:Birkhauser, 1975, pp. 451-462.
19. Taylor, A.W., Booth, M.A. and Rao, S.: Human skeletal muscle glycogen phosphorylase activities with exercise and training. Can. J. Physiol. Pharm. 50:1038-1042, 1972.
20. Taylor, A.W., Lappage, R.S. and Rao, S.: Skeletal muscle glycogen stores after submaximal and maximal work. Med. Sci. Sports 3:75-78, 1971.
21. Taylor, A.W., Thayer, R. and Rao, S.: Human skeletal muscle glycogen synthetase activities with exercise and training. Can. J. Physiol. Pharm. 50:411-415, 1972.
22. Wattenberg, L.W. and Leong, J.L.: Effects of coenzyme Q_{10} and menadione on succinic dehydrogenase activity as measured by tetrazolium salt reduction. J. Histochem. Cytochem. 8:296-303, 1960.

Effect of Eight-Week Physical Training on Muscle and Connective Tissue of the M. Vastus Lateralis in 69-Year-Old Men and Women

H. Suominen, E. Heikkinen
and T. Parkatti

According to some recent reports [1, 6] the trainability of old people is better than previously assumed. The aerobic capacity of skeletal muscle in middle-aged and elderly men can be increased significantly through relatively short endurance training [13] (Suominen et al, manuscript in preparation). However, we are still short of information about the effects of physical training on muscle metabolism in elderly women.

The effect of endurance-type training on connective tissue in skeletal muscle is little understood. Some animal experiments indicate that the biosynthesis of muscle collagen is activated by compensatory hypertrophy [18] as well as running exercise [16]. In our previous studies [17] we have also found an increased activity of prolyl hydroxylase together with that of oxidative enzymes in the m. vastus lateralis of middle-aged and elderly endurance athletes in habitual training. Connective tissue may thus have an important role in the adaptation of skeletal muscle to physical training.

The present paper deals with the trainability of elderly men and women on the basis of a larger gerontological research project, a part of which was undertaken to study the different biological effects of an eight-week physical training program. Among the numerous variables the activity of certain enzymes representing the aerobic and anaerobic energy metabolism as well as the collagen biosynthesis in skeletal muscle will be discussed. In addition the muscle fiber distribution of the subjects involved will be given.

H. Suominen, E. Heikkinen and T. Parkatti, Department of Public Health, University of Jyväskylä, Jyväskylä, Finland.

Supported by a grant from the Ministry of Education, Finland.

The study comprised 32 healthy pensioners (18 men and 14 women) who, except for some of the men, had no previous experience in regular physical training. The physical characteristics of the subjects appear in Table I.

Altogether 14 men and 12 women fulfilled an eight-week supervised physical training program which consisted of five one-hour exercise bouts a week including walking-jogging, swimming, gymnastics and ball games. The subjects had to participate in at least three exercise bouts during each training week. Except for one Achilles tendon rupture, no untoward incidents occurred during the training.

The maximal oxygen uptake of the subjects was determined indirectly [2] during a 12-minute submaximal bicycle ergometer exercise before as well as after the training period.

The muscle samples were taken from the m. vastus lateralis using a needle biopsy technique [3] both before and after the training. One sample was stained for myosin ATPase [15] and used for the determination of the percentage number of slow twitch (ST) muscle fibers [7]. The remaining biopsy specimens were freed from blood, fat and visible connective tissue and assayed for the activity of lactate dehydrogenase (LDH), malate dehydrogenase (MDH) and prolyl hydroxylase (PH) as described earlier [17]. In order to eliminate the effect of the possibly different amount of connective tissue in the more or less "random" muscle samples the concentration of hydroxyproline [20] was determined from the specimens used for the analysis of the PH activity.

As seen in Table I, the maximal oxygen uptake values of the subjects increased significantly during the training, the mean

Table I. Physical Characteristics of 69-Year-Old
Men and Women Participating in Study
Means ± SD Are Given

			Before Training	After Training
Height	Men	(14)	171.1 ± 5.7	171.0 ± 5.9
(cm)	Women	(12)	157.3 ± 4.2	157.2 ± 4.2
Weight	Men	(14)	74.9 ± 7.7	74.8 ± 7.4
(kg)	Women	(12)	69.3 ± 8.8	68.7 ± 7.9
$\dot{V}O_2$ max	Men	(14)	28.9 ± 4.3	32.0 ± 3.9[a]
(ml/kg/min)	Women	(12)	27.9 ± 4.3	31.3 ± 5.4[b]

[a,b]Significantly different (p < .005, p < .05, respectively) from the value before training.

improvement being about 11% in the men and about 12% in the women. This is in agreement with recent results [1, 6] showing that the trainability of old people does not greatly differ from that of young and middle-aged persons if compared on a percentage basis. The findings of the present study indicate a true increase in maximal oxygen uptake because a similar result was obtained in our earlier study of 55- to 70-year-old men [13] (Suominen et al, manuscript in preparation) in which a direct method was used.

Table II presents the activity of the enzymes of energy metabolism and the percentage of ST fibers in the m. vastus lateralis. The MDH activity increased significantly after training in the women, while the change in the men was negligible. The LDH activity remained unchanged or, as in the women, even decreased. Compared to the women the male subjects showed higher activities in both enzymes both before and after the training. The percentage of ST fibers was, however, nearly the same in the two groups, the values ranging from 28% to 65% in the men and from 41% to 68% in the women.

Several authors have earlier reported increased oxidative enzyme activities after endurance-type training in younger subjects [4, 8, 14, 19]. Together with our previous study (Suominen et al, manuscript in preparation) the present results suggest that the aerobic capacity of skeletal muscle can significantly be improved in elderly persons as well. The explanation for the smaller increase in MDH activity in the men in the present study may be that compared to the women they were already more active physically before training. This is also

Table II. Effect of 8-Week Physical Training on Enzyme Activities of M. Vastus Lateralis in 69-Year-Old Men and Women. Percentages of ST Fibers Given are Values Before Training or, in Some Cases, the Means of Values Before and After Training Means ± SD Are Given

			Before Training	After Training
LDH	Men	(13)	121.4 ± 41.4	118.8 ± 37.1
(μmol/g/min)	Women	(8)	107.8 ± 42.0	89.7 ± 29.4
MDH	Men	(13)	116.8 ± 28.5[a]	122.5 ± 21.3
(μmol/g/min)	Women	(8)	88.5 ± 19.1	101.8 ± 21.2[b]
ST fibers	Men	(18)	49.3 ± 10.3	
(%)	Women	(14)	53.5 ± 7.8	

[a] Significantly different (p < .05) from the value of the women.
[b] Significantly different (p < .05) from the value before training.

supported by the significantly higher initial MDH activity of the male subjects.

The unchanged or even decreased LDH activity agrees with the previous results of e.g. Holloszy et al [9] and Morgan et al [14] which indicate that the glycolytic capacity of skeletal muscle does not increase in response to endurance training. Habitually trained endurance athletes actually have lower muscle LDH activity compared to their untrained counterparts [11, 12, 17]. However, it is possible that during the initial phases of endurance training, muscle LDH activity may also increase in sedentary persons [12] (Suominen et al, manuscript in preparation).

The mean percentage of ST fibers in the m. vastus lateralis, as well as the wide distribution of the results in both men and women, was rather similar to those earlier reported in untrained young and middle-aged men [7].

The effect of the training on muscle PH activity is shown in Table III. In conformity with the MDH activity, an increased PH activity was observed after training in the women, while there were hardly any changes to be found in the men. The increase in the women was statistically significant if the values were referred to the amount of hydroxyproline in the muscle samples. Although the results were not quite unambiguous, the changes may be regarded as an indication of the adaptability of muscle connective tissue even in aged persons. Previous animal experiments [5, 10] have shown that the activation of connective tissue cells is an important prerequisite to work-induced muscular growth. In agreement with our earlier results [17] the findings of the present study suggest that endurance-type training also affects the collagen metabolism in human skeletal muscle. The possibly increased turnover of muscle collagen, as well as its importance for older people, remains to be elucidated.

Table III. Effect of 8-Week Physical Training on Prolyl Hydroxylase Activity of M. Vastus Lateralis in 69-Year-Old Men and Women Means ± SD Are Given

			Before Training	After Training
dpm/g/hr	Men	(10)	42400 ± 14720	42810 ± 15820
	Women	(5)	41320 ± 10010	46959 ± 10990
dpm/mg Hyp/hr	Men	(10)	61570 ± 27100	70550 ± 34880
	Women	(5)	33770 ± 12360	88020 ± 17460[a]

[a]Significantly different (p < .01) from the value before training.

References

1. Adams, G.M. and deVries, H.A.: Physiological effects of an exercise training regimen upon women aged 52 to 79. J. Geront. 28:50-55, 1973.
2. Åstrand, P.-O. and Ryhming, I.: A nomogram for calculating of aerobic capacity (physical fitness) from pulse rate during submaximal work. J. Appl. Physiol. 7:218-221, 1954.
3. Bergström, J.: Muscle electrolytes in man. Determination by neutron activation analysis on needle biopsy specimens. A study on normal subjects, kidney patients and patients with chronic diarrhoea. Scand. J. Clin. Lab. Invest. 14 (suppl. 68), 1962.
4. Björntorp, P., Fahlén, M., Holm, J. et al: Determination of succinic oxidase activity in human skeletal muscle. Scand. J. Clin. Lab. Invest. 26:145-150, 1970.
5. Booth, F.W. and Gould, E.W.: Effects of training and disuse on connective tissue. In Wilmore, J.H. and Keogh, J.F. (eds.): Exercise and Sport Sciences Reviews. New York:Academic Press, 1975, pp. 83-112.
6. deVries, H.A.: Physiological effects of an exercise training regimen upon men aged 52 to 88. J. Geront. 25:325-336, 1970.
7. Gollnick, P.D., Armstrong, R.B., Saubert, C.W. IV, et al: Enzyme activity and fiber composition in skeletal muscle of untrained and trained men. J. Appl. Physiol. 33:312-319, 1972.
8. Gollnick, P.D., Armstrong, R.B., Saltin, B. et al: Effect of training on enzyme activity and fiber composition of human skeletal muscle. J. Appl. Physiol. 34:107-111, 1973.
9. Holloszy, J.O., Oscai, L.B., Molé, P.A. and Don, I.J.: Biochemical adaptations to endurance exercise in skeletal muscle. In Pernow, B. and Saltin, B. (eds.): Muscle Metabolism During Exercise. Advances in Experimental Medicine and Biology. New York:Plenum Press, 1971, vol. 11, pp. 51-61.
10. Jablecki, C.K., Heuser, J.E. and Kaufman, S.: Autoradiographic localization of new RNA synthesis in hypertrophying skeletal muscle. J. Cell Biol. 57:743-759, 1973.
11. Karlsson, J., Sjödin, B., Thorstensson, A. et al: LDH isozymes in skeletal muscles of endurance and strength trained athletes. Acta Physiol. Scand. 93:150-156, 1975.
12. Kiessling, K.-H, Pilström, L., Bylund, A.-Ch. et al: Enzyme activities and morphometry in skeletal muscle of middle-aged men after training. Scand. J. Clin. Lab. Invest. 33:63-69, 1974.
13. Liesen, H., Heikkinen, E., Suominen, H. und Michel, D.: Der Effekt eines zwölfwöchigen Ausdauertrainings auf die Leistungsfähigkeit und den Muskelstoffwechsel bei untrainierten Männern des 6. und 7. Lebensjahrzehnts. Sportarzt Sportmedizin 26:26-30, 1975.
14. Morgan, T.E., Cobb, L.A., Short, F.A. et al: Effects of long-term exercise on human muscle mitochondria. In Pernow, B. and Saltin, B. (eds.): Muscle Metabolism During Exercise. Advances in Experimental Medicine and Biology. New York: Plenum Press, 1971, vol 11, pp. 87-95.
15. Padykula, H.A. and Herman, E.: The specificity of the histochemical method of adenosine triphosphatase. J. Histochem. Cytochem. 3:170-195, 1955.

16. Suominen, H. and Heikkinen, E.: Effect of physical training on collagen. Ital. J. Biochem. 24:64-65, 1975.
17. Suominen, H. and Heikkinen, E.: Enzyme activities in muscle and connective tissue of m. vastus lateralis in habitually training and sedentary 33 to 70-year-old men. Europ. J. Appl. Physiol. 34:249-254, 1975.
18. Turto, H., Lindy, S. and Halme, J.: Protocollagen proline hydroxylase activity in work-induced hypertrophy of rat muscle. Am. J. Physiol. 226:63-65, 1974.
19. Varnauskas, E., Björntorp, P., Fahlén, M. et al: Effects of physical training on exercise blood flow and enzymatic activity in skeletal muscle. Cardiovasc. Res. 4:418-422, 1970.
20. Woessner, J.F. Jr.: The determination of hydroxyproline in tissue and protein samples containing small proportions of this amino acid. Arch. Biochem. 93:440-447, 1961.

Metabolic Responses to Noradrenalin in Trained and Nontrained Human Subjects

J. LeBlanc, M. Boulay, S. Dulac,
M. Jobin and A. Labrie

Introduction

Physical training has been shown to produce important changes especially concerning the utilization of energy substrates. One such change is the enhanced lipid mobilization and oxidation which has been shown to have a sparing effect on glycogen reserve [34, 49, 51, 52]. Since available glycogen is a limiting factor in exercise performance [1, 17], the improved lipid utilization is interpreted as having a beneficial effect in exercise training [9, 21, 23, 38]. On the other hand, it has also been shown that exercise and other metabolic stresses, such as cold exposure, cause an activation of the sympathetic nervous system [25, 30, 58]. The increased noradrenalin secretion which results from this stimulation has been shown to produce a marked sensitization to the metabolic effects of noradrenalin in cold-adapted animals [26-29, 53]. In exercise training, only in vitro effects of noradrenalin have been tested in laboratory animals [2, 18, 41, 59]. The present study was aimed at investigating the metabolic responses to noradrenalin perfused in trained and nontrained human subjects in order to assess the presumed importance of this amine in physical training.

Material and Methods

Forty male subjects, 18 to 30 years of age, volunteered for this study. These subjects were picked from a university student

J. LeBlanc, M. Boulay, S. Dulac,* M. Jobin and A. Labrie, Department of Physiology, School of Medicine, and Department of Physical Education, Laval University, Quebec City, Canada.

*Present address: Département des sciences de l'activité physique, Université du Québec, Trois-Rivières.

population to represent a sampling as wide as possible between the lowest and the highest levels of training. The subjects with the highest working capacity were distance runners in marathon, cross-country skiing or bicycle events. A few days prior to the noradrenalin test, physical measurements were obtained and maximum working capacity and total body fat were determined. The maximum oxygen uptake was measured on a bicycle ergometer by a stepwise increase in the workload, oxygen uptake and pulmonary ventilation were determined by a closed circuit gas analysis system (Dargatz Magna Test). Total body fat, expressed as percent of total body weight, was obtained by the hydrostatic weighing technique [40]. The subjects were instructed to fast and to restrain from smoking and unnecessary activity before coming for the test which took place at about 8 AM. Upon arrival the subjects were informed in more detail about the testing and were asked to lie supine for one-half hour before the perfusion was started. Subsequently the left arm was cannulated and a saline solution was perfused at a rate of 1 ml/min. This perfusion lasted 15 minutes and ECG and blood pressures were measured at one-minute intervals during that period as well as during the total duration of the test. At the end of this period three 10 ml blood samples were drawn from the right arm and immediately processed for the determinations of various blood constituents. After blood drawing, which lasted about 1 minute, saline was replaced with noradrenalin perfusion (0.1 μg/kg/min) which was continued for a period of 30 minutes. Three blood samples were again drawn after 15 and after 30 minutes of noradrenalin perfusion. Fifteen minutes after the perfusion was stopped, the last three samples of blood were drawn and this ended the test.

Thus three 10 ml samples of blood were taken at four different periods to give a total of 12 drawings for each subject. Sample one was used to determine serum glycerol by the method of Eggstein [15] and free fatty acids by the method of Dole [14] modified by Novak [37]. Sample two served to determine insulin by a radioimmunoassay method [19] as modified by Nadeau [36], and glucose by autoanalyzer [5]. Sample three was used to determine lactate [20].

Correlations between $\dot{V}O_2$ max and the various blood parameters were calculated and in each case the equation of the regression is given on the figures. When analyzing the effect of noradrenalin perfusion on various blood constituents, a test of pairing was done for each individual subject between the values measured before and after the perfusion. The T test was used to compare results obtained on trained and control subjects.

Results

While the correlations between $\dot{V}O_2$ and the various blood parameters, both during the noradrenalin perfusion and the control periods, were always determined for all subjects, it seemed also interesting to make a comparison between the best and the least trained subjects. To that effect two groups of ten subjects were formed, one from subjects with max $\dot{V}O_2$ smaller than 45 and the other with max $\dot{V}O_2$ larger than 65 ml/kg/min. Table I shows the characteristics of the subjects. As may be seen from the max $\dot{V}O_2$, the trained group have a high level of training while the control have pronounced sedentary habits. The significant difference in body weight between the two groups is due to the percentage of body fat, since the lean body mass shows no significant difference. The high $\dot{V}O_2$ max and the low percentage of body fat associated with training raised the possibility of a negative correlation between these two variables. Figure 1 shows this correlation to be highly significant. For this reason it is necessary to analyze the importance of both $\dot{V}O_2$ max and the percent body fat in any of the differences observed between our two groups of subjects; this point will be studied in the discussion.

Figure 3 shows that the plasma glucose is lower in trained subjects during the pre-infusion period and a highly significant correlation is found between plasma glucose and max $\dot{V}O_2$ (Fig. 2). Figure 3 shows a significant increase in plasma glucose of both groups during the perfusion of noradrenalin which persisted 15

Table I. Characteristics of Subjects

Group	Age (year)	Height (cm)	Weight (kg)	Body Fat (%)	Lean Body Mass (kg)	Max $\dot{V}O_2$ (ml/kg/min)	Max $\dot{V}O_2$ (l/min)
Control subjects (n = 10)	26.9 ±1.7	171. ±7.14	72.95 ±3.29	21.12 ±1.29	57.23 ±1.86	38.76 ±1.04	2.82 ±0.14
Trained subjects (n = 10)	21.0 ±1.9	171. ±8.21	64.24 ±2.93	8.37 ±1.21	58.72 ±2.40	69.61 ±1.02	4.46 ±0.17
All subjects (n = 40)	24.2 ±3.3	173. ±7.31	70.08 ±1.45	12.35 ±0.99	61.17 ±1.12	54.61 ±1.85	3.79 ±0.12

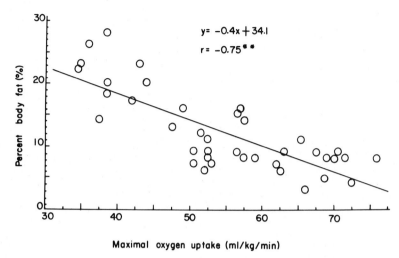

FIG. 1. Correlation between maximal oxygen uptake and percentage of body fat as measured by hydrostatic weighing of subjects.

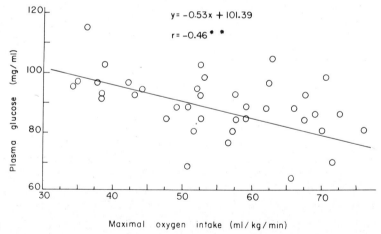

FIG. 2. Correlation between resting plasma glucose before noradrenalin perfusion and maximal oxygen uptake for all 40 subjects.

minutes after the end of noradrenalin perfusion. A significant difference is also noted between both groups during the control period and 15 minutes after the beginning of noradrenalin perfusion. This difference, however, disappears in the later part of the perfusion

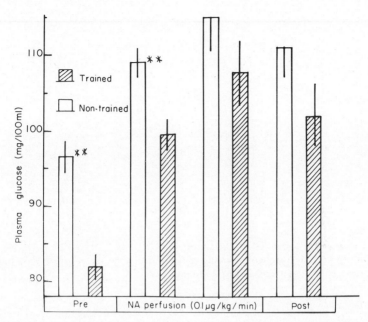

FIG. 3. Levels of plasma glucose in the ten subjects with the highest $\dot{V}O_2$ max (mean 69.61 ± 1.02 ml/kg/min) representing the trained group and the subjects with the lowest $\dot{V}O_2$ max (mean 38.76 ± 1.04 ml/kg/min) representing the untrained group. The determinations were made on samples taken (1) immediately before the perfusion, (pre-infusion period), (2) and (3) 15 and 30 minutes after the beginning of noradrenalin perfusion (perfusion period) and (4) 15 minutes after the end of the perfusion (postperfusion period).

as well as in the postperfusion period. Results on insulin also show a highly significant correlation between plasma insulin and max $\dot{V}O_2$ during the control period (Fig. 4). Lower levels of insulin were noted in the trained subjects during the control and the first part of the perfusion periods (Fig. 5); this difference disappears during the later part of the perfusion. As may also be seen on Figure 5, the levels of insulin again become significantly lower in the trained subjects during the postperfusion period. Figures 2 and 4 show a significant negative correlation during the saline perfusion period, between both glucose and insulin levels and the level of training. For that reason the correlation was tested between glucose and insulin levels during the control period. Figure 6 shows a positive correlation between glucose and insulin levels and indicates by reference to Figures 2 and 4 that trained subjects have lower fasting levels of both glucose and insulin and that these parameters are related to one another. The

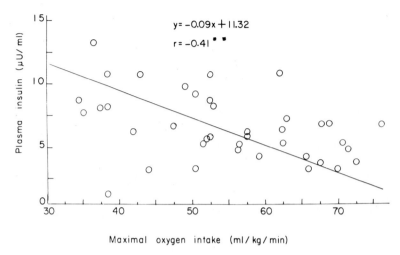

FIG. 4. Correlation between resting plasma insulin before noradrenalin perfusion
and maximal oxygen uptake for all 40 subjects.

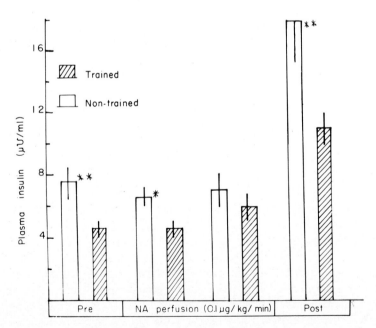

FIG. 5. Levels of plasma insulin in trained and nontrained subjects before,
during and after noradrenalin perfusion. See Figure 3 for additional information.

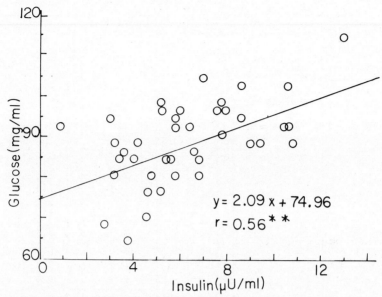

FIG. 6. Correlation between plasma glucose and plasma insulin for all 40 subjects before noradrenalin perfusion.

modalities and implications of the glucose-insulin relationship as affected by noradrenalin perfusion in control and trained subjects will be analyzed further in the discussion (Table II).

Figure 7 shows that noradrenalin perfusion increases serum FFA in both trained and nontrained subjects. The same figure shows that during the control period the difference in serum FFA levels between the trained and the nontrained subjects is not quite significant. In the latter part of the perfusion, the difference in serum FFA between both groups becomes significant and persisted in the postperfusion period. The results obtained on glycerol, which are reported in Figure 8, are somewhat similar to those obtained for FFA with the exception that the difference in FFA levels observed between the two groups in the latter part of noradrenalin perfusion is already present for glycerol during the first part of the perfusion. The results for plasma lactate are given in Figure 9. Despite the variations observed, the level of lactate in the control group is significantly higher than in the trained subjects during the latter part of noradrenalin perfusion.

Discussion

Body weight of trained subjects is smaller than that of nontrained subjects and this difference is explained by different

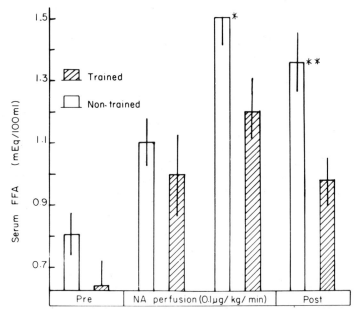

FIG. 7. Levels of serum free fatty acids in trained and nontrained subjects before, during and after noradrenalin perfusion. See Figure 3 for additional information.

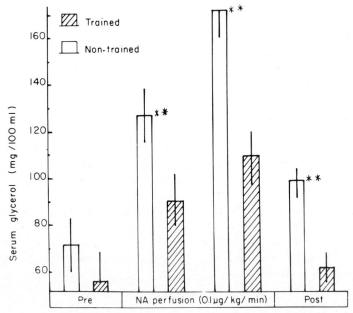

FIG. 8. Levels of serum glycerol in trained and nontrained subjects before, during and after noradrenalin perfusion. See Figure 3 for additional information.

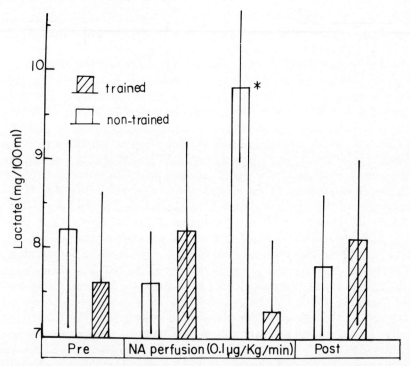

FIG. 9. Levels of blood lactate in trained and nontrained subjects before, during and after noradrenalin perfusion. See Figure 3 for additional information.

percentage of total body fat. This finding confirms previous results showing the effect of physical training on body composition in young normal subjects [40] as well as in middle-aged obese [6, 39] and nonobese men [43, 54]. A decreased uptake of glucose by peripheral tissues [42, 43] and a reduced sensitivity of adipose tissue to insulin [48] have been reported in obese subjects. It has also been shown that a reduction of body weight in obese subjects causes an increase in the sensitivity to insulin [48]. On the other hand, an increased response to insulin was noted in obese subjects following a period of physical training which did not result in a significant change in body weight [7]. In the present study, our subjects could not be considered obese. Just the same, because of the high correlation between level of training and percentage of body fat, a factorial analysis was made for all biochemical and cardiovascular parameters measured in order to see whether the differences observed between the trained and nontrained subjects were really due to physical training and not to difference in body composition.

This analysis has shown that the percentage of body fat was not a significant factor in any of the variations observed in this study; the only important factor was physical training.

Our results show lower level of plasma glucose and insulin in the trained subjects before noradrenalin perfusion. Resting glucose levels have been shown to be diminished by physical training. Low basal plasma insulin levels have also been reported following periods of physical training in both obese [55] and normal subjects [10, 47]. Even if a positive correlation is found between glucose and insulin levels during the control period (Fig. 6), Table II shows that the ratio of glucose over insulin is significantly higher in the trained subject: 19.38 compared to 13.12 in the nontrained subjects. This finding suggests that concomitant with lower insulin levels, the sensitivity to insulin is enhanced in trained subjects. Björntorp reached the same conclusion after submitting trained subjects to a glucose tolerance test [4, 8]. Noradrenalin perfusion produced an elevation of plasma glucose in both groups of subjects. As expected this increase was smaller than that normally found with adrenalin but was comparable to that observed by Porte [45] for comparable doses of nor-adrenalin. The plasma glucose, which was lower in the trained subjects during the pre-infusion period, became comparable in both groups after perfusing noradrenalin for 30 minutes. In other words, the increase in plasma glucose caused by noradrenalin was greater in the trained subjects. As might be expected noradrenalin perfusion prevented an increase in plasma insulin which normally follows an elevation of plasma glucose [44]. During the noradrenalin perfusion the ratio of glucose over insulin becomes significantly higher because of the block on insulin secretion and the difference in this ratio between the two groups of subjects is no more significant. Table II also shows that in the postperfusion period, when insulin secretion is

Table II. Ratio of Glucose (mg/100 ml) Over Insulin (μU/ml) for Trained and Nontrained Subjects Before, During and After Noradrenalin Perfusion

| Subjects | Pre | Noradrenalin Perfusion | | Post |
		15 min	30 min	
Nontrained	13.12	19.44	22.97	6.11
(n = 10)	±2.32	±2.92	±6.04	±0.90
Trained	19.38	25.05	20.50	9.58
(n = 10)	±1.88	±3.01	±2.34	±0.84
P value	<0.05	n.s.	n.s.	<0.05

released, the ratios for both groups are different, indicating an enhanced sensitivity to insulin in trained subjects similar to that observed during the pre-infusion period. Figure 10 summarized these findings. First, a significant difference in the relationship between glucose and insulin was found during the period when noradrenalin was perfused and during the pre- or postperfusion periods. The postperfusion period was particularly revealing about the effect of physical training on causal relationship between glucose and insulin. Indeed, Figure 5 shows that there was a drastic elevation of plasma insulin when the block produced by noradrenalin was released at the end of the perfusion. It is also seen that during that period, at a time when blood glucose was not significantly different between the trained and nontrained subjects (105 compared to 113 mg/ml), the insulin level was much higher in the untrained subjects (17 μU/ml) than in the trained subjects (11 μU/ml). For that reason the ratio of glucose over insulin is higher in the trained subjects in this postperfusion period as it was also higher before the perfusion. These

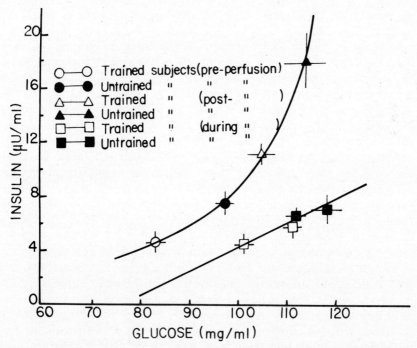

FIG. 10. Correlation between plasma insulin and plasma glucose for trained and nontrained subjects before, during and after noradrenalin perfusion. See Figure 3 for additional information.

results suggest that physical training produces an increase in the sensitivity to insulin.

Fröberg [16] and Rennie et al [46] found a lowering of basal free fatty acids (FFA) in trained subjects whereas other investigators failed to observe this change [16, 23, 46]. This tendency was confirmed in the present study, but the difference between the two groups during the pre-infusion period did not quite reach the level of significance. These various results possibly reflect the state of training, eating habits of the subjects or the conditions in which the determinations were made. When noradrenalin is perfused plasma FFA increase in both groups, but the elevation is significantly greater in the nontrained subjects and this difference is still present during the postperfusion period. These results may indicate an enhanced utilization and/or a reduced mobilization of FFA in trained subjects perfused with noradrenalin. The elevation of FFA during noradrenalin perfusion has also been shown to be significantly smaller in animals adapted to cold which is a metabolic stress comparable to exercise [35]. Furthermore, noradrenalin perfusion causes an increased utilization of FFA in cold-adapted animals [35]. By analogy and because exposure to both cold or exercise is characterized by an enhanced secretion of noradrenalin [3, 30, 32, 57, 58], the results of the present study could indicate that the preferential fat utilization observed in exercise training [13, 20, 21, 23, 33, 49] is mediated by a greater sensitivity to noradrenalin. This hypothesis is corroborated by many in vitro studies which show an increased lipolysis of white adipose tissues of trained animals when incubated with adrenalin [2, 41] and noradrenalin [18, 59]. The results obtained with glycerol are in all respects comparable to those reported for FFA and would then confirm the suggested importance of noradrenalin for the enhanced utilization of body lipids in exercise training. During noradrenalin perfusion blood lactate was found to increase only in the nontrained subjects. This result could indicate a sparing effect of training on glycogen reserves compensated by an increased lipid utilization in response to noradrenalin.

Exercise training produces important changes in the mobilization and utilization of energy substrates. In trained subjects doing moderate exercise a decreased glycogen utilization and an enhanced lipid oxidation have been observed [21, 23, 34, 38, 49]. The reason for these changes is unknown, but some recent findings indicate that noradrenalin may be implicated. We know that noradrenalin is secreted in larger quantities at certain levels of exercise [58]. It is also known that when noradrenalin is secreted during prolonged

Table III. Effects of Physical Training on Response
to Exercise or to Noradrenalin Perfusion

Exercise		Blood Parameter	NA Perfusion*
[50]	↑	Glucose	↑
[11]	↑	Insulin sensitivity	↑
[45, 48, 50, 52]	↓	FFA	↓
[50, 52]	↓	Glycerol	↓
[21, 50]	↓	Lactate	↓

*Present study.
(↑) indicates an enhanced response observed in trained subjects
and (↓) indicates a decreased response.

periods, such as in cold adaptation [25, 30], or when animals are exposed to repeated injections of catecholamines, an increased sensitivity to noradrenalin develops especially with regard to actions mediated by beta receptors [26-29, 53]. In order to establish a causal relationship between noradrenalin and adaptation to exercise a parallelism was drawn between the responses to exercise in trained subjects. Table III shows many similarities between these responses. Indeed, FFA [12, 22, 47, 53], glycerol [22, 47] and lactate [23, 46, 47, 51, 52] elevations in the plasma in response to both exercise and noradrenalin perfusion are significantly smaller in the trained subjects, whereas the increase in plasma glucose [46, 47] and the sensitivity to insulin [8] are augmented by exercise training. In view of the known activation of the sympathetic nervous system during exercise, these results would seem to present valuable arguments to support the possibility of an important role for noradrenalin in physical training.

References

1. Ahlboy, B., Bergström, J., Ekelund, L.G.E. and Hultman, E.: Muscle glycogen and muscle electrolytes during prolonged physical exercise. Acta Physiol. Scand. 70:129-142, 1972.
2. Askew, E.W., Dohm, G.L., Huston, R.L. et al: Response of rat tissue lipases to physical training and exercise. Proc. Soc. Exp. Biol. Med. 141:123-127, 1972.
3. Banister, E.W. and Griffiths, J.: Blood levels of adrenergic amines during exercise. J. Appl. Physiol. 33:674-676, 1972.
4. Berger, M., Hagg, S. and Ruderman, N.B.: Glucose metabolism in perfused skeletal muscle. Biochem. J. 146:231-238, 1975.
5. Bittner, D.L. and McCleary, N.L.: The cupric phenanthraline chelate in the determination of monosaccharides in whole blood. Am. J. Clin. Path. 40:423-428, 1963.

6. Björntorp, P., de Jounge, K., Krotkiewski, M. et al: Physical training in human obesity. III. Effects of long-term physical training on body composition. Metabolism 22:1467-1475, 1973.

7. Björntorp, P., de Jounge, K., Sjöström, L. and Sillivan, L.: The effect of physical training on insulin production in obesity. Metabolism 19:631-639, 1970.

8. Björntorp, P., Fahlen, M., Grimby, G. et al: Carbohydrate and lipid metabolism in middle-aged, physically well-trained men. Metabolism. 21:1037-1042, 1972.

9. Costill, D.L., Gollnick, P.D., Jansson, E.D. et al: Glycogen depletion pattern in human muscle fibers during distance running. Acta Physiol. Scand. 89:374-381, 1973.

10. Davidson, P.C., Shane, S.R. and Albrink, M.J.: Decreased glucose tolerance following a physical conditioning program. Circulation 33:7, 1966.

11. Depocas, F.: Body glucose as fuel in white rats adapted to cold. Am. J. Physiol. 202:1015-1018, 1962.

12. Devlin, J., Varma, M.P. and Prendergast, J.: Effects of training and exercise on growth hormone release in man. Postgraduate Med. J. 49 (suppl. 5):144-147, 1973.

13. Dohm, G.L., Huston, R.L., Askew, E.W. and Weiser, P.C.: Effects of exercise on activity of heart and muscle mitochondria. Am. J. Physiol. 223:783-788, 1972.

14. Dole, V.P.: Determination of free fatty acids in the blood. J. Clin. Invest. 35:150-155, 1956.

15. Eggstein, M.: Enzymatic determination of glycerol in plasma and other biological fluids. Klin. Wschr. 44:262-267, 1966.

16. Fröberg, S.O.: Effects of training and of acute exercise in trained rats. Metabolism 20:1044-1047, 1971.

17. Fröberg, S.O., Carlson, L.A. and Ekelund, G.G.: Local lipid stores and exercise. In Pernow, B. and Saltin, B. (eds.): Muscle Metabolism During Exercise. New York:Plenum Press, 1971, pp. 307-313.

18. Fröberg, S.O., Ostman, I. and Sjostrand, N.O.: Effect of training on esterified fatty acids and carnitine in muscle and on lipolysis in adipose tissue in vitro. Acta Physiol. Scand. 86:166-170, 1972.

19. Hales, C.N. and Randle, P.J.: Immunoassay of insulin with insulin-antibody precipitate. Biochem. J. 88:137-146, 1963.

20. Hohorst, E.J.: Methods of Enzymatic Analysis. New York:Academic Press, 1963, p. 266.

21. Issekutz, B. Jr., Miller, H.I., Paul, P. and Rodahl, K.: Aerobic work capacity and plasma FFA turnover. J. Appl. Physiol. 20:293-298, 1965.

22. Johnson, R.H., Walton, J.L., Krebs, H.A. and Williamson, D.H.: Metabolic fuels during and after severe exercise in athletes and non-athletes. Lancet 2:452-455, 1969.

23. Karlson, J., Nordesjo, L.O. and Saltin, B.: Muscle glycogen utilization during exercise after physical training. Acta Physiol. Scand. 90:210-217, 1974.

24. Kozlowski, S., Brzezinska, Z., Nazar, K. and Kowalsky, W.: Activity of adrenergic system activation during exercise in men: Relation to work load and physical working capacity. Bull. Pol. Acad. Sci. 20:897-901, 1972.

25. LeBlanc, J. and Nadeau, G.: Urinary excretion of adrenaline and noradrenaline in normal and cold adapted animals. Can. J. Biochem. Physiol. 39:215-217, 1961.

26. LeBlanc, J. and Pouliot, M.: Importance of noradrenaline in cold adaptation. Am. J. Physiol. 207:853-856, 1964.

27. LeBlanc, J. and Villemaire, A.: Thyroxine and noradrenaline on noradrenaline sensitivity, cold resistance and brown fat. Am. J. Physiol. 218:1742-1745, 1970.

28. LeBlanc, J., Vallières, J. and Vachon, C.: Beta-receptor sensitization by repeated injections of isoproterenol and by cold adaptation. Am. J. Physiol. 222:1043-1046, 1972.

29. LeBlanc, J., Villemaire, A. and Vallières, J.: Simultaneous sensitization to metabolic and cardiovascular effects of noradrenaline. Arch. Int. Physiol. Biochem. 77:731-740, 1969.

30. Leduc, J.: Catecholamine production and release in exposure and acclimatation to cold. Acta Physiol. Scand. (suppl.) 53:183, 1961.

31. Luft, R., Cerosi, E. and Andersson, B.: Obesity as an additional factor in the pathogenesis of diabetes. Acta Endocr. (Copenhagen) 59:344-350, 1968.

32. Maron, M.B., Horvath, S.M. and Wilkerson, J.E.: Acute blood biochemical alterations in response to marathon running. Europ. J. Appl. Physiol. 34:173-181, 1975.

33. Molé, P.A. and Holloszy, J.O.: Exercise-induced increase in the capacity of skeletal muscle to oxidize palmitate. Proc. Soc. Exp. Biol. Med. 134:789-792, 1970.

34. Molé, P.A., Oscai, L.B. and Holloszy, J.O.: Adaptation of muscle to exercise: Increase in levels of palmityl CoA synthetase, carnitine palmityl transferase, and palmityl CoA dehydrogenase, and in the capacity to oxydise fatty acids. J. Clin. Invest. 50:2323-2328, 1971.

35. Moryia, K., Maekubo, H. and Itoh, S.: Turnover rate of free fatty acids in cold-acclimated rats. Jap. J. Physiol. 24:419-431, 1974.

36. Nadeau, A. and Morissette, J.: Une nouvelle méthode simple de transformation linéaire de la courbe standard dans le dosage radio-immunologique de l'insuline. Union Méd. Canada 102:566-569, 1973.

37. Novak, M.: Colorimetric ultramicro method for the determination of free fatty acids. J. Lip. Res. 6:431-434, 1965.

38. Olsson, O. and Saltin, B.: Diet and fluids in training and competition. Scand. J. Rehabil. Med. 3:31-35, 1971.

39. Oscai, L.B. and Williams, B.T.: Effect of exercise on overweight, middle-aged males. J. Am. Geriatr. Soc. 16:794, 1968.

40. Parizkova, J.: Impact of age, diet, and exercise on man's body composition. Ann. N.Y. Acad. Sci. 110:661-675, 1963.

41. Parizkova, J. and Stankova, L.: Influence of physical activity on a treadmill on the metabolism of adipose tissue in rats. Br. J. Nutrition 18:325-331, 1964.

42. Perley, M.J. and Kipnis, D.M.: Plasma insulin responses to oral and intravenous glucose. Studies in normal and diabetic subjects. J. Clin. Invest. 46:1954-1960, 1967.

43. Pollock, M.L., Miller, H.S. Jr., Janeway, R. et al: Effects of walking on body composition and cardiovascular function of middle-aged men. J. Appl. Physiol. 30:126-130, 1971.

44. Porte, D., Graber, A.L., Kuzuya, T. and Williams, R.H.: The effect of epinephrine on immunoreactive insulin levels in man. J. Clin. Invest. 45:228-236, 1966.

45. Porte, D. and Williams, R.H.: Inhibition of insulin release by norepinephrine in man. Science 152:1248-1250, 1966.

46. Rennie, M.J., Jennett, S. and Johnson, R.H.: The metabolic effects of strenuous exercise: A comparison between untrained subjects and racing cyclists. Q. J. Exp. Physiol. 59:201-212, 1974.

47. Rennie, M.J. and Johnson, R.H.: Alteration of metabolic and hormonal responses to exercise by physical training. Eur. J. Appl. Physiol. 33:215-226, 1974.

48. Salons, L.B., Knittle, J.L. and Kirsch, J.: The role of adipose tissue cell size and adipose tissue insulin sensitivity in the carbohydrate intolerance of human obesity. J. Clin. Invest. 47:153-160, 1968.

49. Saltin, B.: Metabolism fundamentals in exercise. Med. Sci. Sports 5:137-146, 1973.

50. Saltin, B., Blomquist, G., Mitchell, J.H. et al: Response to exercise after bed rest and after training. Am. Heart Assoc. Monogr. 1968.

51. Saltin, B. and Karlsson, J.: Muscle glycogen utilization during work at different intensities. In Pernow, B. and Saltin, B. (eds.): Muscle Metabolism During Exercise. New York:Plenum Press, 1971, pp. 289-299.

52. Saltin, B. and Karlsson, J.: Muscle ATP, CP and lactate during exercise and physical training. In Pernow, B. and Saltin, B. (eds.): Muscle Metabolism During Exercise. New York:Plenum Press, 1971, pp. 395-399.

53. Simko, V. and Chorvathova, V.: Response of free fatty acids and intraperitoneal glucose tolerance test to exercise in trained and untrained rats. Med. Exp. 19:71-74, 1969.

54. Skinner, J.S., Holloszy, J.O. and Cureton, T.: Effects of a program of endurance exercises on physical work. Capacity and anthropometric measurements of fifteen middle-aged men. Am. J. Cardiol. 14:747-753, 1964.

55. Sterky, G.: Clinical and metabolic aspects on obesity in childhood. In Pernow, B. and Saltin, B. (eds.): Muscle Metabolism During Exercise. New York:Plenum Press, 1971, pp. 521-527.

56. Taylor, A.W., McNulty, M., Cary, S. et al: The effects of pair feeding and exercise upon blood and tissue energy substrates. Rev. Can. Biol. 33:27-36, 1974.

57. Vendsatu, A.: Studies on adrenaline and noradrenaline in human plasma. Acta Physiol. Scand. (suppl.) 49:173, 1960.

58. von Euler, U.S.: Sympatho-adrenal activity in physical exercise. Med. Sci. Sports 6:165-173, 1974.

59. Williams, C.: Regulation of Norepinephrine Induced Lipolysis in Fat Cells From Untrained Rats. Master thesis, Washington State Univ., 1969.

Concentrations of Plasma Lipids and Lipoproteins in Male and Female Long-Distance Runners

Peter D. Wood, William L. Haskell, Steven Lewis,
Christopher Perry and Michael P. Stern

Introduction

The possibility of a beneficial influence of a sustained high level of physical fitness upon risk of cardiovascular disease in Westernized countries remains a fascinating, although still controversial issue. The role of exercise in modifying plasma lipid and lipoprotein concentrations in a way that could result in protection from coronary heart disease has not been clear. It is well established that plasma triglyceride levels are lower in well-trained men than in their sedentary counterparts [1] and are reduced by vigorous physical activity in hyperlipemic subjects [12]. However, it appears that elevated plasma triglyceride is probably not a major risk factor for coronary heart disease [4]. A program of vigorous physical activity has been found to be followed by a modest reduction [2, 10] or no change [6, 8] in plasma total cholesterol level. Recently, it has been suggested that relatively *high* concentrations of plasma high density lipoprotein (HDL) cholesterol may in effect be protective against coronary heart disease [11]. Certainly, plasma HDL-cholesterol concentrations are lowered in several conditions associated with an increased risk of heart disease (diabetes mellitus, obesity, hypercholesterolemia) and in patients suffering from coronary heart disease [3]. Rhoads et al have recently shown [13] an increasing prevalence of cardiovascular disease in Hawaiian-Japanese men as plasma HDL-cholesterol concentrations decrease from 53 mg/100 ml

Peter D. Wood, William L. Haskell, Steven Lewis, Christopher Perry and Michael P. Stern, Stanford Heart Disease Prevention Program, Stanford University School of Medicine, Stanford, California, U.S.A.

The research upon which this publication is based was performed pursuant to Contract NHLI 71-2161-L with the National Institutes of Health, Department of Health, Education and Welfare.

and above to 36 mg/100 ml and below. Investigators from the Framingham study have reported similar findings [7].

During a period of several years we noticed on agarose electrophoresis an apparently high concentration of the alpha (HDL) lipoprotein fraction in the plasma of very active people. In view of the recent interest in HDL-cholesterol as a possible protective factor in coronary heart disease we studied cross-sectionally the distribution of lipids and lipoproteins in groups of middle-aged male and female long-distance runners as compared with control groups of similar age.

Methods

Forty-one male and forty-three female runners who had each run at least 15 miles/week for the past year and were aged 30 to 59 were studied (Table I). The control groups were randomly selected men and women aged 35 to 59 living in three northern California towns (response rate, 78%). For the plasma triglyceride and total cholesterol analyses there were 743 male and 923 female controls; for the HDL, low density lipoprotein (LDL) and very low density lipoprotein (VLDL) analyses, random subsets of 147 male and 93 female controls were used.

All subjects were evaluated after a 12- to 16-hour fast during which no exercise was performed. The evaluation for the runners included a questionnaire inquiring about smoking and other habits, body composition by hydrostatic weighing and a maximal treadmill test. Subjects in the control groups underwent similar tests with the exception of the hydrostatic weighing. Plasma total cholesterol and triglyceride levels were determined on the Auto-Analyzer II following the standardized procedures of the Lipid Research Clinics Program [9]. The cholesterol content of plasma lipoprotein fractions was determined by the combined ultracentrifugal-precipitation

Table I. Characteristics of Runners and Controls

| | Runners | | Controls | |
	Males	Females	Males	Females
Number	41	43	743(147)*	923(93)*
Age range	35-59	30-59	35-59	35-59
Age mean	47	42	47	47
Relative weight	1.02	1.04	1.22	1.25
Percent body fat	13	20.5	–	–

*Numbers in parentheses are control groups used for comparisons of plasma lipoprotein cholesterol concentrations and for the treadmill test.

method [9] for the runners and by the "indirect" method [5] for the control subjects. Good agreement between the two methods has been demonstrated in our laboratory and elsewhere [5].

Results and Discussion

As expected, both male and female runners showed evidence of considerably greater physical fitness than was exhibited by the corresponding control groups (Table II). Thus, the runners showed a greater average test duration on the Bruce treadmill test, greater predicted maximum $\dot{V}O_2$, lower heart rate at six minutes and lower systolic blood pressure at six minutes.

Plasma lipid and lipoprotein concentrations for runners and control groups are shown in Table III. Mean total cholesterol levels were modestly, but significantly, lower in both male and female runners, confirming the experience of several previous investigators. The *distribution* of this total cholesterol among the major lipoprotein classes was different for runners and controls, however. HDL-cholesterol concentrations were considerably *higher* in runners of both sexes than in their corresponding (relatively sedentary) control groups (75 vs. 55 for women; 64 vs. 43 mg/100 ml for men). LDL-cholesterol, conversely, was significantly *lower* in runners than in controls (113 vs. 128 for women; 125 vs. 139 mg/100 ml for men). Similar differences between runners and controls were seen when ten-year age groups within the total 30- to 59-year-old group were considered.

Large differences were observed in plasma triglyceride concentrations between runners and controls (56 vs. 122 for women; 70 vs. 146 mg/100 ml for men). Although lower triglyceride levels have been reported quite often in active compared with inactive individuals, the extent of the differences in the present study (runners

Table II. Bruce Treadmill Exercise Test Responses for Male and Female Runners and Controls

| | Runners | | Controls | |
	Males	Females	Males	Females
Number	41	43	147	93
Test duration (minutes)	16.0	13.0	9.5	9.0
Predicted max $\dot{V}O_2$ (ml/kg/min)	57.6	45.0	33.0	31.5
Heart rate at six minutes (beats/min)	103	116	131	148
Systolic blood pressure at six minutes (mm Hg)	142	156	184	175

All test differences between runners and appropriate control group are significant (p <0.05 or less).

have one-half the mean levels of sedentary controls) is particularly striking. The low standard deviations obtained for plasma triglycerides of runners compared to controls (Table III) are noteworthy and reflect the complete absence among the runners of individuals with elevated triglycerides. High standard deviations for this measurement are characteristic of survey data obtained in U.S. populations [14].

Of course, there are several further differences between runners and controls other than the greater physical activity level of the runners. None of the runners in our study currently smoked cigarettes, although many were ex-smokers. Both male and female runners exhibited considerably less adiposity than controls (Table I). Values for percent body weight as fat in runners (13% and 20.5% for males and females, respectively) were considerably lower than has been reported for the general population of similar age. Clearly, leanness is part of the running "package" and probably is in part responsible for the observed characteristic pattern of plasma lipoproteins. However, linear correlation coefficients for indices of adiposity versus plasma HDL-cholesterol or plasma triglyceride concentration were of a low order (for instance, for control group men $r = -0.233$, $p < 0.05$, for relative weight versus plasma HDL—cholesterol concentration). The differences between runners and controls for plasma triglyceride concentrations remain statistically significant when age, relative weight, cigarette smoking and plasma cholesterol level are controlled for. Also, plasma lipoprotein concentration differences do not seem to be due to differences in diet (including alcohol intake) between runners and controls, as judged from preliminary examination of three-day food records obtained recently for the runners and for a random subset of controls.

Whatever the mechanism responsible for the characteristic lipoprotein pattern found in long-distance runners, current information suggests strongly that it is a desirable state of affairs with respect to future risk of cardiovascular disease. Since elevations of LDL-cholesterol have long been associated with increased risk of heart disease, and since more recently decreasing HDL-cholesterol levels have been shown to be associated with *increasing* risk of heart disease [13], we propose the ratio: HDL-cholesterol concentration/ LDL-cholesterol concentration as an "atherosclerotic index" or, more accurately, as a "safety index." As shown in Table III, there is a progression in this ratio among the groups we studied from "most risk" to "least risk" as follows: sedentary men, 0.31; sedentary women, 0.43; male runners, 0.51; female runners, 0.66. The

Table III. Plasma Lipid and Lipoprotein Concentrations (mean ± SD; mg/100 ml) and Ratio HDL/LDL-Cholesterol in Runners and Controls

| | Runners | | Controls | |
	Males	Females	Males	Females
Total Cholesterol	200 ± 23	193 ± 33	210 ± 35	210 ± 39
VLDL-cholesterol	11	5	28	27
LDL-cholesterol	125 ± 21	113 ± 33	139 ± 31	128 ± 29
HDL-cholesterol	64 ± 13	75 ± 14	43 ± 10	55 ± 12
Ratio: HDL/LDL-cholesterol	0.51	0.66	0.31	0.43
Triglycerides	70 ± 25	56 ± 19	146 ± 108	122 ± 96

See Table I for numbers of runners and controls. All differences between runners and corresponding control group are statistically significant at $p < 0.05$ or less (for values where a standard deviation is given).

increasing ratio is due, of course, to modestly lower levels of LDL-cholesterol in runners vs. controls (and in women vs. men) and to considerably higher levels of HDL-cholesterol in runners vs. controls (and in women vs. men).

When these apparently beneficial plasma lipoprotein patterns are considered together with other characteristics of long-distance runners (leanness, nonsmoking habits, relatively low systolic blood pressure during exercise — see Table II), it seems clear that these very active middle-aged people form a group with remarkably low risk of cardiovascular disease, at least by North American standards.

Summary

Male and female long-distance runners in the age range of 30 to 59 show a plasma lipoprotein pattern significantly different from relatively sedentary controls matched for age and sex. Plasma LDL- and VLDL-cholesterol concentrations and triglyceride concentrations are *lower* in the runners, while HDL-cholesterol concentration is considerably *higher*. Current evidence suggests strongly that this characteristic pattern in runners is advantageous with respect to risk of cardiovascular disease.

At least part of the differences in lipoprotein pattern appears to be due to exercise per se — independent of degree of adiposity or other life-style habits.

When considered together with the leanness and freedom from cigarette smoking exhibited by these runners, these groups of very active middle-aged men and women appear to be at unusually low risk of cardiovascular disease.

References

1. Bjorntorp, P., Fahlen, M., Grimby, G. et al: Carbohydrate and lipid metabolism in middle-aged physically well-trained men. Metabolism 21:1037-1044, 1972.
2. Campbell, D.E.: Influence of several physical activities on serum cholesterol concentrations in young men. J. Lipid Res. 6:478-480, 1965.
3. Carlson, L.A. and Ericsson, M.: Quantitative and qualitative serum lipoprotein analysis. II. Studies in male survivors of myocardial infarction. Atherosclerosis 21:435-450, 1975.
4. Cohn, P.F., Gabbay, S.I. and Weglicki, W.B.: Serum lipid levels in angiographically defined coronary artery disease. Ann. Intern. Med. 84:241-245, 1976.
,5. Friedewald, W.T., Levy, R.I. and Fredrickson, D.S.: Estimation of the concentration of low-density lipoprotein cholesterol in plasma, without use of the preparative ultracentrifuge. Clin. Chem. 18:499-502, 1972.
6. Goode, R.C., First Brook, J.B. and Shepard, R.J.: Effects of exercise and a cholesterol-free diet on human serum lipids. Can. J. Physiol. Pharmacol. 44:575-580, 1966.
,7. Gordon, T., Castelli, W.P., McNamara, P.M. et al: HDL-cholesterol and the optimal CHD lipid risk profile: The Framingham Study. CVD Epidemiology Newsletter, Council on Epidemiology, American Heart Association, March 1976, abstract #17.
8. Holloszy, J.O., Skinner, J.S., Toro, G. and Cureton, T.K.: The effects of a six month program of endurance exercise on serum lipids of middle-aged men. Am. J. Cardiol. 14:753-760, 1964.
9. Lipid Research Clinics Manual of Laboratory Operations, Vol. 1. Lipid and Lipoprotein Analysis. Dept. Health, Educ. Welfare Pub. No. (NIH) 75-628. U.S. Govt. Print. Off., 1974.
10. Mann, G.V., Garrett, H.L., Farhi, A. et al: Exercise to prevent coronary heart disease. Am. J. Med. 46:12-27, 1969.
11. Miller, G.J. and Miller, N.E.: Plasma high-density-lipoprotein concentration and development of ischemic heart disease. Lancet 1:16-19, 1975.
12. Oscai, L.B., Patterson, J.A., Bogard, D.L. et al: Normalization of serum triglycerides and lipoprotein electrophoretic patterns by exercise. Am. J. Cardiol. 30:775-780, 1972.
13. Rhoads, G.G., Gulbrandsen, C.L. and Kagan, A.: Serum lipoproteins and coronary heart disease in a population study of Hawaii Japanese men. N. Engl. J. Med. 294:293-298, 1976.
14. Wood, P.D.S., Stern, M.P., Silvers, A. et al: Prevalence of plasma lipoprotein abnormalities in a free-living population of the Central Valley, California. Circulation 45:114-126, 1972.

Effects of a Carbohydrate-Rich Diet on Nutritional Status and Aerobic Performance

Maurice Jetté, Omer Pelletier, James Thoden
and Louise Parker

Introduction

Recent studies have reported that carbohydrate-rich diets could improve the capacity for prolonged exercise. This increase in performance is said to be the result of enhanced muscle glycogen stores. It has also been indicated that muscle glycogen stores could be further increased if existing stores were first depleted by exhaustive exercise followed by a protein-fat diet prior to saturating the diet with carbohydrate-rich foods.

Like many others, we have recommended this glycogen depletion-saturation procedure as a means of improving the performance of those athletes involved in prolonged and exhaustive exercise such as cross-country skiing and running. We also have repeated the suggestion that this training regimen could possibly be useful to those athletes involved in activities requiring short but repeated bursts of intense activity over extended periods of time, such as in hockey. As a result of discussions with nutritionists, three questions came to mind which led to the aims of this study:

1. What should be the detailed composition of a "protein-fat" and a carbohydrate-rich diet?

2. Would such diets, even if employed for short periods of time, cause nutritional imbalance and/or deficiency?

3. Would glycogen saturation of the muscle fibers modify serum lactate production during short periods of exercise intensity of relative workloads?

Maurice Jetté and James Thoden, Department of Kinanthropology; Louise Parker, Department of Dietetics, University of Ottawa, Ontario; and Omer Pelletier, Surveillance Laboratory, Health and Welfare, Canada.

Methodology

Subjects

Four male subjects participated in the study. Their age, anthropometric and $\dot{V}O_2$ max measurements are outlined in Table I. The subjects were not permitted to participate in any form of intense vigorous activity during the entire period of the study except as required by the experimental protocol.

Protocol

Table II outlines the five-week experimental protocol which was rigidly followed for each subject.

The first three weeks were devoted to control measurements of their habitual diet, anthropometric, metabolic, biochemical measurements and aerobic test.

The experimental week consisted of the glycogen-depletion exercise stress, followed by three days of a protein-fat diet, three days of a carbohydrate-rich diet, followed by the aerobic tests.

Diet Assessment and Elaboration

Diet assessment, elaboration and control were under the supervision of a nutritionist. Information from food kept by the subjects was used for a detail analysis of food consumption dietary habits, nutrient content and the determination of isocaloric experimental diets. The nutrient content of food was evaluated by computer based on the data from the Agriculture Handbook # 8.

The experimental protein-fat diet provided no more than 10% carbohydrates while the high carbohydrate diet contained approximately 80% carbohydrate.

Parameters

Basic anthropometric and BMR measurements were recorded at regular intervals under basal conditions during the five weeks.

Table I. Age and Anthropometric Measurements of Subjects

Subject	Age	Weight (kg)	Height (cm)	BSA (m 2)	$\dot{V}O_2$ max ml/kg/min
J.M.	20	67.27	179.71	1.86	55.5
C.M.	21	76.14	179.71	1.95	44.4
J.D.	21	80.00	178.44	1.99	47.7
M.R.	21	68.18	165.10	1.75	44.5
$\overline{X}$	20.75	72.9	175.7	1.89	48.0
σ	.50	6.19	7.12	.11	5.2

Table II. Five-Week Experimental Protocol

Week	Mon	Tue	Wed	Thu	Fri
Control 1.	Anthro. BMR EKG	← Usual normal diet assessment →			Serum + Urine + BMR
Control 2.		Work Capacity ($\dot{V}O_2$ max)	,,	Work Capacity ($\dot{V}O_2$ max)	as above
Control 3.			,,		as above
Exper. 1	Exhaustion run	Protein-fat diet		Serum Urine BMR	CHO diet (A) incl. Sat. and Sun.
Exper. 2	Serum Urine BMR	Work Capacity CHO diet (B) ($\dot{V}O_2$ max)		Serum Urine BMR	

Twenty-five cubic centimeters of venous blood was withdrawn under basal condition in appropriate vacutainers for the analysis of the parameters indicated in Tables III and IV.

A 24-hour urine collection was also returned at this time and analyzed for the parameters indicated in Table V. These data from urine and blood analysis provided the "nutritional profile" indicated in Table II.

Exercise Stress Tests

The exercise stress test employed to evaluate $\dot{V}O_2$ max and production was a progressive treadmill test with a constant speed of 3.75 mph.

Elevation was increased by 2.5% at every two minutes until the subject could not complete a further increase.

One cubic centimeter of venous blood was collected for lactate analysis in conjunction with $\dot{V}O_2$ analysis, i.e., at 5%, 10%, 15%, 17.5% and at each further elevation until the test was completed.

Glycogen Depletion

In order to deplete glycogen stores the subject was exercised to exhaustion on a motor-driven treadmill at 5% elevation at 70% of his $\dot{V}O_2$ max.

**Table III. Blood Serum Analysis Prior to and Following
Protein-Fat and Carbohydrate-Rich Diets**

Variable	Units		Control Values ($\bar{X}$)	Post Protein-Fat Diet	Post CHO-Rich Diet (A)	Post CHO-Rich Diet (B)
Hematocrit	%	$\bar{X}$	43.2	41.6	41.9	42.5
		σ	3.6	3.0	3.9	3.7
Hemoglobin	g%	$\bar{X}$	15.4	14.9	15.1	15.2
		σ	.9	.6	1.2	1.1
Cholesterol	mg%	$\bar{X}$	165.4	174.0	160.8	150.3
		σ	15.3	15.3	16.1	16.0
Triglycerides	mg%	$\bar{X}$	74.2	60.5	108.8	148.9
		σ	13.8	6.7	14.3	29.1
Total protein	g%	$\bar{X}$	6.86	6.80	6.75	6.88
		σ	.45	.43	.40	.46
Albumin	g%	$\bar{X}$	4.63	4.48	4.55	4.55
		σ	.35	.17	.19	.10
Calcium	mg%	$\bar{X}$	9.46	9.35	9.73	9.83
		σ	.13	.29	.21	.38
Inorg. phosphorus	mg%	$\bar{X}$	3.48	3.25	3.40	3.40
		σ	.33	.38	.36	.50
Glucose	mg%	$\bar{X}$	100.5	93.2	101.0	100.8
		σ	4.2	9.1	11.0	7.4
BUN	mg%	$\bar{X}$	18.2	22.3	11.3	10.0
		σ	3.3	3.9	2.1	1.4
Uric acid	mg%	$\bar{X}$	6.2	5.9	5.7	6.0
		σ	1.4	.8	1.3	1.5
Creatinine	mg%	$\bar{X}$	1.1	.95	1.0	1.0
		σ	.1	.06	.1	.1
Total bilirubin	mg%	$\bar{X}$	.78	.75	.93	.93
		σ	.14	.13	.29	.15
Alkaline phos.	mU/ml	$\bar{X}$	52.1	49.5	50.5	53.5
		σ	4.7	2.1	6.4	7.9
SGOT	mU/ml	$\bar{X}$	33.8	35.5	27.8	26.8
		σ	9.1	14.2	8.5	5.9

Endurance Test

Following the final $\dot{V}O_2$ max test, the subject was again put on a
two-day carbohydrate-rich diet and then subjected to run to
exhaustion as employed in the glycogen-depletion protocol.

Table IV. Blood Serum Vitamin Profile Following
Protein-Fat and Carbohydrate-Rich Diets

Variable	Units		Control Values ($\overline{X}$)	Post Protein-Fat Diet	Post CHO-Rich Diet (A)	Post CHO-Rich Diet (B)
Vitamin A	μg/%	$\overline{X}$	62.2	60.3	54.9	60.3
		σ	2.4	10.4	5.5	6.1
Vitamin C	mg%	$\overline{X}$	.99	1.06	1.52	1.72
		σ	.07	.08	.10	.07
Vitamin E	μg/ml	$\overline{X}$	9.86	10.03	9.55	9.43
		σ	.29	.72	.94	.29
Folate	ng/ml	$\overline{X}$	4.33	5.58	4.33	4.02
		σ	1.23	1.76	1.60	1.00

Table V. Urine Analysis Prior to and Following
Protein-Fat and Carbohydrate-Rich Diets

Variable	Units		Control Values ($\overline{X}$)	Post Protein-Fat Diet	Post CHO-Rich Diet (A)	Post CHO-Rich Diet (B)
Creatinine	mg%	$\overline{X}$	181.0	128.5	133.5	125.3
		σ	55.2	40.9	40.9	54.6
Creatinine (c)	g/day	$\overline{X}$	2.33	2.27	2.10	2.04
		σ	.55	.72	.44	.43
Thiamine	μg/g c	$\overline{X}$	287.3	292.3	360.8	418.3
		σ	122.1	78.0	78.8	113.6
Riboflavin	μg/g c	$\overline{X}$	940.8	670.0	1192.0	1166.0
		σ	357.4	192.2	302.6	270.0
N^1-M nicotinamide	mg/g c	$\overline{X}$	3.24	6.11	2.36	2.20
		σ	0.87	1.5	0.74	0.99
Vitamin B_6	μg/g c	$\overline{X}$	34.7	41.0	39.9	34.1
		σ	7.5	14.2	10.0	7.4
Iodine	μg/g c	$\overline{X}$	380.5	278.5	171.5	187.75
		σ	115.4	78.3	13.9	14.3

Results

Dietary Analysis and Weight

Food data evaluation revealed a wide variation in the diet of our subjects during the control weeks. Nonetheless, the results indicated adequate protein, vitamin and mineral intake during this period.

The experimental protein-fat diet supplied from 26% to 32% proteins while fats constituted 55% to 62% of the total diet. There was adequate vitamin and mineral intake. During the high carbohydrate diet, all four subjects decreased their caloric consumption. Notwithstanding, they demonstrated increases in weight — as much as 2.26 kg in one subject (Fig. 1), probably the result of increased water retention. Protein intake during this diet was reduced from 0.6 to 0.8 gm/kg of body weight.

Food consumption evaluation during this period revealed a decrease in niacin and riboflavin intake and an increase in the intake of vitamin C.

BMR Measurements

The RQ measured from the BMR reflected quite well the changes in the diet of the subjects: a decreased RQ with the protein-lipid diet, and an increased RQ with the carbohydrate diet (Fig. 2).

Blood and Urine Analysis

The triglycerides, as expected, mirrored the increased carbohydrate intake (Fig. 3). The same pattern was seen with the serum

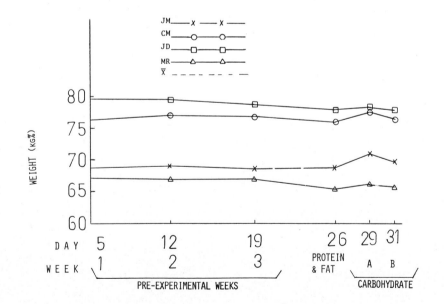

FIG. 1. Weight of subjects prior to and following the protein-fat and carbohydrate-rich diets.

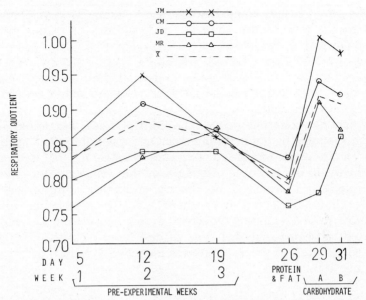

FIG. 2. Basal metabolic rate (RQ) prior to and following the protein-fat and carbohydrate-rich diets.

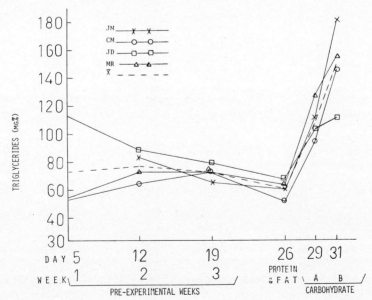

FIG. 3. Triglyceride measurements prior to and following the protein-fat and carbohydrate-rich diets.

glucose (Fig. 4) and coincidentally with vitamin C (Fig. 5). Serum
BUN results reflected the increase and decrease of dietary protein
intake during the two experimental diets (Fig. 6).

As for the other vitamins monitored there were no changes in
vitamins A, B$_6$ and E during the course of the five weeks, neither
were there any changes in serum folic acid and serum and urinary
excretion of creatinine.

Thiamine excretion during the control week was found to be
generally above the population median and risk criteria in all subjects
(Fig. 7). The acute changes in two subjects J.D. and J.M. during the
control weeks are a simple reflection of the changes in the amounts
they ingested as revealed by dietary evaluation. During the high
carbohydrate diet, however, there was an increase in urinary
excretion notwithstanding that there were no changes in the amounts
ingested. It seems that this type of diet caused less thiamine to be
utilized or retained unless there was increased synthesis of thiamine
by the intestinal flora.

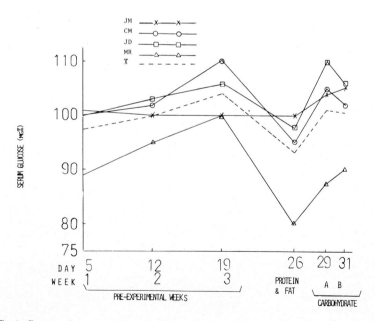

FIG. 4. Serum glucose measurements prior to and following the protein-fat and
carbohydrate-rich diets.

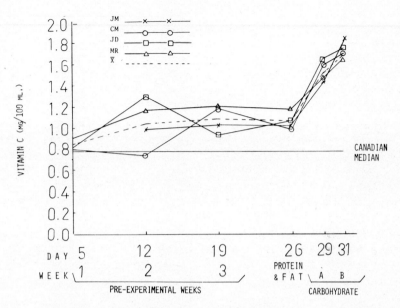

FIG. 5. Vitamin C measurements prior to and following the protein-fat and carbohydrate-rich diets.

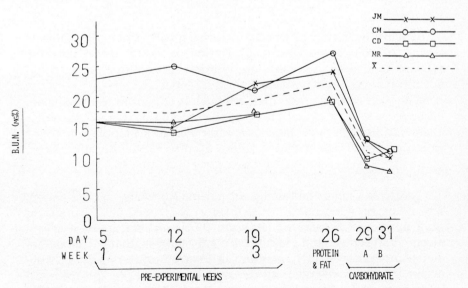

FIG. 6. Serum BUN measurements prior to and following the protein-fat and carbohydrate-rich diets.

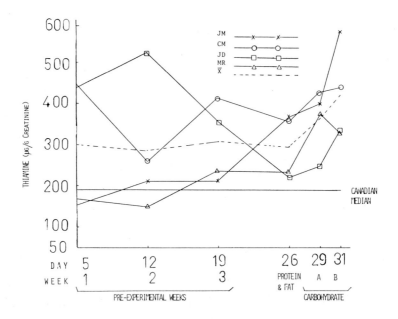

FIG. 7. Urinary thiamine measurements prior to and following the protein-fat and carbohydrate-rich diets.

Riboflavin

Urinary excretion of riboflavin varied greatly among the subjects during the control weeks (Fig. 8). During the experimental diets, the subjects tended to become more uniform in excretion which could not be attributed to a uniformity in their intake.

The high carbohydrate diet, although it contained less riboflavin, produced a greater excretion of riboflavin. This could indicate either a lesser utilization or retention for carbohydrate metabolism than for amino acids and fats or that synthesis occurred in the intestinal flora.

N^1-Methyl Nicotinamide (N-MN)

N-MN is a major metabolite of niacin. Normally, approximately 25% of niacin is excreted in the form of N-MN and 50% in the form of 2 pyridone. A value of less than 0.5 is an indication of severe niacin deficiency and values of 1.6 suggest that a moderate deficiency exists. N-MN excretion in Figure 9 mirrors very well the niacin intake as revealed by dietary evaluation. The subjects who ingested more niacin eliminated more N-MN. The increased excretion seen during the protein-fat diet corresponds to a measured increase in

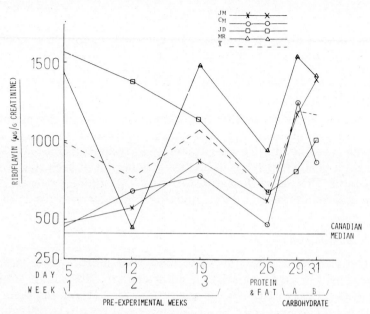

FIG. 8. Urinary riboflavin measurements prior to and following the protein-fat and carbohydrate-rich diets.

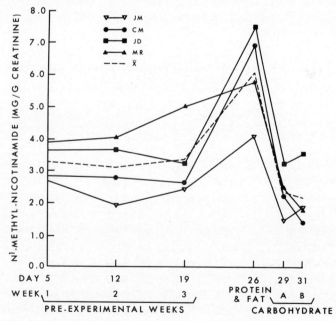

FIG. 9. Urinary N^1-methyl-nicotinamide prior to and following the protein-fat and carbohydrate-rich diets.

niacin intake during this period. The decreased excretion seen during the carbohydrate diet corresponds to a dietary decrease in niacin intake.

Aerobic Performance

The $\dot{V}O_2$ max expressed in milliliters per kilogram per minute of the subjects following the high carbohydrate diet showed a slight decrease possibly due to their increase in weight (Table VI). There was also a general increase in lactate production at each stage of the test (Table VII) as well as a decrease in $\dot{V}O_2$ uptake at each stage. There was no increase in $\dot{V}O_2$ max performance as a result of this diet.

Endurance Performance

The endurance run was performed on a motor-driven treadmill inclined at 5% grade at a speed equivalent to 70% of the subjects' $\dot{V}O_2$ max (Table VIII). Of the four subjects, J.M. ran the same time as his pre-diet time (120 min); C.M. decreased his run by 20 minutes; C.M. could no longer continue after 50 minutes of running following the rich carbohydrate diet, although his pre-diet time was 147 minutes. The fourth subject (M.R.) developed knee trouble following the final $\dot{V}O_2$ max test and was unable to perform the endurance run.

Table VI. Maximal Work Capacity Response of Subjects
Prior to and Following Carbohydrate-Rich Diet

Subject		Max Heart Rate b/m	RQ	$\dot{V}O_2$ (l/min)	$\dot{V}O_2$ max (ml/kg/min)	Post Ex. Lactate
J.M.	Control	200	1.22	3.76	55.5	–
	Post diet	198	1.20	3.57	51.0	–
C.M.	Control	195	1.18	3.68	47.8	121.2
	Post diet	192	1.28	3.37	43.4	128.7
J.D.	Control	190	1.23	3.82	47.8	89.1
	Post diet	192	1.22	3.28	41.9	93.5
M.R.	Control	192	1.22	3.00	44.5	81.6
	Post diet	190	1.25	2.57	43.3	105.5
	Control $\overline{X}$	194	1.23	3.57	48.90	97.3
	σ	4	.02	.38	4.66	21.0
	Post diet $\overline{X}$	193	1.23	3.20	44.90	109.2
	σ	3	.03	.43	4.12	17.9

Table VII. Lactate Levels (mg%) During Maximal Voluntary Work
Prior to and Following a Carbohydrate-Rich Diet

Subject		Rest	5%	10%	15%	20%	22.5%	25%	Post Ex. 1 min
				Treadmill Elevation — Constant Speed of 3.75 mph					
J.M.	Pre diet	8.0	8.5	9.8	19.4	33.0	39.8	46.7	76.0
	Post diet	17.3	11.8	20.8	26.1	–	–	–	–
C.M.	Pre diet	10.7	17.3	21.7	36.8	79.5	105.8	X	121.2
	Post diet	19.9	16.9	20.2	40.6	80.7	117.2	X	128.7
J.D.	Pre diet	15.0	11.3	13.1	28.9	53.9	X	X	89.1
	Post diet	18.3	19.5	–	30.8	64.7	X	X	93.5
M.R.	Pre diet	10.8	19.4	22.7	42.4	X	X	X	81.6
	Post diet	24.4	23.2	25.1	42.8	88.6	X	X	105.5

– Insufficient amount of blood for analysis.
X Work not completed.

Table VIII. Endurance Run at 70% $\dot{V}O_2$ max
Prior to and Following a Carbohydrate-Rich Diet

Subject		Speed mph	Duration min	$\dot{V}O_2$ max ml/kg/min	RQ	Heart Rate 1 min
J.M.	Pre diet	5.00	120	39.4	.955	191
	Post diet	5.00	120	46.3	.849	–
C.M.	Pre diet	4.75	90	36.1	.926	200
	Post diet	4.75	70	37.4	.986	191
J.D.	Pre diet	4.25	147	39.5	1.029	187
	Post diet	4.25	50	22.8	1.044	157

Discussion

It is tempting to ask if the increased urinary excretion of thiamine and riboflavin during the carbohydrate-rich diet is the result of a decreased quantity of NAD secondary to reduced niacin intake. This is a possible explanation if niacin, the precursor to NAD, had reached a "suboptimal" level.

Increased NAD production would result in increased glucose oxidation by favoring conversion of glyceraldehyde-3-P in 1-3 diphosphoglycerate and subsequently increase decarboxylation of pyruvate and of α-ketoglytarate in the Krebs cycle.

This increased aerobic oxidation in the Krebs cycle would help to maintain better NAD/NADH NADP/NADPH ratios. The consequence could be a reduction in lactate production where NADH is required and a possible reduction of fatty acids synthesis where NADPH is required. The apparent decreased aerobic oxidation seen in the performance test as revealed by a decrease in proportion of $\dot{V}O_2$ uptake and an increase in lactate production at a given workload could be related to a lower intake of niacin during the carbohydrate diet.

It is also possible that an increase in dietary niacin would only lead to increased NMN excretion. Nonetheless, it would appear of interest to study the effects of additional niacin when ingesting a high carbohydrate diet. However, there is no suggestion on our part that supplementing niacin to the normal diet would improve oxidative mechanisms.

Bibliography

Bergstrom, J., Hermansen, L., Hultman E. et al: Diet muscle glycogen and physical performance. Acta Physiol. Scand. 7:140, 1967.

Bergstrom, J. and Hultman, E.: Nutrition for maximal sports performance. JAMA 221:999, 1972.

Consolazio, C.F., Johnson, R.E. and Pecora, L.J.: Physiological Measurements of Metabolic Functions in Man. New York:McGraw-Hill Book Company, 1963.

Frankel, S. and Reitman, S. (eds.): Microtechnic for Hematocrit Determination, Wintrobe. Gradwhols Clinical Laboratory Methods and Diagnosis, Vol. 2. St. Louis:C.J. Mosley Company, 1963.

Garry, P.J., Lashley, W. and Owen, G.M.: Automated measurement of urinary iodine. Clin. Chem. 19:950, 1973.

Hermansen, L., Hultman, E. and Saltin, B.: Muscle glycogen during prolonged severe exercise. Acta Physiol. Scand. 71:129, 1967.

Hohorst, H.J.: In Bergmeyer: Methods of Enzymatic Analysis. Verlag Chemie Weinheim, 1st ed., 1962, p. 622.

Jellife, D.B.: The Assessment of the Nutritional Status of the Community. Geneva:World Health Organization, 1966.

Karlsson, J. and Saltin, B.: Diet, muscle glycogen, and endurance performance. J. Appl. Physiol. 31:203, 1971.

Nutrition Canada, National Survey, Ottawa: Bureau of Nutritional Sciences, Department of National Health and Welfare, 1973.

Nutrition Canada, Ontario Survey, Ottawa: Bureau of Nutritional Sciences, Department of National Health and Welfare, 1975.

Pelletier, O. and Brassard, R.: New automated method for serum Vitamin C. In Advance in Automated Analysis, 1972. Technicon International Congress. Pharmaceutical Sciences. Tarrytown, N.Y.:Medical Inc., 1973, p. 73.

Pelletier, O. and Campbell, J.A.: A rapid method for the determination of N^1-methylnicotinamide in urine. Anal. Biochem. 3:60, 1962.

Pelletier, O. and Madere, R.: Automated determination of riboflavin (vitamin B_2) in urine. In Advance in Automated Analysis, 1970. Technicon International Congress. Miami, Florida:Thurman Associates, 1971, 11:413.

Pelletier, O. and Madere, R.: New automated method for measuring thiamine (vitamin B_1) in urine. Clin. Chem. 18:937, 1972.

Slovic, P.: What helps the long distance runner. Nutrition Today 10:18, 1975.

Thompson, J.N., Erdody, P. and Maxwell, W.B.: Simultaneous fluorometric determinations of vitamins A and E in human serum and plasma. Biochem. Med. 8:403, 1973.

Wyatt, B.K. and Merrill, A.L.: Composition of foods: Raw, processed, prepared. Agriculture Handbook No. 8, Washington:U.S. Department of Agriculture, 1963.

Diet and Muscle Glycogen in Runners

Angelo Tremblay, Jeannine Sevigny, Michel Jobin
and Claude Allard

Introduction

The present experiment was undertaken to evaluate the respective role of exercise, feeding frequency and a three-day carbohydrate overload on muscle glycogen in man. Three dietary patterns were studied: the first was a standard diet eaten three meals a day (Sd 3), the second was also a standard diet, but eaten six meals a day during six days (Sd 6), and the third consisted of high fat-protein diet for the first three days and high carbohydrate diet in the following three days also given three times a day (Hc 3).

Methods

Seven male runners who had participated for at least one year in competitive events volunteered for this experiment. They were submitted to the three regimens during three consecutive weeks. During the first week, three subjects received the Sd 3 diet, two received the Sd 6 diet, and the other two had the Hc 3 diet. In the following weeks, the diets were interchanged in such a manner that each subject had followed the three diet patterns at the end of the experiment. Except for the Sd 6 diet while three prepared meals were given to be eaten outside, all the meals were taken in the laboratory. The daily caloric content for six days was the same for each regimen (Table I). The percentage of calories as protein, fat and carbohydrate was also the same for each diet (Table II).

The mean daily caloric content was calculated to meet the estimated needs of each subject.

At the end of day 0, just before the first controlled meal, the subjects ran for a minimum of 150 minutes at about 70% of their individual maximal oxygen uptake. On the following three days, the prescribed exercise lasted about 70 minutes per day. In the last three

Angelo Tremblay, Jeannine Sevigny, Michel Jobin and Claude Allard, Departments of Dietetics, Physiology and Physical Education, Laval University, Quebec, Canada.

Table I. Daily Caloric Content (kcal) for Each Diet
(Mean ± SD)

		Diets		
Sd 3	Sd 6		Hc 3 Days	
		1, 2, 3	4, 5, 6	Mean (1 to 6)
3139 ± 284	3142 ± 284	2060 ± 180	4224 ± 348	3143 ± 260

Table II. Mean Composition of the Diets*

Nutriments			Diets		
	Sd 3	Sd 6		Hc 3 Days	
			1, 2, 3	4, 5, 6	Mean (1 to 6)
Protein	15.4	15.3	25.0	11.5	15.5
Lipid	33.8	33.9	58.3	23.3	33.7
Carbohydrate	50.8	50.8	16.7	65.2	50.8

*Percentage of total caloric content.

days of each regimen, training was not allowed. The amount of work performed by each subject was adjusted according to the maximal oxygen uptake and previous performances and remained the same for the three experimental periods.

Muscle biopsies were obtained just before the controlled diet period and about four hours after the last meal of this period which was theoretically *the moment to start a long distance competitive race.* Muscle specimens were taken from the vastus lateralis by the biopsy needle technique of Bergström, weighed on a Cahn torsion balance and immediately frozen at −40 C. Glycogen concentration was determined the same day as described by Lo and collaborators.

Results

The body weight was not influenced by the various regimens (Table III). The body weight of the subjects did not change after the three weeks of the experiment, indicating that the estimated caloric needs were met.

The mean glycogen content after the long distance run was the same at the beginning of each regimen period (mean = 0.83). At the end of the diets (end of day 6), muscle glycogen averaged 2.13, 2.17

Table III. Body Weight and Muscle Glycogen After
the Three Different Diet Patterns
(Mean ± SD)

Body Weight and Muscle Glycogen	Diets		
n = 6	Sd 3	Sd 6	Hc 3
Body weight, kg	63.9 ± 4.2	63.9 ± 4.3	64.8 ± 4.7
Muscle glycogen, gm/100 gm wet muscle	2.13 ± 0.35	2.17 ± 1.18	2.56 ± 1.08

and 2.56 gm/100 gm wet muscle for the Sd 3, Sd 6 and Hc 3 diet, respectively. These values did not differ significantly ($P > 0.05$).

Discussion

The results of this study showed that the Hc 3 diet was not superior to the Sd 3 or the Sd 6 diets in building up muscle glycogen stores. This is not in complete agreement with the results of Karlsson and Saltin which indicated that three days of a combination of severe exercise and fat-protein diet followed by rest and a high carbohydrate diet produces higher muscle glycogen concentration as compared to a mixed diet. In the study of Karlsson and Saltin, when the subjects ate the mixed diet, there was no control over the food consumed and the exercise performed. In the present experiment, the program of exercise and the cumulative food intake were identical for the experimental weeks and therefore the treatments differed only by the way of distributing food over the six days of controlled diets. Our treatments were also more comparable between each other because the initial levels of muscle glycogen measured after the long distance runs were the same.

In this investigation, no significant difference was observed between the Sd 3 and Sd 6 diets, indicating that feeding frequency is not a factor which can produce a large variation of the muscle glycogen in man.

One possible limiting factor of glycogen accumulation is the total caloric content of the diet. In the present study, the daily caloric content, which amounted to 3141 ± 1 calories, was calculated to meet as accurately as possible the energy expenditure of each subject. These values were however much less than the spontaneous caloric intake of runners of similar body weight in the study of Rennie and Johnson.

Together with the fact that our final values of muscle glycogen were not as high as those reported by other authors, this may suggest that the caloric content of our diets was not sufficiently high to allow optimal rise of muscle glycogen. However, the body weight of our subjects did not change after the three weeks of the experiment, indicating that the caloric intake was sufficient to keep an equilibrium with energy expenditure.

Concerning the specificity of the site of the muscle biopsy with respect to the type of exercise, it is to be recalled that our subjects were runners and that muscle specimens were obtained from the vastus lateralis. It is possible that muscle biopsy in other muscle, for instance gastrocnemius, would have shown greater glycogen changes in the runners and would have revealed differences between the diets. Thus, in further experiments, muscle biopsies might be taken at various sites to verify these assumptions.

From the present results, which were obtained in rigorously controlled conditions, it cannot be concluded that one of the specific dietary patterns studied is particularly essential to raise muscle glycogen content in preparation for endurance events. It cannot be stated at the present time whether a larger caloric allowance would have revealed differences between the dietary patterns.

Myokinase Activity and Isozyme Pattern in Human Skeletal Muscle

Alf Thorstensson

Several key enzymes in the energy yielding metabolism of the human muscle have been shown to have different activity characteristics depending upon the relative distribution of slow twitch (ST or type I), and fast twitch (FT or type II) muscle fibers [3, 4]. This paper provides a short review of our recent results concerning the possible muscle fiber specific properties of the enzyme myokinase (MK), also referred to as adenylate kinase (E.C. 2.7.4.3.).

MK catalyzes the reaction: 2 ADP ⇌ ATP + AMP. It is thereby regulating what has been referred to as "energy charge" of the muscle cell [1], i.e., the interplay between the energy rich adenylate nucleotides. Since the ratio between these nucleotides influences the kinetics of enzymes in key positions, e.g., glycogen phosphorylase and phosphofructokinase, MK must be considered to be an essential step in regulating the overall metabolism of the muscle cells. Furthermore, the MK reaction constitutes a possible way of rapid ATP replenishment from ADP, e.g., in connection with muscle contractions. Any difference between muscle fiber types in MK enzymatic properties could thus imply fundamental differences in regulation of metabolism.

Muscle samples for this investigation were obtained from m. vastus lateralis of healthy young men (17 to 24 years) by means of the conventional needle biopsy technique [2]. Total MK activity in the direction of ATP formation, as well as the MK isozyme distribution, was studied. These analyses were performed both on muscle homogenates containing a mixture of FT and ST fibers and on pooled single FT and ST fibers dissected out from freeze-dried muscle specimens [3]. In both cases FT and ST muscle fibers were distinguished according to myofibrillar ATPase staining at pH 9.4 [6] after pre-incubation at pH 10.3. Total MK activity was determined fluorometrically as the initial rate of NADPH formation

Alf Thorstensson, Department of Physiology, Gymnastik- och idrotts-högskolan, Stockholm, Sweden.

via a coupled enzymatic assay [5]. The isozyme separation was performed by isoelectric focusing on Sephadex G-75 Superfine flat bed gels [7]. Identification of MK isozymes was done by a modified print technique [7]. Sepraphor electrophoretic strips were layered on top of the gel and subsequently immersed in specific MK staining medium. Comparison between the isozyme bands was carried out on the basis of densitometric scanning of the stained strips. Conventional statistical methods were used, including Student's t test for evaluation of the significance of differences and linear correlation coefficients.

Total MK activity ranged from 0.4 to 1.4×10^{-4} moles $\times g^{-1}$ wet weight $\times min^{-1}$ in the investigated muscle samples (n = 30). The corresponding range in muscle fiber composition was 15% to 64% FT fibers. In this material a significant linear correlation was found between MK activity and fiber distribution (r = 0.69, p <0.01), indicating higher activity values with an increase in percent FT fibers (Fig. 1). A similar relationship has earlier been shown in a smaller material [10].

The analysis of pooled FT and ST fibers showed a markedly higher MK activity in FT fibers. The FT/ST ratio in MK activity was about 2:1. Thus, the values obtained on mixed muscle homogenates were confirmed by the single fiber analysis, although the activity ratio was somewhat lower than indicated by the regression line in Figure 1.

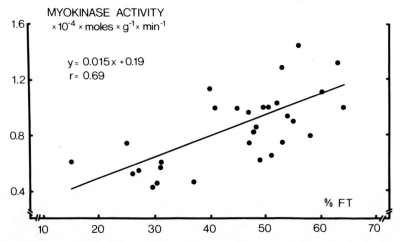

FIG. 1. Total activity of myokinase in the direction of ATP formation versus percent fast twitch (FT) muscle fibers in biopsy specimens obtained from m. vastus lateralis of 30 subjects.

Being able to conclude a higher MK activity in FT fibers, we wanted to examine if this difference was caused by a difference in MK isozyme pattern between the fiber types. Such a relationship had earlier been indicated for the enzyme lactate dehydrogenase in human muscle [8].

After isoelectric focusing of crude muscle homogenates, two bands were demonstrated by specific staining for MK (Fig. 2). Both bands, in the following called MK-1 and MK-2, were found in the alkaline region of the gel. The isoelectric points, pI:s, were on the average 9.8 and 8.9, respectively (Fig. 2). MK-1 was the predominating isozyme in all instances, constituting an average of about 75% of total staining density. The relative distribution of isozymes seemed, however, to vary with the fiber composition of the muscle specimens investigated. In a sample of 13 biopsies ranging from 25 to

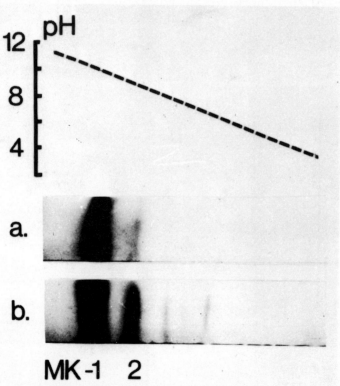

FIG. 2. Two prints specifically stained for myokinase (MK) are shown after isoelectric focusing. Muscle fiber compositions of the two samples were 25% FT (a), and 76% FT (b), respectively. The corresponding pH gradient is shown on top.

76 in percent FT fibers a linear correlation was present between the contribution of MK-2 to total stain density and percent FT fibers (r = 0.67, p <0.05) (Fig. 3).

The indicated higher proportion of MK-2 in FT as compared to ST muscle fibers was supported by similar experiments on pooled single FT and ST fibers. Relative to total stain density MK-2 constituted 27% in FT and 13% in ST fibers, respectively (Fig. 3).

Thus, not only total MK activity but also the relative distribution of MK isozymes appeared to be related to the metabolic profile of human skeletal muscle in terms of its fiber composition, which in turn is considered to be largely determined by genetic factors [8]. However, MK can also be influenced by environmental factors, such as physical training. Thus, eight weeks of sprint training resulted in an increase of MK activity with 20% (n = 4) [9], whereas systematic weight training for a corresponding time period caused a mean increase of 8% (n = 14) [10]. Studies are now in progress to investigate the possible effects of physical training also on the distribution of MK isozymes.

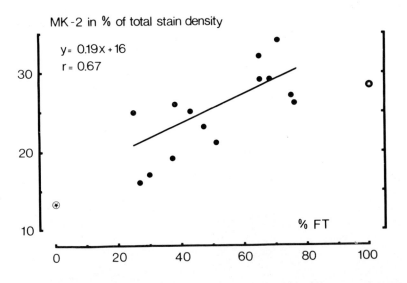

FIG. 3. The relative contribution of MK-2 to total stain density versus percent fast twitch (FT) muscle fibers in biopsy samples obtained from m. vastus lateralis of 13 subjects. Included are also the corresponding scanning results for pooled FT (✮) and ST (★) muscle fibers dissected out from freeze-dried biopsy material.

References

1. Atkinson, D.E.: The energy charge of the adenylate pool as a regulatory parameter. Interaction with feedback modifiers. Biochemistry 7:4030-4034, 1968.
2. Bergström, J.: Muscle electrolytes in man. Scand. J. Clin. Lab. Invest. Suppl. 68, 1962.
3. Essén, B., Jansson, E. Henriksson, J. et al: Metabolic characteristics of fibre types in human skeletal muscle. Acta Physiol. Scand. 95:153-165, 1975.
4. Gollnick, P.D., Sjödin, B., Karlsson, J. et al: Human soleus muscle: A comparison of fiber composition and enzyme activities with other leg muscles. Pflügers Arch. 348:247-255, 1974.
5. Lowry, O.H. and Passonneau, J.V.: A Flexible System of Enzymatic Analysis. New York:Academic Press, 1972.
6. Padykula, H.A. and Herman, E.: The specificity of the histochemical method for adenosine triphosphatase. J. Histochem. Cytochem. 3:170-195, 1955.
7. Radola, B.J.: Isoelectric focusing in layers of granulated gels. I. Thin-layer isoelectric focusing of proteins. Biochim. Biophys. Acta 295:412-428, 1973.
8. Sjödin, B.: Lactate dehydrogenase in human skeletal muscle. Acta Physiol. Scand. Suppl. 436, 1976.
9. Thorstensson, A., Sjödin, B. and Karlsson, J.: Enzyme activities and muscle strength after "sprint training" in man. Acta Physiol. Scand. 94:313-318, 1975.
10. Thorstensson, A., Hultén, B., von Döbeln, W. and Karlsson, J.: Effect of strength training on enzyme activities and fibre characteristics in human skeletal muscle. Acta Physiol. Scand. 96:392-398, 1976.

Glycogen Depletion in Human Skeletal Muscle as a Function of Four Fiber Types

J. A. Thomson, H. J. Green and M. E. Houston

A selective glycogen depletion pattern in human skeletal muscle in response to exercise of different kinds and intensities has been well demonstrated. This is important metabolic evidence for the usage of motor units and their recruitment. At submaximal workloads the slow twitch (ST) fibers are preferentially depleted whereas at supramaximal loads the fast twitch (FT) fibers are exhausted first.

The muscle fibers are routinely characterized by their myofibrillar ATPase activity in histochemical staining at pH 9.4 after preincubation at pH 10.3. Myosin ATPase activity, however, is quite sensitive to changes in the preincubation acidity. Brooke and Kaiser have based their system of fiber typing on this fact. Alkaline labile activity is found in type 1 fibers (ST above). Type 2 fibers (FT) show acid labile activity but of three identifiable responses which yield the fiber subclasses of 2A, 2B and 2C. Preincubation of serial sections of tissue at pH's 10.3, 4.3 and 4.6 allow the four fiber types to be differentiated in human skeletal muscle.

These fiber types histochemically demonstrate differing metabolic properties as seen using the stains NADH — tetrazolium reductase and alpha-glycerophosphate dehydrogenase. Type 1 fibers are highly oxidative with low glycolytic capacity. The type 2 fibers have high glycolytic capacity (type 2B being the highest) and oxidative properties below those of type 1 fibers but by differing amounts. The highest in capacity is the 2C fiber which Brooke and Kaiser view as a primitive or undifferentiated fiber: few are normally seen in tissue from adults. Less than 1% of the fibers identified in this study were type 2C. Hence the data with regard to this fiber are incomplete and won't be stressed further. The lowest oxidative capacity is found in type 2B fibers with type 2A fibers intermediate

J. A. Thomson, H. J. Green and M. E. Houston, Department of Kinesiology, University of Waterloo, Waterloo, Ontario, Canada.

in their capacity. The PAS stain for glycogen shows no differences between the four fiber types.

Very recently, workers in Copenhagen and Stockholm, applying the single-fiber techniques, confirmed biochemically the relationships just discussed.

It was of interest to see if the metabolic differences now recognized in the four fiber classifications were reflected in fiber utilization during exercise of different intensities. Glycogen depletion in human skeletal muscle with exercise was therefore reexamined considering four fiber types.

Eight fully formed, healthy male adults volunteered to perform bicycle ergometer work at a pedal rate of 60 rev min^{-1}. They were instructed to undertake no prolonged activity the day before testing and to report in a postabsorptive state. Four subjects worked submaximally at a load corresponding to 60% of their $\dot{V}O_2$ max while the remaining four performed supramaximal loads at 120% $\dot{V}O_2$max. The submaximal work was performed continuously for two hours. The supramaximal load was intermittent, one minute work to five minutes rest for ten work bouts or to exhaustion. Venous blood, muscle (vastus lateralis) and gas samples were collected at specified times during the work sessions. The blood samples were analyzed for glucose, lactate and plasma free fatty acid concentration and also for hematocrit readings. Muscle samples were analyzed for lactate, glucose 6-phosphate, glycogen and phosphagen concentrations. Other tissue samples were serially sectioned and stained histochemically as above.

The gas, blood and muscle data considered collectively reveal a detailed profile of subjects working in the manner expected.

The distribution of fiber types of the two groups are given in Table I. These data are in agreement with literature values.

One of the subjects exhibited no type 2B fibers. This finding, too, has been reported elsewhere.

Table I. The Fiber Distribution of the Subjects

| % Workload | No. of Fibers | | Percent Type Distribution* | | |
		1	2A	2B	2C
60	1548	46 (35-60)	43 (37-54)	10 (0-20)	1 (0-2)
120	2650	46 (32-55)	38 (29-47)	16 (8-26)	1 (0-1)
Total	4198	46	40	14	1

*Values are means with ranges in parentheses.

PAS histochemical sections were rated for the stain intensity of fibers whose type was known. Three levels of intensity were used; dark for the darkest staining fibers, light for the lightest and intermediate for all others in a particular section. While the ranking is subjective, the simplicity of this system probably minimized making gross errors in judgment. Others have expressed confidence in a more complex four level ranking. The disadvantage of the simpler system is that overall shifts in stain intensity are masked; i.e., an initially dark fiber would still be rated dark after a period of exercise which more properly should be classed "moderate." When fluctuations in the quality of the stain and the individual responses of the subjects to the work are considered, the more conservative system may be justified.

Fibers obtained at rest before each exercise condition were, with only minor exceptions, classed as PAS-dark staining, independent of fiber type.

Only for the end of exercise samples were definitive results obtained for all of the subjects.

In the 60% condition, the type 1 fibers were highly depleted as expected. Examples of each intensity rank could be found in the type 2 fibers. A much greater portion, however, of the type 2B fibers remained darkly stained while a great many 2A fibers were classed light.

This pattern was reversed in the 120% condition. Type 1 fibers were classed dark, or more accurately moderate, as were a few 2A fibers. Most of this type were intermediate with many light staining. The majority of the 2B fibers were light staining and none were ranked dark. Two subjects in this work condition did show a distinct depletion after five work bouts; these data confirm that the 2B fiber is preferentially depleted.

The results are summarized in Table II.

Eight type 2C fibers were found in the submaximal condition — one was full, four partially depleted and three depleted. The one 2C fiber seen in the supramaximal condition was full.

Andersen and Sjøgaard in a brief report published after our data were collected found that at 85% $\dot{V}O_2$ max the recruitment of fiber types was in the identical order as here reported: type 1, 2A and then 2B.

As the exercise intensity increased above maximal load, the order of depletion changes to type 2B first, then 2A, followed by type 1.

That this depletion order parallels the known metabolic properties of the three fiber types strongly supports availability of oxygen

Table II. Glycogen Depletion as a Function of
Fiber Type and Exercise Condition

| Work Condition | | PAS Staining Intensity (% of Fiber Type) | | |
(% $\dot{V}O_2$ max)	Fiber Type	Dark	Intermediate	Light
60	1	0	5	95
	2A	32	21	47
	2B	72	11	17
120-Bout 5	1	92	8	0
	2A	61	36	3
	2B	26	55	20
120-End of	1	87	13	0
Exercise	2A	8	67	25
	2B	0	24	76

as a governing factor in depletion patterns. By recognizing in man
principally three fiber types of varying oxidative capacities — type
1 > 2A > 2B, glycogen depletion in order of oxidative capacity in
man then is similar to that in animals such as the horse or rat.

It is concluded that the fiber types based on myofibrillar ATPase
activity do have physiological significance.

Bibliography

Andersen, P.: Acta Physiol. Scand. 95:203, 1975.
Andersen, P. and Sjogaard, G.: Acta Physiol. Scand. 96:26A, 1976
Brooke, M.H. and Kaiser, K.K.: Arch. Neurol. 23:369, 1970.
Costill, D.L., Gollnick, P.D., Jansson, E.C. et al: Acta Physiol. Scand. 89:374,
    1973.
Costill, D.L., Jansson, E., Gollnick, P.D. and Saltin, B.: Acta Physiol. Scand.
    91:475, 1974.
Eriksson, E.: Med. Sci. Sports 8:133, 1976.
Essen, B., Jansson, E., Henriksson, J. et al: Acta Physiol. Scand. 95:153, 1975.
Gollnick, P.D., Armstrong, R.B., Sembrowich, W.L. et al: J. Appl. Physiol.
    34:615, 1973.
Gollnick, P.D., Piehl, K. and Saltin, B.: J. Physiol. 241:45, 1974.
Jansson, E.: Acta Physiol. Scand. 95:47A, 1975.
Lindholm, A., Bjerneld, H. and Saltin, B.: Acta Physiol. Scand. 90:475, 1974.

Participation d'un réservoir lipidique intramusculaire au maintien de l'oxydation des acides gras libres dans le muscle squelettique humain au repos

Gilles R. Dagenais, Robert G. Tancredi et Kenneth L. Zierler

Introduction

Durant une période de jeûne d'au moins 8 heures, les acides gras libres constituent les principaux substrats du muscle squelettique humain au repos et pendant l'exercice. Cependant, les différentes voies maintenant l'oxydation de ces substrats n'ont pas encore été démontrées définitivement. La figure 1 illustre quatre hypothèses pouvant expliquer comment le muscle squelettique humain au repos peut maintenir le processus oxydatif des acides gras libres. Première-ment, les acides gras libres plasmatiques captés par le muscle squelettique au repos sont immédiatement et totalement oxydés. La seconde hypothèse est la même que la première, sauf qu'un réservoir lipidique constitué surtout de triglycérides, décrit chez l'animal [1-3], est ajouté. Cependant ce réservoir, pour cette deuxième hypothèse, ne participerait pas à l'oxydation des acides gras libres. Dans la troisième hypothèse, une partie des acides gras libres captés par le muscle squelettique au repos serait immédiatement oxydée tandis que l'autre partie serait incorporée sous forme de triglycérides dans un réservoir intramusculaire. Ces triglycérides seraient ultérieurement hydrolysés et deviendraient alors une source d'acides gras libres pour

Gilles R. Dagenais, Robert G. Tancredi et Kenneth L. Zierler, Institut de cardiologie de Québec, Québec, Canada et The Johns Hopkins University Hospital, Baltimore, Maryland, U.S.A.

L'étude sur laquelle cette publication est basée fut effectuée lorsque le docteur Dagenais était fellow des Fondations Canadiennes du coeur et le docteur Tancredi récipiendaire d'un fellowship du U.S. Public Health Service (1F03HE44504). Cette étude fut subventionnée par le N.I.H. (AM05524), la compagnie G.M. (15989) et le Muscular Dystrophy Associations Inc.

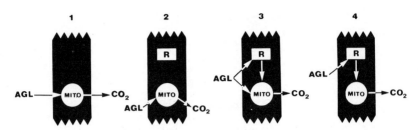

FIG. 1. Quatre hypothèses illustrant schématiquement les différentes voies maintenant le métabolisme oxydatif des acides gras libres (AGL). R = réservoir lipidique. MITO = mitochondrie (voir texte).

maintenir le processus oxydatif lipidique. Cette hypothèse a été émise par le groupe de Havel [4] et par le groupe de Malmendier [5] en se basant sur des données recueillies chez cinq sujets pour ces deux études. Cependant, ces deux groupes ont évalué l'oxydation des acides gras libres par le muscle squelettique au repos en mesurant le taux de CO_2 radioactif expiré. Cette approche n'est pas entièrement valide puisqu'elle représente le métabolisme oxydatif des acides gras libres provenant non seulement des muscles squelettiques au repos mais aussi des muscles en état d'exercice comme les muscles respiratoires et cardiaque. La quatrième hypothèse évoque l'existence d'un réservoir intramusculaire qui, d'une part s'approvisionne en acides gras libres du plasma et d'autre part est la source d'acides gras pour l'oxydation par le muscle squelettique.

Pour vérifier ces hypothèses nous avons tenté de répondre aux deux questions suivantes: (a) Quels arguments soutiennent l'existence d'un réservoir lipidique dans le muscle squelettique au repos? (b) S'il existe un tel réservoir, quel est son rôle dans le maintien de l'oxydation des acides gras libres par le muscle squelettique au repos? Les aspects méthodologiques et les résultats de cette étude ont été détaillés récemment [6]. Nous nous bornerons donc à fournir brièvement les détails essentiels.

Sujets et méthodes

Neuf étudiants, sans problème de santé et âgés de 21 à 31 ans acceptèrent de participer à ces expériences. Après une période de 12 heures de jeûne, les sujets furent couchés confortablement durant toute l'étude qui débutait toujours vers 9 h 00 A.M..

Sous anesthésie locale, une veine antécubitale profonde et une veine superficielle de l'avant-bras droit furent cathétérisées par voie transcutanée d'une façon rétrograde. L'artère humérale droite fut cannulée à l'aide d'une aiguille 18 comportant une double lumière. La lumière distale de l'aiguille artérielle servait à l'échantillonnage du sang artériel tandis que la lumière proximale était utilisée pour la perfusion continue. Chez 7 des 9 sujets, cette perfusion fut constituée d'une solution de sérum physiologique, de bleu d'Evans (T-1824) et de 2.5 μC d'acide oléique -1-^{14}C couplé à l'albumine humaine. Cette solution fut infusée à un débit constant de 0.1 ml/min. dans l'artère humérale. Chez les deux autres sujets, la même procédure fut effectuée mais l'acide oléique isotopique fut remplacé par du bicarbonate de soude contenant un carbone radioactif.

Pour obtenir les données métaboliques des muscles de l'avant-bras seulement, un brassard pédiatrique d'un appareil de pression fut appliqué au poignet et gonflé à une pression de 200 mmHg pendant chaque période expérimentale qui durait 20 à 30 minutes. Chaque expérience comporta 7 à 8 périodes expérimentales. Durant ces périodes, des échantillonnages de sang artériel et veineux furent obtenus simultanément à la 10 ième, 20 ième ou 30 ième minutes après l'inflation du brassard. Entre les périodes expérimentales le brassard était complètement dégonflé.

Sur chaque échantillon de sang artériel et veineux nous avons mesuré l'hématocrite, la concentration de bleu d'Evans et celle du CO_2 et de l'acide oléique radioactifs. Durant 4 périodes expérimentales différentes, nous avons effectué une collection supplémentaire de sang artériel et veineux pour la détermination d'acides gras libres totaux et individuels et du contenu d'oxygène et de CO_2. Le débit plasmatique de l'avant-bras fut évalué selon la technique d'indicateur de dilution par infusion constante selon l'approche décrite par Zierler.

Resultats

Le Tableau I indique les résultats moyens de l'hématocrite, du débit plasmatique et des données métaboliques pendant l'infusion continue d'acide oléique -1-^{14}C. Durant les 4 heures d'infusion, l'hématocrite, le débit plasmatique, la concentration artérielle de l'acide oléique isotopique et non isotopique et la consommation musculaire squelettique d'oxygène ne varient pas de façon significative. Il en est de même pour l'extraction de l'acide oléique -1-^{14}C, sauf durant la période de 211 à 240 minutes. Cependant, la captation de cet indicateur radioactif ne change pas d'une façon significative puisque le débit plasmatique est légèrement plus élevé durant cette période.

Durant l'infusion continue de l'acide oléique -1-^{14}C, nous ne documentons pas de CO_2 radioactif dans le sang veineux pendant les

Tableau I. Hématocrite, débit plasmatique et données métaboliques obtenus chez les sujets qui ont reçu une infusion constante d'acide oléique $-1-C^{14}$ (moyenne ± E.S.M.)

Temps (min	0-120	121-150	151-180	181-210	210-240	241-270
Hématocrite	41.8 ± 0.7	41.8 ± 0.9	41.4 ± 0.8	41.6 ± 0.7	41.3 ± 0.9	40.9 ± 0.8
Débit plasmatique (ml/min ^{1}/100g muscle)	2.4 ± 0.4	2.2 ± 0.4	2.1 ± 0.3	2.3 ± 0.4	2.8 ± 0.7	2.4 ± 0.6
Concentration artérielle de l'acide oléique -1-^{14}C (dpm/ml)	378 ± 52	382 ± 52	379 ± 78	341 ± 49	344 ± 93	436 ± 104
Extraction de l'acide oléique -1-^{14}C (%)	46 ± 3.5	46 ± 4.0	44 ± 3.5	41 ± 3.6	30 ± 3.4	42 ± 2.9
Concentration artérielle de l'acide oléique (μ mol/ml)	0.44 ± 0.09		0.40 ± 0.08		0.48 ± 0.04	
Consommation d'oxygène (μ mol/min ^{1}/100g muscle)	10.4 ± 1.7		9.8 ± 1.3		9.1 ± 0.8	
CO_2 provenant de l'oxydation de l'acide oléique (%)	7.1 ± 2.4		10.2 ± 2.6		19.3 ± 6.1	18.0 ± 0.6

30 premières minutes d'infusion. Par la suite, le CO_2 radioactif augmente lentement, mais progressivement jusqu'à la 150 ième minute d'infusion pour atteindre un plateau relativement stable vers la 200 ième minute (Tableau I).

Le Tableau II démontre le pourcentage d'oxygène consommé par le muscle squelettique qui est utilisé pour l'oxydation des lipides par les muscles de l'avant-bras chez les 7 sujets. Le quotient respiratoire des muscles de l'avant-bras se chiffre à 0.76 et implique donc que 80% de l'oxygène consommé par ces muscles est requis pour l'oxydation des lipides. Si tout l'acide oléique capté par le muscle est immédiatement et totalement oxydé, il existerait un déficit de 17% d'oxygène au niveau du muscle. Cependant, d'après la production de CO_2 radioactif, toutes les molécules d'acide oléique ne sont pas oxydées. En effet, après 3 heures d'infusion, seulement 15% de l'acide oléique capté est oxydé nécessitant 17% de l'oxygène consommé par le muscle squelettique.

Tableau II. Pourcentage (%) d'oxygène consommé par le muscle squelettique
requis pour l'oxydation des lipides (moyenne ± E.S.M.)

Quotient respiratoire musculaire (0.76 ± 0.06)	80 ± 22%
Pourcentage d'O_2 consommé, requis pour oxyder complètement tout l'acide oléique capté par le muscle	117 ± 23%
Pourcentage d'O_2 consommé, requis pour l'oxydation réelle de l'acide oléique	17 ± 5%

Si l'on émet l'hypothèse que les acides gras libres doivent passer
par un réservoir lipidique avant d'être oxydés, on devrait observer
une oxydation continue de l'acide oléique après la cessation de
l'infusion de l'acide oléique isotopique. Chez 3 sujets, l'infusion
continue de l'acide oléique isotopique est cessé après 200 minutes.
On observe durant les 100 minutes qui suivent la cessation de
l'infusion, une production de CO_2 radioactif qui est à un niveau
d'environ 10 à 20% inférieure à la valeur observée pendant l'infusion
(Fig. 2). La persistance de la production de $^{14}CO_2$ ne résulte pas de

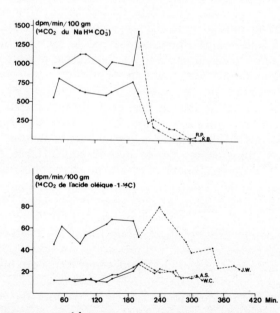

FIG. 2. Production de $^{14}CO_2$ par les muscles squelettiques de l'avant-bras
durant la perfusion continue (ligne continue) et après la perfusion (ligne brisée).
La partie du haut représente l'expérience effectuée chez 2 sujets qui ont reçu
une perfusion de bicarbonate isotopique. La partie du bas illustre l'expérience de
la perfusion de l'acide oléique $-1-^{14}C$ chez 3 sujets.

la recirculation de l'acide oléique isotopique lié à l'albumine plasmatique ou incorporé dans des triglycérides plasmatiques. Serait-il possible que cette persistance de la production de $^{14}CO_2$ provienne d'un long transport (transit time) tissulaire du $^{14}CO_2$? Pour refuter ou confirmer cette possibilité, 2 sujets reçoivent une infusion continue de bicarbonate isotopique au lieu d'acide oléique -1-^{14}C. Pendant l'infusion continue de bicarbonate isotopique on obtient un plateau de la production de $^{14}CO_2$ après 40 minutes. Soixante minutes après la cessation de cette dernière infusion, la production du $^{14}CO_2$ diminue de plus de 90%. Cette dernière valeur contraste avec la baisse de 15% observée après l'infusion de l'acide oléique $-1-^{14}C$.

Discussion

Les résultats de la présente étude démontrent (a) qu'il existe un réservoir de lipides dans le muscle squelettique humain au repos et (b) que ce réservoir lipidique est une source d'acides gras maintenant la métabolisme oxydatif lipidique au muscle squelettique.

Les évidences plaidant en faveur de l'existence d'un tel réservoir lipidique dans le muscle squelettique, reposent particulièrement sur la quantité d'acides gras libres captés par le muscle. Si toutes les molécules d'acide oléique captées par le muscle étaient immédiatement et totalement oxydées, une telle oxydation requierrait 117% de l'oxygène consommé par le muscle. Il faut mentionner que l'acide oléique constitue 43% des acides gras totaux mesurés (C:12 à C:18-2). La captation et l'oxydation de ces autres acides gras ne sont probablement pas différentes de celles de l'acide oléique. Donc, tous les acides gras libres captés par le muscle squelettique ne sont pas totalement et immédiatement oxydés puisque plus de 200% de l'oxygène consommé serait nécessaire pour effectuer une telle oxydation. Ces observations et celles rapportées chez l'animal [1-3] évoquent que la plupart des acides gras captés s'incorporent, en présende de l'α-glycérophosphate, sous forme de triglycérides et se localisent dans des réservoirs lipidiques situés près des mitochondries.

Ce réservoir serait la source d'acides gras libres qui maintiendrait le métabolisme oxydatif du muscle squelettique. Le calcul du quotient respiratoire musculaire squelettique lors de cette étude, implique que 80% de l'oxygène consommé par le muscle est utilisé pour l'oxydation des lipides. Or, seulement 17% de l'oxygène consommé sert à l'oxydation de l'acide oléique capté. Comme les autres acides gras libres se "metabolisent" comme l'acide oléique, 40% de l'oxygène serait utilisé pour l'oxydation de tous les acides gras libres captés par le muscle squelettique au respos. Si l'on tient compte du quotient respiratoire musculaire, il faut postuler qu'il existe une autre source des acides gras libres oxydés requiérant le 40% d'oxygène consommé restant. Cette autre source d'acides gras oxydés provient de l'hydrolyse de triglycérides emmagasinés dans les réservoirs lipidiques. Donc, les évidences actuelles indiquent qu'il existe un réservoir lipidique dans le muscle squelettique humain au repos et que ce réservoir joue un rôle actif dans le métabolisme lipidique oxydatif en étant la source de substrats.

La présente étude révèle de plus la possibilité d'une autre facette. Les acides gras libres captés par le muscle squelettique ne sont pas oxydés immédiatement. Avec la préparation utilisée, la captation musculaire squelettique d'acide oléique -1-^{14}C est stable après 10 à 15 minutes d'infusion continue. Cependant, la production de $^{14}CO_2$ n'est pas détectée dans les premières 30 minutes d'infusion. De plus, l'oxydation de l'acide oléique -1-^{14}C persiste à un haut taux après l'arrêt de l'infusion. Les résultats des expériences avec le bicarbonate radioactif indiquent que la persistance de la production de $^{14}CO_2$ ne résulte pas d'une dilution de $^{14}CO_2$ dans le "pool" de CO_2 de l'avant-bras. Il est fort probable que les acides gras libres captés par le muscle squelettique soient orientés vers les réservoirs lipidiques et oxydés ultérieurement. Ces réservoirs lipidiques ont sûrement un turnover lent lorsque le muscle est au repos. En effet, pour retracer tout le ^{14}C provenant d'une infusion de 3 heures d'acide oléique, il faudrait effectuer un échantillonnage pendant au moins une semaine. Cependant, durant l'exercice, le turnover dans ces réservoirs lipidiques est sûrement accéléré.

En conclusion, cette étude démontre que la plupart sinon tous les acides gras captés par le muscle squelettique au repos ne sont pas oxydés immédiatement, mais entrent probablement dans un réservoir lipidique intramusculaire qui a un turnover lent. Ce réservoir assurerait par hydrolyse des triglycérides la source immédiate et continue des substrats lipidiques oxydés.

Références

1. George, J.C. and Naik, R.M.: Relative distribution and chemical nature of the fuel store of the two types of fibres in the pectoralis major muscle of the pigeon. Nature (Lond.) 181:709-711, 1958.
2. Volk, M.E., Millington, R.H. and Weinhouse, S.: Oxidation of endogenous fatty acids of rat tissues in vitro. J. Biol. Chem. 195:493-501, 1952.
3. Neptune, E.M. Jr., Sudduth, H.C., Foreman, D.R. and Fash, F.J.: Phospholipid and triglyceride metabolism of excised rat diaphragm and the role of these lipids in fatty acid uptake and oxidation. J. Lipid Res. 1:229-235, 1960.

4. Havel, R.J., Naimark, A. and Borchgrevink, C.F.: Turnover rate and oxidation of free fatty acids of blood plasma in man during exercise: Studies during continuous infusion of palmitate -1-^{14}C. J. Clin. Invest. 42:1054-1063, 1963.

5. Malmendier, C.L., Delcroix, C. and Berman, M.: Interrelations in the oxidative metabolism of free fatty acids, glucose, and glycerol in normal and hyperlipemic patients. A compartmental model. J. Clin. Invest. 54:461-476, 1974.

6. Dagenais, G.R., Tancredi, R.G. and Zierler, K.L.: Free fatty oxidation by forearm muscle at rest, and evidence for an intramuscular lipid pool in the human forearm. J. Clin. Invest. 58:421-431, 1976.

Quantitative Aspects of the Anaerobic Capacity of Perfused Rat Hind Quarter

H. G. Westra, E. J. de Haan and A. de Haan

Introduction

Measurement of the lactate concentration in muscle biopsy, venous or capillary blood is generally used to obtain information about the anaerobic muscle metabolism [1]. For example, the rate of lactate production is considered to be a good measure of the anaerobic capacity of the muscle, whereas the disappearance of lactate from the blood is determined to follow the recovery of the muscle after a period of work. Furthermore, the effect of physical training on muscle metabolism is often described in terms of lactate production during exercise. However, in most of these experiments measurements are performed on volunteers or intact animals. These measurements suffer from the disadvantage that the system is complicated by the presence of other organs (e.g., nonactivated muscle, heart, liver) that may even utilize metabolites like lactate. Furthermore, it is often not possible to obtain venous blood directly draining the active muscle, thus a direct comparison between the intra- and extracellular lactate concentration cannot be made. Finally, in these experiments the possibilities to influence the metabolism or to create a fixed condition are very limited.

Therefore, we decided to follow the metabolism of muscle during artificial perfusion. In this paper we present preliminary data on experiments with a perfused rat hind quarter. Anaerobic metabolism measured as lactate production is studied under conditions where it is expected to be stimulated, i.e., when oxidative energy production is blocked either by inhibition of the mitochondrial respiratory chain by azide (N_3^-) or by the uncoupler of oxidative phosphorylation 2,4-dinitrophenol. By means of freeze-clamping of the quadriceps muscle it was possible under those conditions to determine the intracellular lactate concentration and the concentration gradient

H. G. Westra, E. J. de Haan and A. de Haan, Coronel Laboratory and Laboratory of Biochemistry, University of Amsterdam, Amsterdam, The Netherlands.

345

over the cell membrane. Experiments on the effect of electric stimulation and of training on the lactate production under various conditions are in progress.

Methods

Surgical Preparation of the Hind Quarter

Male Wistar rats weighing 165 to 175 gm were used. The animals were fed ad libitum. Rats were anesthetized by intraperitoneal injection of nembutal. Before operation, the rats were heparinized via a tail vein. The operation technique used was partly according to Ruderman [6] as modified by M. Schwenen (personal communication). In essence in this method the hind quarter is infused via the abdominal aorta and the perfusate is collected from the inferior vena cava. Using this technique no loss of perfusate during the experiments, lasting 90 minutes, could be measured. The time of operation until cannulation of the aorta and vena cava was about 25 minutes; the cannulation time was 0.5 to 3.0 minutes.

Perfusion Medium

The standard perfusion medium consisted of Krebs-Henseleit bicarbonate buffer (118.5 mM NaCl, 4.74 mM KCl, 2.54 mM $CaCl_2$, 1.19 mM KH_2PO_4, 1.19 mM $MgSO_4$ and 25 mM $NaHCO_3$) containing 2.5% dialyzed bovine serum albumin (BSA), 10 to 15 mM glucose and three to seven weeks aged human erythrocytes, washed five times (Hb about 5 mM). Some lactate was always present at the beginning of the perfusions, originating from the erythrocytes. Other additions are indicated in the figures and tables. The medium was gassed with O_2, CO_2 and N_2. Arterial P_{O_2} was kept at 150 to 250 mm Hg and the P_{CO_2} at about 40 mm Hg during the whole experiment. The pH was kept constant during the experiment by addition of $NaHCO_3$ using an automatic titrator.

Perfusion Set-up

A scheme of the perfusion set-up is given in Figure 1. The flow through the hind quarter of the rat was fixed at 12 ml/min. After a pre-perfusion of 15 minutes, in which the blood of the rat was washed out, at zero time the hind quarter was connected with the recirculating perfusion system, containing 150 ml perfusate. The first 20 to 30 minutes were used to equilibrate the flow, P_{O_2}, P_{CO_2} and pH at the desired levels. The perfusions were carried out in a thermostatically controlled cabinet at 37 C, relative humidity 30% to 40%.

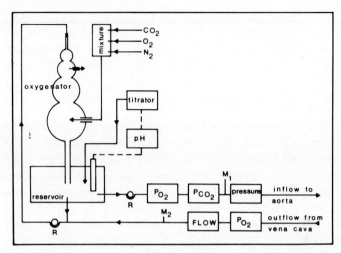

FIG. 1. Scheme of the perfusion set-up used for rat hind quarter. pH, P_{O_2}, P_{CO_2}, flow and "blood" pressure are registrated at points given in the scheme. R = roller pump; M = points, where samples were taken: M_1 = arterial; M_2 = venous. The perfusions were carried out in a thermostatically controlled cabinet at 37 C, relative humidity 30% to 40%.

Criteria of Tissue Integrity

As criterion for tissue integrity served the "blood" pressure during the whole experiment. The mean blood pressure at the beginning of the experiment was 70 (63-74) mm Hg. The increase in blood pressure towards the end of the experiment varied only from 4 to 28 mm Hg. No cyanosis was observed.

In most experiments at the beginning and at the end the LDH activity in the perfusate without erythrocytes was determined. No changes could be found.

At the beginning and at the end of each experiment the hemoglobin concentration of the perfusate after separation of the erythrocytes was determined. No detectable hemolysis took place.

Although on the basis of these criteria the perfused muscle apparently was not damaged, it must be mentioned that at the end of the perfusions in the presence of 2,4-dinitrophenol the muscle appeared edematic in a cross section.

Analytical Methods

Samples, 1.3 ml, were taken from the perfusate at points M_1 and M_2 before and after the hind quarter, respectively (Fig. 1). The samples were directly centrifuged (Eppendorf micro centrifuge) to remove the erythrocytes. From the supernatant 0.6 ml was taken and added to 0.06 ml 70% ice-cooled $HClO_4$. After mixing followed by removal of the precipitate by centrifugation 0.4 ml of the supernatant was neutralized to pH 6-7. The samples were kept at -18 C. Lactate was determined enzymatically with NAD^+ and lactate dehydrogenase [3].

Freeze-clamping

In some experiments the muscle metabolism was fixed by rapid freeze-clamping of the tissue. For this purpose the skin of the upper limb was removed, the quadriceps muscle was dissected free from the patella without damaging the tissue. The muscle was clamped in a pair of clamps and precooled in liquid nitrogen. The freeze-clamped material was ground in a precooled mortar with continuous addition of liquid nitrogen and quickly weighed at O C. Subsequently, the material was homogenized at 0 C in 10% $HClO_4$ using a Potter-Elvehjem homogenizer. After centrifugation and neutralization the extract was analyzed.

Measurement of the Sucrose Impermeable Space

In a series of experiments (n = 12) $[^{14}C]$-labeled sucrose and $[^3H]H_2O$ was added to the perfusate in order to determine the sucrose impermeable space, which is equivalent to the extracellular space. The experiments lasted for 20 minutes, in which time sucrose is known to be divided equally over the extracellular fluid, but not to permeate the cells; $[^3H]H_2O$ diffuses in all compartments. In these experiments no preflow was used. From the ratio of $^{14}C/^3H$ in the perfusate and the freeze-clamped muscle after 20 minutes the sucrose impermeable space, i.e., the extracellular space, was calculated.

Weight of the Perfused Muscle Mass

From the dilution of $[^3H]H_2O$ in several experiments the total weight of the perfused tissue (including skin, bone, etc.) was calculated to be 35 to 40 gm for rats weighing 170 to 190 gm. These measurements were confirmed by direct weighing of the perfused tissue [6]. According to Ruderman [6] 77% of this total tissue consists of muscle. Thus we have used an amount of 30 gm muscle mass in our calculations.

Results and Discussion

Rate of Lactate Production in the Presence
of an Uncoupler of the Oxidative Phosphorylation

2,4-Dinitrophenol (DNP) is known to uncouple the mito-chondrial respiratory chain phosphorylation. This results in (1) lack of ATP synthesis via the oxidative phosphorylation whereas the respiratory chain is not inhibited, so that oxygen consumption is not depressed and (2) the introduction of an ATPase activity in the mitochondria with concomitant depression of the cellular ATP concentration. Thus, in the presence of DNP the production of ATP can take place only via glycolysis. Pyruvate as a product of glycolysis can either be converted to lactate or be oxidized by the mito-chondria.

In Figure 2 and Table I the results of experiments on lactate production in the presence of 0.33 mM DNP are presented. As expected, addition of DNP caused an increase in the lactate production due to stimulation of the glycolysis. The rate of lactate formation (0.61 μmol/min/gm wet weight) is an underestimation of the rate of glycolysis, since part of the pyruvate could be oxidized by the mitochondria under this condition.

From the results of curve 2 of Figure 2 it is clear that the rate of lactate formation did not decline as the extracellular lactate

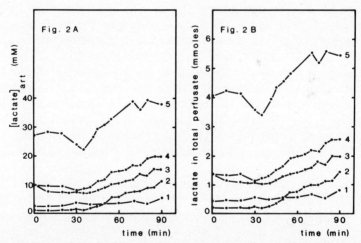

FIG. 2. Effect of 2,4-dinitrophenol (DNP) on lactate production in perfused hind quarter of the rat. Thirty minutes after a perfusion with Krebs-Henseleit buffer, including 10-15 mM glucose, 2.5% bovine serum albumin, aged human erythrocytes (Hb about 5 mM) and, if added, lactate, 0.33 mM DNP was added. In the perfusions the pH was kept constant at pH 7.35 except for curve 3, where it was 7.00. Samples were taken and analyzed as described under "Methods." Perfusions: (1) control without DNP; (2) no lactate; (3) 10 mM lactate, pH 7.00; (4) 10 mM lactate, pH 7.35; (5) 25 mM lactate. *Fig.* 2A; actual arterial lactate concentration: *Fig.* 2B; total lactate production after correction for sampling.

Table I. Rate of Lactate Production in Perfused Hind Quarter of the Rat
in Presence of 2,4-Dinitrophenol (DNP)

Additions	Rate of Lactate Production (μmoles/min/gm Wet Weight)
None	0.14
DNP (0.33 mM)	0.61
DNP, lactate (10 mM), pH 7.00	0.52
DNP, lactate (10 mM)	0.79
DNP, lactate (25 mM)	1.03
DNP, lactate (25 mM), initial rate	1.67

Rates were calculated from the perfusions described in Figure 2. For the perfusion
with the high lactate concentration the initial rate (calculated between 30 and 70
min) is also presented. The wet weight of the perfused muscle mass was taken as
30 gm per rat (see text).

concentration increased, indicating that glycolysis was not inhibited
by these lactate concentrations. Since during intermittent exercise
blood lactate concentrations of maximally about 30 mM were
reached [1, 2], we determined the rate of lactate production in the
presence of DNP and extra lactate added to the perfusate. In the
experiments of curves 4 and 5 of Figure 2 the effects of addition of
10 and 25 mM lactate were investigated. From the rates of lactate
formation it can be concluded that increasing extracellular lactate
concentration did not inhibit the initial rate of lactate production
under these conditions. In contrast even a stimulation of lactate
formation was found. Only at very high extracellular lactate
concentration (above 35 mM) lactate production leveled off.

These results are not in agreement with the experiments of
Hermansen [2] with human subjects who performed intermittent
exercise until exhaustion. In these experiments the rate of lactate
production already slows down at concentrations of 15 to 20 mM.
One principal difference between the experiments of Hermansen [2]
and ours is that in the perfusion system it was possible to keep the
extracellular pH constant, whereas in the in vivo experiments there
was a simultaneous decrease in pH during exercise. In curve 3 of
Figure 2 it is shown that lowering of the extracellular pH to a value
of 7.0 causes an inhibition of the lactate production of 34%, without
changing the linearity of the process (see also Table I). These results
are in agreement with experiments of Mainwood et al [5] with
isolated superfused frog muscle.

Rate of Lactate Production in the Presence of an Inhibitor of the Mitochondrial Respiratory Chain

Azide is known to inhibit cytochrome c oxidase, the terminal enzyme of the respiratory chain. Thus in the presence of azide pyruvate oxidation and concomitant ATP production is inhibited. In Figure 3 and Table II the results of perfusions in the presence of azide are presented. In a titration with azide (curve 2 of Figure 3) it appeared that maximal lactate production was obtained at azide concentrations of 3 to 6.5 mM; under these conditions some oxygen consumption was still detectable. As expected the rate of lactate formation in the presence of azide was higher than in the presence of DNP under otherwise comparable conditions. Further addition of DNP did not influence lactate production significantly (curve 3). At high initial lactate concentration (curve 4) initially a rapid lactate extrusion was found, followed by a slower increase after about 40 minutes at an extracellular concentration of 30 to 35 mM. Therefore, the effect of added lactate is difficult to interpret.

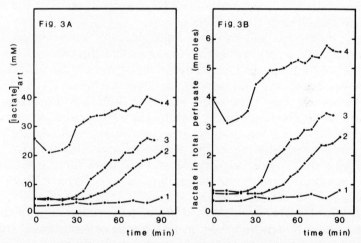

FIG. 3. Effect of azide (N_3^-) with and without 2,4-dinitrophenol (DNP) on lactate production. Perfusions were performed as described in Figure 2, except that azide was added instead of DNP. Perfusions: (1) control without azide; (2) no lactate, titration with azide; 2.3 mM at 30 min, 3.1 mM at 40 min, 6.5 mM at 50 min, 8.8 mM at 55 min, 11.6 mM at 60 min and 14.5 mM at 68 min; (3) no lactate, 3.2 mM azide at 20 min and 6.5 mM azide at 28 min followed by 0.33 mM DNP at 55 min; (4) 25 mM lactate, 3.2 mM azide added after 20 min; *Fig. 3A*: actual arterial lactate concentration; *Fig. 3B*: total lactate production corrected for sampling.

Table II. Rate of Lactate Production in Perfused Hind Quarter of the Rat
in Presence of Azide (N_3^-)

Additions	Rate of Lactate Production ($\mu moles/min/gm$ Wet Weight)
None	0.14
Azide (6.5 mM)	1.35
Azide (6.5 mM) + DNP (0.33 mM)	0.92
Azide (3.2 mM), lactate (25 mM)	1.05
Azide (3.2 mM), lactate (25 mM), initial rate	2.65

Rates were calculated from the perfusions described in Figure 3. For the perfusion with the high lactate concentration the initial rate (calculated between 20 and 40 min) is also presented. The wet weight of the perfused muscle mass was taken as 30 gm per rat (see text).

Since we wanted to estimate the lactate gradient across the cell membrane, in some of the experiments presented in Figures 2 and 3 the perfused muscle of the hind quarter was freeze-clamped as described under "Methods." Lactate was determined in the muscle extract as well as in the perfusate.

In order to be able to calculate the intracellular lactate concentration, it was necessary to determine the value of the intra- and extracellular space of the muscle. For this purpose a method was adopted, based on the assumption that the intracellular space is equivalent to the sucrose-impermeable part of the tissue. This procedure is described under "Methods." Measurements, under our conditions, in 12 leg muscles (six perfusions) resulted in a mean sucrose impermeable space ($\equiv$ extracellular space) of 13% (range 12.5% to 15%). For our calculations we used for the total water content of the muscle the generally accepted figure of 80% of the muscle weight.

In Table III the results of the freeze-clamp experiments are shown. Lactate concentration in the muscle was calculated from the lactate content of the freeze-clamped muscle applying the percentages mentioned. The values given in column 4 of Table III are of the same order of magnitude as those obtained from biopsies of working muscle [2, 4]. From Table III it appears that only in the presence of DNP and 25 mM lactate the intracellular lactate concentration is somewhat higher than the concentration in the perfusate. In all other measurements the intracellular concentration of lactate is found to be lower than that in the perfusate.

Table III. Lactate and pH Gradient Across the Cell Membrane

Expt.	[Lactate] in Perfusate (mM)	Lactate in Total Muscle (μmoles/g ww)	Intracellular [Lactate] (mM)	F	ΔpH	pH_in
1	37.7	31	38.9	1.03	+0.02	7.37
		33	41.8	1.11	+0.04	7.39
2	25.3	14.5	17.1	0.68	−0.17	7.18
		16	19.2	0.76	−0.12	7.23
3	38.1	23	27.3	0.72	−0.14	7.21

The intracellular lactate concentration was determined after freeze-clamping as described in the text. The intracellular lactate concentration in column 4 is calculated from the lactate content in column 3 by assuming a water content of 80% and correcting for an extracellular space of 13%. The gradient [lactate] intracellular/[lactate] extracellular is in column 5 expressed as F. For calculation of ΔpH and pH_in see text.

Conditions: Expt. 1: DNP, 25 mM lactate (curve 5 of Fig. 2); Expt. 2: azide, DNP (curve 3 of Fig. 3); Expt. 3: azide, 25 mM lactate (curve 4 of Fig. 3); in Expts 1 and 2 both leg muscles were analyzed separately.

In column 5 of Table III these results are presented as a concentration gradient (F) which is slightly larger than 1 in the first two measurements, but distinctly smaller in the other cases. These results are unexpected, since it is generally assumed that due to a rapid diffusion of lactic acid the concentration gradient over the cell membrane will be equal to or at most somewhat higher than 1. However, in in vivo experiments a gradient of about 1.5 is found, the difference being explained by the fact that in these experiments the extracellular lactate concentration is underestimated due to a dilution of lactate by blood draining nonactivated muscle fibers [1]. In our experiments the metabolism of *all* muscle fibers is influenced by azide or DNP; thus, this dilution phenomenon does not take place.

It is mostly accepted that the lactate diffuses freely across the cell membrane in the uncharged form. If the cell membrane is freely permeable to the uncharged form of lactate and not to the ionized species, the equilibrium distribution of the acid is characterized by an equal concentration of the uncharged form on both sides of the membrane. According to the Henderson-Hasselbalch relation, a pH differential will result in an unequal concentration of the charged species and thus in a difference in total concentration of the acid in the intra- and extracellular spaces. The ratio of internal to external concentrations of the acid is then related to the intracellular pH (pH_{in}) by the formula:

$$pH_{in} = pK_a + \log \left[\frac{[A]_{in}}{[A]_{out}} (1 + 10^{pH_{out} - pK_a}) - 1 \right] \text{, where}$$

pK_a = dissociation constant of the acid (for lactate pK_a = 3.8)
$[A]_{in}$ = concentration of acid in intracellular space
$[A]_{out}$= concentration of acid in extracellular space

If the pK_a of the acid is much lower than pH_{out}, as is the case with lactate, the relation is reduced to

$$pH_{in} = pH_{out} + \log \frac{[A]_{in}}{[A]_{out}}$$

Substituting for $\dfrac{[A]_{in}}{[A]_{out}} = F$ and for $pH_{in} - pH_{out} = \Delta pH$

the equation will become:
$$\Delta pH = \log F.$$

From our experiments we have calculated the ΔpH across the membrane (Table III, column 6), and from that the intracellular pH at a pH_{out} = 7.35 (column 7).

The results of experiments 2 and 3 indicate that if we convert the observed lactate gradient into an intracellular pH, values are obtained that lie within the experimentally found range for muscle [7], although most of these measurements indicate a somewhat lower pH_{in}. The latter would suggest a still smaller value for F than those presented in Table III. The lack of pH gradient in the presence of DNP and lactate (Experiment 1) is under investigation.

References

1. Gollnick, P.D. and Hermansen, L.: *In* Wilmore, J.H. (ed.): Exercise and Sport Sciences Reviews, Vol. 1. New York and London:Academic Press, 1973, pp. 1-45.
2. Hermansen, L.: *In* Pernow, B. and Saltin, B. (eds.): Muscle Metabolism During Exercise. New York:Plenum Press, 1971, pp. 401-407.
3. Hohorst, H.J.: *In* Bergmeyer, H.U. (ed.): Methoden der Enzymatischen Analyse. Verlag Chemie, Weinheim, Bergstrasse, 1970, pp. 1425-1430.
4. Karlsson, J.: *In* Pernow, B. and Saltin, B. (eds.): Muscle Metabolism During Exercise. New York:Plenum Press, 1971, pp. 383-394.
5. Mainwood, G.W., Worsley-Brown, P. and Paterson, R.A.: Can. J. Physiol. Pharmacol. 50:143-155, 1972.
6. Ruderman, N.B., Houghton, C.R.S. and Hems, R.: Biochem. J. 124:639-651, 1971.
7. Waddell, W.J. and Bates, R.G.: Physiol. Rev. 49:285-330, 1969.

Relationship Between Blood Constituents and the Metabolism of Glycogen and Protein in Muscle and Liver

Gerhard Gerber, Hannelore Böhme, Gerhard Feustel,
Heinz Langer and Rudolf Lorenz

Long-lasting physical exercise at low intensity produces in man and animals (1) a decline of the glycogen content in working muscles and in the liver, (2) a diminished rate of protein synthesis and an acceleration of gluconeogenesis, (3) an increased rate of fat mobilization and ketone body formation and (4) a drop of the glucose and insulin levels in blood. Due to different experimental conditions in the various laboratories a critical examination into details of the data published is not possible. The present investigations with rats were performed under standardized conditions to obtain information about concomitant changes in metabolites of blood and tissues.

Male rats of a Wistar strain weighing about 250 gm swam at 32 C two hours per day for two weeks. At the day of the experiment the animals swam up to six hours and were decapitated at several terms of the swimming and recovery period. Glycogen was extracted from M. rectus, the red and white portion of M. vastus, M. soleus and from liver according to the procedure of Good et al [3] and determined chemically according to the anthrone principle. Lactate [6] and beta-hydroxybutyrate [14] of blood were assayed using the optical test and the concentration of plasma insulin was measured radio-immunologically [5]. Uniformly labeled ^{14}C-glucose and ^{14}C-lysine were taken for the determination of the formation rate of glycogen and protein, respectively, in liver and muscles.

Figure 1 shows the relationship between the immunoreactive insulin in plasma and the concentration of glycogen in liver and M. vastus. The degradation of glycogen in both organs is in accord with

Gerhard Gerber, Hannelore Böhme, Gerhard Feustel, Heinz Langer and Rudolf Lorenz, Forschungsinstitut für Körperkultur und Sport, Leipzig, German Democratic Republic.

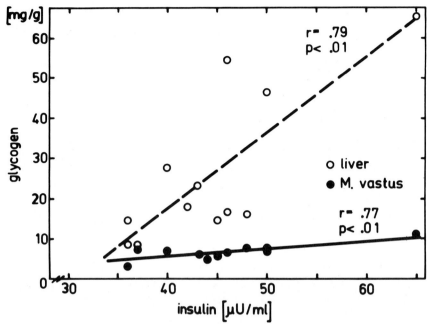

FIG. 1. Relationship between immunoreactive insulin in plasma and the glycogen level of liver and muscle.

earlier observations of Leschkewitsch [9] and Armstrong et al [1] on animals and of Hultman et al [7, 8] and Edgerton et al [2] in man. The drop of insulin in the course of exercise was discussed by several authors [4, 10, 13, 15]. It is obvious from the data of Figure 1 that there is a proportional decrease between glycogen and insulin. However, the slope is very much steeper in liver. In this way the organism may utilize the pool of liver glycogen for the energy metabolism in muscle and thereby spare the glycogen in muscle. The molecular mechanism of the greater sensitivity of liver glycogen with respect to changes in insulin concentration is not clear. It may be due to a different number of insulin receptors at the cellular membrane or to different kinetic properties of the phosphorylase. In this investigation there were no differences in the glycogen/insulin ratio among the various muscles studied.

The decrease in the rate of protein synthesis in liver and muscle during a four-hour swimming load (Fig. 2) is in harmony with the observations of Zimmer et al after one hour of exercise [17]. Figure 3 demonstrates the proportional relation between the diminution of glycogen and the rate of protein synthesis. This relation may be

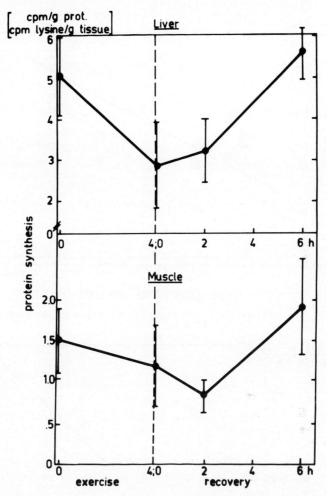

FIG. 2. Rate of protein synthesis in liver and muscle after swimming load.

explained by the results of Wagle et al [16]. These authors found no stimulation in amino acid incorporation into protein of rat liver hepatocytes by insulin when the cells contained low or no glycogen.

The enhanced availability of amino acids on account of the lower protein synthesis and the accelerated rate of proteolysis and lipolysis which were not determined here are accompanied by an increased formation of ketone bodies in the liver [12]. According to Parilla et al [11] approximately 85% of the ketone bodies produced in the liver are transported via the blood circulation in the form of beta-hydroxybutyrate. Thus this parameter reflects the production

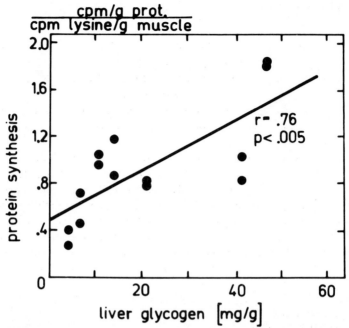

FIG. 3. Dependence of the rate of protein synthesis on liver glycogen.

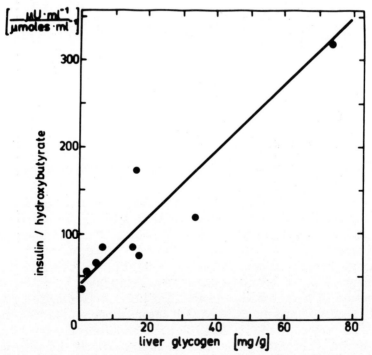

FIG. 4. Relation between the insulin/beta-hydroxybutyrate quotient in blood and the glycogen content of liver.

of ketone bodies and it was chosen for the determinations. A quotient was made from the plasma concentrations of insulin and beta-hydroxybutyrate and it was related to the glycogen level in liver. As it is presented in Figure 4 these parameters show a correlation. Therefore, the possibility increases for estimating the glycogen state in the liver by determining both of these blood constituents.

Owing to the activating effect of insulin on the glycogen synthesis this hormone may be assumed to play an important role in the recovery of the carbohydrate pools following exercise. We injected uniformly labeled ^{14}C-glucose into the animals after the swimming load and determined the rate of its incorporation into glycogen of M. rectus and M. vastus in dependence on the level of immunoreactive insulin in plasma (Fig. 5). There is no indication of elevated glucose incorporation at higher insulin levels. In the first

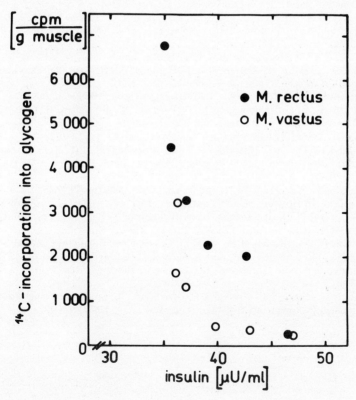

FIG. 5. Comparison of the rate of ^{14}C-glucose incorporation into muscle glycogen and the plasma insulin level during the early recovery period.

hour of the recovery period the maximal rate of glucose incorporation was detected, although in this phase the insulin level remains low.

It is concluded from these data that insulin and beta-hydroxybutyrate are appropriate for estimation of the glycogen depletion and the inhibition of protein synthesis in liver immediately after long-lasting exercise. One can not draw conclusions about the synthesis and state of glycogen in the recovery period from the level of immunoreactive insulin in plasma.

References

1. Armstrong, R.B., Saubert, C.W., Sembrowich, W.L. et al: *In* Howald, H. and Poortmans, J.R. (eds.): Metabolic Adaptation to Prolonged Physical Exercise. Basel:Birkhäuser Verlag, 1975, p. 397.
2. Edgerton, V.R., Essen, B., Saltin, B. and Simpson, D.R.: *In* Howald, H. and Poortmans, J.R. (eds.): Metabolic Adaptation to Prolonged Physical Exercise. Basel:Birkhäuser Verlag, 1975, p. 402.
3. Good, C.A., Kramer, H. and Somogyi, M.: J. Biol. Chem. 100:485, 1933.
4. Hartley, L.H., Mason, J.W., Hogan, R.P. et al: J. Appl. Physiol. 33:602, 1972.
5. Heding, L.G.: Horm. Metabol. Res. 1:145, 1969.
6. Hohorst, H.J.: *In* Bergmeyer, H.U. (ed.): Methoden der enzymatischen Analyse. Berlin:Akademie-Verlag, 1970, p. 1425.
7. Hultman, E.: Scand. J. Clin. Lab. Invest. 19:209, 1967.
8. Hultman, E. and Nilsson, L.H.: *In* Pernow, B. and Saltin, B. (eds.): Muscle Metabolism During Exercise. New York:Plenum Press, 1971, p. 143.
9. Leschkewitsch, L.G.: Fisiolog. Zhourn. USSR 37:475, 1951.
10. Metivier, G.: *In* Howald, H. and Poortmans, J.R. (eds.): Metabolic Adaptation to Prolonged Physical Exercise. Basel:Birkhäuser Verlag, 1975, p. 276.
11. Parilla, R., Goodman, M.N. and Toenz, C.J.: Diabetes 23:725, 1974.
12. Paul, P.: *In* Howald, H. and Poortmans, J.R. (eds.): Metabolic Adaptation to Prolonged Physical Exercise. Basel:Birkhäuser Verlag, 1975, p. 156.
13. Pruett, E.D.R.: J. Appl. Physiol. 28:199, 1970.
14. Stein, G. and Bässler, K.H.: Z. Klin. Chem. Klin. Biochem. 6:27, 1968.
15. Vranic, M., Kawamori, R. and Wrenshall, G.A.: Med. Sci. Sports 7:27, 1975.
16. Wagle, S.R. and Sampson, L.: Biochem. Biophys. Res. Commun. 64:72, 1975.
17. Zimmer, H.G. and Gerlach, E.: *In* Keul, J. (ed.): Limiting Factors of Physical Performance. Stuttgart:Thieme-Verlag, 1973, p. 102.

Metabolic Factors Associated with Tension Decrement in Electrically Stimulated Dog Gastrocnemius Muscle

P. F. Gardiner, H. A. Wenger, D. C. Secord
and A. W. Taylor

Introduction

The study of metabolic occurrences in skeletal muscle during contractile activity has posed the suggestion that continued voluntary exercise of specific types, intensities and durations may be limited by muscle-localized factors as opposed to limitations in the capacities of the cardiovascular, respiratory and other "support" systems. Factors such as depletion of high-energy phosphates [16, 24, 33], depletion of fiber glycogen [1, 12, 14], the accumulation of lactate and the concomitant decrease in muscle pH [17, 19, 31], alterations in muscle temperature [5, 7, 32] or electrolyte balance [4, 21], and changes in the structural integrity of muscle enzymes [23, 31] and mitochondria [11, 13, 15] have all been put forth as possible muscle fatigue mechanisms during contractile activity. In addition, it has been suggested that the limiting component in muscle may well be localized to a specific population of motor units being recruited during the type of activity being studied [1, 12, 14].

The investigation of muscle-localized limiting factors during voluntary exercise poses technical difficulties, mainly those associated with psychological motivation, the extrication of fluid and tissue samples and the accurate measurement of muscle work performance. A more direct approach is via the use of an isolated in situ muscle preparation. The purpose of this study was to assay specific plasma and muscle metabolites in an isolated, electrically stimulated in situ muscle preparation and attempt to relate these to measured work indices of the contracting muscle.

P. F. Gardiner, H. A. Wenger, D. C. Secord and A. W. Taylor, Surgical-Medical Research Institute and Department of Physical Education, University of Alberta, Edmonton, Alberta, Canada.

361

Methods and Procedures

Twenty-nine healthy mongrel dogs of both sexes were used as experimental animals. Dogs were anesthetized with halothane, with a 95% O_2/5% CO_2 mixture administered to maintain arterial pO_2 at 90 to 110 mm Hg. The gastrocnemius muscle and its venous drainage were surgically isolated as described by other authors [3, 34]. Blood flow from the muscle group was measured using an electromagnetic square-wave flowmeter (Zepeda Instruments, Seattle) with a 3 mm I.D. flowthrough probe. The venous drainage from the muscle group was routed via a polyethylene catheter inserted in the popliteal vein, through the flow probe and was returned to the animal via a catheter inserted in the cephalic vein. Heparin was used as an anticoagulant.

Muscle tension development during contractions was measured using a myograph-linear displacement transducer complex designed for this purpose. The femur was fixed by drilling through the femur near the origin of the muscle group, and the exposed ends of the drill bit clamped to two upright steel rods which were bolted to a firm base. The calcaneus was severed distally from the hindpaw, drilled, and the exposed ends of the drill bit were attached to the myograph-linear displacement transducer system by means of a steel cable. Muscles were loaded with 2 kg. The muscle group was stimulated to contract using an Electronic Stimulator (American Electronic Labs, Philadelphia) modified to yield specified trains of impulses. Supramaximal stimuli were delivered directly to the muscle belly. Contractions were elicited using trains of impulses delivered at a rate of 22 Hz, with each train lasting 0.7 seconds. One contraction occurred every 2.2 seconds, and contractions were isometric.

Animals were randomly assigned to either an 80%, 65%, 50% or 50%L group, which designated the tension during contractions, relative to initial maximum levels, at which freeze-clamped tissue samples were to be taken. The 50%L group represented those experiments in which the muscle group was allowed to level off in work output (change in tension of less than 5% over 30 minutes). Pilot studies had revealed this level off occurred at approximately 50% of initial work output. Freeze-clamped tissue plugs were taken simultaneously from the working muscle and the contralateral control muscle which had been similarly surgically isolated.

In all experiments, paired arterial and venous samples were taken during the prestimulation period and at predetermined tension levels during the contraction period until the termination of the experiment when tissue samples were obtained. Venous samples were taken from a stopcock distal to the flow probe, and arterial samples were taken from the contralateral femoral artery.

Plasma glucose and lactate were measured enzymatically, and plasma FFA were measured using a colorimetric technique [29]. Muscle oxygen consumption was estimated using the Fick relationship [30]. Enzymatic assays for tissue ATP, CP, lactate and pyruvate were performed on perchloric acid extracts as outlined by Lowry and Passonneau [27]. Tissue β-hydroxybutyrate and acetoacetate assays were modified slightly from those described by Edington, Ward and Saville [6].

Results

The tension curve of the stimulated muscle group (Fig. 1) is similar to trends reported for similar preparations [2, 8, 18, 35, 36]. Muscle blood flow and oxygen consumption levels during the contraction were highest early in the contraction period and gradually decreased thereafter. Muscle blood flow and oxygen consumption were below reported maximum values for this preparation [19, 28, 35, 36].

Arteriovenous differences of lactate, FFA, glucose and plasma water are summarized in Table I. When (A-V) dynamics were correlated individually with tension-time indices of the contracting muscle, the highest single correlation was that between lactate (A-V) difference and time from beginning of stimulation (r = +.63). Lactate (A-V) difference was significantly correlated (p<.01) with all tension-time indices, which was not the case with any other single tension-time index (Table II).

Muscle metabolite profiles at the tension levels studied are presented in Figure 2. ATP and CP reached a steady state by the 80% sampling interval and did not significantly (p>.05) change thereafter. Muscle glycogen content decreased gradually, showing a significant (p<.05) decrease, as compared to the control muscles, by the 50% interval. Muscle pyruvate did not change significantly during contractions. Muscle lactate concentration was highest at the 80% interval, then gradually decreased to levels at 50% and 50%L, which were significantly (p<.01) lower than the 80% and 65% levels and not different from the control muscles. Estimated mitochondrial $NAD^+/NADH$ ratios showed no significant trends, while the cytoplasmic $NAD^+/NADH$ ratio in the contracting muscles of the 80% group was significantly (p<.05) lower than in the contralateral control muscle.

The highest correlation between any single muscle metabolite parameter and tension-time index was that between muscle lactate

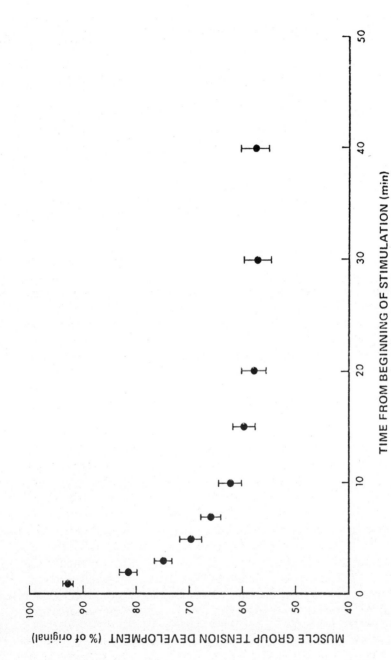

FIG. 1. Tension development changes of combined groups with time in maximally stimulated gastrocnemius muscle group ($\bar{X} \pm$ SEM).

Table I. Blood Flow, Oxygen Consumption and Arteriovenous Oxygen Difference at Rest and at Different Relative Tension Levels During Contractions[a]

| Parameter | Rest | Tension Level (% of Original) | | | | | |
		80%	70%	65%	60%	50%	50%L
Muscle blood flow (ml/g/min)	0.22 ± 0.02	0.66 ± 0.08**	0.73 ± 0.12**	0.63 ± 0.06**	0.64 ± 0.06**	0.65 ± 0.07**	0.64 ± 0.07**
Muscle oxygen uptake (μl/g/min)	7.1 ± 0.7	84.0 ± 9.0**	83.7 ± 8.5**	79.2 ± 9.4**	78.6 ± 8.0**	63.8 ± 6.8**	58.3 ± 6.2**
Oxygen (A-V) difference (mm Hg)	37.8 ± 1.0	66.4 ± 2.8**	63.3 ± 4.1**	62.6 ± 2.4**	59.9 ± 3.4*	52.5 ± 3.4**	52.2 ± 3.7**

[a]Values are $\overline{X}$ ± SEM
*Significantly different from corresponding resting mean $(p < .05)$
**Significantly different from corresponding resting mean $(p < .01)$

concentration and the rate of tension decline (gm/min) at sample time (r = +.80, Fig. 3). Muscle lactate concentration was significantly (p<.01) correlated with all expressions of tension decrement rate (Table III).

Discussion

The relationships between lactate parameters and tension-time indices suggest a possible role of muscle lactate presence in determining muscle work capabilities. This is particularly evident with reference to the high relationship (r = +.80) between muscle lactate concentration and the rate of tension decrement at sample time. The fact that lactate (A-V) difference showed the highest relationship (r = +.63) to time as opposed to any tension index suggests an accumulation of lactate in muscle tissue and a subsequent efflux which is time-related. Hirche et al [19, 20] have illustrated this accumulation of lactate in muscle tissue in a similar preparation and attribute it to the muscle cell membrane constituting a barrier to the diffusion of the non-ionized form of lactate.

It appears that the relationships between tension indices and muscle lactate are not due to a common relationship of these parameters to hypoxia in the muscle. Profiles of muscle ATP and CP, and mitochondrial NAD^+/NADH ratios suggested that the muscle was working under conditions of oxygen sufficiency by the 80% interval and thereafter, despite variations in tension decline. Jobsis

Table II. Summary of Significant (p < .01) Correlations
Between Arteriovenous and Tension-time Parameters

Parameters Correlated	Number of Observations	r	Probability that r = 0
Lactate (A-V) Difference			
(μM/g/min) vs:			
Time from beginning of stimulation (min)	75	.63	.000
Muscle tension development (kg)	75	−.41	.000
Muscle tension development (% of original)	75	−.37	.001
Muscle tension development (g/g)	75	−.37	.001
Rate of tension decline (g/g/min)	75	−.37	.001
Rate of tension decline (%/min)	75	−.35	.002
Rate of tension decline (g/min)	75	−.35	.002
Muscle Blood Flow			
(ml/g/min) vs:			
Rate of tension decline (g/min)	74	−.35	.002
Rate of tension decline (%/min)	74	−.34	.003
Muscle tension development (kg)	74	−.34	.004
Rate of tension decline (g/g/min)	74	−.33	.004
Venous Blood pH vs:			
Rate of tension decline (%/min)	75	−.42	.000
Rate of tension decline (g/min)	75	−.41	.000
Rate of tension decline (g/g/min)	75	−.39	.001
Muscle tension development (kg)	75	−.30	.009
Venous Blood pCO$_2$			
(mm Hg) vs:			
Muscle tension development (kg)	75	.61	.000
Muscle tension development (% of original)	75	.46	.000
Time from beginning of stimulation (min)	75	−.44	.000
Rate of tension decline (g/min)	75	.38	.001
Rate of tension decline (g/g/min)	75	.35	.002
Rate of tension decline (%/min)	75	.33	.004
Venous Blood pO$_2$			
(mm Hg) vs:			
Time from beginning of stimulation (min)	75	.28	.000
Oxygen (A-V) Difference			
(mm Hg) vs:			
Muscle tension development (kg)	75	.39	.001

and Stainsby [25] have shown similar metabolic tendencies in their working muscle groups, where lactate production occurred despite evidence of well-oxygenated mitochondria. It has been suggested by Katz [26] and Fuchs et al [10] that acidosis in muscle tissue may result in a decrease in actin-myosin interaction due to displacement of troponin-bound calcium ion by hydrogen ion. Such a mechanism could explain the relationship of lactate and tension decline seen here. Current experiments are under way at present to investigate

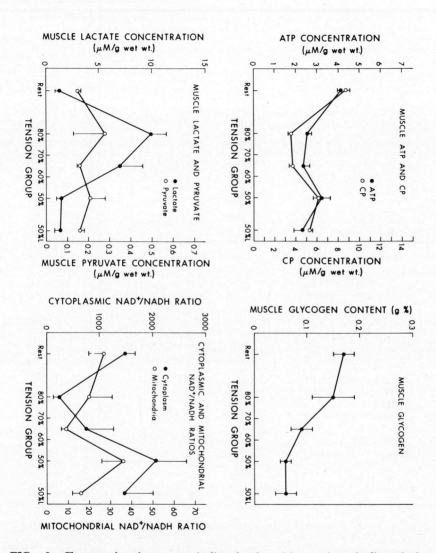

FIG. 2. Changes in tissue metabolite levels with tension decline during contractions.

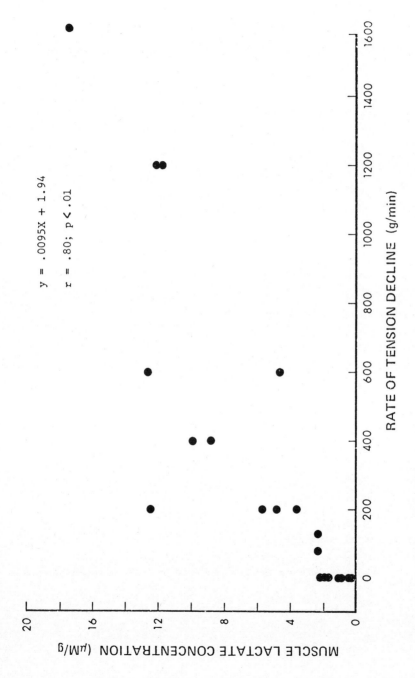

FIG. 3. Relationship between muscle lactate concentration and rate of tension decline at sample time.

Table III. Summary of Significant (p < .01) Correlations
Between Muscle Metabolite Concentrations and Tension-time Parameters

Parameters Correlated	Number of Observations	r	Probability that r = 0
Left Muscle Lactate Concentration (μM/g/min) vs:			
Rate of tension decline (g/min)	28	.80	.000
Rate of tension decline (g/g/min)	28	.78	.000
Rate of tension decline (%/min)	28	.76	.000
Muscle tension development at sample (kg)	28	.63	.000
Time from beginning of stimulation (min)	28	−.63	.000
Muscle Tension Development at Sample (% of Original) vs:			
Left muscle CP concentration (μM/g)	23	−.63	.001
Left muscle glycogen concentration (g%)	29	.52	.004
Muscle Tension Development at Sample (kg) vs:			
Right muscle weight (g)	26	.66	.000
Left muscle weight (g)	25	.62	.001
Muscle glycogen concentration (g%)	29	.57	.001

simulated "warm-up" conditions in this preparation and their effects on metabolite and work performance profiles.

References

1. Armstrong, R., Saubert, C., Sembrowich, W. et al: Glycogen depletion in rat skeletal muscle fibers at different intensities and durations of exercise. Pflügers Arch. 352:243-256, 1974.
2. Baldwin, K. and Tipton, C.: Work and metabolic patterns of fast and slow twitch skeletal muscle contracting in situ. Pflügers Arch. 334:345-356, 1972.
3. Barclay, J. and Stainsby, W.: The role of blood flow in limiting maximal metabolic rate in muscle. Med. Sci. Sports 7:116-119, 1975.
4. Bergström, J., Guarnieri, G. and Hultman, E.: Carbohydrate metabolism and electrolyte changes in human muscle tissue during heavy work. J. Appl. Physiol. 30:122-125, 1971.
5. Brooks, G., Hittelman, K., Faulkner, J. and Beyer, R.: Temperature, skeletal muscle mitochondrial functions, and oxygen debt. Am. J. Physiol. 220:1053-1059, 1971.
6. Edington, D., Ward, G. and Saville, W.: Energy metabolism of working muscle: Concentration profiles of selected metabolites. Am. J. Physiol. 224:1375-1380, 1973.
7. Edwards, R., Harris, R., Hultman, E. et al: Effect of temperature on muscle energy metabolism and endurance during successive isometric contractions sustained to fatigue, of the quadriceps muscle in man. J. Physiol. 220:335-352, 1972.

8. Fitch, C., Jellinek, M., Fitts, R. et al: Phosphorylated -quanidino-propionate as a substitute for phosphocreatine in rat muscle. Am. J. Physiol. 228:1123-1125, 1975.

9. Fitts, R., Campion, D., Nagle, F. and Cassens, R.: Contractile properties of skeletal muscle from trained miniature pig. Pflügers Arch. 343:133-141, 1973.

10. Fuchs, F., Reddy, Y. and Briggs, F.: The interaction of cations with the calcium-binding site of troponin. Biochim. Biophys. Acta 221:407-409, 1970.

11. Gale, J.: Mitochondrial swelling associated with exercise and method of fixation. Med. Sci. Sports 6:182-187, 1974.

12. Gollnick, P., Armstrong, R., Saubert, C. et al: Glycogen depletion patterns in human skeletal muscle fibers during prolonged work. Pflügers Arch 344:1-12, 1973.

13. Gollnick, P., Ianuzzo, C. and King, D.: Ultrastructural and enzyme changes in muscles with exercise. In Pernow, B. and Saltin, B. (eds.): Muscle Metabolism During Exercise. New York:Plenum Press, 1971.

14. Gollnick, P., Karlsson, J., Piehl, K. and Saltin, B.: Selective glycogen depletion in skeletal muscle fibers of man following sustained contractions. J. Physiol. 241:59-67, 1974.

15. Gonzalez-Serratos, H., Borrero, L. and Franzini-Armstrong, C.: Changes in mitochondria and intracellular pH during muscle fatigue. Fed. Proc. 33:1401, 1974.

16. Gubjarnason, S., Mathes, P. and Ravens, K.: Functional compartmentation of ATP and creatine phosphate in heart muscle. J. Mol. Cell. Cardiol. 1:325-339, 1970.

17. Hermansen, L. and Osnes, J.: Blood and muscle pH after maximal exercise in man. J. Appl. Physiol. 32:304-308, 1972.

18. Hirche, H., Grun, D. and Waller, W.: Utilization of carbohydrates and free fatty acids by the gastrocnemius of the dog during long lasting rhythmical exercise. Pflügers Arch. 321:121-132, 1970.

19. Hirche, H., Hombach, V., Langohr, H. et al: Lactic acid permeation rate in working gastrocnemii of dogs during metabolic alkalosis and acidosis. Pflügers Arch. 356:209-222, 1975.

20. Hirche, H., Langohr, H. and Wacker, U.: Lactic acid accumulation in working skeletal muscle. In Keul, J. (ed.): Limiting Factors of Physical Performance. Stuttgart:Georg Thieme, 1973.

21. Hudlicka, O.: Differences in development of fatigue in slow and fast muscles. In Keul, J. (ed.): Limiting Factors of Physical Performance. Stuttgart:Georg Thieme, 1973.

22. Hulten, B., Thortensson, A., Sjodin, B. and Karlsson, J.: Relationship between isometric endurance and fibre types in human leg muscles. Acta Physiol. Scand. 93:135-138, 1975.

23. Hultman, E. and Bergström, J.: Local energy-supplying substrates as limiting factors in different types of leg muscle work in normal man. In Keul, J. (ed.): Limiting Factors of Physical Performance. Stuttgart:Georg Thieme, 1973.

24. Hultman, E., Bergström, J. and Anderson, N.: Breakdown and resynthesis of phosphorylcreatine and adenosine triphosphate in connection with muscular work in man. Scand. J. Clin. Lab. Invest. 19:56-66, 1967.

25. Jobsis, F. and Stainsby, W.: Oxidation of NADH during contractions of circulated mammalian skeletal muscle. Resp. Physiol. 4:292-300, 1968.
26. Katz, A.: Contractile proteins of the heart. Physiol. Rev. 50:63-158, 1970.
27. Lowry, O. and Passonneau, J.: A Flexible System of Enzymatic Analysis. New York:Academic Press, 1972.
28. Piiper, J., DiPrampero, P. and Cerretelli, P.: Oxygen debt and high-energy phosphates in gastrocnemius muscle of the dog. Am. J. Physiol. 215:523-531, 1968.
29. Pinelli, A.: A new colorimetric method for plasma fatty acid analysis. Clin. Chim. Acta 44:385-390, 1973.
30. Rushmer, R.: Cardiovascular Dynamics. Philadelphia:W. B. Saunders, 1970.
31. Sahlin, K., Harris, R. and Hultman, E.: Creatine kinase equilibrium and lactate content compared with muscle pH in tissue samples obtained after isometric exercise. Biochem. J. 152:173-180, 1975.
32. Saltin, B., Gagge, A., Bergh, U. and Stolwijk, J.: Body temperatures and sweating during exhaustive exercise. J. Appl. Physiol. 32:635-643, 1972.
33. Spande, J. and Schottelius, B.: Chemical basis of fatigue in isolated mouse soleus muscle. Am. J. Physiol. 219:1490-1495, 1970.
34. Stainsby, W.: Oxygen uptake for isotonic and isometric twitch contractions of dog skeletal muscle in situ. Am. J. Physiol. 219:435-439, 1970.
35. Stainsby, W. and Welch, H.: Lactate metabolism of contracting dog skeletal muscle in situ. Am. J. Physiol. 211:177-183, 1966.
36. Welch, H. and Stainsby, W.: Oxygen debt in contracting dog skeletal muscle in situ. Resp. Physiol. 3:229-242, 1967.

Effects of Methandrostenolone on the Acute Compensatory Growth of Rat Skeletal Muscle

C. David Ianuzzo and Victor Chen

Introduction

A certain component of the athletic population, i.e., those participating primarily in power events, are known to utilize synthetic or semisynthetic analogues of steroids with the purpose of achieving anabolic myotrophic benefits. At present the findings are conflicting concerning the effects of anabolic steroids on compensatory hypertrophy of skeletal muscle [1, 8, 9, 16, 21, 29]. These contradictory results are difficult to resolve because of the various experimental methods used (e.g., the differences in steroids utilized, dosages administered, training and testing methods, the population of subjects studied and control of psychological factors, etc.). Our approach to this problem was to investigate the effects of the anabolic steroid, methandrostenolone (Dianabol, Ciba) on the acute compensatory growth of skeletal muscle using a well-studied animal model. This model has the following advantages: a quick and simple surgical myectomy results in a rapid and dramatic increase in muscle mass; the corresponding contralateral leg muscle serves as a control; ample tissue is provided for several different types of biochemical analyses; and it eliminates contending with certain human psychological variables.

Methods

Male Sprague-Dawley albino rats with initial body weights of 180-200 gm were administered subcutaneously either 3, 6, 9 or 18 mg/kg/day of methandrostenolone (17α-methyl-17β-hydroxy-androsta-1,4-dien-3-one) for a total of seven days. The steroid was

C. David Ianuzzo and Victor Chen, Departments of Physical Education and Biology, York University,, Toronto, Ontario, Canada.
Supported by a York University President's NRC grant.

injected as a suspension in the vehicle (i.e., 0.9% sodium chloride, 0.9% benzyl alcohol, 0.5% carboxymethylcellulose and 0.4% polysorbate 80 in distilled water) described by Boris et al [3]. Control animals received sham injections of the vehicle. Two days following the commencement of injections, compensatory hypertrophy of the plantaris muscle was induced by the functional overload imposed by ipsilateral gastrocnemius myectomy [15]. Two days were allowed following the initial administering of the steroid before inducing hypertrophy to allow for the hormone to establish myotrophic activity [25]. Animals were killed five days postsurgery. The levator ani muscle was excised in toto and weighed. There was a significant increase (p < .01) in wet weight of the levator ani muscle in all the steroid treated groups, which indicated the administered dosages of methandrostenolone were anabolically active (Table I). The control and hypertrophied plantaris muscles were immediately excised, cleaned of excess connective tissue, blotted and weighed. The muscles were homogenized in 33 mM phosphate buffer (1:20 w/v) at pH 7.4. The Vmax enzyme activities of phosphofructokinase (PFK) [28], succinate dehydrogenase (SDH) [6] and 3-hydroxy-acyl-CoA dehydrogenase (HADH) [2] were determined spectrophotometrically at 25 C. DNA was assayed using the Ceriotti indole method [5] as recently modified by Hubbard et al [18, 19]. Protein content was determined as described by Lowry et al [23].

Results

A significant increase in mass of the overloaded plantaris muscle ranging from 36% to 57% occurred in all groups (Table II). There was no trend toward a greater relative enlargement of the muscles from the steroid-treated animals, but a less than normal hypertrophy was

Table I. Animal and Levator Ani Muscle Weights

	Control	3 mg/kg	Groups 6 mg/kg	9 mg/kg	18 mg/kg
Body wts. (gm)	242 ± 16	262 ± 7[a]	253 ± 12	236 ± 7	242 ± 18
Levator ani muscle wet wts. (mg)	145 ± 16	184 ± 18[b]	209 ± 22[b]	191 ± 16[b]	221 ± 41[b]

Values are expressed as mean ± S.D.
Each group consisted of five animals.
[a,b]Control vs. steroid group statistically significant p < .05 and p < .01, respectively.

Table II. Muscle Wet Weights, Total DNA Content, DNA Concentration and Protein Concentrations of Control and Hypertrophied Muscles From Normal and Steroid-Treated Rats

Groups	Muscle Wet Wts. (mg)		Total DNA Content (µg/muscle)		DNA Concentration (µg/mg wet wt.)		Protein Concentration (mg/g wet wt.)	
	Control	Hypertrophied	Control	Hypertrophied	Control	Hypertrophied	Control	Hypertrophied
Control	213 ± 7	334 ± 24^a	240 ± 20	672 ± 76^a	$1.10 \pm .12$	$2.01 \pm .12^a$	171 ± 18	139 ± 15^c
3 mg/kg	219 ± 8	300 ± 11^a	176 ± 20	660 ± 140^a	$0.81 \pm .12$	$2.19 \pm .42^b$	165 ± 22	132 ± 14^c
6 mg/kg	216 ± 6	291 ± 8^a	268 ± 44	568 ± 80^c	$1.25 \pm .18$	$1.95 \pm .32^b$	165 ± 12	156 ± 7
9 mg/kg	219 ± 8	312 ± 3^a	232 ± 20	544 ± 36^a	$1.04 \pm .05$	$1.75 \pm .11^a$	170 ± 25	164 ± 28
18 mg/kg	215 ± 20	324 ± 26^a	236 ± 36	620 ± 72^a	$1.08 \pm .02$	$1.87 \pm .29^b$	168 ± 4	153 ± 6^b

Groups consisted of five animals with exception of four animals for the 18 mg/kg DNA content and DNA concentration.
Values are expressed as mean ± S.D.
[a],[b],[c] Control vs. hypertrophied muscles are statistically significant at $p < .001$, $p < .01$, and $p < .05$, respectively.

observed for the 3 mg/kg and 6 mg/kg groups (Table III). The hypertrophied plantaris muscles from all groups tended to have a lower than normal protein content (-4% to -17%). Total DNA content increased 110% to 276% during the five-day compensatory growth period. The greater increase in total DNA content than in muscle mass resulted in a significant increase in DNA concentration (Table II). The ratios of DNA concentration of hypertrophied/control plantaris muscle were similar in the steroid groups to that of the control group with the exception of the higher value for the 9 mg/kg group (Table III). The enzyme activities of PFK (-32% to -49%), SDH (-25% to -31%) and HADH (-30% to -48%) were significantly lower in the hypertrophied muscles of the control and steroid-treated animals (Table IV). The ratio of enzyme activities indicated no differences between the metabolic potential of the control and steroid-treated animals with the exception of the lower PFK activities in the hypertrophied muscle of the 9 mg/kg and 18 mg/kg groups (Table III).

Discussion

This study has demonstrated that the synthetic anabolic steroid, methandrostenolone, does not facilitate the early phase of compensatory growth of fast-twitch rat skeletal muscle. This finding is not surprising, since it is widely accepted that short-term work-induced growth of skeletal muscle is not hormone-dependent [12]. Goldberg has shown compensatory growth of both fast- and slow-twitch muscle to occur to the same relative extent in hypophysectomized as

Table III. Ratio of Hypertrophied/Control Plantaris Muscle With Respect to Wet Weight, DNA and Protein Concentrations, and Enzyme Activities

Groups	Muscle Wet Wt.	DNA Concentration	Protein Concentration	Succinate Dehydrogenase	Phosphofructokinase	3-Hydroxylacyl-CoA Dehydrogenase
Control	1.57 ± .12	1.84 ± .21	.88 ± .10	.70 ± .10	.68 ± .07	.64 ± .08
3 mg/kg	1.37 ± .07[b]	2.79 ± .78	.83 ± .08	.70 ± .09	.63 ± .13	.64 ± .08
6 mg/kg	1.36 ± .06[b]	1.57 ± .24	.95 ± .05	.70 ± .09	.64 ± .04	.67 ± .08
9 mg/kg	1.43 ± .11	1.68 ± .16	.96 ± .05[b]	.75 ± .11	.51 ± .06[a]	.70 ± .05
18 mg/kg	1.52 ± .20	1.73 ± .28	.91 ± .03	.70 ± .10	.49 ± .09[a]	.53 ± .10

Values are mean ± S.D.
Five animals per group with the exception of four for DNA concentration of 18 mg/kg.
[a,b]Control vs. steroid-treated groups are statistically significant at $P < .01$ and $P < .05$, respectively.

Table IV. Enzyme Activities of Control and Hypertrophied Plantaris Muscles

Groups	Succinate Dehydrogenase Activity Control	Hypertrophied	Phosphofructokinase Activity Control	Hypertrophied	3-Hydroxyacyl-CoA Dehydrogenase Activity Control	Hypertrophied
Control	3.49 ± .35	2.42 ± .17[b]	46.0 ± 2.3	31.2 ± 3.1[a]	4.39 ± .45	2.82 ± .36[b]
3 mg/kg	3.86 ± .38	2.70 ± .48[b]	48.0 ± 3.5	30.0 ± 6.2[b]	3.87 ± .31	2.48 ± .31[a]
6 mg/kg	4.11 ± .40	2.85 ± .37[b]	48.4 ± 6.4	31.0 ± 3.7[b]	4.07 ± .25	2.74 ± .31[a]
9 mg/kg	3.21 ± .41	2.39 ± .19[b]	51.8 ± 7.0	26.4 ± 4.4[a]	3.90 ± .27	2.74 ± .24[a]
18 mg/kg	3.69 ± .34	2.58 ± .36[b]	55.3 ± 3.6	27.9 ± 5.5[a]	5.25 ± .82	2.72 ± .27[a]

Mean ± S.D. are in μmoles $\cdot$ gm^{-1} $\cdot$ min^{-1}
Each group consisted of six animals
[a,b]Control vs. hypertrophied muscles are statistically significant at p < .001 and p < .01, respectively.

in normal animals [12]. He has also observed that administering of growth hormone results in a proportional increase in mass of both the control and compensating muscles [10]. This suggests that the anabolic hormone, somatotrophin, functions to amplify muscle growth without selectively benefiting the compensatory response. Insulin, another anabolic hormone, has not been found to influence short-term compensatory growth [11, 20]. Muscles of animals with chemically induced hypoinsulinism hypertrophy to the same relative amount as those of normal animals during the early phase, even though severe muscle wasting is occurring in the non-overloaded muscles. A further indication that hormonal alterations do not influence compensatory growth is the similar hypertrophy of muscles of male and female rats [24]. The high priority given to this compensatory adaptation has also been emphasized by the occurrence of a similar relative amount of muscular hypertrophy in fasted as in normal animals [13]. As inferred from these studies and found in the present study, the administration of a synthetic anabolic steroid would not be expected to complement compensatory muscle growth, since it apparently is not hormone-dependent.

The tendency of the compensating muscles to have a reduced protein content suggests an added hydration. This has been discussed previously [20]. It may be the result of an increased intracellular osmolarity from the added rate of amino transport that occurs during hypertrophy [14]. The 6, 9 and 18 mg/kg steroid-treated animals showed a lesser decline in protein concentration. This may be the result of increased amino acid transport reported to occur following the administration of methandrostenolone [25].

The ratio of the enzyme activities of the hypertrophied to control muscles indicated a significant decline in the metabolic potentials of glycolysis, Krebs cycle and beta-oxidation of fatty acids. Methandrostenolone has been shown to protect mitochondria from glucocorticoid attack; however, when administered alone it does not alter mitochondrial morphology [4] or enzyme activities of the Krebs cycle and electron transport system [7, 22]. This agrees with the present study showing the acute decline in metabolic potential of the compensating muscle was not altered by the administration of the anabolic steroid.

An early response of compensating muscle is a dramatic increase in DNA proliferation [20]. The locale of this nuclear proliferation during the acute phase of hypertrophy has been observed to occur almost exclusively in nonmuscle cells [27]. Since the greatest relative increase is initially in the stromal proteins [17], this added DNA most likely functions in "fathering" intermuscle cell proteins. However, it is possible that at a later time this DNA may be redistributed to hypertrophying muscle fibers to provide genetic material either for polyploidy or for nuclei for new fiber formation. This is supported by the findings of Moss and Leblond [26], indicating the satellite cell has the ability to provide genetic material to growing muscle fibers. The similar amounts of DNA proliferation observed in the control and steroid-treated animals of this study indicate that this commonly used anabolic steroid does not influence the dramatic and probably obligatory compensatory DNA proliferation that occurs in the early phase of hypertrophy.

Summary

The effect of the anabolic steroid, methandrostenolone, on short-term compensatory muscle hypertrophy was investigated. Male Sprague-Dawley albino rats (180 to 200 gm) were subcutaneously administered either 3, 6, 9 or 18 mg/kg/day of the steroid. Compensatory growth of the plantaris muscle was initiated two days following the commencement of injections. Animals were sacrificed five days post-surgery, at which time the following determinations were accomplished: levator ani and plantaris muscles wet weights; phosphofructokinase (PFK), 3-hydroxyacyl-CoA dehydrogenase (HADH) and succinate dehydrogenase (SDH) activities; DNA and protein content. There was a significant increase in the wet weights of the levator ani muscle of all groups receiving the steroid. The hypertrophied plantaris muscle wet weights increased 36% to 57% with no significant difference between groups. Enzyme activities of PFK, HADH and SDH were significantly less (20% to 50%) in the hypertrophied muscles of all groups. There were significant increases in the

DNA concentration (57% to 84%) and DNA content (110% to 276%) within groups with no difference between groups. The protein content of the hypertrophied muscle tended to be lower in all groups. It has been concluded from these findings that the anabolic steroid, methandrostenolone, does not facilitate the short-term compensatory growth of skeletal muscle in the rat.

References

1. Ariel, G.: Prolonged effects of anabolic steroid upon muscular contractile force. Med. Sci. Sports 6:62-64, 1974.
2. Bass, A., Brdiczka, D., Eyer, P. et al: Metabolic differentiation of distinct muscle types at the level of enzymatic organization. Eur. J. Biochem. 10:198-206, 1969.
3. Boris, A., Stevenson, R.H. and Trmal, T.: A comparison of the androgenic and myotropic activities of some anabolic steroids in the castrated rat. J. Steroid Biochem. 1:349-354, 1970.
4. Bullock, G.R., Christian, R.A., Peters, R.F. and White, A.M.: Rapid mitochondrial enlargement in muscle as a response to triamcinolone acetonide and its relationship to the ribosomal defect. Biochem. Pharm. 20:943-953, 1971.
5. Ceriotti, G.: A microchemical determination of desoxyribonuclei acid. J. Biol. Chem. 198:297-303, 1952.
6. Cooperstein, S.J., Lazarow, A. and Kurfess, N.J.: A microspectrophotometric method for the determination of succinic dehydrogenase. J. Biol. Chem. 186:129-139, 1950.
7. Endahl, G. and Kochakian, C.: Influences of androgens on enzymes of the Krebs cycle. Endocrinology 64:833-835, 1959.
8. Fahey, J.D. and Brown, C.H.: The effects of an anabolic steroid on the strength, body composition, and endurance of college males when accompanied by a weight training program. Med. Sci. Sports 5:272-276, 1973.
9. Fowler, W.M. Jr., Gardner, G.W. and Egstrom, G.H.: Effect of an anabolic steroid on physical performance of young men. J. Appl. Physiol. 20:1038-1040, 1965.
10. Goldberg, A.L.: Relationship between hormones and muscular work in determining muscle size. In Alpert, N.R. (ed.): Cardiac Hypertrophy. New York:Academic Press, 1971, pp. 39-53.
11. Goldberg, A.L.: Role of insulin in work-induced growth of skeletal muscle. Endocrinology 83:1071-1073, 1968.
12. Goldberg, A.L.: Work-induced growth of skeletal muscle in normal and hypophysectomized rats. Am. J. Physiol. 312:1193-1198, 1967.
13. Goldberg, A.L., Etlinger, J.D., Goldspink, D.F. and Jablecki, C.: Mechanism of work-induced hypertrophy of skeletal muscle. Med. Sci. Sports 7:248-261, 1975.
14. Goldberg, A.L. and Goodman, H.M.: Amino acid transport during work-induced growth of skeletal muscle. Am. J. Physiol. 216:1111-1115, 1969.
15. Guth, L. and Yellin, H.: The dynamic nature of the so-called "fiber types" of mammalian skeletal muscle. Exp. Neurol. 31:277-300, 1971.

16. Hervey, G.R., Hutchinson, I. and Knubbs, A.V.: Effects of methandrostenolone on body composition in male students undergoing athletic training. J. Endocrinol. 65:49P, 1975.

17. Hubbard, R.W., Ianuzzo, C.D., Matthew, W.T. and Linduska, J.D.: Compensatory adaptations of skeletal muscle composition to a long-term functional overload. Growth 39:85-93, 1975.

18. Hubbard, R.W., Matthew, W.T. and Dubowik, D.A.: Factors influencing the determination of DNA with indole. Anal. Biochem. 38:190-201, 1970.

19. Hubbard, R.W., Matthew, W.T. and Moulton, D.W.: Factors influencing the determination of DNA with indole II. Recovery of hydrolyzed DNA from protein precipitates. Anal. Biochem. 46:461-472, 1972.

20. Ianuzzo, C.D. and Armstrong, R.B.: DNA proliferation in normal and diabetic muscle during short-term compensatory growth. Int. J. Biochem. 6:889-892, 1975.

21. Johnson, L.C. and O'Shea, J.P.: Anabolic steroid: Effects on strength development. Science 164:957-959, 1969.

22. Kowalewski, K.: Activity of succinic dehydrogenase and cytochrome oxydase of liver mitochondria in rats treated with cortisone and with an anabolic androgen. Proc. Soc. Exp. Bio. Med. 109:971-973, 1962.

23. Lowry, O.H., Rosebrough, H.J., Farr, A.L. and Randall, R.J.: Protein measurement with Folin phenol reagent. J. Biol. Chem. 193:265-275, 1951.

24. Mackova, E. and Hnik, P.: Time course of compensatory hypertrophy of slow and fast rat muscles in relation to age. Physiol. Bohemoslov. 21:9-17, 1972.

25. Metcalf, W. and Gross, E.: Influence of anabolic steroids on uptake of alpha-aminoisobutyric acid by levator ani muscle. Science 132:41, 1960.

26. Moss, F.P. and Leblond, C.P.: Nature of dividing nuclei in skeletal muscle of growing rats. J. Cell. Biol. 44:459-462, 1970.

27. Schiaffino, S., Bormioli, S.P. and Aloisi, M.: Cell proliferation in rat skeletal muscle during early stages of compensatory hypertrophy. Virchows Arch. Abt. B:Zellpath. 11:268-273, 1972.

28. Shonk, C.E. and Boxer, G.E.: Enzyme patterns in human tissue. I. Methods for the determination of glycolytic enzymes. Cancer Res. 24:709-724, 1964.

29. Ward, P.: The effect of an anabolic steroid on strength and lean body mass. Med. Sci. Sports 5:277-282, 1973.

Firing Patterns of Slow and Fast Twitch Motor Units

V. Reggie Edgerton,* T. Collatos,
J. L. Smith* and B. Betts

Introduction

Mammalian skeletal muscle consists of muscle fibers characterized by variable biochemical and physiological properties with a wide range in enzyme activities, substrate concentrations, contraction times, tensions and fatigue resistance [3, 4]. These ranges in values have resulted in the classification of motor units into three somewhat distinct populations in the cat [3].

But, the role of different types of motor units in the execution of routine movements has not been determined. In order to study this problem, a technique was developed which permits telemetered electromyographic (EMG) recordings of predominantly slow and fast twitch muscle while the unrestrained movements of the cat are recorded on videotape.

Procedures

Three adult female cats have been implanted with up to eight electrodes and a common ground wire which permit bipolar recordings of four muscles simultaneously. These wires are encased in silastic tubing and led subcutaneously to a connector which is secured to the skull with four screws and dental cement. Each electrode wire (O.D. = 0.28 mm) is made of 19 stainless steel strands which are insulated with a nylon coating. The lateral head of the gastrocnemius (fast twitch), soleus (slow twitch), lateral tricep (fast twitch), and accessory portion of the medial tricep muscles (slow twitch) have been implanted. These implants have remained functional for up to five months. A detailed description of the implantation procedures has been reported [1]. The physiological

V. Reggie Edgerton, T. Collatos, J. L. Smith and B. Betts, Department of Kinesiology, University of California, Los Angeles, Calif., U.S.A.
*Members of Brain Research Institute, U.C.L.A.

properties of the forelimb muscles involved in this report have been published [5].

A 125 cm³ PAM-FM telemetry transmitter weighing 83 gm is attached to the head connector for transmission of the EMG signal. The EMG signals are matched with the associated movements of the cat with a video system consisting of one camera which follows the cat and another which records the EMG signals from an oscilloscope. The images recorded from the two cameras are combined on a single monitor.

All signals, including a code for identification, were recorded on 0.5 inch FM tape. Raw and rectified, averaged EMG were analyzed with the aid of a Hewlett-Packard 21 MX mini-computer and x-y plotter.

To assess the relationship between the changes in EMG activity of two muscles, the onset, peak and termination of the raw and averaged EMG signal of selected movements were plotted on graph paper. In all cases, the relative rates of change in the raw and averaged EMG signals were the same. All of the figures in this paper were derived from the raw EMG signal.

Results

Figure 1 represents the relationship between the raw EMG amplitude of the soleus and lateral head of the gastrocnemius muscles during a step, a 30 cm jump and a 91 cm jump of the same cat. During the initial stages of each movement, changes in slow and fast muscle EMG amplitude are directly related. During the 30 and 91 cm jumps, changes in the gastrocnemius and soleus EMG amplitude become inversely related at the point which the EMG of the slow twitch soleus reaches the peak of that movement. The significance of the differences in the raw or averaged EMG activity between two muscles is the rate of change and not the absolute value of the signal. Note also that in the progression from a step to a 91 cm jump, the gastrocnemius peak EMG amplitudes increased considerably while the soleus peak EMG amplitude remained relatively constant.

Figure 2 represents similar data taken from a relatively homogeneous fast (lateral head of the triceps brachii) and slow (accessory head of the medial triceps brachii) muscles of the forelimb during a step, a pawing action and a rapid extension of the elbow with the forelimb lifted off the ground (swipe). The pawing action is similar to the swiping except the elbow is not as fully extended. As in Figure 1, the initial stages of EMG activity are characterized by an

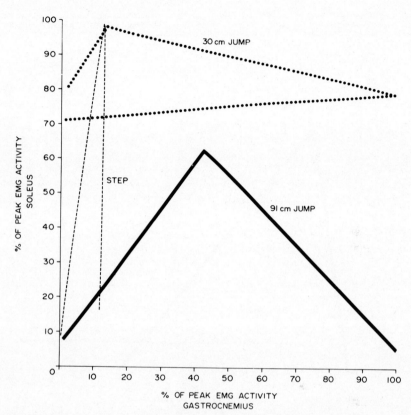

FIG. 1. The relationship of the EMG amplitude of the gastrocnemius and soleus muscles during a step, 30 cm jump and a 91 cm jump. The amplitude is normalized so that the muscle with its peak EMG amplitude during the movement represented is equal to 100%. Note that in a step, the peak EMG amplitude occurred in the soleus, whereas the gastrocnemius yielded a higher amplitude during both jumps. The EMG of the two muscles during a 30 cm jump were directly related initially, then the relationship became an inverse one, followed by another direct relationship. A direct relationship indicates that as the EMG of one muscle was increasing, the other muscle was increasing also, or vice versa.

increasing amplitude in the slow and fast muscle while this relationship is reversed or becomes unrelated after the peak of the slow muscle EMG is evident. Note particularly that the EMG amplitude of the fast muscle ranges from about 15% to 100% of the peak with essentially no variation in amplitude of the slow muscle EMG activity.

The onset and termination of EMG activity of slow and fast muscle also reflected the level of interdependence that existed

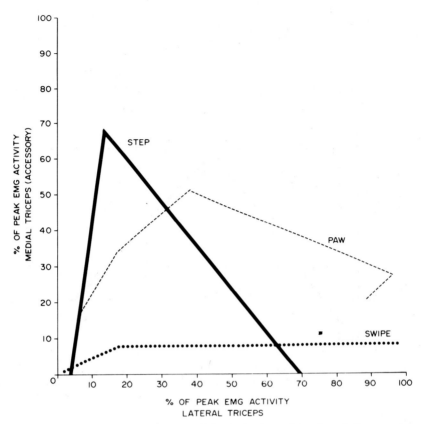

FIG. 2. The relationship of peak EMG of the lateral head and the accessory portion of the medial head of the triceps are plotted during a step, pawing movement and a swipe. The pawing and swiping action are movements involving extension of the elbow while the forelimb is free of providing support for the body. The swiping action differs from the pawing action in that it is a more complete extension.

between synergistic slow and fast muscles. During a step, the onset and termination of the slow accessory portion of the medial head of the triceps relative to the fast lateral head was markedly variable (Figs. 3 and 4). During a jump, the soleus muscle was usually activated at approximately the same time or slightly after the gastrocnemius muscle. The relationship between the termination point of the two muscles was more variable. During a more rapid swiping movement, usually both were activated simultaneously, but the EMG of the slow portion of the medial triceps terminated much earlier than the lateral head of the triceps.

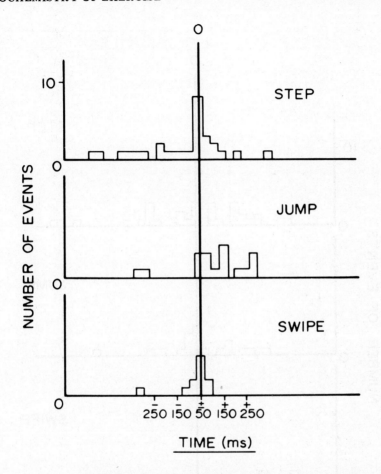

ONSET OF EMG ACTIVITY OF SLOW
RELATIVE TO FAST MUSCLE

FIG. 3. The point at which the EMG signal of the slow muscle increased in relation to the onset of the fast muscle. The step and jump data were derived from the soleus and gastrocnemius while the swipe was derived from the accessory portion of the medial head of the triceps and the lateral triceps.

Discussion

The concept that the "size principle" determines the order of recruitment of motoneurons within a given motoneuron pool has been proposed by Henneman and co-workers [9, 10]. That is, in a movement in which a range of motoneuron sizes within a given pool

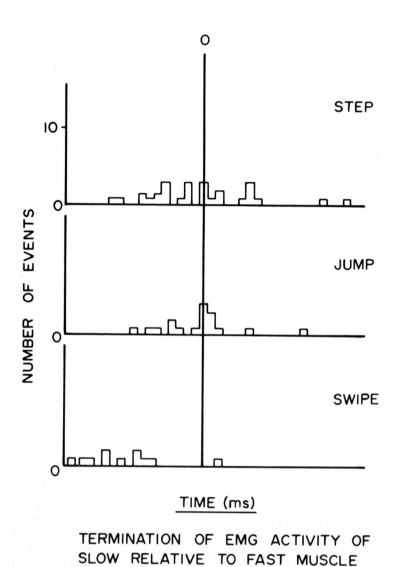

TERMINATION OF EMG ACTIVITY OF
SLOW RELATIVE TO FAST MUSCLE

FIG. 4. Data representing the point of termination of the slow relation to the fast muscle are shown. As in Figure 3, the hind limb slow and fast muscles are represented in the step and jump, whereas the forelimb slow and fast muscle is represented for the rapid swiping action.

is recruited, the smaller ones will be recruited before the larger ones. Because it is known that the smaller motoneurons generally innervated slow twitch and the larger ones innervated fast twitch, [2, 9] the size principle leaves one to conclude that the recruitment order of motoneurons begins with the slow twitch motor units, followed by the fast twitch units. This principle, based on anesthetized, decerebrated preparations, for the most part, has been interpreted in general to apply to all normal voluntary movement [9, 10]. To extend the size principle of a group of synergistic muscles to its logical conclusion, one would expect that in all movements, activation of slow units would precede fast units and that in the cessation of movement, the fast units would be the first to become disfacilitated [10].

It could be questioned whether the size principle is applicable in the comparison of two separate muscles even though they are synergists. But the experiments of Henneman et al [10] demonstrated the existence of the small-to-large motoneuron recruitment order in a large majority of filaments from L_7 and S_1 of decerebrated cats in response to ipsilateral monosynaptic and disynaptic reflexes, flexor reflexes, crossed-extension reflexes and stretch reflexes. They also found the consistency of the stereotyped recruitment order in a single pool to be indistinguishable from that observed in motoneurons from several pools.

The raw EMG pattern of synergistic slow and fast muscles of either the hind limb or forelimb does not support the idea that the size principle is always a dominant factor in normal cats during a variety of voluntary movements. In most cases, the initial stages of an EMG burst were characterized by a positive relationship between the changes in EMG amplitude of the slow and fast muscle. However, it was common for this relation to become a negative one or totally absent in the later stages of most EMG bursts (Figs. 1 and 2). If the size principle was applicable to normal unanesthetized cats, these EMG relationships between synergists probably would not occur. It could be argued that because of the difference in their proximal attachments [7], the validity of comparing the soleus and lateral gastrocnemius muscles for the purpose of evaluating the utilization of slow and fast motor units in normal movement is questionable. However, the morphological and mechanical comparisons of these two muscles during stepping, galloping and jumping by Goslow et al [7] and of muscle length tension relationships by Grillner [8] suggest that the difference in their mechanics is not a major factor for the nervous system to consider in the synchronization of coordinated movement. Furthermore, calculations made from the data presented by Goslow et al [7] on the mechanics of a 2-meter jump and gallop demonstrate that it is highly unlikely that slow motor units could make any contribution in such a movement except at the very early stages when the movement was relatively slow. For example, if one assumes time-to-peak tension of 100 ms for a slow twitch and 30 ms for a fast twitch unit and a 10% shortening in length, these muscles could shorten at a rate of 0.1 and 0.3 mm/ms, respectively [3]. In the analyses of a gallop made by Goslow et al [7] the soleus would have had to shorten 14 mm in 31 ms (average velocity = 0.45 mm/ms) and the gastrocnemius 10 mm in 31 ms (0.32 mm/ms). Similar figures for the jump were 0.26 and 0.20 mm/ms, respectively. It is clear that the soleus could not have contributed any force during the latter stages of the gallop or jump when the average velocity of shortening appears to be two- to fourfold greater than that which most soleus units are capable. Because the order in which any pair of motor units in L_7 or S_1 were activated in the decerebrated cat [10] was reversed upon inactivation, one would expect a direct relationship in EMG activity of synergistic muscles throughout the falling as well as the rising phase of the EMG burst. Clearly, this was not the case in the forelimb or hind limb slow and fast muscles during normal movements of unrestrained cats.

The precise relationship between time of onset and termination of EMG activity in slow and fast muscles is variable. Gambaryan [6] reports that the soleus is activated approximately the same time as the gastrocnemius during a step or gallop, but that the soleus terminates earlier. Our data in general illustrate that the relative times of onset and termination of slow and fast muscles are highly variable.

Data based on muscle glycogen depletion or EMG activity of single motor units during different types of movements suggest that recruitment order of slow and fast motor units is variable in normal movement. These reports have been reviewed recently [3]. In general, the data of this report provide further evidence, but do not prove that the order of recruitment of motoneurons in normal movement in part is a function of the nature of the movement.

References

1. Betts, B., Smith, J.L., Edgerton, V.R. and Collatos, T.C.: Telemetered EMG of fast and slow muscles of the cat. Brain Res. (Submitted 1976.)

2. Burke, R.E.: On the central nervous system control of fast and slow twitch motor units. *In* Desmedt, J.E. (ed.): New Developments in Electromyography and Clinical Neurophysiology. Vol. 3, 1973, pp. 69-94.

3. Burke, R.E. and Edgerton, V.R.: Motor unit properties and selective involvement in movement. Exerc. Sport. Sci. Rev. 3:31-81, 1975.

4. Close, R.I.: Dynamic properties of mammalian skeletal muscle. Physiol. Rev. 52:129-197, 1972.

5. Collatos, T.C. and Smith, J.L.: Histochemical and electromyographic studies of elbow joint muscles in the cat. Med. Sci. Sports 8:69, 1976.

6. Gambaryan, P.P.: How Mammals Run. Anatomical Adaptations. Hardin, H. (trans.). New York:J. Wiley & Sons, 1974, p. 220.

7. Goslow, G.E. Jr., Reinking, R.M. and Stuart, D.S.: The cat step cycle: Hind limb joint angles and muscle lengths during unrestrained locomotion. J. Morphol. 141:1-42, 1973.

8. Grillner, S.: The role of muscle stiffness in meeting changing postural and locomotor requirements for force development by ankle extensors. Acta Physiol. Scand. 86:92-108, 1972.

9. Henneman, E. and Olson, C.B.: Relations between structure and function in the design of skeletal muscles. J. Neurophysiol. 28:581-598, 1965.

10. Henneman, E., Somjen, G. and Carpenter, D.O.: Excitability and inhibitability of motoneurons of different sizes. J. Neurophysiol. 28:599-620, 1965.

Author Index   Auteurs

AUTHOR INDEX/AUTEURS

Subject Index ⊗ Sujets

SUBJECT INDEX/SUJETS

A listing of the COMPLETE SERIES from the International Congress of Physical Activity Sciences Meeting

SERIE COMPLETE des ouvrages du Congrès international des sciences de l'activité physique

NOTICE

By decision of the Scientific Commission, *French* and *English* were adopted as the two official languages of the International Congress of Physical Activity Sciences – 1976.

In these Proceedings, the communications appear *in the language in which they were presented* for French and English and *in English* as concerns the papers which were delivered in either German, Russian or Spanish. Abstracts in the two official languages accompany each paper included in Books 1 and 2 and the seminar presentations in the other books of the series.

AVERTISSEMENT

Les langues *anglaise* et *française* furent adoptées par la Commission scientifique comme langues officielles du Congrès international des sciences de l'activité physique – 1976. De ce fait, les communications apparaissent au présent rapport officiel *dans la langue où elles ont été présentées* pour ce qui est de l'anglais et du français, et dans la langue *anglaise* pour ce qui est des communications qui furent faites dans les langues allemande, russe et espagnole.

Des résumés dans chacune des deux langues officielles accompagnent chacune des communications qui paraissent aux Volumes 1 et 2 ainsi que les présentations faites par les conférenciers invités dans les autres volumes de la série.

QUARTER